Also by Kate Simon

New York: Places and Pleasures

New York (with Andreas Feininger)

Mexico: Places and Pleasures

Kate Simon's Paris

Kate Simon's London

Italy: The Places In Between

ROME: Places and Pleasures

ROME

PLACES AND PLEASURES

by Kate Simon

ALFRED A. KNOPF   New York   1972

THIS IS A BORZOI BOOK
PUBLISHED BY ALFRED A. KNOPF, INC.

Copyright © 1972 by Kate Simon

The lines from Martial on page 374 come from *Selected
Epigrams of Martial*, translated by Rolfe Humphries,
copyright © 1963 by Indiana University Press.

Library of Congress Cataloging in Publication Data

Simon, Kate.
   Rome: places and pleasures.

   1. Rome (City)—Description and travel—
   Guide-books.
I. Title.
DG804.S47   914.5′632′0492   70-38320
ISBN 0-394-46824-4
ISBN 0-394-70763-2 (pbk.)

Manufactured in the United States of America

FIRST EDITION

In memory of Herbert Weinstock

Acknowledgments

Many thanks to my friends in Rome for suggestions, information, and the pleasure of their company, especially Mr. and Mrs. Sandro Bennati and Mr. Piero Bozzetti. My thanks, too, to the Ladies of Bethany of the Foyer Unitas for their boundless store of shared information and their buoyant spirits.

Kate Simon

Contents

Contents

Introduction

Goethe: "I find it is a difficult and melancholy business, I must confess, separating the old Rome from the new, but it has to be done and I can only hope that, in the end, my efforts will prove worth while. One comes upon traces of magnificence and of devastation which stagger the imagination."

James Joyce: "Rome is like an old cemetery with broken columns of temples and slabs," "flowers of death, ruins, piles of bones and skeletons." "Rome reminds me of a man who lives by exhibiting to travellers his grandmother's corpse."

Shelley, in a parallel context: "Look on my works, ye Mighty, and despair!"

Moderate, slightly frightened statement; immoderate, exasperated snarl; romantic-tragic view—all reflect the recoil of many travelers. There is no spot in the city that does not bear ancient footprints. A bare oval that now serves to divide lines of traffic is scored with chariot tracks, a patch of grass is scorched with Norman fire, a handful of pebbles casts the shadow of a Roman altar. Where ruins have been battered by man and time to total shapelessness they are battlegrounds of mad giants. Where there is recognizable shape—the Colosseum, the Theater of Marcellus, the Basilica of Maxentius—there remains unspeakable anger.

Immortal Rome is a triumph of mortality constantly revived; the Roman eagle dies to rise as a phoenix, changing with each flight from its ashes, discarding here, reshaping there. Following the density of changes in their confused logics of chronology and influences, of the simple proliferating into the complex, is difficult in the rapid spinning of a voyager's time and especially difficult when one is confronted with the interlaced threads of two major empires, the Church and classical Rome, by no means dead since some of their institutions, habits, and arts still wield influence.

Rome gives much and asks much: the agility to leap back and forth over the centuries, following mazes in several dimensions, swooping, darting, rising, and falling through layers of time. The bewildering chase from St. Peter's to Forum to Colosseum to S. Maria Maggiore to Pantheon to S. Giovanni in Laterano to the Campidoglio, quick glimpses of baroque fountains and the sinking, for a moment, into twentieth-century seats for hamburgers and then on to a mass of old wall near the modern railroad station, a surge of triumphal column surrounded by bright shops, two abandoned stalks of marble, a medieval slope of roof, rococo fancies on dismayed doorways, creates a twirling set of kinetic collages, more the art of mobiles bathed in shifting light than solid, descriptive scenes and portraits and not easy to absorb and remember.

It is the excess and heaped, muddled riches that *is* Rome, its frenetic pleasures enhanced by the city's systole and diastole, the pattern of quick, short breaths of tight alleys that exhale luxuriously at their neighboring piazze, an almost human breathing that unites city and man in the harmony which makes walking in Rome, in spite of the traffic, an easy, tireless progress. To share such and other delights of Rome is, of course, the primary purpose of this book and, tangentially, to make more appealing that which might initially be appalling, to touch with an attempt at comprehensibility that which seems incomprehensible, to isolate a number of representative entities that symbolize the restless broken waves that carved out the city.

An early guidebook, the twelfth-century *Mirabilia Urbis Romae*, was designed to point pilgrims from one shrine to another. Several centuries later a cleric wrote a book on Rome whose purpose was to plot paths between churches in such a manner that the devout might be always in the shade. A renowned German work that deals exclusively with medieval Rome spreads through numerous volumes; the building of St. Peter's in its various aspects through the centuries absorbs tome after tome; large and many books are devoted to the Roman works of one architect or one painter, to a sole palazzo. Although the hard-working Italian Touring Club guide, unfortunately not translated, tries, there is no one compete book on Rome, nor can there be, nor should it be attempted. This book joins the hordes of the truncated with several "famouses" explored lightly and from a personal point of view because they *are* so famous and exhaustively studied, with stress on the more obscure for their charm or glittering history or their singular "Romanness," which can mean many things. The arrangement here is not a strict plotting of courses—no musts, merely suggestions from which to choose. Nor do the sections follow an order of importance upward or down. The scheme is arbitrary and hopefully permits the reader to select and concentrate here and there according to his time, his energy, and his tastes.

A caveat before you are launched. No matter what guides say, not every building in Rome was built by Bramante or Bernini, not every massive sculpture is the work of Michelangelo, not every painting is by Raphael or Guido Reni. This warning extends to historical "fact" as well, often an amalgam of gossip, legend, tradition, and fancy woven into a thin scrim of recorded information. And that accounts for the recurrence of "it is said," "probably," "possibly," as irritating to write as to read, and one asks indulgence of the reader in the interests of skirting the wilder, fascinating shores of inaccuracy.

ROME: *Places and Pleasures*

VATICAN

St. Peter's

Everyone, of course, sees St. Peter's, and a first encounter is a bewildering Alice-in-Wonderland fall into a forest of gigantic marbles with golden fronds, skies of pocked and pierced gold; the flora climbing vines of cherubim, the fauna large white agitated figures with supplicating eyes. There is a tendency to escape, as from the Forum, to recoil from the vastness and its accretions, the outcome of invasions, sacking, earthquakes, and rebuilding that became increasingly grandiose with luxurious tastes and wealth and the challenge of the Reformation, not to mention the extraordinary tide of talent that washed into the portals. In architecture alone, Bramante, Raphael, Vignola, the Sangallos, Michelangelo, Peruzzi, Giacomo Della Porta, Maderna, Bernini, to neglect a few others.

The first "must" is that you must be decently dressed—no shorts on men, no bare chests male or female, and discreet length of skirt. Already, gossip-legend is mushrooming about attempted expulsions and fights that may never have taken place. A guardian-inspector proved too harsh, vulnerable and hot-tempered, and he was replaced by a nun whose low, calm speech and chaste black would discourage the boys in the ragged loincloths and the braless see-through girls. The latest piece of information is that, after a tormented week, the nun had a nervous breakdown and is now resting, recovering smoothly in the sickrooms of a sheltered convent far from the shocking, irreverent world.

The other "musts," and they truly must be seen, are the baldacchino of Bernini, wrapped in the bronze that once belonged to the Pantheon, and the *Pietà* of the young Michelangelo, which is placed so high that one cannot see

Christ's face but can marvel at the flaccidity of the upper
arm and shoulder as they drag from Mary's supporting
hand. The seeming lack of expression on the face of Mary,
no older than Christ, is often interpreted as that of total
resignation learned through years of foreknowledge, and
the sculptor himself said that Mary's youth symbolized her
innocence. The bronze St. Peter, whose metal doily halo was
given him in the late nineteenth century and is too dainty
for the stern, remote head, is generally attributed to the
thirteenth-century Arnolfo di Cambio. Some think it might
be a pagan figure (the blessing gesture and papal keys
added later) whose provenance was one of the local temples that shared the area with the earliest basilica. If that
were so, it managed to stay whole, as did the statue of
Marcus Aurelius on the Capitoline, through the fortunate
intervention of mistaken identity. If the light is right, a
blaze of glory and flights of angels will tear through the
clouds that sustain the Cathedra (throne) of St. Peter,
devised with the operatic effects characteristic of Bernini.
The elaborately worked bronze seat encloses (if it has been
returned after recent study) a wooden inlaid chair which
may (we are almost always clouded by nebulous Roman
uncertainty) be a Roman judge's seat or a throne brought
by Charles the Bald for his anointing ceremonies in Rome.
It is not the actual cathedra used by St. Peter. The gilded
stucco angels and babies are so boisterously happy one can
hear them sing, and the active drapery gives dynamic support to the gestures of four doctors of the Church, two
mitered to represent the Western and two bareheaded for
the Eastern Church, all four touching, taking strength from,
the cathedra and sharing it as a sign of church unity. Your
guide, either as person or as a compact little booklet worth
buying in the shops or from the gentlemen near St. Peter's,
may take you next to the Bernini monument for Pope
Alexander VII, a rich, rich, rich Chigi from Siena who prays
in effulgent Bernini lighting and is, in turn, adored by a
woman holding a child, who testifies to the many charities

of the Pope. At the other end of the arch, a figure who represents Faith. Her head leans slightly abashed like those of Filippo Lippi angels, but more interesting is her foot, which rests on a globe, the toes carefully obliterating England's place in the Catholic universe. (Bernini was a playful as well as gifted man.) The *pièce* here for sheer technical mastery, however, is the brown drape lifted by a skeleton holding an hourglass in marble as smooth and supple as heavy silk.

For the slow seeker, not easily engulfed, there are several worthy obscure works and details to be found in the supersplendor. For instance, look at the tomb of Clement XIII, by Canova, not too far in design from the Chigi tomb, though a white neoclassic deadness has set in. The lions alert and sleeping, clearly points of major concentration, are charmers, and the thin cones that emerge from the head of a stolid lady may remind you of the rays on the Statue of Liberty. Return to the baldacchino and look for one column pedestal whose shields, swarming with Barberini bees, hold a female head which expresses various degrees of agony and calm. She is said to represent a pregnant Barberini niece, and it seems a curious compliment to show her in labor—or could it have been Bernini's ingenious statement of good wishes that all might turn out well?

As you walk through the opulence jammed into corners of awesome, belittling space, notice that all the paintings but one are mosaic reproductions made to replace works which were disintegrating and have been moved to the kinder atmosphere of the Pinacoteca. Try to find—not if it is a fatiguing chore—the tomb of the eccentric, intellectual, sexually uncertain Christina of Sweden, which shows her big-nosed and bold-faced, light-years away from the beauty of Greta Garbo, and if it interests you, a tomb of the last of the exiled Stuarts, by Canova. When you pass St. Peter watch again the many people who put their hands to his foot, almost erased with years of touching and kissing, and then to their mouths; watch them lift their children to kiss the foot directly. One thinks, for the hundredth time, how healthy these people must be to live in littered streets with cats who have forgotten how to wash, people who pinch and heft market fruits and vegetables freely and thoroughly, who kiss each other and sacred images constantly, and still remain free of epidemics. As you wonder whether this might not be a subtle, steady miracle of the Church, examine the distinguished modern metal sculpture on a Paschal candle that now stands before St. Peter. In the center aisle, a piece of *bella figura* that belongs to the particularly resplendent Mother Church, bronze markings that show the comparative lesser lengths of other great cathedrals: Prague, Hagia Sofia, Reims, St. Patrick's, Westminster, and so on downward, none to match St. Peter's.

The dearly loved Pope John XXIII figures in a panel by Greco (of the controversial Orvieto doors) whose craggy, energetic angels accompany the comfortable, plump, egalitarian Pope in the progress of his life, the concepts and techniques especially successful in a section that deals with a visit made to prisoners shortly after John took the papacy, when he told them—a statement Romans are fond of quoting—that one of his ancestors was also imprisoned, for poaching.

The important modern work is the bronze door used for the funerals of dignitaries of the Church made by Manzù, an atheist and great friend of Papa Giovanni. The doors do not close tightly and harshly but curl back gently as they meet; a violent death is symbolized by the flight of stones, a peaceful death is an angel gently summoning the old Pope, and a convocation is etched as the slant of many cloaks. Spare and august, it makes its statements with economy and deep emotion, and gathers them together into ancient symbols of life and the Church: a gnarled old vine which will yet bear grapes and a heavy sheaf of wheat which will yield new seed.

The centuries meet in an unconscious gesture here, Manzu gazing across the portico at Giotto. The panel was once an ornament of the old basilica, hung in a place of honor, then it wandered in and out of a number of other places before it found its way back, damaged and tampered with, but still Giotto.

The roof of the basilica (stairs or elevator) reveals a few stimulating aspects of design and adornment unsuspected, unrevealed from below. The magniloquent statues, close up, are crude and backless; in spite of their size they lack impact and significance. They are poor relations of Roman colossi, awkwardly unfinished and made feeble by the cords of lightning conductor that run up their backs and end in spikes on their heads. The surrounding clusters of Vatican building are still too close, still too much an immense warren to define clearly the units that grew into, around, atop each other. Clarity returns on the billowing tropical-leaf shape of the Nervi roof of a new Assembly building and its clever insert of Art Nouveau window at the crest of the swell, at the domed glass cases that conduct light into the church, and especially Michelangelo's dome. Divorced from the structure below, from the majestic height and size that dominate the city, the dome becomes smaller, more inti-mate. The deceptively light, swinging festoons and ivory ribs that hold three perfectly spaced orders of window make of the dome, in this close view, a graceful temple, a singular small church of unique design.

Sad and tatty little strivings for immortality—names and dates crayoned, inked, scratched—darken the walls of the stairs that turn up and up, interminably, inside the drum and then begin to narrow and slant in a fun-house disloca-tion of space as they coil, narrower and narrower, to the top of the dome and its low iron-ringed balcony.

A map is helpful, sturdy legs important, and an ease with heights essential. Blocked by photographers who snap each other on a background of anonymous sky, and blocking their work and pleasure, one makes the circuit that ar-

ranges the Vatican city into simpler masses. The huge pine
cone of bronze found near the Pantheon (whose rione is
called Pigna—pine cone) glows from a neoclassical screen
that adjoins Bramante's Belvedere court. From this height,
the escape walk between the Vatican Palace and the Castel
S. Angelo becomes a barbed arrow and the formal gardens
reveal their skillful patterns—shrubs and grasses that make
concentric curves, as a drop of water might in a green
pool, around a charming shell fountain; intertwined bands
of yellow lying plumply on a bed of green; a papal insignia
of tiara, keys, the Chigi mounds and Farnese lilies embroidered in bright, controlled flowers and low, clipped bushes.
Now one can see just how the new Nervi museum hugs
the neoclassic Pinacoteca, which is, in turn, linked with the
lengths of older Vatican museums, the turret chosen for
his apartment by John XXIII shortly before he died and
the turret that functions as the Vatican's radio station,
incompletely linked by runs of papal wall.

Above, far above, the city's observatory, and semihidden
in the woods below, Raphael's Palazzo Madama, and to the
west, open ground waiting, the anticlerical say, for the
Vatican to fill with enterprising real-estate projects to join
their apartment blocks farther up on the rise of Monte
Mario. Still turning, the Janiculum, the endless park of the
Doria-Pamphili, St. Peter in Montorio, the Vatican railroad
and office buildings below, an Esso sign on the roof of a
gas station, painted especially for you, and an ordinary
street whose normally unseen core is a colorful, irregular
yardful of inner houses. The leafy fan of the Nervi roof now
looks like the lid of an ivory box, and one is back to the
façade side and identification of the heirs of St. Peter's
dome, with strong resemblances to their parent, that swell
the sky from the smooth ribbon of river to the rise of
Trinità dei Monti above the Spanish Steps. Very close,
behind you and dug firmly into the volutes that edge the
dome, the big hooks from which the *sanpietrini* lowered
their ropes to dangle over the dome, lighting the flares that

once upon a not too long time ago illuminated the dome on high ceremonial occasions. The rusty disks for oil still spot the rays, and the hooks remain as helpful aids for the agoraphobic, but the *sanpietrini* no longer make their firefly flights. Electricity has made their function obsolete except as sweepers and rearrangers of stanchions and temporary platforms in and outside the cathedral.

For some time closed, maybe at some time to be reopened, there is still a higher viewing point from the golden finial ball, but this lower ring should be quite enough, giving a total command of the city into its misty horizons.

The Mass that begins punctually at 11 o'clock in the vast atrium of St. Peter's on Easter Sunday is an occasion not to be slighted, no matter what your particular religion or lack of it tells you. Behind one group of statues on the colonnades, visiting priests, nuns, and guests of functionaries; between other rhetorical saints in their customary agonies of expression and draperies, photographers, cinematographers, television cameramen. The huge crowd, as many as 200,000, that drops from street buses, cars, and innumerable tourist caravans to find places in the embrace of Bernini's colonnade is orderly, respectable, and it speaks every language in the world including Italian dialects. The young find uncertain perches on wooden barriers beneath the obelisk and try for the curlicues of the nineteenth-century Place de l'Opéra lamplights.

If you haven't done so before and the crowd still permits, look for the marble spots at the sides of the obelisk, vantage points that align the double rows of colonnade columns as one. See if your glasses can pick out a Renaissance composition in the vicinity of the altar of red and purple robes and faces of bishops and cardinals reminiscent of the painting by Melozzo da Forlì in the Pinacoteca. Notice how Michelangelo's dome, visible from almost any rise in the city, has disappeared behind Maderna's façade, an eventuality that Michelangelo feared. Notice—if you are not too desperately jostled by a short man whose binoculars show him only napes of necks and backs and he muttering at all the thousands of them to get out of his way— that the obelisk does not stand on a flat base but is, for the sheer showiness of it, resting on the backs of four flattened lions. Probably because of the importance of its position, each step of the raising of the obelisk was carefully recorded, and there are extant prints taken from an old volume which demonstrate with painstaking exactitude the types of ropes used and the manner in which they were knotted, the diversity of pulleyed wheels, platforms, scaffolds, and supports, each a precision instrument, that add up to a grand tutti of nearly a thousand men, dozens of machines, more than one hundred horses and miles of rope pulling at the obelisk in an infinity of rayed lines. A story, not necessarily fact, tells of an order of silence on pain of death during the concerted effort to set the Egyptian pillar upright. One version of the story says that a rope caught fire because of friction; another insists that one rope was slackened. If the slack-rope version is told, it is a sailor who shouts, "Pour on water." Advice taken, rope tightens, sailor absolved and given honors. If "pour on water" is meant to quench fire, forgiveness and honor go to a member of the Braschi of the Piazza Navona, and because the family held southern lands in which palm trees flourished, they were given the concession of supplying the city's churches in preparation for Palm Sunday.

No fuss accompanied the placing of the Chigi mounds and star and the relic of the True Cross they contain at the top of the obelisk. The relic replaced a golden urn full of the ashes of Julius Caesar, it was rumored, placed on the spire when it came from Egypt to be used as a marker in the circus of Caligula (later expanded by Nero), a short distance from the present basilica. Here, where St. Peter was martyred, Constantine built a noble church on his tomb, the proof of its existence becoming more clearly visible as excavations continue under the Vatican.

But we return to the Easter celebration of the 262nd pope after Peter, the "rock" on which the church was founded. The choir, whose amplified, rich sounds float through the piazza and into the Via della Conciliazione, intone old liturgical music in the responses of the service. The tired old voice burred with the French "r" of the north retires after the Mass to be heard almost immediately later from a red-draped balcony where the pope delivers his sermon, a brief one in the spring of 1971, which deplored the decay of morals and the explosions of violence and added consolations of better things to come promised in the words of Christ. "Happy Easter" is spoken in all European languages, including several Slavic tongues, and in Arabic, Korean, Japanese, and Chinese. This is followed by the benediction and the immediate dismantling by an army of ant-men of the red-robed door and balcony, a holy image is lowered with unholy speed, the altar is taken apart with marked dispatch, and it's all over for another year.

The babble of languages and gestures of deaf-mute pilgrims stroll out past a sign that insists on the repeal of the divorce act and another that asks for higher wages for parish priests. It is a pleasant, relaxed crowd, its joints easy as it saunters toward the bus pens, sunburned, unawed by the weight of the experience—benediction by the Vicar of God on the day of Resurrection, greetings in a universe of languages proper to the Universal Church. The gelato wagon and the souvenir shops are mobbed while a man with a fortunetelling machine that is an ingenious jumble of flashlights, bells, primitive typewriter, whirring ineffectual wheels—something like the jukebox in Saroyan's *Time of Your Life,* if you remember that far back—bemoans his lack of an interpreter to call and explain his magic machine. The sidewalk caffès rush coffees, pizza droops from a good number of hands, a boy with hair as dirty as his bare feet asks directions of a pristine policeman who answers him with great courtesy. A family from New

Jersey asks if a policeman in a white helmet and gloves will pose with them. "Volentieri," and they take him home in their camera wreathed in Rosie and Joe.

Rising from the mouth of the traffic tunnel at the bottom of the street of the penitents (Penitenzieri), southeast of St. Peter's, the slapdash working-class Salita di S. Onofrio darts up to the heights of the Janiculum, grounds sacred to Janus. Follow the walk upward to the left, leaving below receding streets and unsuspected green plots, as perfectly designed and varied as only Italians can make a garden. A drop from the path (the Passeggiata del Gianicolo) takes one to a small amphitheater, used at times for plays, usually for necking, picnicking and viewing Rome, and, back on the path, the shattered trunk of an oak bound and crutched with iron, accompanied by a stone that describes the place as a peaceful refuge of the delicately balanced poet Tasso. The Passeggiata opens to a brisk open-air caffè, a lighthouse, and a generous expanse of city. A springtime visitor may still see snow on the Alban hills and closer in (opera glasses will help, and a monuments map if you enjoy picking out specific buildings) the cityscape of domes and famous landmarks. To the south—right—the ivory crown of statuary on S. Giovanni; to the left, the green of the Pincian hills; across the river, the Palatine and Aventine, and, conspicuous in the tangle of palazzi and monuments, the dulled leaden dome of the denuded Pantheon; the leap of the leaning Torre delle Milizie; the uncharacteristic roof of the synagogue, and if the sky is clear and your glasses cooperative, the top of S. Maria Maggiore and, closer to, the swirl of Borromini's spire on S. Ivo. It makes a good game if you already know the face of the city, an impressive ensemble if you don't.

Below, at the end of the rows of artichokes and fruit trees, the botanical gardens attached to the Villa Corsini, its arches smoothed by distance into an attractiveness it lacks face to face. Back of you, a heroic, agitated equestrian Anita Garibaldi, the South American Pasionaria buried here, and—an odd way to serve heroes—busts in rows, circles, ovals, with and without hats, staring, thoroughly dead descendants of the weakest of Roman portraits, meant to represent the fervent men who followed Garibaldi and died defending the short-lived Republic in 1849.

The Passeggiata which has given you glimpses of villas close and far and the sea of green that is the park (now public) of the Villa Doria-Pamphili will, with a couple of downward turns, take you through the Via di S. Pancrazio, past the villa of Garibaldi's last-stand battle, to drop you in Trastevere. Continuing southward and turning left leaves one at S. Pietro in Montorio, the church given an innocent night light that glows softly across the Tiber. S. Pietro in Montorio was the scene of a major event in church tradition. Here, far above the temples of the Capitoline, St. Peter was crucified and taken to be entombed on the lower adjoining hill of the Vatican. There is no sign of the Apostle's presence in or near the church, nor of Beatrice Cenci, although it is more certain that she was buried in the chancel after her execution on the banks of the river. The usual competent and unadventurous church art doesn't hold one long; the attraction is inside the gate next to the church in the yard it shares with the Spanish Academy of Fine Arts. It shocks at first, like an untrustworthy optical illusion, and seems to be enormously outsized for the meager space of the yard. This tempietto of Bramante, built in 1502, is an appealing miniature adorned with granite columns, a tasteful balustrade to introduce the dome, and alternations of niches and chaste ornaments: a charming, rare, expensive toy. Why was it built? To show what Bramante could do if he were appointed architect of St. Peter's. Julius II gave him the job a few years later, and between them they destroyed venerable areas of the older church with the enthusiasm of the Huns before and the Barberinis later. Bramante may also have been playing a favorite Renaissance game, how to translate the strict principles of the Roman architect Vitruvius and the buildings his tenets produced into grace, suavity, and humanity rarely seen in the original models.

Turn back (on the Via Garibaldi) for variants of architecture: a harsh, stiff-jawed forties monument and, nearby, the Fontana Paola, built in the triumphal arch manner awash with vigorous Roman waters, and an improved repetition, built by Paul V in 1612, of the unfortunate Acqua Felice fountain downtown.

Westward and up to the Porta S. Pancrazio opens the Doria-Pamphili park, a vastness of woods and open field punctuated with a small lake fed by a sloping arrangement of fountains and self-contained fountains, among them a frolicsome bundle of dolphins designed by Bernini. Then, back for a drop into Trastevere. (A map is absolutely essential here.)

NOTE: A walk through the Vatican gardens is not too difficult to manage with accredited guides. The gardens are, as you might suppose, exquisitely manicured and afford a look into the mosaic workshop on the grounds and a survey in garden planning and fountain tastes of several periods. The walk usually ends with two dramatic late paintings by Michelangelo in the Pauline Chapel.

To visit St. Peter's Tomb, or the deep cavity claimed for it, requires more serious planning—a letter long in advance to your legation to the Holy See, a priest with good connections in Rome, and sometimes the guides already mentioned. Groups admitted are small and the visits infrequent. Although easing through the narrow streets of a tombal city and its ornaments of paint and building detail to reach an empty pause in a long shaft of earth has its interest—and a touch of upmanship when comparing notes with traveling friends—similar structures are easily available to the eye in the necropolis outside of Ostia Antica, open any reasonable time you choose to go.

For the Wednesday morning papal audiences—en masse—arrange with guides, the North American College in Rome, 30 Via dell' Umiltà, or Foyer Unitas, 30 Via dell'Anima.

Museum—Pagan and Paleo-Christian

Near the turnstile and checkroom, up a few stairs and to the right, a startling modernity of museum display, the new Nervi wing designed to hold the archaeological finds of the nineteenth century (plus some objects formerly in other sections of the Vatican museums) that were gathered together by Pope Gregory XVI (1831–1846) as the museums of the Lateran Palace. Pope John XXIII commissioned the new section, and as it expands, an increasing number of classical and early Christian objects make their way across the city, traversing the route of medieval and Renaissance papal processions.

The first effect is shocking. What is the connection between headless classical torsos, bodiless marble heads, crushing cornices, richly adorned sarcophagi, with steely gray pillars and crossbars held together with big, raw bolts like the skeletons of modern buildings or park jungle-gyms? It works, and very well, particularly when one begins to understand the loose flow of spaces that separate but never close off objects from one another and notices the ingeniously planned windows through which glows a faint dawn light, enhancing the distance and mystery of the figures without obscuring them. Nothing lurks, everything is given its due in air and space. The relentless long-gallery imprisonment of other sections of the Vatican museums, the stiff funereal progress of effigies in strictly placed arches, has been dissolved, and the viewer released into stimulating irregularities that lead him up, down, around (mapped out by a chart at the entrance, if he needs it), in clear, if understated, rational progress.

For the visitor with limited time and only so much interest in classical antiquities this area, the Belvedere court, and the monumental torso may be quite enough of Vatican museums. Though incomplete in the summer of 1971, with much to come (including identifying labels), there was still, for the amateur, quite enough—and maybe too much. It is too soon to say surely, but there seems to be a dichotomy of thinking in this new annex: architecture and placement of the late twentieth century combined with a nineteenth-century unwillingness to consign to archives or basements innumerable repetitions. (One can only hope that the stuttering of which so many Roman collections suffer will stop here and other museums will follow suit, pruning mercilessly and storing the excess for scholars and intense enthusiasts.)

Among the torsos and heads of Roman copies of Greek sculpture and of indigenous Roman work (frequently representatives of a flourishing commercial art that reproduced thousands of satyrs, Apollos, bearded terms and portraits, each copy of a copy moving farther from the virtues of the original) try to find a head of Sophocles, severely damaged and yet a meaningful work. At one turn or another you should come on a large mosaic, probably from an Imperial banqueting hall. In tiles so minute and subtly matched that they achieve the shades of brush painting, the craftsmen designed an amusing "after the feast" composition not unlike a Dutch genre painting. Three grapes drooping from a stem, a discarded chicken's foot and bones, the empty shells of snails and lobsters, an olive, a mouse gnawing at a nut, a wishbone, the skeleton of a fish, all given depth by fine creamy-gray shadows on a white background. As a cadenza, the designer edged his tablecloth with black-mouthed, black abyss-eyed Fury masks and on a dark background of Egyptian figures drew Egyptian waterfowl among papyrus plants.

A great marble bulge thrusts at you the garlanded bull's skull, the festoons and other traditional motifs of the first century A.D. that decorated what must have been an important mausoleum. It offers a tentative image of the vast circular mausoleum, now the Castel S. Angelo, Hadrian designed for himself one hundred years later. Making note as you go that there are no fig leaves in this part of the Vatican—and little need for them, since penises, and noses, are the most frangible parts of archaeological anatomy— you should come shortly to a room marked "Nobide Chiaramonti" that confronts you with a flying headless figure in a fury of draperies and her calmer sister in slightly less wind-swept robes. Back of the sisters, sitting quite alone on a pedestal numbered 9969, there is an enchanting head worthy of Praxiteles, though it is a Roman copy of a young woman whose musing head bends like a flower from the strong stem of neck. It is a compelling work that speaks, however softly and pensively, across the centuries.

A mercifully small number of sarcophagi frame stiff scrawny couples staring severely out at their lost world and couples who look at or touch each other in mutual, friendly consolation. Life again flourishes in a big-bellied sleeping Bacchus, his head lolling on a wineskin, one plump breast drooping as relaxedly as his half-open drunken mouth. He, large and conspicuous as he is, was merely part of a fountain designed for a theater, another detail to add to the image of the monumental that was, and still is, Roman.

As in similar collections, some of the bits of frieze that cling modestly to the walls deserve considerably more attention than they are usually given. Here a fragment of joyful women dancers and musicians, there a ritual procession; and on fragments of column, deeply carved clusters of lyres, fruits, sheaves of grain densely and complexly designed, pieces of Roman baroque. (Perhaps every period in art history had and has its baroque.) The rococo might be the light-handed plasterwork, extremely refined, that places a young Pan among fruit trees and the embrace of tendrils, leaves, and berries floating together in a perfumed breeze.

Not remarkable as art, though informative as contemporary reports of Roman architecture and life, are slabs that depict theaters, temples, statues, musicians, funeral processions, a wheel-like machine turned by men who walk the spokes to activate attached pulleys and ropes, a curious figure that seems to be sitting on his own tomb, and another stretched on a bier, like a medieval knight misplaced in time. Look, also, for a group of Negroid heads perhaps brought from Egypt or creations generated by the presence of Africans in Rome. See if you can find, not too far away (nothing is, yet), a kneeling man forced down by another. There is no label, no knowing whether this is the beginning of a beheading or enslavement, but, again, you are in the presence of a work that speaks vigorously. You cannot possibly miss a figure, semiprotected by a coarse brown curve of wall, which is considerably larger than life, blunt-nosed and shaggy-haired, wrapped in heavy winter garments. The frowning, saddened face might be that of a captured Barbarian or, judging from his size, more likely a leader of Roman troops in the north; whoever he is, the man and his setting are eminently impressive.

The inescapable sarcophagi return, this particular group no more attractive than their million counterparts, though the skill of these carvings, the exactitude of anatomical detail and adroitness in rendering strain and activity— attacking and being attacked by animals, for example— deserve more than a passing glance. One casket crams every inch of space with figures large and small who dance and sing and consort with lyre-playing centaurs, with lions, fauns, and nymphs. Out of the background poke the heads of a giraffe and two elephants with frilled ears whose African presence relates to the plump-nosed and ripe-lipped dancing figures at the sides of the sarcophagus.

As essential as sarcophagi for any such collection is a large, very white, bemused Antinous, and here he is again, holding flowers in a fold of his toga. As "required" are the Roman portraits, and one wishes, as before and after, that some of them had been left wherever they had previously been. Concentrate instead on a lyrical panel, surprisingly sentimental for a Roman piece, of Ceres offering nourishment from a cornucopia to a baby, near a pair of domesticated goats. Behind them a young Pan trying out a syrinx; above, an eagle with a dead rabbit in his claws; in a spreading tree, birds gazing at a nestful of their young threatened by a coiled snake. (It is entertaining to conjecture whether or not this presentation of the bounty and cruelty of Nature gave Italian painters patterns of composition for Adam and Eve, the Virgin and Child, and manger scenes.)

The section set aside for Eastern religions brought to Rome leaves art entirely but is, in its own mystifying way, stimulating. Who could the soft-faced woman be who is dressed in the skin usually worn by Hercules, peering out of his lion's head and carrying his knobbed club? Mithras is familiar, but who is the fierce lion-headed figure wrapped tightly in the coils of a snake and in its human hands a set of keylike symbols? Barring Aztec gods, one of the most repellent is Diana of Ephesus, who carries lions on her arms, small griffons in rows on her tight skirt, turrets on her sullen head, and the rest of her garlands on garlands of teats, like a human papaya tree. Obviously a fertility goddess, but why so unattractive and stern-faced?

The Christian section stems from finds in the catacombs and the earliest Christian basilicas. They bring from the Romans scenes of the wine harvest and the gathering of wheat and from the Greeks, with Roman adaptations, the Good Shepherd playing a prominent role. The vineyard and fields disappear and give place to the rows of lambs who walk so meekly and charmingly across innumerable church apses. We have come to know them as representatives of the followers of Peter and Paul, and as the twelve apostles,

six on each side. Why are there seven and seven here? The
affable guards cannot explain, though labels later may.
Roman habits die hard, so you will see the old ram's horns
still hanging on to the angles of Christian sarcophagi, as
well as pagan mythology, though somewhere you will find
a circle around an X and P or a variation of the word
"deposit." That is, placed here temporarily to await Christian resurrection. The Good Shepherd loses out at some
point to a fashion for Jonah and his whale, who gives way
in his turn to Roman-style processionals of Old and New
Testament figures. Suddenly, the masks and languid gods
and goddesses and cupids reappear, too irresistibly attractive to lose, and then the seesaw returns again to Christian
scenes, often in landscapes of temples, fortresses, and
houses that show the alternation of angular and rounded
niches like those of the Pantheon and the swirled columns
that still stand in the church of S. Sabina.

These big tombs—as lavish as those of the Romans—
setting their scenes of the Magi, of Christ's miracles, of the
slaughter of the innocents, the sacrifice of Isaac, as if they
were theater pieces, may counter the frequently expressed
theory that Christianity was a religion of the enslaved and
poor. However, they may have been of a later time when
Christianity was well and legally established, when the
jeweled cross began to appear in churches, and Roman
sculpture—an interesting thread to follow among the sarcophagi—began to show characteristics of the Romanesque.

This, as mentioned, is a beginning; there is a great deal
more to come of what was an important collection. Let
your feet, allotted Vatican time, and your own taste be your
guide, and keep in mind that not every nude, head, sarcophagus, Christian or Roman, necessarily merits close
scrutiny.

Pinacoteca

It is assumed that you will see the Vatican famouses. First, the Sistine Chapel, named for the late fifteenth-century Pope Sixtus IV, in whose time it was planned and partially decorated. As everyone knows, this is the hall of the sixteenth-century Michelangelo frescoes, larger than life in several ways, more than a little appalling in their naked, distraught *terribilità*. It must be said, regretfully, that in the high tourist seasons it is almost impossible to see the ceiling frescoes and *The Last Judgment*. One is simply in their presence; the chapel is too jammed with busloads of tourists to allow for the slow neck-craning and the viewing of detail with opera glasses. *The Last Judgment*, furthermore, is fading; the boiling multitude of extraordinary forms is beginning to melt together, joining, overlapping, even more turbulent in their "Hebraic ferocity," as Stendhal called it, than Michelangelo might have meant them to be. Vasari says of *The Last Judgment*: "This great painting is sent by God to men as an example to show what can be done when supreme intellects descend upon the earth, infused with grace and divine knowledge. It takes captive those who think they know art, who tremble at the genius of the master in seeing his handiwork, while in regarding his labours their senses are overcome by thinking how other pictures can possibly bear comparison with them." A more precise authority, Maurizio Calvesi, speaks of the artist's departure from the classicism of the Renaissance, "which now the Counter-Reformation identified negatively with paganism. The very notion of non-perspective space must have seemed distinctly anti-classical, furthermore the figures, as if deformed by the surging currents of empty space, are elongated and compressed, doing violence to the classical canon of proportions. Their swollen forms are no longer the sculpturesque expression of an internal plastic tension, but seem to expand under the action of some obscure fermentation."

The sack of Rome by Charles V had affected Michelangelo, as it did many Italians, deeply; hellfire was real —it had happened and could happen again. Always an introspective man, and old when he worked on the fresco, his mind turned more constantly to thoughts of sin and death, and the uncertainties of the afterlife, preoccupations reflected in his own distorted face, twisted and agonized, drooping from the flayed skin of St. Bartholomew. (And should you be able to approach the fresco, try to identify the drapes ordered later to cover unseemly nudity, the humiliating job assigned to Daniele da Volterra, a younger contemporary of Michelangelo, who earned the name of Il Braghettone, the pantsmaker.)

In the craning, crushing, anxious, "I'm not getting my money's worth" atmosphere, one tends to neglect the chapel's fifteenth-century frescoes by great artists who were not so much interested in tremendous *Dies Irae* statements as harmonies of color and form, the pleasures of painting dreamy landscapes, solid aristocratic bodies, fine portraits and courtly adornments: Botticelli, Signorelli, Ghirlandaio, Pinturicchio and Perugino. Whatever the crush or rush, don't pass them by.

It will be assumed, also, that one sees the Raphael rooms (Stanze di Raffaello) painted by the short-lived, meteorically successful artist, with the assistance of his favorite disciple, Giulio Romano. Raphael is not everyone's painter; the sheer versatility and enameled perfection put some people off, as they did that conspicuous, verbal and minor school of art, the Pre-Raphaelites. If you are a latter-day Pre-Raphaelite, you might let the Stanze go. Viewing the musts of Rome creates some of the exigencies of a "required course." There are no penalties for cutting a class or two. If you do go through the Stanze, as you probably should, since they contain several of Raphael's (and Romano's) most famous paintings, don't neglect the Cappella di Nicolò V, suffused with the genial modesty of Fra Angelico.

By way of Roman mosaic insets in wall and floor beyond the turnstile, one arrives at a loggia that offers two views: a shapely open court and the closeness of St. Peter's dome; and, at the right, the angles, shallow arches and spurs of the Nervi museum building and a medieval tower with a ballooning hat. At the end of the loggia, the Pinacoteca. The primitive art galleries that open the chronological progress are notable mainly for a few icons from the Eastern Church, holy scenes that emerge from a cut-out plate of stamped silver, a small triptych whose formal miniature figures are like those of a *Book of Hours*, and another, packed full of violently lively minute figures. A *Last Judgment* of neat rows of saints and sinners etched in hard colors on dark grounds may remind you of Tibetan painting, and a remote, dark-eyed Virgin and lady saints recall Eastern monasteries. These dourly devout panels alternate with the sunny, prosperous, placid heavens and earths of Siena of the early fourteenth century, before the plague blackened the glowing visions. Look for the orderliness of Sano di Pietro's *Saint George Converting the King's Daughter*, with its impeccable grouping of figures, its play of naïve perspective, and the effect of strong black strokes that crown the doors and compel the eye to the subtle pinks and lavenders of wall. Spend some time with the several fanciful paintings by Giovanni de Paolo, and by Giovanni del Biondo, a big, golden pregnant matron, her hand resting on an exaggerated pink brocade belly, to represent the Virgin Mary.

Sala III moves into the Renaissance, opening with Fra Angelico's interpretation of an episode in the life of S. Nicola da Bari, all of it reasonably of its time except for waves and walls in impossible terra cotta folds, very primitive or very Dali. For Gozzoli the Virgin moves through her life in the regal pace of a richly dressed Florentine lady. Francesco di Gentile sees her less triumphant in his *Madonna della Farfalla*. A disturbingly old and doughy child, beset by a mortal disease, sits on the lap of a worried but rigidly controlled Madonna. Behind them, light foam on pale waves, and to the right, an utterly dissociated, bright butterfly which turns into an ominous symbol in the total context of the painting. You needn't be told to look for the grand Melozzo da Forlì representation of Sixtus IV with several other ecclesiasts, all luxuriously dressed figures, conducting their business under a golden coffered ceiling and pilaster capitals picked out in gold. We are now in Sala IV, where another Melozzo da Forlì work, less strained and obviously more enjoyed than the churchly portraits, appears as frescoed musician-angels, appealing heads worked in muted colors, one of them a blond English child violist who happened to wander into an Italian angel chorus.

The late fifteenth into sixteenth centuries (Sala V) produced some strange things. By Francesco del Cossa a cold, chalky, sharply painted mad landscape of broken buildings and arches that lead nowhere or serve as a frame for distant figures on tortured stone bridges. Completely of this earth is the *Pietà* of Lucas Cranach, close, intimate, blocked out starkly in broad areas of red, blue-white, and black.

The Italian love of decoration and displays of virtuosity take over in the next gallery. A Carlo Crivelli Virgin is a Persian princess, all pearls, brocade, and disdain, sitting under jewels shaped like fruit. Crivelli vitiates the emotion of his *Pietà*, in spite of its tortured Flemish-influenced faces, by placing it in a background of angels' heads, wings, and halos, close on each other like densely patterned wallpaper, which catches and holds the attention. The sweet, becalmed Peruginos and Pinturicchios lead into the great hall of tapestries designed by Raphael (Sala VIII) and woven in Brussels. In spite of the limitations of the medium—the tendency toward ragged, harsh contrasts, the stiff, unreal modeling of faces—the drawing remains surprisingly supple and expressive, especially in the panel that depicts the miraculous fish-seining with its three robust figures, writhing fish in the water, and, on the bank, three long-beaked, long-legged eager birds as minutely observed and detailed as Chinese paintings. In the same hall, Raphael's famous *Madonna di Foligno*, whose plump lively Child is ready to slip off the maternal lap to join myriad baby angels, and the *Transfiguration* washed in a broad, golden light that emanates from Christ. This was the last Raphael painting, completed by assistants and placed at the head of his deathbed, according to Vasari, when he died at the age of 37.

One drops from greatness to two long thin paintings of saints standing one above the other on Gothic pedestals, silly, engaging, and perfect models for Florentine souvenirs. Of another art universe is the large *Pietà* of Giovanni Bellini, a work of passionate, controlled movement that sounds of lamentation. Across the room (IX) the incredible monochrome sketch for a St. Jerome by Leonardo da Vinci, not too clear except for the sunken-cheeked old head and the strained neck and shoulder muscles, yet enough to display a medical mastery of anatomy and the magic which could, with a quick wash of brown on brown, make an immortal portrait of a rapt, humble old man speaking with God.

The Venetians arrive; dexterous, clever, absolute masters of perspective—upside down and backwards and upward— and the colors and shine of cut velvet, satins, and brocades. Veronese makes a Spanish queen of St. Helena, and Titian dresses the Virgin in sensuous deep red. Less famous, less fancy, and more moving is the big, straightforward St. Francis by Girolamo Muziano of the latter half of the sixteenth century.

The next few paces will bring you into the uneasy presence of Mannerism or Anti-Mannerism or whatever you choose (the field is open and of uncertain definitions and dimensions) to call the strong contrasts, the conspicuously emphasized gesture, and the fervid composition which strives to burst the limits of space. Like other schools of painting, it works well for some and not for others. A San Lorenzo by Ribera, an impassioned St. Matthew of Guido Reni, the expressive peasant heads and bodies of Caravaggio's *Deposition* and the head of Judith's maid in Gentileschi's *Giuditta* use the style masterfully. But look at Judith herself and the enormous *Madonna and Child* by Carlo Maratta, designed for a large billboard on a busy highway, to experience some of the mistakes the style could make.

St. Jerome, a great favorite, shows up again with his skull and book, listens to a trumpet that appears out of brown clouds, and then conducts us to fruits and flowers as only seventeenth-century Neapolitans could paint them. Figs and pomegranates open like trumpet calls or D. H. Lawrence heroines, and flowers are full, brilliant, and shockingly candid. They are quite wonderful and easily translate to fantasies, which they were probably meant to do, or at least to imply a fruitiness, a ripeness not necessarily that of edibles and the earth's colorful embroideries. Knowing how Italian words, including those for fruits, can turn into obscenities—a twist at which Neapolitans are masters—there is no reason to doubt a possibility of double meanings.

The popes and doge (by Titian) whose unbeautiful faces line the portrait hall (XV) are dimmed in the effulgence of a full-length Lawrence portrait of a round, stylish, sound-legged, full-panoplied, happy George IV, and what is he, a successor of Henry VIII, doing among popes in the Vatican?

The last galleries, the "modern," are extraordinarily feeble. Nineteenth- and twentieth-century popes had apparently lost the joy—or no longer thought it seemly—of ordering hundreds of feet of frescoes, or goblets by Cellini, or portraits by Titian. There is no sample of Italian Futurist painting; nothing much but imitations of Pre-Raphaelites, Gustave Moreau, and the French Impressionists. Among these inconsequentials, one rather accomplished flat-planed green painting of huts, a bronze bust of a young girl, and the Manzù bronze of John XXIII, an affectionate portrait of the knowing smile and the wise, hooded eyes above the long slope of Manzù cloak.

The Bus

One of the most powerful men in Rome, more intimately and consistently effective than local politicians, is the coin collector and dispenser of tickets who sits enthroned at the back of the one-tiered bus. Not since the Antonines has Rome enjoyed such benevolent despotism, and rarely so aware and capable a ruler. Ruler he is, make no mistake, the driver his valued right-hand man, his domain the citizenry in the bus, the juggernaut itself, and the inviolable space immediately surrounding it.

He is seriously attentive—except in slow, empty summer hours when he concentrates on a crossword puzzle or a *giallo* (the color of inexpensive detective novels)—to every detail of his varied responsibilities and, except in traffic conflicts, benign and unharried. He will ask a young man sitting nearby to read out the day's headlines and will explain what they really mean, not as reported in the corrupt press. He may require all children to say "Grazie" when he hands them the fare receipt, taking on himself the improvement of *educazione* and sense of *civiltà* among the young. An old woman laden with plastic sacks can engage him in a long, patient discussion of where she is going and why and is this the bus she should take and where must she change? He explains in detail while he collects money, hands out receipt slips, and urges the crowd forward in the bus. He has an efficient sign language and often some English to guide or soothe tourists whose anxious hands poke maps or bits of paper into his unruffled face. Rarely, if ever, does he forget to warn a charge, foreign or native, that his stop is arriving soon. It is he who is the guardian of those who almost miss buses. He keeps a sharp eye out for desperate sprinters and calls to the driver to wait until the gasping body has leaped aboard, an extraordinary act of kindness for big-city buses.

As a sharp-eyed evaluator of traffic space (he must be an experienced driver capable of taking over the wheel if necessary), it is he who leaps off the bus to direct a tight turn that will not rip off the backs of parked cars or crush curbs. Should there be a sudden sharp stop (and keep yourself well braced for these and swooping turns) and a woman thrown against the seat in front of her and then to the floor, sustaining fast-rising swellings and discolorations, it is he who will thunder at the owner of the offending car while the bus driver meekly asks the lady if she would like to be driven back to S. Giacomo hospital or get off in front of a hospital in Trastevere. The king, taking a few seconds out of his eruptions of insulting vocabulary, will commandeer another bus and get his subjects on their ways while he, car owner, and a policeman who has finally sauntered on the scene shout an operatic trio.

A woman frantically rummages in her bag, among her bundles, and screams lustily, "I've been robbed! I had a bill of five thousand lire and now it's gone! Stop the bus, get the police!" The bus stops, our Leader turns detective and asks wise, laconic questions which she answers inco-

herently. Inevitably, everyone gets into the act; someone
saw her with her purse open, someone saw it clasped tightly
under her arm; someone else saw a young man dart away
rapidly from the bus stop, probably the thief. She isn't
calmed (that will take weeks), but the boss convinces her
that a busload of people do not want to accompany her to
the offices of the head of police where she insists on going,
that you can't scour Rome for one pickpocket, but he will
take her name and address and make a report. To whom
and for what purpose is not clear, but stating her name and
address to have it recorded by the Jove of the bus gives
her a bit of grumbling satisfaction. The fixer is back on
his high seat, and the assemblage relaxes into stories of
thefts, exchanges advice on how to carry money safely,
examines each other's pocketbooks for their theft-proof
qualities, and the bus bumbles along.

A night or two after a Fascist victory in Sicilian and
Roman local elections, the 26 bus did not make its customary turn at the Ara Pacis of Augustus to follow the Corso
into the Piazza del Popolo. The collector announced, "Those
slob Fascists are holding a victory rally in the Piazza; we're
by-passing it," and the bus continued up the river without
a stop until it had reached a point considerably north of
the Flaminian gate and its Piazza del Popolo. The closed
bus became a meeting hall of vehement politics. One woman's response to the collector's order was: "Why can't they
have a meeting? Isn't this a free country?"

"Free?" he bellows. "Who was free under Mussolini and
Hitler? Who's free in Spain? And in Sicily, what's the victory, what's changed? The Mafia is Fascism and Fascism
the Mafia, those bloody pigs who don't know how to exist
without slaughtering each other."

The lady doesn't answer but settles back with her own
libertarian thoughts and a smug smile. A large elderly
woman now takes the floor: "My one and only son was
killed in Mussolini's war; the Fascists want more blood
now. Look at my husband"—poking a shriveled old man

half her size. "He was in two wars and fought in the Resistance, and where are we now? On pensions that hardly feed us, as poor as we ever were." The little husband takes over, spluttering angrily, "The only answer is Communism; we must have a Communist Italy and to hell with all those Demo-Christians who eat and drink wine and talk and do nothing for the people." A young man carrying a copy of the works of Lenin moves up to an empty seat closer to the old man, who keeps repeating his protest, trembling with anger. A group up in front argues, one voice leaping over the other, sounds growing more confused and urgent, blaming the Communists for the Fascist victory—"Always strikes; people have had them up to here, and they're showing the Commies how they feel about closed schools and post offices, no water and mountains of garbage in the streets"—heaping scorn on the Christian Democrats who kept none of their promises for reforms. Enthroned sits the smiling catalyst who enlivened his route and that of his subjects with a good, loud, rousing free-for-all and made his contribution to Italian political life by refusing to deliver anyone to the Fascist block party.

A good number of buses and trams (go between 2 and 4 P.M.—not on Sunday—the best hours for seats) run excellent sightseeing routes, and the cost is only 50 lire. The 26 is an amusement park whip ride. Descending from Parioli, where it has gathered momentum, the bus flies and bumps around every corner it can find between the Piazza del Popolo and Trastevere, and beyond, flashing snapshots of the Ara Pacis, a wedge of river, a glimpse of the Piazza Navona, almost straight into the columns of the Pantheon, and then, snorting and indignant, creeps through the narrow street, clogged with traffic that lets it approach the Largo Argentina and continue its charge across the river. Hold on tight whether you are standing or seated.

The 11 tram serves one of the lustier slum areas, Garba-

tella, which is featured in Rome crime pages with fair
regularity, passes the wholesale markets on the Via Ostiense,
touches the pyramid at the gate of S. Paolo and the Circus
Maximus, circles the Colosseum, plunges into the Suburra
to emerge at the Basilica of S. Lorenzo and the vast city
cemetery, Campo Verano. The ED tram circles the city from
the Viale Belle Arti (north of the Piazza del Popolo), skirting the Borghese Gardens, then turning for a dash to S.
Lorenzo, followed by a few twists that end at S. Giovanni
in Laterano. It, too, strokes the Colosseum, the feet of the
Palatine and the Pyramid, and hugs the river for a span
after it crosses to give Trastevere and Prati (near the Vatican museums) the pleasure of its company before the
return to Belle Arti, and off we go again.

The 20 takes off from Piazzale Flaminio (extension of
Piazza del Popolo), makes for the Tiber and tears down its
right bank, passing near the Castel S. Angelo and the Isola
Tiberina. Back across the river to the Colosseum, eastward
toward S. Maria Maggiore and the Station. North from the
Station to trundle along the Pincio and, being a *circolare*,
back to the Piazzale Flaminio. If the 5 and 13 are handy,
follow their baroque routes, and the 94 from the Pantheon
to the Aventine, or the 52 or 56 from S. Silvestro to modern
gardened housing in Parioli.

PANTHEON

What is there left to say about the Pantheon? It holds the tombs of Italian royalty, the tomb of Peruzzi, and that of Raphael, decorously near a memorial tablet, placed at the painter's request, for the cardinal's niece whom he never got around to marrying, not at least while there was a Fornarina (or several) in Rome, and she outlived them both. It is a marvel of engineering whose dome (actually two light shells filled with rubble) became the master dome of the Western world. Brunelleschi climbed along the dome, poked into and examined it, being one of those men who, as Vasari says, "cannot rest unless they undertake things of almost impossible difficulty." "He attentively observed all the difficulties of the vaulting of the Rotonda" and used his observations in vaulting the Duomo in Florence. The Pantheon has been judged the most beautiful, the most perfect building in the world, sketched, etched, painted, photographed from every possible angle, and no representation can evoke the sensation of standing in its incomparable light, the slow, tranquil rhythm of its alternating niches and frames, the regal gesture of coffered dome rising to cup of sky; no screen, no glass, nothing to impede the intimacy of dome with rain, snow, drifting clouds, and shafts of sunlight.

A building with so long a history of being brutalized, rebuilt, and denuded of its luster in successive centuries, its purposes several times perverted, should by all the rules be a mess. The first builder (27 B.C.) was the Agrippa whose name stands grandly over the portico columns, and this section, believed originally to have been rectangular, was part of his baths, of which a few other traces can be seen on streets to the south of the Pantheon, where a circular bit has given its street the name of doughnut, Ciambella. There is a tendency to blame the rape of temples and their demolition on Barbarians and popes (everyone knows the phrase: "What the Barbarians didn't manage to destroy, the Barberini [specifically Pope Urban VIII] did"). Not necessarily so. The Pantheon was ruined and restored in the time of Domitian, severely injured in Trajan's day, and given its present circular form by Hadrian, a man of advanced learning, taste, and judgment. Caracalla, the obverse of the Imperial coin, added the portico. Genseric, the Barbarian, was modest in his demands of the temple; he removed only some of the gilded bronze that covered the dome. Although it had already been consecrated as a church earlier, the Christian Emperor Constans II, come to do his devotions in the holy city, didn't hesitate to pry off and carry back the remaining bronze tiles to Constantinople, where, according to some reports, they fell into the hands of the Saracens. In 731 it was decided that the church of St. Mary of the Martyrs, as it was then called, needed the dignity of roofing, so lead tiles were used to cover the dome. Some centuries later, during the incessant medieval struggles for power, the Pantheon was the fortress for an antipope. After the medieval smashing and battering, low, brooding houses encrusted themselves on the building, leaving even less breathing space than the surrounding present strips. Several later popes pulled away the stifling buildings and tried to improve the looks of the church, the most startling improvement made by Urban VIII, who had Bernini erect inept campaniles which were immediately dubbed by the irreverent Romans "the asses' ears." (In spite of popular contempt they remained until 1885.) Urban VIII spent a solid sum of money for his architect's folly, but as fair exchange, he took whatever bronze was left in the portico and supports to make the famous Bernini baldacchino in St. Peter's and cast the rest of the metal as dozens of cannon to guard the Castel S. Angelo. He replaced a column or two, but one of his successors fancied the marble, and that was stripped off to use in churches and palazzi. The only bronze left untouched is that which rings the eye of the dome and in the doors, and one wonders why these were not long since lifted off their massive hinges. Despoiled and distorted, but never a ruin, always alive, maintaining its unassailable perfection for two thousand years, the Pantheon, unlike other Roman ruins whose strong skeletal fingers bespeak mortality, *is* immortality. One can imagine St. Peter's cracking, its statues toppled into scattered pieces of colonnade and butchered column, but not the Pantheon. Much lower in the ground than it originally was, one can see it sinking, but its unity and integrity of design dissolved—never.

If your time at the Pantheon should be a Sunday morning, you may observe a certain Pantheon-like stubbornness in the men who gather near the fountain. They are plumbers, glaziers, carpenters, taxi drivers, and other working class Romans who put on their black hats and gather, often from outlying distances of the city, to stand and talk as they did when young, and as their fathers and grandfathers did, in the piazze of their native villages in Calabria, Maccarese, Puglia, Umbria, discussing first of all the hometown crops they haven't helped to gather for years, the gossip carried by letters, and, always, politics. A hundred years ago this Piazza della Rotonda was the bird market of chirping yellows and reds, the round silence of owls' eyes, the purling whisper of doves. Now the sounds are more often those of old political enmities. "Where were you when we were freezing in mountain caves in the north? Sucking up to the Germans, that's what you were doing." "And you? You didn't stay away long. As soon as the capitalist Americans came you were licking their boots, ready to sell your daughter for a carton of cigarettes to peddle on the black market."

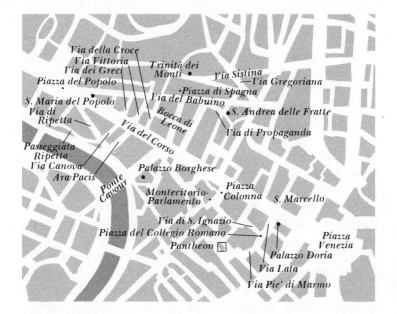

Walk 1

Piazza del Popolo to Pantheon

Where two main streets, Babuino and the Corso, join with a third, Ripetta, which never made it and doesn't seem to care; where two caffès, one a strutting ground for peacocks searching television, screen, and journalism attachments, the other younger and less colorful (both used indiscriminately by panting, thirsty tourists) face each other; where a pair of not quite twin churches, dubbed by American residents "his" and "hers," sit side by side, the city pauses at the immense piazza of the people. The name Popolo has no reference to a democratic gesture but rather to the church, built by money asked of the popoli, which stands near the gateway where the old Porta Flaminia conducted the Flaminian road out of the city. The great, wide, buoyantly designed screen was one high arch attributed to Michelangelo, later reshaped and embellished by Bernini with ample curves from a central loop that enclosed the Chigi star. This was done to please Christina of Sweden, who came through the gate in 1655, having left her kingdom as a Catholic convert to take up an eventful life in Rome. To make doubly sure that this prime and frequently onerous prize would feel well loved, a marble marker welcomes her most warmly in a stately Latin strophe.

One hundred years ago, half a century after Napoleon's architect, Valadier, stretched the piazza to accommodate unabashed neoclassic images, ornaments, and fountains, the piazza was the northern limit of the city, giving way to country and a few scattered villas that sharpened the endless flatness. Favorite subjects for painters were a shepherd and his sheep, a coachman in his *carrozza* drowsing in the undisturbed largesse of space around the obelisk whose hieroglyphs tell of Egyptian kings of 1200 B.C. and which was carted from its site in Egypt to beautify the Circus Maximus many centuries before. Whisked up from that ruin and wafted across the city, the obelisk was placed here in the sixteenth century and depaganized by a topping of Chigi mounds that support a cross. Progress has made of the piazza a parking lot, a taxi stand, a trial by brake for pedestrians and drivers who shoot down at roller-coaster speed from unexpected slots and, most recently, a meeting place of black-leathered motorcycle drivers with unsavory reputations, moral and political. The churches have, fortunately, protective ledges, and from S. Maria del Popolo at the northern end of the piazza one can look back at the tasteful punctuation created by the other S. Marias—di Montesanto and dei Miracoli—to close the meeting of the three streets, and up to the wall that holds back the eager trees of the Pincio and a triple-arched fountain high on the wall which, in its night lighting, resembles the rippling plastics of cocktail lounge waterfalls. From one of the porches at the south of the piazza you can stare at the inhabitants of the sprawling caffès, the sphinxes, the doughty *Seasons*, river-gods and lions, and the swiftly paced traffic minuets of cars not quite meeting, skirting, swerving, repeating the slide, curve, and leap forward with the next, and innumerable, partners.

S. Maria del Popolo doesn't deserve its fate of going almost unnoticed in a fog of gas fumes and motor hysteria. Its important purpose, when it was built at the end of the eleventh century, was to trap and hold the ghost of Nero buried in the family tomb below and still apparently a lively, evil spirit after a thousand years of ghostly mischief. The facade has of course changed since the spirit-trapping days and is now a well-ordered example of Renaissance design with a reasonable touch of the baroque as broken pediment cornices traced with facsimiles of the gateway garlands sketched by Bernini.

Immediately to the left of the main portal, there is a large caged yellow marble skull and neck cloaked in white marble, the leitmotif for the usual concentrations of tombs, not a dour theme necessarily. The peaceable medieval dead lie under their spare motionless drawings, the Renaissance entombs itself in large, cool, reasonable monuments embroidered with classical patterns adroitly carved out of the marble; the baroque permits itself everything that is large and rich, soaring in several directions simultaneously. The peak in necrophiliac show is reached in the Chigi Chapel, second on the left as one enters. It was ordered by Agostino Chigi, the Sienese who was called the Magnificent (the rivalry with Florence affected even such details). Raphael designed the chapel and the hard-blue mosaics in the dome; Bernini carved Daniel and his lion; on the altar is a chalky, Mannerist *Birth of the Virgin* by Sebastiano del Piombo, and at the sides are the tombs of Agostino and his brother Sigismondo, huge red marble metronomes meant to remind the viewer of the obelisks and pyramids of Egyptian kings. Chigis were not meant to die in a meaner fashion than Pharaohs.

Theme two is athletic saints and angels who sit slenderly,

tentatively, about to take flight among the arches, to support for a moment the twin organs, to lift, with a light touch, several yards of marble drapery. They are all aristocratically tall, Graces in the Bernini style which grasped and held Italian sculpture in its shapely hands for a lengthy time.

Theme three is paintings. By Pinturicchio and assistant, an *Adoration of the Child* in the first chapel on the right, and, behind the altar, in what was an extension of the apse built by Bramante, several ceiling medallions that reflect an ideal world of orderly, serene people in a glossy never-never land. In the same broad apsidal space, two stained glass windows, unusual for a Roman church, and two magnificent tombs of a della Rovere and a Sforza cardinal, both designed by Andrea Sansovino. Another eye, manner, and world of painting is represented by the Byzantine Madonna, attributed to St. Luke, which hangs over the altar. Art of yet another universe and vision appears in the chapel to the left of the Madonna. In space much too small for their size, the impact of their drama, the solidity of their forms and breadth of gesture, hang Caravaggio's *Conversion of St. Paul* and the *Crucifixion of St. Peter.* Painting at the very opening of the seventeenth century, he discarded the musical dreaminess, the elegance, and the sensuality of religious painting and turned to the direct impact of naturalism. The furrowed face of a peasant, the rump of a horse, St. Paul lying on the ground, outstretched, reaching to and guarding from the blazing light that suffuses the whole painting, force a here-and-now religious experience for a long time before lost in Italian painting.

There is nothing in an adjoining undistinguished chapel near the altar to betray the fact that somewhere in these walls were tombstones for two of *the* family of Renaissance license. One was the Duke of Gandia, son of Pope Alexander VI, brother of Lucrezia Borgia (who prayed here after her betrothal to Alfonso d'Este) and brother of Cesare. The other was their mother, Vannozza Cattanei, who was given a plaque sometime later in the church of San Marco, behind the Palazzo Venezia. The most strait-laced ghost is that of Martin Luther, who lived during his stay in Rome (1511) in the convent attached to the church, which he entered, according to a French biographer, as a pilgrim and left as an embattled warrior.

The Corso was the last stretch of the Flaminian road, long ago arched over by triumphal monuments and less long ago the street of carnival, confetti and flowers thrown from jostling carriages and innumerable balconies. According to Dickens, "... if year after year, and season after season, it had rained balconies, hailed balconies, snowed balconies, blown balconies, they could scarcely have come into existence in a more disorderly manner." A number of the balconies still exist, but the Corso has gone into trade; journeying along it means window-shopping over the shoulders and behind the elbows of other shoppers and during the "passeggiata" hours, immediately before lunch and dinner, a death struggle to maintain at least one foot on the slip of sidewalk, semisafe from the plunging, snorting traffic, which is as heedless as stampeding horses and considerably more lethal.

The Via del Babuino—named "baboon" for a leering moss- and dust-covered stone Silenus with a yellowed cigarette butt in his mouth who lounges near the Via dei Greci —functions as arts and antiques market and as a screen for the Via Margutta, also called "Carnaby Street" for several shops of kinky clothing, gleefully impertinent tinsely, papery, and freaky adornments that have about had their day, one hopes. Besides duplicating Soho, the street busies itself with art galleries, rugs, jewelry, clothing, and cold, large studios undergoing fission to become small, expensive apartments. Which has not yet marred its older charms, its seclusion, its shape as a long salon, an old frame shop, the ramble of slopes and stairs (beyond the Vicolo d'Alibert) toward the Pincian Hill, a raffish little wineshop that serves drinks and conversation—lounging at the counter or seated on one wooden crate—to painters and antiquarians. Theoretically, it is almost entirely closed to traffic—not quite enough to suspend wariness—and on fair evenings and Sunday mornings becomes a passeggiata court for art lovers, the young in their floating, costly glad rags, and the intellectual older, more somberly shaped and tinted. Theoretically it is still an "artists' street," with an inept fountain of easels, buckets and masks to prove it and a few studios that resist improvement, but the neighborhood is less colorful than it was a century ago, when there were cheap eating places for artists, like those in Montmartre, where models also ate if they could or sauntered through, posturing paintably. A number of the street floor areas were then stables, and the horses cared for in the street added their dung to the garbage, the mixture settling as a warm-colored odoriferous carpet, freshened by the drops of laundry that hung in decorative loops across the street. Neither odor nor uncertain footing discouraged the fashionable who came to the theater of the Alibert, for whom the local vicolo is named, to examine art and to taste the deliciously frightening atmosphere of a bohemian quarter.

(A street show of paintings that lasts for a few days takes place each spring and fall. Much of it, like the Spanish Steps displays and those on the Piazza Navona, is distinctly "tourist" art, turned out like buns from a vast oven and equally interesting, true of all outdoor shows in touristed areas: Paris' Montmartre, London's parks, New York's several Villages, Mexico's cities, art colonies everywhere, which seem to share an international cartel of art with minimal though rigid standards.)

The baroque ancestry of the neighborhood still lives engagingly on the main streets and in the short silent alleys that bridge the street of the Baboon with the Corso. An arch on the Via dei Greci, a tiny yard of craftsmen and shoemakers' enclosure on the Via Vittoria, the inner courts of palazzi modernized and converted into proud enclaves of gallery, bookshop, and furnishings in the advanced styles of Milano on parallel streets. Via della Croce is a thick minestra of foods, boutiques, cars, shopping baskets and female bodies. The butcher shops are jewel boxes, the pizzicherie sell caviar, Cadbury's chocolates, macrobiotic dainties, stalactites of sausages short, tall, slender, thick, spicy and blander (but never truly bland), fatter and less fatty (but never lean); squeezed in among the sirens, an old-fashioned hole-in-the-wall greengrocer's, and a cotton, buttons, detergents, and toilet paper clutter, both left of a more modest time. A fruit and vegetable street market lights up the stones of the Via Bocca di Leone, as it undoubtedly warmed the lives of Elizabeth and Robert Browning, whose house was at the northern edge of the market, near the Via Vittoria. A large marker remembers their stay and their passion for Italy, the famous phrases quoted in Italian. She: "Le sue memorie eterne attestano che l'Italia è immortale." He: "Aprendo il mio cuore vi trovaste incisio Italia."

The Via di Ripetta is, for a short stretch from the Piazza del Popolo, an easygoing Cinderella, willing to serve inexpensive meals, sell domestic supplies and odds and ends of hardware. (Look for a shop that arranges fine tools, sculptors' burins and painters' knives in a display that makes a good piece of Renaissance ironwork.) The street may have lost its ambition when it lost its port, where the Ponte Cavour now begins to cross the river. Old drawings show it to have been bustling with sailboats and sailors and porters dragging sacks up wide swings of steps gathered around a semicircular platform, a fountain and church, in a common, satisfying Roman street design. Between Ripetta and the Tiber, a few secretive short streets that are yielding space to art galleries. The most secretive, wrapped in its own cocoon of atmosphere, the slip called the Passeggiata Ripetta, hides under the river embankment until it is frightened out of existence by a thunderous Mussolini-

built expanse. The showiest of Ripetta's riches are its
nineteenth-century Beaux-Arts buildings linked by a neoclassical rounded court and, on the street named for the
sculptor, the studio of Canova, a headless draped worthy
at its corner, the rest voluptuously pimpled with bits and
pieces of classical stone, a most enthusiastic example of
Roman measles, an endemic disease. At the very end of
Ripetta (73) another divertissement, the entrance to a
business building as thoroughly muraled as the grand salon
of a papal apartment. The anonymous artist has chosen to
record the modest charms of his neighborhood as it once
was—the Spanish Steps fronted by an intellectual or a
scribe reading a letter to a peasant woman, horse racing
around the obelisk of the Piazza del Popolo, the Ripetta
port unloading barrels of wine from its boats, and in the
foreground a relaxed fisherman, pipe in mouth. Each scene
is framed in columns under draperies in the classy Venetian
manner.

Improved recently, when glass was substituted for the
stone and concrete that made it a huge repellent coffin,
Augustus' Ara Pacis is still uncomfortable in its surroundings and rarely solaced by visitors. Improved yes, lovable
no, and interesting enough to justify stealing a half-hour
from the shopping a few paces away. Misplaced as it seems,
like a gigantic container dropped carelessly from a behemoth truck, the contents of the box belong here, placed in
a time when its position was an undisturbed grassy slope
to the Tiber. Following a persistent military habit of mind,
conquest spelled peace to Augustus, and thus, after his
seizure of Spain and Gaul (13 B.C.), he dedicated the
immense altar to Pax. The approach and the surroundings
of the altar must have in their day been more awe-inspiring,
according to contemporary descriptions, than they now are.
Certainly not all of the altar is in its original stone. Much
of it had to be retrieved from depths under surrounding
buildings, from the Uffizi in Florence, where several marble
reliefs found themselves, from the Vatican Museum and

the museum in Diocletian's baths; pieces dispersed and gathered over the centuries. The fortunes of several sections are unknown; they may have been pulverized in one of the hundreds of medieval mashing, burning, and reducing to rubble and limestone establishments of the city.

The rebuilt altar exemplifies the approved best in sculpture of Augustus' Golden Age. The friezes of personages in hieratic progress close on each other; the allegorical and ceremonial scenes and the skillful hand on garlands and fruits deserve respect, though they rarely evoke—and this is frequently true of Roman art—emotion. Except when they take on common life, as it breathes and moves in the figure of a small child tugging tearfully at his father's toga.

A few paces from the Ara Pacis there is a rather forbidding, impenetrable mound ringed with funeral cypress, whose only company is boys racing around its depths and dogs out for a supervised airing. Elderly Romans speak of a riding ring on one of the levels; others attended concerts and theater performances there. In the twelfth century it was a fortress of the Colonna, built in a ruin left by the Goths of the royal mausoleum of Augustus, his wife Livia, their successors, and their wives, intertwined by marriage, ancestry, poison plots, banishments, assassinations, and untold riches. The last interment was that of Nerva in A.D. 98. It was not a very long time from the first burial to the last in the niches off circular corridors reserved for the Olympians of Rome, yet there was a considerable number of urns. These dignitaries divorced or killed their spouses, remarried, and adopted each other's children, who in turn killed each other with rare frequency, keeping a fairly steady flame of funeral pyres burning, the streets crowded with the funeral processions, ancestral masks (even those of recently bought ancestors) held high while the rhetoric of funeral orations swelled the air. It is difficult to think of a vase of passive ashes as the corrupt Tiberius; as his son Drusus, poisoned; as Caligula, murdered; as Britannicus, the son of Claudius, murdered by Nero; as Claudius, murdered. Only Livia, who probably had a number of her gnarled fingers in several of these mortal pies, lived to be a very old woman, one of the more remarkable feats of survival.

Augustus' death, many years before, was accompanied by a supernatural act which confirmed his godhood. According to Suetonius, one of the ex-praetors said he saw, after the pyre had done its work, the form of the emperor rise to the heavens. Other reporters change the rising form to that of an eagle and the ex-praetor to a senator paid an immense sum by Livia—in tatters, barefoot, and wracked with mourning—to say so. Tacitus neglects the episode but would not put such an act beyond her, "a catastrophe to the nation as a mother and to the house of the Caesars as a stepmother." He is pleased to repeat the gossip which ran through the forum holding Livia responsible for the deterioration in Augustus' health. Unrelenting, he mentions the early natural deaths of two potential heirs to the succession —"unless their stepmother Livia had a secret hand in them." And in a swift cloak-and-dagger résumé, he describes Livia's manipulations to eliminate, one way or another, possible rivals of her son Tiberius in the fierce contest for the imperial crown. "When he arrived at Nola [from Dalmatia] it is unknown whether he found Augustus alive or dead. For the house and neighboring streets were carefully sealed by Livia's guards. At intervals, hopeful reports were published—until the steps demanded by the situation had been taken. Then two pieces of news became known simultaneously. Augustus was dead, and Tiberius was in control." So much for the sweet patient lady who sat in her painted indoor garden of rollicking birds in a dainty orchard (now in the Baths of Diocletian museum), weaving poisoned webs.

Sharing the bend of the river and cheering it out of the sepulchral black-cypress mood, there is a babbling jollity of balconies that form the river side of the Palazzo Borghese, which spreads wide and wider and then irregularly

narrows, a shape that earned it the name of "harpsichord."
A spur of the palazzo piazza, the Fontanella di Borghese,
makes room for a used books, prints, small *objets* antiques
market whose vendors are a varied lot, from "go-away-can't-
you-see-I'm-reading?" taciturn to the inviting, beckoning
old man with slipping eyeglasses, a Dickens-Cruikshank
beam and entertainingly voluble.

Back to shopping or merely for the felicitous rise of the
Spanish Steps to Trinità dei Monti, daubed with pink azaleas in the spring, invaded by a crèche during the Christmas
season, and unless the weather is malevolent, draped in a
carpet of lounging young bodies in raggle-taggle gypsy-o
costumes, pounds of hair lank or crisp, the swell of guitars,
and the glitter of wire trinkets for sale. The grotesquery
of costume and ornament rises on the stairs to meet an
ancient grotesque, a rococo façade on the Via Gregoriana,
whose entrance is a monstrous face, the door-mouth open
in the insatiable gauping greed of Bosch demons. Squares
of lettered stone indicate that this and its neighbor, the
Via Sistina, were part of a local colony of foreign artists
and writers who flocked to Rome in the eighteenth and
nineteenth centuries. (At 125 Via Sistina, a bust, a wreath,
and lettering in Russian and Italian to say that Gogol lived
here from 1836 to 1842.) The Gregoriana ogre was added to
a small palace owned by the artist Federico Zuccari, who
painted Queen Elizabeth I in a series of world-conquest
stances. Later, the expanded house was inhabited by
another royal patroness of the arts and learning, the Polish
Queen Maria Casimira, and in its lists of associations, often
vague, one also finds mentioned Domenico Scarlatti, the
archaeologist Winckelmann, the painters David and Reynolds
and Angelica Kauffman.

Borromini posthumous is not much luckier than Borromini
alive, still overshadowed by the Cavaliere Bernini, whose
work stands in open, frank space while that of his short-

term assistant and short-term rival is often obscured, peeping out of impenetrable walls or strangled by narrow streets. The church of S. Andrea delle Fratte, the Scottish National church lost centuries ago, was only partially built by Borromini. That which bears his unique stamp, the unfinished cupola and tower, require crossing and recrossing and keeping a firm foothold on the corners of Capo le Case and Due Macelli. Jostled as you will be, hold your ground (preferably equipped with binoculars), and take your time with what Sacheverell Sitwell calls Borromini's most sensational work, which "resembles nothing built before or since." Let your eye travel with the large, brick areas of light and shade in the unfolding of convex and concave, the emphases and retractions of answering curves. A circle of balustrade eases the solid squareness of the tower base which begins to soar as herm-angels with long folded wings moving out of the depths of garlanded niches. Up and up the flight, stopping for a restatement of balanced rhythms, a spurt of slender torches, and above, four magnificent springs of stone to a crown whose sharp thin supports continue the gesture of flight. Sitwell: "The tower of Sant'Andrea, an unimportant Roman church is conceived as a piece of sculpture to hold the attention but it could also be a table ornament, or a pyx or other sacred vessel in a sacristy or treasury."

The Via di Propaganda turns back to the Piazza di Spagna, taking with it a few shops, a bar that sells choice coffees to drink or carry away dry, a (or *the*) Japanese restaurant, and facing them all across mean space, the Palace of the Propagation of the Faith. The short side facing the Piazza di Spagna was a respectable lesser accomplishment of Bernini. The long side, in a subtle combination of earth-red and brown, affords an intimate view of a Borromini contented to arrange and rearrange his blocks, circles, ovals, and ornaments, pulling them forward, forcing them back to form a screen that closes on an equally gracious corridor and a small church, a characteristic song of fluid movement. (The portiere is proud of the church, and if you don't disturb his lunch, and tip him 200 lire, he will be most hospitable.)

It might be time for tea and Italianized Viennese melodies in the Galleria Colonna or, for the more conscientious, a search for a foothold on the Piazza Colonna from which to study, with those binoculars, the spiraling triumphs of Marcus Aurelius, somewhat reduced by the supreme triumph of St. Paul, who stands at the very top of the column. The presence of tall policemen in ceremonial Napoleonic hats, gloved hands resting on anachronistic swords, or the more proletarian sight and sound of demonstrators, on Montecitorio-Parlamento, reveal quickly enough that you are among government buildings, one of them partially designed by Bernini (the Chamber of Deputies) and all of them sitting on the area once reserved for glorifying Marcus Aurelius. He may not, as a civilized skeptic, have enjoyed such cloying flattery, but as an emperor he must have made compromises similar to those he arranged for gladiatorial games. Accompanied by secretaries, he conducted the business of the empire in the arena, appeasing the public by his presence, appeasing himself by averting his attention from the brutal pleasures of his subjects.

The Corso holds an excellent example of dexterous smooth bending of baroque space into a narrow area in the façade of S. Marcello. You may want to see what a few of the omnipresent Frangipane looked like as imagined by an artist who never saw them, a piece of carved Roman stone in the altar (no novelty), the tomb of a Cardinal Giovanni Michele, for whom Alexander VI ordered death by poisoning (no novelty either), and below, and more novel, his bishop nephew resting uncomfortably on stacks of books to remind the viewer of the collection of rare books and papers he donated to the convent of S. Marcello.

The Via Lata, off the Corso near its halt at the Piazza Venezia where the Romans gathered to hear Mussolini declaim from the balcony of the Venetian palazzo, is a short street in which is imbedded a figure of an old porter holding a barrel. A fountain, and one of the ironical "speaking" figures of Rome, like Pasquino near the Piazza Navona, he actually existed, and if your Latin can face it, make out his name—Rizio—and a jaunty, laudatory epigraph. Rizio's street leads to the Piazza del Collegio Romano and the visitors' entrance to the Palazzo Doria. (A fairly young legend, possibly apocryphal, has it that an anti-Fascist Doria refused to adorn his palace with patriotic symbols, as the surrounding palaces did, to celebrate Italy's conquest of Ethiopia. Il Duce had the name of the Vicolo Doria changed to Vespasiano, a synonym for pissoir, after the emperor-builder of public toilets. The spur of street is now again Doria.)

Before entering, walk around the palace, which occupies the whole of a sizable block, to enjoy the eighteenth-century façade (Corso) and the spirited ironwork design on its windows, to try to get a glimpse of the courtyard, and to consider the upkeep of such a palace. Estimates vary, but it is generally said that about 200 families rent flats in the palace, and there must be substantial revenues from the fee paid by visitors who come to see the gallery and several of the salons. The gallery is a typical example of the no-air, one set of paintings pressing its forms and colors into the other, which makes uneasy, impatient looking for the modern eye accustomed to pictures more generously spaced. Though only a minority of the paintings deserve rapt study, don't go too fast; the collection is an excellent example of what was considered good and fashionable in Italian and Flemish paintings in the sixteenth, seventeenth, and eighteenth centuries and, in the gathering, a few masterpieces and a few mistakes by masters. *Spain Rescuing Religion* (10) is a windy piece of nonsense by Titian, done, one hopes, reluctantly and for a bountiful fee. Forget it and look at several male portraits, one by Tintoretto, a double portrait attributed to Raphael, and Lorenzo Lotto's version of St. Jerome, that favorite for the pleasure of studying an old man's characterful head, the dry depths of skull, a book, a lion, a desert landscape. The next place for a long pause is at number 40, a muted portrait of a disconsolate girl sitting in a bare room. If it weren't for the meticulous painting of the jewelry she has dropped to the floor, one would accept it as a late-nineteenth-century work. Actually it is a Caravaggio of the end of the sixteenth century, and the tired, despairing *puttana* is Mary Magdalene. This quiet early work marks a revolution in Italian painting, the Caravaggian rebellion that used earthy common people to enact situations and emotions of the Scriptures. Another painting (42), *The Rest on the Flight into Egypt* by Caravaggio, reveals similar elements, the Virgin and Child sleeping like a tired market woman cradling her child, Joseph a gray-haired carpenter sitting on a bundle of his few household goods, holding—and here one loses naturalism and emotion—a musical score for a seductive boy angel-fiddler with Mannerist face and wings. It is a charming work, boldly composed, miraculously painted, and curiously Pre-Raphaelite in its painstaking details, the burnished surface, and the solidity of its supernatural figure.

Greeting the famous marble Olimpia who looks like a conquering armada in full sail, you should soon be in a hall of statuary standing before tapestries that celebrate the deeds of Andrea Doria, the Genoese admiral who helped the Venetians conquer the Turks at Lepanto. The Carraccis and several of their sixteenth-century fellow artists take over in the next sections of the gallery and then give way to the Flemish (242 to 317) represented by Breughels (260, 280, 295, 316, 317), a portrait by Rubens (291), and by no imposing name, Jan van Schorel (279), the small portrait of Agatha Schoonhoven, as precise and gemlike as a Memling, as luminous as a Vermeer, and an interesting contrast to the bombastic Titian ladies you met earlier.

The goal of this visit is justifiably the Velázquez portrait of Innocent X of the Pamphili-Dorias, set off in a small enclosure of its own accompanied by the marble bust of

the Pope by Bernini. These twin pinnacles of skill might
be the place and time to leave the palace, although you may
feel the admission price (500 lire) warrants the complete
visit: more Italian paintings rather like those you have seen
before, a group by Claude Lorrain (343, 346, 348), the first
version of Bernini's bust of Innocent X. If the guide is
feeling energetic and good-natured he should take you the
full course, through classic busts and Brussels tapestries,
several family portraits painted by illustrious artists, rooms
luxuriously furnished in the Venetian style and several
other styles tolerant enough to admit a chinoiserie ceiling.
Somewhere among the imposing Doria portraits, a modest
Deposition by Memling, a naïve, dexterous allegory of the
seasons and the elements by the Breughel called "The Velvet," and, if the idea stirs you, look for a portrait of the
pretender to the English throne, James Edward Stuart.

A street called Pie' di Marmo (marble foot) leads out of
the misshapen piazza at the back of the palazzo to present
a gigantic sandaled marble foot, left of some unidentified
colossus and brought to spark up a studious neighborhood,
the center of training established by St. Ignatius Loyola
three hundred years ago. The street named for the saint
leads past the Ministry of Communications, a building
wrapped around a hospitable court of benches among the
trees and flowers, a fountain, and the inescapable souvenir
of broken marble. Hospitality is limited to employees, but
the portiere usually permits a leisured look from the gates.
St. Ignatius' church is a very serious church in the Jesuit
style—gray, frowning, and naked of frippery except for the
trompe l'oeil that makes a flat ceiling surface a cloudy,
turbulent "Ascension" rising to a deep nonexistent dome.
(A marble plate in the center of the main aisle is the best
place for viewing the trickery.)
    The determinedly heavy façade gives on a bonbonnière
box of piazza, a rococo building plan unique in the baroque

city, designed by Filippo Raguzzini in 1727. It has been called an operetta set, a jigsaw puzzle with well-fitted pieces, and compared to curvaceous French desks of the period, *burrò*, which actually names one of the curves of street enclosed in the design. Follow the piazza's lines, tracing the attractive shapes of the gay, faded rose palazzetti as they compliment and bow to each other, then return to the center of the pattern to admire the window proportions and their ornaments. Ideally, the piazza should be seen from a helicopter as bands of pink ribbon, billowing, held, billowing, held, in a design that might pattern a Watteau dress or the wallpaper of a palace in Vienna, but a good visual sense will do it amply well.

Solidness thumps to earth on the Piazza di Pietra in sight of the mighty ravaged columns that support one side of the Stock Exchange, reminders of a temple for the deified Hadrian built by his adopted son, Antoninus Pius. An easy few steps eastward and there it is, the Pantheon.

NOTE: The Palazzo Doria collection is open from 10 to 1 on Tuesday, Friday, Saturday, and Sunday.

In the course of this walk or at some time in need for seclusion from the cacophony of cars, the Babel of languages, and the Lorelei calls of shops on the Piazza di Spagna, go into the Keats-Shelley Memorial House, whose hours are 9 to 12 and 3 to 5. Keats never actually saw Rome except as he envisioned it in Shakespeare and the reports of the poets who spoke of the overwhelming somber beauty of its desolation, "that High Capital, where kingly Death/ Keeps his pale court in beauty and decay," according to Shelley. He came in desperation and fear: "There is no doubt that an English winter would put an end to me. . . . Therefore I must either voyage or travel to Italy as a soldier marches up to a battery." For three months, from

November 1820 to February 1821, he spent what he called his "posthumous life," fighting death, welcoming it, delirious, resigned, bitter, silent, staring at the roses painted on the ceiling of his small room, feeling them growing out of his grave, writing neither poetry nor letters, except one farewell to friends and an unbearably short meager will.

A plaque on an inconspicuous house on the side of the Spanish Steps leads up three stories into quiet and the placid comforting odor of leather-bound books, a library that specializes in the English romantic poets, their works and biographies, and then into the rooms of Joseph Severn and Keats. One finds in the glass cases a copy of a letter that Byron's daughter Allegra wrote to him when she was five, asking that he visit her. He did not, and she died within the year, not necessarily the fault of "caro papà," though it offers one aspect of the man. An aspect of Shelley emerges from a letter asking that Keats be brought to him in Pisa. "I intend to be the physician both of his body and his soul, to keep the one warm and to teach the other Greek and Spanish. I am aware, indeed, in part that I am nourishing a rival who will far surpass me, and this is an additional motive and will be an added pleasure." Significant, too, the fact that Shelley went to visit Allegra before she died and was haunted by the child as her father was apparently not. Mary Shelley writes of her husband's death and their fancifying friend, Trevelyan, of the high romantic gesture of plucking Shelley's heart from his funeral pyre.

The Keats room has copies of manuscripts, letters, and portraits of Keats and his family: of frail sweet-faced Tom, who died very young of the tuberculosis that destroyed most of the family; of married George, who migrated to America and for whom John wished a son who would be the first poet of America; of the sister Fanny, who lived to a reasonably old age as her brothers did not. A small conventional painting of a moderately pretty girl gives us Fanny Brawne, the girl who inspired incandescent love letters, whom Keats might have married, whose absence was so agonizing that he could not read, or even open, her letters.

Among the various portraits and bits of manuscript and the few lines of will, there is a new acquisition which expands the field of English literary memorabilia. It is a silver reliquary owned by a late Renaissance pope that found its way to England as a container for a few hairs of John Milton and then came into the possession of Addison, Johnson, and a literary line that led to the Brownings, whose initials it now bears along with a lock of Elizabeth's hair.

The sketch made by the exhausted, infinitely devoted Severn "to keep myself awake" as Keats was dying is terrible to look at, the young face wasted, the eyelids drooping toward death, the sweat-covered hair hanging in bitter strands. More terrible is the scene outside the window, and, if one loves Keats, hardly to be borne on a bright spring afternoon when the umbrellas spread like triumphant flags over the flower stalls, the young sit in the boat fountain of Bernini's father washing their feet, or stretch their lithe bodies in the full sun, while the vendors flash color views of Rome and tourists totter to the bright green taxis. It is said that Sinclair Lewis, who was not a crying man, cried in Keats's room, possibly while he was looking out the window at the heedless profligacy of color, flesh, sound, comfortable stupidity, sharp awareness, and he asked the protesting, unanswerable question, "Why?"

RENDER UNTO CAESAR

Ostia Antica

Staring down into the Forum and walking its adjoining lengths and widths from the heights of the Palatine to the upper stories of Trajan's market and down to Nero's buried house, visualizing the high solemnities at Augustus' Ara Pacis, standing in the mellow light of the Pantheon, will give you only a vast necropolis of Imperial will and wealth, not the functioning overpopulated center of world commerce Rome was for several centuries. A sensible way —if one has the time for sense—to see a small version of ancient Rome as an entire city is to head first for Ostia Antica, reachable by the Metropolitana from the central railroad station or the Colosseum or 24 kilometers by automobile over the road that passes EUR, the broad-avenued, marble-pavemented city built for an international fair that never came off.

The small sleepy modern town dozes in the shadow of a fifteenth-century fortress, occasionally open to the public, the visit included in the price of the admission ticket (150 lire) to the ruins. At the end of the town, the entrance to the ruined port. Its beginnings as a particularized site are lost in clouds of prehistory which disclose the figure of Aeneas, who landed here after his long travels. More surely, it was a fortified commercial center with a large complement of soldiers by the mid-fourth century B.C., strategically positioned at the meeting of the Tiber and the sea. (Silting and violent flooding of the river in much later centuries changed the useful position, but by that time the port was already ruins.) As the Empire expanded, the city grew. The large harbor built by Claudius proved to be unsatisfactory in stormy weather. Trajan, to accommodate more safely the commercial activities of the Empire, added a better-sheltered hexagonal port which gave space for the wheat, oil, exotic fruits, plants and seafood, marbles, rare woods, conquered works of art and men from its limitless fiefs. Offices, temples dedicated to the orthodox and foreign religions, insulae (apartment houses), villas, gardens, shops, and inns increased in number and luxury to house and amuse the enterprising city whose polyglot population and military personnel were estimated to be as many as 100,000. (A number of authorities consider that an exaggerated figure.) Whether 50,000 or 100,000, Constantine first spelled their doom by declaring the town an adjunct of Rome rather than its own well-organized municipality, thus reducing the prosperity and population of the town which Trajan had helped make rich and Hadrian had embellished. By the time the Barbarians arrived there was little of importance to destroy. When the early waves of barbaric invasions ebbed, the land was taken over by agriculture, malaria, and substantial looting. Excavations and reconstruction—always with material found on the site—were begun systematically in the nineteenth century and rushed in the twentieth when Mussolini ordered that Ostia be readied as an antique show-piece to accompany his exposition area, EUR.

The street called Porta Romana was the main boulevard of Republican times, now left a few tombs in several styles and a few decapitated statues. The road becomes the spine of Imperial times, Decumano Massimo, which shows remains of shops and warehouses, the indispensable baths, and a big, imperious Minerva denuded of the temple that once cloaked her. In the remains of a temple immediately beyond there might have been an Isis or Diana of Ephesus to serve her worshipers among the internationals of the town. The main road leads on to tall porticoes, mosaics, the heating vents of baths, rather like the vestiges you may

see in Rome. Gone or hidden from the mother city, however, but clearly visible in Ostia, are the specific symbols,
repeated, lively mosaic ideographs, of commercial links
with the principal provinces: Spain is a sprig of olives,
Africa is an elephant's trunk, on the narrow street of the
Vigili, the firemen who protected the grain which fed Rome.
Ruins that might have been barracks and columns of
temple take one to the Via Fullonica and its remnants of a
public laundry among shops and an inn (Via della Fontana)
whose sign was and is a wine cup. Return to D. Massimo
for scattered pillars and statues and sketches of building
bound in concrete to prevent further decay (this lends
some of the edifices the soft contours of Arab houses) and
the stairs that lead to the top of the handsome, comfortably
sized theater bearing the appropriate masks.

You are now a few paces from the Piazzale delle
Corporazioni, the heart of the living matter and one of the
essential reasons for coming to Ostia—a witness, a chunk
of reality that evokes the bustle and many-tongued noise
of the port. The neat divisions you see were the offices of
more than fifty representatives of importing and shipping
companies, their interests explained entertainingly and well
by black and white mosaics in the pavement of each section. An extraordinary kneeling figure measuring grain
from a vat represents *navicularii* who dealt with Egypt or
Puglia. There is a Sicilian concern, one from Carthage,
another from Sardinia, and the wine corporation which
advertises itself with the mosaic of a porter carrying an
amphora across the plank of one ship to another may have
brought its wine from Gaul. There were ropemakers and
oil importers, repairers of ships and transporters of cloth.
The piazzale, in short, was rather like the old shipping
streets of New York before they were entirely consumed,
not left the dignity of a shred of ruin. Nor did they ever
have the exuberant signs that include, in one large square,
animals, circles, knots, and the Eastern swastika amid a
gay splash of abstract designs. Rounding this aisle, one

comes on a box of more formal design to contain a fierce lunging boar, a leaping deer, and a torpid elephant.

Returning along the side of the theater, among vestiges of a roomy private house and a number of temples, one of them dedicated to Mithras (scholars say that there were eighteen temples dedicated to this popular, imported god in Ostia), one stands in another nexus of the living city, crowded with shops, apartment houses, and taverns. The Casa of Diana had nothing to do with that goddess, but is an arbitrary name for one of the first balconied houses— the supports visible—and inner stairs to climb which were the model of many apartment houses in Ostia and in Rome. Imaginative sketches of what these flat blocks looked like show them to be, with their curved balconies and proportions of height to width, curiously like the few Art Nouveau houses still standing in London. Except that they lacked water on the upper floors, had no fireplaces, no glass for the windows; if one can judge from the low boxes near the Aracaeli stairs, they were depressingly cavelike, and to believe the complaints of Roman poets, they were exhausting to climb. Conveniently close to the tenements is the Thermopolium, the tavern with deep pits for cooking, benches for lounging on, vats for wine and, on the wall, a beguiling panel of fruits and foodstuffs airily spaced and simplified, the work of a Roman Braque. The twentieth century seems to return for a moment in a view from a nearby alley, of an ample room in the Casa dei Dipinti (painted house) whose glass enclosure and broad striped walls imitate a modern studio. The original room, built and decorated in the time of Hadrian, had no windows but made do with oddly perspectived, yet convincing, painted openings to lend air and space to the dancers, myths, and landscapes worked on the walls. The upper sections are more crudely painted than the lower, testimony to changes of technique from working directly on a rough surface to treating the surface for a smoother, more absorbent ground to hold the earth reds and sea blues.

A nymph, or part of her, stands at the curve of a once cool, placid nymphaeum; a huge basin against slabs of marble and spiraled columns marks another. A tall, stern building designated the Capitol has steps made of broken, contemporary stone taken from a variety of local sources, several lettered, many gouged by the posts of destroyed doors, the top step a massive stretch of grained, gray Egyptian marble. Isolated columns and mutilated figures rise in the serene, remote landscape. Man persists in noisily returning, however, on neat sets of public toilets, some cruder than others, one sanctified by a small temple, another witness to the city's decline when a well-carved side of a sarcophagus or a building ornament replaced a pair of seats; the city was decaying, and there wasn't the money for a new stretch of marble.

There is much else to see, including a good, small museum (closed—same dismal story—in the summer of 1971 for *restauro* and lack of personnel) and a Christian basilica, but concentrate if time is short on the dense inner city with its shops and villas surmounted by apartment buildings, shipping agencies, and public toilets and taverns, and listen for the bawling of drunken sailors, the loud arguments of merchants, the call of women for children, the exchanges of quips in the toilets, the gossip of women carrying water up the stairs to their waterless apartments or lolling, if they are lucky tenants of a street-level flat, in the air cooled by a garden fountain.

Right at the fortress and hugging the fields of corn that disclose spurts of ruin, you should shortly come to the synagogue. It is the oldest synagogue in Rome, unearthed only a few years ago during the construction of a new highway to the airport, and closed from intimate view because excavations, as elsewhere in the area, are still going on. About a kilometer or so from the opposite bank of the Tiber, a well-marked turn into a dirt road ends at the necropolis of the port. Not a large place and blessedly free of "great" works, the necropolis makes an interesting, peaceable stroll of an hour or so. Quite close to the entrance you will come on a joined group of stone boxes that resemble public laundry vats. These held the remains of the poor, in death as in life in Rome, intermingled with the rich. At this point the prosperous are represented by a sarcophagus whose talented carver cut a few jolly babies into the stone and, with a stroke of mystical symbolism not too commonly seen in pragmatic Rome, pushed one of his putti through the mask of a fearsome old man, the little round buttocks disappearing at the back of the mask, a tiny hand emerging from the mouth. Life into death into life, perhaps.

Some of the tombs resemble in decoration and form the houselike family tombs under St. Peter's, sarcophagi and statue niches for the leading members of a household, columbaria niches for the ashes of lesser members, and in thin, cheap amphorae half-imbedded in the earth, the ashes of servants and slaves; again, the physical proximity, as in the insulae among the palaces, of the rich and the poor. Look around in the alleys off the central road to find faint traces of dancing figures in some tombs, others half-eaten by salt air. Leave a heavy footprint in one tomb or other to realize that its floor is dark, damp sea sand. Notice the dense explosions of fern growing from tomb niches. Search out mosaics on walls, mosaics used as lettering to identify a tomb, mosaics as two charming birds to brighten a damp tomb. Stop for a moment to admire the vigorous Roman lettering and wonder at the presence of uncharacteristic, unadorned rounded tombs. In them lie the remains of Egyptian sailors or functionaries or merchants. Try not to miss several plaster panels, near the end of the central walk, which keep immortal a man's work. One was a miller or dealer in grain, to judge from the figure turning a large grindstone. Another advertises a neat arrangement of tools and instruments which he made or used as a carpenter; the presence of a horse might mean a groomer or breeder of horses or a racer in a *circo* which must have existed in Ostia as it did in Rome. And the markers bring back the

sounds of men working, drinking, betting, living, and dying
—many of them far from home—that drift across the Tiber
from the port.

NOTE: Coordinate your Ostia and necropolis visits carefully.
The ruins of the town may be seen throughout the day and
the necropolis only from 10 A.M. to noon and 2 to 5 during
the fall and winter months, 3 to 6 in the spring and summer.
Rome's summer heat shouldn't discourage a trip to Ostia
Antica. The traffic is distant, the nearby sea sends its
breezes, and the walls and trees make shade for a tranquil
picnic. If you prefer, there is a snack bar back of the
theater or a plate of pasta in the village.

Forum

A few visitors find the Forum repellent as a snake-pit womb
of dictatorships, from early Etruscan kings through Caesars, Flavians, and Antonines, through the medieval and
Renaissance church supremacy to the revival by Mussolini;
in short, a pool of dried blood crusted with scabs of gilt-
specked marble. There are those who, not quite con-
sciously, hope to see an arch buckle, sway, and sink into
its rubble or a column crack and bend at one glued knuckle.
And there are those who stare at it blankly, unable to
derive any meaning, any response, to the long showcase
of rubble.

There are several ways to "do" the Forum: to look down
on it from the platform behind the Campidoglio, drama-
tized and romanticized by night illumination; or in full
sunlight, which mists the stumps, the crippled columns,
the cracked architraves; or in late daylight, which lends
them the gentling tact of shadows, and then leave. It can
be done in a speedy guided tour which gives the satisfac-

tions of having accomplished a difficult, essential task without the burdens of understanding or sensing anything but the cemetery mood. It can be a pleasant, uninformed stroll. Another approach is to buy the booklet sold at the entrance to the Forum and follow its maps, stopping at a shaded pedestal or slice of column to read the background material. It is a not too difficult, certainly not dull, manner of spending a couple of hours and may rebuild—the cement must be imagination—the Forum in its various epochs from marshy necropolis to Imperial grandiosity so crammed that there was hardly room to move among the splendors and Augustus, Vespasian, Domitian, and Trajan had to build forums outside the ancient rectangle.

The ideal way to reconstruct the area and some of its history is to study briefly the maps of the growth of Empire on the Via dei Fori Imperiali, near the Baths of Maxentius, then to zigzag, cross, and recross the area in chronological order from the necropolis to the last monument, the column of Phocus. But that requires planning beforehand, and most travelers must submit to leaping from century to century, looking down to ancient levels and up to less ancient heights, erecting temples and basilicas and honorific columns, in geographical progress.

From the back of the Campidoglio, take the roadway that leads toward the Mamertine Prison, early dungeons and execution grounds where medieval tradition placed St. Peter as prisoner, and below, an isolated depth of broken stone bones, keystones in useless arches and a trio of three surviving columns to mark the expansion that was the forum of Julius Caesar. Before you make the descent which will lead along the Via dei Fori Imperiali to the entrance proper of the Forum, look up at the Tabularium, whose remaining chipped arches (walking through them gives curious, broken glimpses of the Forum) represent the oldest surviving Roman arcade, built in 78 B.C. to flank the repository of the state archives. On the street below, a trio of columns that remain of a temple dedicated by Domitian to Vespasian and Titus. Of the accompanying Temple of Concord, built several centuries before, there is not much left except notes in Roman history. It was erected (367 B.C.) to mark the end of an early revolution, the discord between the patricians and the people, and thereafter from time to time rebuilt to contain, at a high point, an unusual collection, in size and quality, of art dedicated to peace. A low set of columns awkwardly supported by iron bars wedged into the Senate building propels us through centuries again, into early Christian times (fourth century), when a prefect of Rome, finding it wise to follow the return to paganism of Julian the Apostate, placed in his portico coupled ancient images of the major gods, Mars with Venus, Apollo with Diana, Jove with Juno, Mercury with Ceres, Vulcan and Vesta. The imposing set of columns immediately south, which look almost complete compared to the wreckage surrounding them, are the residue of the Temple of Saturn as it was restored in the time of Caesar. The first temple, of the fifth century B.C., was the public treasury and, more famously, the point of gathering for the Saturnalia, a December week of roistering and gift giving, a Republican Christmas and carnival rolled into one immortal uninhibited celebration, as its name, still in use, implies.

Once through the entrance and down the slope into the Forum, let your eyes scan the whole—from the enormous old road stones at your feet up to the heights and gardens of the Palatine, back to the Tabularium, the campanile and medieval tower on the Capitol, ahead to the Arch of Titus and curve of the Colosseum. As you begin to wander among bare spaces with thunderous names, scraps that represent marble edifices shining of gilded bronze statues, let your eyes gather together the immense numbers of broken columns, scattered here, stacked there, some inscribed or crowned in their acanthus fronds, some slender, others heavy, in pinkish marble, in striped gray, in darkened tones of white, and consider the tonnage of marble that must have entered the port at Ostia, or been carted over endless distances along Roman roads.

An oval-shaped lightweight exploration might start beyond the Basilica Emilia, with little to show except size and a form that was an innovation for its time, the second century B.C., and then head along the Sacred Way (Sacra Via) to a shed that guards slabs of black marble and a stairway to the Lapis Niger, often referred to as the tomb of Romulus. Glass casing shows only blocks of coarse tufa that might be one large tomb or sections of several, one corner embroidered with spurts of fernery which may receive their sustenance from depths of marsh or seepage from the Cloaca Maxima, which passes nearby on its way to the Tiber. Either deeply hidden under the blocks of tufa or carried off elsewhere, the Black Stone itself is not visible except as a copy in the Antiquarium of the Forum. Whether it was the tomb of Romulus, the founder of the city, or not is and may forever be in dispute. That it is a tomb of the fifth or sixth century B.C. seems to have been proven by the type of tufa and structure. That it was the burial place of a king is indicated by an inscription in crude Greek letters that read as early Latin (the irregular lines run from left to right, then right to left, etc.) which proscribes defilement with refuse or the approach of draft animals by order of "the king," proof that kings and areas sacred to them existed at that time.

The Arch of Septimius Severus (third century A.D.) represents victories, the function of these triumphal arches, in a slanting manner that tries for the spirals of victorious events on the more successful columns of Trajan and Marcus Aurelius. A high broad platform marks the rostrum, once covered with marble and gilded bronze, which was the columned stage where emperors spoke, distributed largess to the people, and conducted state ceremonies from the time of Caesar. Shards of older rostra have been detected near the Lapis Niger (the Comitium) and, according to some authorities, in the very fabric of Caesar's dais. Two small ruins near the curved back of the platform are the Vulcanale, a shrine to Vulcan of a most ancient time, now diminished to a few steplike stones and rounded brick wall,

and a basic edifice like the inside of a chimney, the Umbili-
cus Urbis, the center of the city—at which particular point
in its growth is not stated. Between the far side of the
rostra and the almost invisible Arch of Tiberius, the Mili-
arium Aureum (golden milestone), which was inscribed
with the names and distances of the major places of the
Empire in the time, and by order, of Augustus.

Behind the column of Phocus—a usurper who is remembered primarily as the last emperor to teeter on a marble
column in the Forum and as the ruler who gave the
Pantheon to Pope Boniface IV, who converted it into a
church—there is another protective fence, this to enclose
the last vestige or reminder of the marsh and/or a sacred
depth into which the Roman citizenry dropped coins as
offerings for the health and safety of the emperors. The
plaque of a young warrior on a horse that stands near the
opening refers to the willingness of a young Marcus Curtius
to throw himself and his horse into a whirlpool that suddenly opened here as a sacrifice to appease the angry gods.

The Basilica Giulia is, like its neighbor across the road,
nothing but steps and bases of column and size, except for
one earthy vestige. The building, initiated by Caesar and
completed by Augustus on the site of an earlier basilica,
was concerned primarily with the law. The sessions were
not closed, and the populace, when there weren't games to
attend, or before the baths were opened, hung around to
listen. As often happens, there were dull stretches in the
proceedings, and in moments of boredom, citizens or soldiers or police or court attendants, or all, scratched wheels
and circles into the marble floor to play a form of check-
ers. (There are scholars who idealize the graffiti as sketches
of ornaments in the basilica, but it is difficult to see anything but gaming boards in the primitive forms.)

Skirting the miles of cable and innumerable lights used
for the Son et Lumière representations and paying strict
attention to "danger" signs in three languages, go on to
the temple of Castor and Pollux, reduced to three superb

columns of Parian marble that stand high over a defunct arch of Augustus. Corinthian columns of the Empire may not say it (Forum temples and basilicas underwent the same ruthless destruction by fire, earthquake, plunder, and reconstruction as did the Roman churches in their time), but the temple dates back to the fifth century B.C. and commemorates the intervention of the twin sons of Leda and the Swan in a battle between the Romans and the Tarquins and friends. The battle won, the twins appeared in the Forum to announce the victory and, having watered their horses in the pool of the goddess Juturna, disappeared. The pool and its surrounding reliefs of the twins, the Swan and Leda, a small temple, and a room behind the pool with a headless figure holding a snake accompanied by a child and a large, domesticated fowl make an attractive, almost intimate enclave among the uncommunicative spaces. The headless figure is thought to be Aesculapius, and he may very well have been, since legendary waters that fed supernatural horses would surely have curative magic for humans. There is a plaque on the temple of Castor and Pollux that is worth straining your Italian for, or that of a friend. It describes the pomp of the legions returning victorious in wreaths of olive leaves and shining togas with purple borders. They came from a temple of Mars outside the city and crossed Rome and the Forum to arrive at the temple of the Dioscuri carrying their "prizes" (read "spoils of war").

S. Maria Antiqua was built into an entrance of a Palatine mansion. Its irregular cavelike walls are placed around awkwardly shaped and reshaped spaces, and it is a place of semidestroyed and extremely interesting early church paintings, one period often visibly imposed on another, or two others. (Like the Antiquarium, the House of Livia, the Curia, the church is frequently closed, and although the guards say there is a schedule of alternating personnel among these places, no one will commit himself to saying when what will be open. Perhaps yours will be the lucky day for S. Maria Antiqua.)

From a hut where a woman or two guarded the precious single source of fire in a primitive hamlet grew the ornate temple and spacious house of the Vestals, refurbished and enlarged to suit the swollen tastes of the Empire. Mysterious, tainted with a touch of the sinister—or is one simply remembering *Norma*?—the vestals who served for a period of thirty years as the traditional keepers of the flame had extraordinary privileges. The six were among the few who could ride about in their chariots at will, and they were probably custodians of treasures of a ritual nature to warrant so large a house. As a matter of fact, excavations during the early part of our century turned up a large store of ancient coins at the base of the house. If a vestal strayed from virginity, she was taken from the luxurious temple and gardened house and buried alive. This may have been the fate of one vestal among the rows in nunlike hoods and somber faces that line their garden pools. Whether they lack a head or not—and most do—there is always an identifying inscription at the base of the statue, except one which has been blanked out. Was she, as guides like to say, a convert to Christianity, or was she overwhelmed by profane love?

Entering a peaceful, blank area where history is too well buried to be disturbing, except for a shed that demonstrates layers of Roman building styles and the stairway that mounts to the Farnese Gardens of the Palatine, one is soon accosted by the Arch of Titus (and Vespasian, who is mentioned twice on the inscriptions) and its famous procession out of conquered Jerusalem, the ceremonial candles, the long trumpets, and the tablets of the Temple held triumphantly high on one side. On the other, the emperor riding his chariot drawn by a quadriga, and above him a winged Victory.

At this point, exhausted with hopscotching back and forth across the centuries, you may leave the Forum for the Colosseum and the Arch of Constantine by way of the largest temple of them all, that of Venus and the goddess

Roma designed by Hadrian over a long hallway of Nero's dream house. Or you may round back to the church of S. Francesca Romana and the Antiquarium Forense. When it is open, the hours are strict, 9 to 9:30, and so on, on the hour, and closed at 12:30. The museum concerns itself with funerary finds in the Forum and nearby, charred narrow wooden boxes and their inhabiting skeletons, photos and sketches of large urns holding smaller urns, an actual tomb with bones and pottery as they were found, bits of crude jewelry and small vials of glass turned opalescent by time and burial; black pottery rather like the Etruscan and the urn shaped like a small house found in primitive burials of several civilizations; coins, needles, fibulae, figurines, small lamps, a remnant of wall painting, and three especially interesting objects. One is an ancient lead baptismal font, large enough for total immersion, marked with crude X's which may represent the cross and one side melted by fire into leaden waves. The other is a replica of the Lapis Niger broken at the top and incised with its crude message; the third a model of an archaic necropolis.

Beyond the tall arches and bold coffers of the Basilica of Maxentius, a medieval portico embraced by vines. Inside a closed gate next to the temple of Romulus there is a dumpheap of bits of stone drapery, medieval network carving, fragments of egg-and-dart ledge, a thigh, a torso, and skittering among the disordered piles, a bright green lizard whose color is close to that of the temple, tentatively identified as that built by Maxentius for his deified young son Romulus. The greened bronze doors, although stripped of their adornments, are the originals of the fourth century, and whoever is in charge of checking these matters says the lock still works although it is rarely, if ever, used.

At the foot of the audacious columns and stairs of the temple of Antoninus and Faustina, several patches of grass forming lozenges, circles, and rectangles echo the shapes of archaic sepulchers, the necropolis that yielded the shards and bones in the museum and, in its forgotten time, served as cemetery for the primitive village of the early Palatine.

By order of the Senate, possibly nudged by Antoninus, his wife Faustina was deified and a temple erected to her in A.D. 141. On his death in 161, the deified emperor shared the temple. High up, and surprisingly fresh, a frieze of griffons and vases and acanthus coils, and at the top of the stairs the lower half of a substantially built goddess. The truncated goddess looks out on two piles of meaningless stone that once had great significance. The Regia is claimed by some scholars as the palace of a pre-Republican king. During the Republic it was the major religious temple, where the Pontifex Maximus, the precursor of the pope who still bears the Roman title, supervised religious practices and adherence to religious law and kept under watch sacred objects—the lances that trembled to warn of impending danger, the shield of Mars that descended from the sky. There was a period when the Regia was attached to the house of the Vestals, and their large house may have shared these and other awesome objects to be hidden from plebeian eyes. The accompanying pile is the sad remains of the temple of Caesar, where Antony made his moving oration and the listening crowd built a pyre on which the body was burned.

The Sacred Way continues to the dark mottled rows of marble thumbs of the Basilica of the Emilians and along the wall at the back sections of frieze that may have adorned this or other buildings. They might represent the rape of the Sabine women or Persephone wrenched from her mother's arms by Pluto; the concentration is, in any case, on violently uprooted ladies.

The tall Curia owes its intact form to restoration early in this century. The bronze doors are copies of the originals that now hum in S. Giovanni in Laterano, and if they are not open—a too common event—you are out of considerable luck, since some of the best and most informative art of the Forum is enclosed in the old Senate building. The regal hall has, like its neighbors, a long past that stems from the seventh century B.C., according to popular belief, through reconstructions by Caesar and Diocletian and the Church and back to the third-century image of Diocletian's era. The regal space speaks its purpose more lucidly than do the other buildings in the Forum. On either side of the multicolored marble floor are rises for the seats of senators, the pros ranged on one side, their adversaries on the other, and toward the back, the low podium of the authority who presided. Next to the podium, a base which is said to have held the golden figure of Victory brought to Rome from Magna Grecia by Augustus and a serious cause for contention between pagans and early Christian powers who wanted the image removed and destroyed.

Destroyed she was, one way or another, but there should still be in the austere space reliefs that may have decorated the side of the large rostrum, a possibility still in dispute among archaeologists. The sacrificial pig, sheep, and bull adorned in their ceremonial garlands appear on the side of the plaques that depict an enlightened Emperor standing on the rostrum of the Forum, canceling debts by ordering that a fire be built under a heap of tablets and, in the second, seated to receive a woman and her children to give them, or be thanked for, the dole he established for the children of the poor.

From prehistoric grave to Byzantine Mafioso, from Caesar to Septimius Severus, from Romulo to Constantine, we have wandered with silence. Where is the noise and movement? Set in a Frangipane fortress, where important documents and books of the Lateran palace were placed for safekeeping and disappeared when the tower was destroyed by antipapal forces in 1244. Spot the rest of the Forum with enough tower-fortresses to have earned the rectangle the name of Campo Torrechiano in the Middle Ages, and have them mass their soldiers for melees. For earlier noises, bookshops and copyists in a tight row along the Argiletum, at the side of the Curia; huge warehouses under the Palatine, near S. Maria Antiqua; drunken men and ululating women

around the temple of Saturn; milling crowds waiting to be
diverted or edified or fed from the rostrum; gamers and
gawkers and idlers in the law courts and in the narrow
alleys; makers of jewelry and trumpets and harps and drums
on the Sacred Way; vendors and purchasers of fish in the
porticoes of the basilicas; the wanderers and wonderers
from Palestine, Syria, Egypt, Germany, France, England, and
the thieves and prostitutes who followed them through the
shaded alleys. Noise, people working, people idling happily,
gaping foreigners; splendid, frenetic, and thief-ridden Rome
as it was and not too different from what it is.

Outside the Arch of Titus, before you enter the Colosseum,
try to reconstruct, from the breadth of column and huge
arch, the probable size of the temple of Venus immediately
to the north. To the south, walk up the Via di S. Bonaventura which rises with the Palatine. It is an oasis of rural
quiet—except for wedding parties which use its churches—
that stops at a hidden corner, so secluded that it provides
undisturbed calm for friars who pace back and forth reading their breviaries as they might in a cloister garden.

Difficult but possible for the intrepid is the daring of
converging lines of traffic to reach the isolated Arch of
Constantine at the side of the Colosseum built to celebrate
Constantine's victory over Maxentius in the fourth century. The bands of crude, quasi-Romanesque notables
meeting at the Forum and soldiers going forth to war carrying Mithraic symbols, and a rough-cut moon-goddess in a
roundel above are of the fourth century. Contrast these
with the reliefs of the uppermost section and finely incised
medallions—hunting scene, sacrificial rites—above the side
arches, the elegance of the columns and the strength of
the freestanding figures near the top. The latter came from
an edifice built for Trajan, the eight medallions from a
monument of Hadrian's reign; the uppermost reliefs are of
the time of Marcus Aurelius and the Corinthian columns

from a building of Domitian. Obviously, the Roman habit of reusing pieces of ancient edifice is as ancient as the edifices.

Capitoline Museums

The reiterated question: How much Greco-Roman or purely Roman art have you seen and how much do you still want to see? The recommendations here are the peerless Michelangelo piazza and the buildings in which the museums live, their proximity and links to the Forum, the fact that they (or more precisely, the Capitoline Museum) constitute the oldest museum in the world, established in 1471 by Sixtus IV, embellished by later popes. And, as always in this numberless field, a good number of objects of artistic or historic value that one might regret overlooking.

The Capitoline Museum (left of the central building) uses as greeter the god Oceano, listed as "Marforio" among the "talking statues" who make wry comments on Roman events, a co-worker of the prolific Pasquino off the Piazza Navona. In colossal indolence he sits in an early baroque flood of light at the end of a dark frame-passage. His friends are Pans who once skittered among the decorations of the theater of Pompey. Authentic and imitation Egyptian figures line an inner court, many of them disinterred from the temple of Isis that also yielded the obelisk and the Minerva of the church near the Pantheon. It must have been a remarkable thing to see, the matronly Roman goddess among the effete Egyptians—perhaps sent for by Caligula, who was a devotee of Isis.

The same strain of Eastern music sounds through the adjoining galleries; inevitably Mithras slaying his bull, Isis in several guises, and adjustable Jove compartmentalized to suit a number of sects and functions. The more conventional aspects of the gods on and off sarcophagi, copies of the Greek and local products, fill the rest of the lower galleries and a few of the upper until, in the Sala delle Colombe, one is stopped by a most celebrated mosaic copied as objects and jewelry over the centuries and throughout Europe, the four doves drinking from a vase, a reproduction from the Greek found in Hadrian's villa. An equally notable work, also Greek in origin, is the Capitoline Venus, who stands in her own niche, soon followed by rows of very unbeautiful people in the Sala degli Imperatori, and their wives and *their* hairstyles. These sixty-five, ranged neatly and constrictedly like supermarket packages, give way to several dozen philosophers and writers, an actor or two, and someone who may be Aesculapius.

In a larger room matters begin to improve, with several Greek figures and good copies leading to the celebrated wounded Amazon resting on her lance, saddened by her wound rather than infuriated or frightened; she bears it with Spartan poise. A Greek bronze of a jocund satyr dangling a bunch of grapes is exceedingly well translated here into a marble that lends its name to the Sala del Fauno, which then regrettably returns to Roman portraits and sarcophagi in more of their inexhaustible number. The star of the next room is the dying gladiator or warrior, a unique Greek work, prayerfully copied by an artist who may easily have been a Greek slave. Certainly not as moving but equally distinguished is the well-known figure, believed to be that of Praxiteles—again exceedingly well copied—of the relaxed satyr (probably Hawthorne's "Marble Faun") easing his wine-filled limbs against a tree trunk and a gratifying contrast to the tragic Antinous, now dressed like Hermes, and next to him, the purposeful head of Alexander the Great.

To match the river-god across the square, the court of the Museo dei Conservatori (hung with marriage notices) shows off *its* colossi, an immense hook-nosed head of Constantine, one of his arms, a leg with carefully traced veins, and two pointing fingers. The second giant's head is that of Constantine II, and both induce the conviction that Rome must have been a sequoia forest of colossi during several epochs of its Imperial life, an appalling reflection of megalomania and vulgarity. Less scrambled Forum personae appear in characteristic action on the first landing of the staircase. Three reliefs of the second century A.D. taken from an edifice built to honor Marcus Aurelius show the emperor in a triumphal chariot pulled by the usual four spirited horses, in a gesture of mercy toward a group of the vanquished, and participating in a sacrifice, the sacrificial bull almost lost in the crowd, a piper blowing heartily. A fourth frieze gives us Hadrian making his ceremonious entrance into Rome and again, on an upper landing, making a speech in the Roman Forum, his head almost crushed by the monument above him. Perhaps this squeezing of space, in the Marcus Aurelius panels as well, was meant to indicate the crowding of buildings and people on the Forum or is simply a manifestation of decay in Roman art, as compared to the handling of groups in processions and ceremonies in the Ara Pacis, of an earlier century. To observe how a king should be ennobled by art, stand for a while with Arnolfo di Cambio's thirteenth-century portrait of the enthroned Charles of Anjou, king of Sicily.

The sections and rooms in this portion of the museums are as confusing—some closed, others rushing off in unexpected directions—as portions of the Vatican museums. Do what you can, if you can. The first of the Sale dei Conservatori, those of the big red chairs and carpets and big frescoes, can be dashed through quickly until one comes on a group of bronzes: the always astonishing Diana of Ephesus, who stands on a base more tastefully decorated than the lady herself; the *Spinario*, the justly prized first-century B.C. boy whose young, concentrated face is bent to the thorn in his foot; an eerie bronze head of an earlier period whose marble eyes stare inimically through tunnels of dark time. The Sala della Lupa is gathered around The Ancestors, the bronze wolf of Rome with dugs like those of the many-breasted Diana-Isis-Astarte, an exceedingly old (fifth or sixth century B.C.) girl to be nursing twins born in the Renaissance or later. Although they may not say much to the casual viewer, old lists attached to the walls are texts of Roman history, lists of consuls and triumphant military leaders that start in a misty era and finish at about the time Christ was born. There is some debate about where these panels stood in the Forum, whether attached to one of the rostra or to the walls of the almost invisible Arch of Augustus; the latter supposition is generally favored. The scored, sadly contemplative face of Michelangelo, a copy of the head by Daniele da Volterra in Florence, refuses to respond to the excitements of a Medusa by Bernini, or be cheered by the foolish agitation of several irritated ducks, or lured by the compelling archaic eyes of a small Isis. An attractive small Venus-like figure, asleep with her arms leaning on her knee, brightens her sala (delle Aquile), and then you can start running again until you reach a pair of children playing leapfrog. The fact that they are headless scarcely impairs their fun and your fun in them.

At the end of a passage that holds six engaging seventeenth- into eighteenth-century views of Rome by the Dutchman the Italians call Vanvitelli, one is ushered into the Museo del Palazzo dei Conservatori proper, where the pace once again becomes swifter, blurring empresses and sarcophagi to halt (the Galleria degli Orti Lamiani) at a Hellenistic enchantment. She is young, sitting in total ease, her legs crossed, one arm on the edge of a bench. The raised shoulder against the smooth diagonal of bent arm, the turn and droop of head moving toward an extended leg, set in motion a delicate rippling rhythm that breathes youth in the momentary serenity, a pause in a dance, a footrace won. She creates a stimulating contrast with the sturdy, armless Esquiline Venus nearby.

The Sala dei Magistrati offers honorary Roman citizenship to Petrarch, who was crowned poet laureate on this hill, to Titian and Michelangelo and, among others, Queen Christina, whose portrait shows a wilderness of curly hair lapping at a witch's profile. Long-lined archaic controls the next room, styling a tombstone of a young girl holding a dove and a Nike whose drapes are light, slender lines, and in the center of the room a stylized female torso that might almost be Egyptian were it not for the dynamic slant and thrust of the shoulder and legs, ready for action, probably kneeling to pull a bow.

One meets again with pleasure King Charles in his illuminated niche and, turning a bit to his left, comes on another gigantic foot (Isis, once more), a relief landscape of a section of Rome as seen before the birth of Christ, and a *scena dionisiaca*, a Hellenistic frieze that deals with a ritual act, two people whose hands cover their genitals being led into a grove in which stands a leering priapic satyr. Interest dulls in the return of empresses and sarcophagi and picks up in the galleries of Etruscan and contemporaneous Greek art, a quintessence of naturalism achieved in the frieze of a young man leaning on a counter, holding a pitcher to be filled with wine and, waiting at his side, the faithful dog, a scene by a Norman Rockwell of Etruscan Caere (Cerveteri).

The colossi will not for long be obscured, and since there is something in the human face that makes it stupid in elephantiasis, Constant II, separated from his hand nearby, looks colossally stupid. "Sad and bewildered" better describes a bronze hermaphrodite not quite capable of coping with breasts and an erection. Hecate manages with confidence her three bodies in a compact bronze unit, and inconquerably proud is the funeral bier embroidered in bronze and silver which takes the center of the stage in the Sala dei Bronzi.

The room named for the gardens of Maecenas (Orti di Mecenate) indicates that the objects in it were found in the Esquiline gardens of that very rich friend of Augustus. You have seen Herculeses, Venuses, and Amazons in abundance at this stage, but little like the Roman copy of a Marsyas from Rhodes, his arms pulled and tied above his head, a tight rope joining his ankles (about to be flayed because he dared a musical contest against Apollo and lost), inevitably reminiscent of later crucifixions; nor a relief of a maenad, head down, trampling the ground, hair, body, and draperies swirling in delirium.

The Braccio Nuovo is often closed, but, from reports, it apparently contains variations of what has gone before, and at any rate, a rest in the somber shaded gardens might prove a grateful substitute before you return to the Museo Nuovo, by way of the Muro Romano, the remains of the great temple of Jove that stood on this peak of the Capitoline. The rooms of this wing are not all open all the time either, and if they were, you might find yourself again in the company of gods and goddesses, supervised by their stocky forelady, Athena.

Diversion rests in the Pinacoteca, a good sampling of Italian and Dutch paintings of the sixteenth through eighteenth centuries that encompass several flat Renis which appear to be unfinished or badly repainted; Guercinos acting out their dramas against vast, murky, threatening skies; a slow rape of Europa delayed by ladies-in-waiting who must see to it that she is lavishly dressed for the event (Veronese); a Magdalene, of the younger Tintoretto, who lies on straw mats so artfully worked that the eye lingers on them rather than the woman. In the respectable miscellany, a portrait of Bernini by Velázquez, Orpheus soothing his animals in a Poussin twilight, a distinguished double portrait of two Dutch painters by Van Dyke, two small, glistening landscapes by Domenichino and a group of Carracci paintings. With room and objects to spare, the painting gallery decides to include a few minor primitive paintings, tapestries, and a large collection of snuffboxes, watches, hundreds of pieces of Italian, German, and Chinese porcelain, and many-sectioned jewel chests, one entirely of lapis, another of tortoise shell in bronze bands. On your way down the stairs, if you haven't already seen it, look for a marble sturgeon cut through to the first fin. It is a highly ornamented edition of the slab in the ghetto that assured the right of the *conservatori* (governors) to dispose as they saw fit of the head of a large fish, a privilege spelled out in Latin not too difficult to decipher, the opening words *Capita Piscium Hoc Marmoreo Schemate.*

Below lies the greatest work on the hill, the not-quite square itself, designed by Michelangelo. Standing on the steps of the central building helps reveal the brilliance of conception, the several sloping roads of easy access so drawn as not to interfere with the integrity of the piazza, the sides not parallel (which would constrict the square) but widening subtly to let in the city and sky above the regal stairway, the black and white pattern of irregular lozenges that have a look of flexibility, like wire mesh, which intensifies the sense of movement to and from the almost imperceptible rise on which Marcus Aurelius stands. Many people deplore the incongruously small statues on the cornices of the side buildings, but were they larger they might compete with the magnificent equestrian statue—the model for Donatello's *Gattamelata* in Padua, to mention only one of many later equestrian sculptures—or disturb the calm godliness of Castor and Pollux. The eye easily erases the cornice figures to dwell on the symmetry of the buildings in their superb space, a just concentration of emphasis.

Turn now to Castor and Pollux in their little eggshell caps, notice that the horses are small for such big boys, and then go into the arch at the left nearest the stairs. If the cars permit, you should soon be standing among the trees below the Palazzo Caffarelli looking down on whipping traffic, onto bell towers, undulating tiles, domes, the three tragic columns of Apollo's temple at the entrance to the ghetto, and beyond the lead of the synagogue roof, mounds of houses caught in wooded patches. At your foot, one of the few dim-witted cats of Rome who hasn't yet found out that here there is no food depot. Walking down one path or up another (Via di Monte Caprino, perhaps) shifts the view to obliterate the Vittorio Emanuele monument and accept the Teatro di Marcello, a considerable improvement. The Via del Tempio di Giove drops from the rise of Caprino to a broad vista of the Palatine and the Fori Imperiali, fringed in the distance by the chess pieces at the crest of S. Giovanni in Laterano, and offers the choice of returning to the Campidoglio or following the curving slopes down to the Forum, or up to the Palatine hill.

Palatine

The empty sockets and eviscerated depths of the Palatine, as they stare out across the barren Circus Maximus, in thin light threaten, loom, warn like Shelley's "Ozymandias." The full, flat sun washes some of the threat from the Palatine; it simply looks forlorn. As the sun pulls away from its gutted caves they darken and, depending on your mood, the mass resembles an enormous veined cheese or a maze of traps. Under the night illumination it may be a huge golden mesh of looped necklaces or a thing of hidden rites, madness, poisons. These are exaggerated responses, of course, elicited by a collection of the most exaggerated of Imperial gestures, the arches on arches of the Septizonium which Septimius Severus (A.D. 211, born in Africa) built tall, very tall and majestic on rows of richly crested columns of the finest African marble to flank noble statues and provide space for viewing the games in the circus below. Its primary purpose was *bella figura*, how magnificent, how eye-boggling his Rome could be, particularly in the eyes of foreign dignitaries approaching from the south, from Africa maybe, to be stunned by how very well the local boy had made out.

Such pride and total, uncensored control of moneys and labor in the indulgence of maniacal whims was the divine right of emperors, with a few reasonable exceptions, and except when it reached the highest vortices of madness, quite acceptable. Augustus, who was born on the hill, had for a loving wife Livia, reputed, as mentioned, to be a skillful manipulator of poisoners. The merciless distrustful Domitian, afraid to walk in the portico of his palace, yet obsessed with expanding it endlessly and adorning it with precious metal and rare stone, had a type of mirror-like marble, kept highly polished, put into its side so that he might see if someone were lurking behind him with a knife. He was murdered nevertheless, bleeding into the gold of his chamber. The vicious Caligula, who was Jove or a charioteer or a horse as the mood took him, was murdered in an approach to his house here. The famous Imperial excesses of all appetites—food, sex in several varieties, love of intrigue and destruction—reached their pinnacle on this crowded, resplendent rise from which we have taken the word "palace."

As it witnessed the collapse of ancient Rome, the Palatine saw the beginning. Before it was leveled, filled, and built upon by the emperors, the hill was three, populated by three peoples of Latin, Sabine, and Etruscan roots who were united under one system of laws. These may not have been the earliest inhabitants of the mounds, according to archaeologists, but history contents itself with the coalition of the three tribes and places the founding of the city proper in the mid-eighth century B.C. Around this nucleus there was erected a box of wall which gave the city its name of "Roma quadrata," and from the settlement on the Palatine, the village grew by conquest and the natural intermixtures of neighboring peoples to include the other hills. As the city expanded and the population spread, the Palatine remained primarily a place for religious worship, and since it offered pleasant views and cool air, the villas of the respected prosperous (Cicero, Cataline, and Mark Anthony) began to appear among the temples. After Augustus' comparatively modest house, there sprang up magnificences of marble halls built by his successors. Occupied with conquests and rebellions in an ever changing empire, later rulers lacked the time or the taste for sybaritic mansions, and the Palatine faded, its decayed palaces used for brief periods by Gothic kings, members of the ecclesiastical hierarchy, and Eastern emperors. The search for high positions on which to build fortresses brought the troops and bastions of the Frangipani family to the hill. Centuries later, the Renaissance Farnese bought a major stretch of the area and built a luxurious villa and gardens. To balance the costs, they took vast quantities of marble and treasures under the guise of exploration. The Bourbons of Naples later owned the hill, and in 1860 they sold it to Napoleon III, who began systematic excavation which continued with vigor after the Palatine reverted to the Italian government.

There is no reasonable way to follow ruins chronologically when they have been built on, dug up, destroyed, and are still in the course of being discovered in deep and deeper pits. To reach the height, one might use the Clivus Palatinus, which leads up from the Arch of Titus, or enter through the imposing Vignola arch on the Via di S. Gregorio, keeping in mind as a vague chronological signpost that the oldest buildings discovered to date are situated above the corner of the Via di S. Teodoro as it meets the Circus Maximus. For the studious there are the booklets with detailed maps sold near the Colosseum, along the broad Via dei Fori Imperiali and souvenir-bookshops that fringe tourist centers. For the collectors of moods and dreamers of lost times, a few hours, a small picnic basket, and enthusiasm for the suggestive and fragmentary are enough.

A century ago the Palatine was reported to be a confusion of goalless arcades, meaningless rooms, domestic animals, vegetable patches and a puzzling lyricism. The arches and rooms have been given connections and names derived from descriptions by Latin authors; the animals, vegetables, and their keepers are gone. Lyricism remains under the deep pines, as light breezes that hardly ruffle the stillness in the broad high undisturbed spaces and the views over the city whose traffic noise floats upward as a distant purr. The Vignola gate which once led to the Farnese gardens takes one to clumps of pines over upward paths to the grandiose stadium of Domitian. No one can say certainly how the sunken area, once surrounded by a double portico, was used; some suggest a garden full of fountains and statues, others that it was a private gymnasium and athletic field, still others that it was a public stadium devoted to games and races. Once marble-faced portico columns now stand as small heaps of brick: between the rows, stones that shape an oval which was—maybe—a horse ring ordered by Theodoric, and at one side the Imperial Tribune built by Hadrian. The viewing stand for the Imperial family and its guests is an impressive semicircular loggia on two levels that probably held works of classical art, selected by Hadrian's informed eye, and was gaily painted, as evidenced by faded areas in the lower level. The curved corridor that leads into the Tribune is vaulted by rows of coffering like that of the Basilica of Maxentius and the Pantheon. Behind the curve of the viewing box, the palace of Septimius Severus and his baths and the great arches and supports he built to extend the Palatine hill.

From the palace of this last of the obsessed builders, there is a remarkable view downward to low and high arches, white patches of mosaic which may have been the floors of pools and thermal rooms, lower paths that disappear into pine groves, a depth of green and more green below, and the blankness of the Circus Maximus. From a railed walk above, a gift of significant sites of Rome: a fan that opens to the Baths of Caracalla, the campaniles of small basilicas beyond, a curious slice of the Colosseum, the smooth, green sweep of the Aventine, and across the river, St. Peter's and the heights of the Janiculum. Straight downward, the heavy, obdurate piles of the arch supports and, at one edge of the platform, an area cut out to demonstrate the heating system of hollow brick columns filled with hot water, devised for the baths. The abysses of great depth, one realizes, are not necessarily depth at all but a level of height, a recurrent element of Rome's tricks, where up and down are comparative, depending upon which layer was ground level at a given time.

Returning to the crest of the hill via a number of bridge-paths, past sprinklings of brick and stone, one comes to the enormous Domus Augustana, immediately west of the stadium. The name has little to do with Augustus, but rather means the "house of the emperors," part of Domitian's engulfment of the hill and actually used as Imperial and papal house for several centuries. The site in classical times was larger than it now appears to be. Beginning with the Mattei in the sixteenth century, and passing to other families which absorbed increasing amounts of land that covered Domitian's mansion, the northern section took on several aspects. In the early nineteenth century it was Gothic orange-red scallops over fake Gothic archways, heraldic designs of the British Isles' thistles and roses. These were the improvements of Charles Andrew Mills, rich Scotsman, as eccentric as any emperor and deeply enamored, like many Anglos of his time, of the brooding neo-Gothic.

If the museum on the site (9 to 1, closed Tuesdays) is available to you, see some of the material collected locally, then return to the nearby pits of excavation which have uncovered several ornamental shapes—that of a pool surrounded by flower paths and a sketch of a small temple, walls not quite as indomitable as their owner expected them to be, surrounding an endless courtyard dressed in marble and leading to rooms lined with precious metals, paved with mosaics, ornamented with paintings and choice statuary.

Of equal if not greater splendor was the palace of the Flavii, also by Domitian, meant for official business and state ceremonies, which parallels the Domus on the other side of the museum. Its porticoes and gigantic public rooms cover sections of earlier buildings of several periods. In the middle of the vast peristyled central court, a hedge maze surrounded by pieces of marble column and pavements, a ledge gravid with heavy eggs and darts and a few excavation pits covered with screening which allows only a glimpse of great depth. On the side toward the Circus Maximus, the Triclinium, the state dining hall, paved with colored marbles now cracked in lively waves of rose and green lapping at the apselike area where the emperor sat enthroned, above and apart from his guests. Where there was a banqueting hall there was usually a nymphaeum; here there were two whose flowered waters cooled and scented the air of the banqueting hall. A lower remnant of porphyry and serpentine may be remains of earlier constructions, perhaps of a house of Nero burned in A.D. 64, and, almost adjacent, a closed room whose fine plasterwork and painting of the time of Trajan should be in the local Antiquarium.

A group of marbles and niches at the front of the Triclinium is all that remains of the library, and from the very front, one can look down on a long ledge that marks the building which was an academy for court pages. At the other side, the Aula Regia, whose first rooms mark the Lararium, the private chapel where were gathered the sacred symbols of Rome. Next to that, a state reception room described by contemporaries as dazzlingly splendid with a raised apse for the throne of the emperors and black stone statues in the many niches that alternated with columns of lustrous stone. The third area, now a tall spur of ruin, was the court where the emperor sat but did not necessarily hand down judgments. (Imaginative historians like to see St. Paul in this basilica and Nero listening as the saint is accused of treason and ultimately freed.) Under the basilica and visitable if the guardian of the Antiquarium is about and will cooperate there is an elaborately painted chamber adorned with a frieze of Egyptian symbols that is said to have been a chapel dedicated by Caligula to the worship of Isis.

Sauntering westward, sometimes up, sometimes down, one approaches a sign that indicates an Augustan temple of Apollo, where the Sibylline books enclosed in metal chests were buried, in its time an awesome place whose

portico was spaced with dozens of statues circled around
the effulgent god who probably bore a close resemblance
to the handsome Augustus. In the pediment, the chariot of
the Sun; and on the doors of carved ivory, Greek myths. A
group of Muses introduced the library which held a famous
collection of Greek and Latin books, rare art treasures, and
another statue of Apollo, reported as fifty feet tall, all
destroyed by the fire of A.D. 64.

Turn from the emptiness to see a view of crippled stone
and tall pines that beg for a camera, and back to the house
of Livia. It is hardly the "small house" where Augustus
humbled himself once a year by sitting with a begging bowl
at the threshold, nor is it the ambitious halls of the megalo-
maniacs, but 'twill serve. Architecturally of interest because
it is a good example of a commodious villa of Augustan
times, its essential importance lies in the frescoes, some of
them quite faded and some still briskly, smartly drawn in
Pompeian curlicues. The floors retain their precise mosaic
patterns; a set of lead sewer pipes stamped with Livia's
family name, Julia, hang on one of the walls; in several
rooms, small paintings which have lost their color but kept
their lively drawing. A broad, large headless Cybele, whose
primitive head was a sacred conical meteorite, stands in
one of the niches. Best, by far, is a small room festooned
with fruits and flowers and a bounding, innocent gaiety
rather like that of the room from Livia's villa on the Flaminia, now at the Baths of Diocletian.

Close to Livia, between her house and the temple of
Cybele to the west, one finds the oldest remains yet dug out
of the hill, an archaic cistern made of handsome stone
blocks and the rudiments of cabins that go back to the
ninth century B.C. Here, it is believed, stood the cabin of
Romulus, which was ceremoniously rethatched each year
into the time of the Empire. Among these dark antiquities,
in the shade of a clump of trees, stands the platform of the
ancient temple dedicated to Cybele, the supreme fertility
goddess, the mother of the gods. A smaller, similar neigh-

boring temple of a later time has been appointed by archaeologists the Auguratorium, the place from which the augurs
observed the flight of birds to pronounce their prophecies.

The rest returns to confusion, the palaces of Tiberius
and Caligula mixed with rooms and arches built by Trajan
and Hadrian and most of it covered by once formal Farnese
gardens. The northeast corner of the gardens brings one
back into Rome, above the insistent whiteness of the Vittorio
Emanuele monument, the Campidoglio and its widening
tower, outcroppings of Tiberius' palace, the listing medieval
Torre delle Milizie, Trajan's column, the arches of the
Basilica of Maxentius, the chic penthouses and terraces on
the Via del Foro Romano, and the traffic arrowing through
the Imperial forums.

Whether you care about pleasure gardens which have
shrunk and aged dustily over the last four hundred years,
or about the plinth that held a meteorite-headed goddess,
or choose to trace out which part, if any, of Septimius
Severus' bastion was planned by Hadrian, whether or not
you care to envision Tiberius lolling at a royal banquet
or Claudius dipping into his dish untouched by the news
(probably anticipated) that his wife Messalina was killed,
climb and walk in the Palatine. In spite of its history and
forbidding faces, it is now a docile place, a place of flowers,
shade among pines, a place for mild, unpressing curiosity
and conjecture, the cradle of Rome and still capable of
lulling.

Colosseum and
Domus Aurea

As you stand at the edge of the Parco Oppio across from
the Colosseum, stare back at the arena. Replace the statuary long ago removed from its arches, watch the crowd

pour into its tunnels and scramble to their seats under the ingeniously devised canopies that assured a show come rain or too much shine. Hear the howling of the beasts set against each other, listen to the shrilling of the crowd as a favorite gladiator makes his kill. Smell the perfumes of courtesans and the scent of spices and herbs meant to cover the odor of blood.

Yesterday, sauntering in the illumination that cloaks the night city in a delicacy totally foreign to the day city, you saw the unexpectedly tender arcs of light etched in the heavy entrances. The day before yesterday you may have been reading nineteenth-century accounts of promenades in the Colosseum, an essential exercise of the Romantic spirit which survives as lovers' meeting ground for men and boys, with or without the exchange of moneys.

Between the grand opening by Vespasian in A.D. 75, celebrated with daily "games" for more than three months, and the recent Holy Week Mass when the Pope progressed through the Stations of the Cross above the ruts and passages bitten into the ground for caged men and animals, the Colosseum has suffered earthquakes and avid, systematic flaying of its marbles, and has witnessed many curious lesser events. Benvenuto Cellini was an actor in one of these bizarre incidents. A Sicilian priest, "a man of most lofty mind, and with an excellent knowledge of Latin and Greek," fancied himself a necromancer and found the goldsmith enthusiastic to study his mysteries. With two friends, Cellini went to the Colosseum on the appointed night and there found the priest dressed as a magician, drawing magic circles and making mysterious signs, sprinkling perfumes and stenches. He drew the friends into the circle and mumbo-jumboed for an hour and a half, eliciting "many legions of spirits, so that the Colosseum was full of them." Cellini asked the spirits to bring him back his Sicilian girl, Angelica. No satisfaction. The priest-necromancer said that a young boy of perfect purity was needed. Cellini brought a shopboy of twelve, and again the circle was drawn and the ritual ceremonies performed while Cellini held a potent amulet over the boy's head. "This done, the necromancer began to utter the most terrible invocations, and to call by their names many of the princes of the demoniac legions (speaking the while in Hebrew words, also in Greek and Latin) and commanding them, by the strength and power of God incarnate, living, and eternal, so that in a brief space the whole Colosseum was full of them, and there was a hundred times more than there had been the first night." The terrified boy saw a million threatening men and four armed giants, a report that frightened the necromancer, who "tried with all the soft and gentle words he could think of to bid them to go." Cellini, as usual, inspired them with his show of courage, although they were all sure that they were about to die, especially the boy, who saw the whole arena on fire and "the fire is upon us." On instructions from the priest, Cellini ordered one of his friends to put asafoetida on the fire. "At the instant when he moved to do this, he yielded so powerfully to the needs of nature that it served better than the asafoetida." This touch of the ordinary basic improved everyone's spirits, and at dawn they marched off, still pursued by two demons, "now leaping, now running over the roofs, not along the grounds," as the boy described them. Angelica never showed up, and further mystical searches stopped because "so in love was I with my medal [for the pope] that I never gave a thought to Angelica or anything of the sort. My work was everything to me"—perhaps the reason Angelica left in the first place.

The unconstant moon by which Cellini's group and countless later visitors viewed the Colosseum has been exchanged for constant and effective interior illumination. Away from the full glare of the lamps, one huge block turns lavender, the arches dissolve into each other and grow shadows like giant black lizards. Below, the depths and spurs of animal runs change to infinitely deep gorges that seem to be miles wide, as if one were looking down at the Grand Canyon through a distorting glass. As one circles the arena, the shadows shift, the color clears, and the accustomed shapes return to fade again into violet fantasy.

If you haven't noticed them before, look up into the very tall entrance arches for shreds of exquisitely delicate frieze, an exercise in art for art's sake, since they never were clear to the normal eye, and compare the monumentality of the travertine blocks, in a conception that is truly "colossal," with the pinched faces of the boys and the pallid plumpness of the men who lounge against them.

Across from the theater of demonic events real and imagined, the site of—if not demonic—deranged events, Nero's Golden House. For background we refer to Tacitus' description of the fire of A.D. 64 which destroyed most of Rome. "Nobody dared fight the flames. Attempts to do so were prevented by menacing gangs. Torches, too, were openly thrown in, by men crying that they acted under orders." Nero returned to the city when the fire was approaching the mansion he had built to link the Gardens of Maecenas (on the Esquiline) to the Palatine. The flames could not be prevented from overwhelming the whole of the Palatine, including his palace. Nero arranged temporary housing for the homeless and the distribution of inexpensive corn. "Yet these measures, for all their popular character, earned no gratitude: for a rumor had spread that, while the city was burning, Nero had gone to his private stage and, comparing modern calamities with ancient, had sung of the destruction of Troy. [The famous fiddling?] By the sixth day enormous demolitions had confronted the raging flames with bare ground and open sky, and the fire was finally stamped out. But—flames broke out again. This new conflagration caused additional ill-feeling because it started on [Nero's henchman] Tigellinus' estate. For people believed that Nero was ambitious to found a new city to be called after himself."

Nero did replan the city, Tacitus tells us sourly, "in parts of Rome unfilled by Nero's palace," by regulating the height and materials—more stone in proportion to timber—of houses, creating broad straight avenues and protective colonnades, himself paying a good portion of the costs and offering aid to homeowners for clearing debris and rebuilding damaged houses. Nevertheless, "Nero profited by his country's ruin to build a new palace. Its wonders were not so much customary and commonplace luxuries like gold and jewels, but lawns and lakes and faked rusticity—woods here, open spaces and views there."

Suetonius, writing a century or more later, is not as interested in city planning as Tacitus, nor in maintaining the cool Taciturnity (irresistible!) with which the earlier historian described Nero's excesses, disdainfully holding the events away from himself as if they were stinking rags. Suetonius enjoys Nero. Although he tries to be properly censorious, there is an unmistakable yeasty enthusiasm in his accounts of Nero's debauchery, from the youthful thefts he and his gangs committed—being beaten by and beating up citizens in dark shop streets—and the thieves' market he established for his own profit, to detailed descriptions of his ardent showmanship. He was charioteer, actor, and musician, not only in Rome but in Greece as well, where it pleased him to participate in the games of a fancied Periclean age, and he, Nero, a versatile luminary of that lost time. (Needless to say, he won all contests.) Suetonius happily describes marriages with castrated men, complete with nuptial ceremonies, dowries, bridal veils, numerous wedding guests, and "going so far as to imitate the cries and lamentations of a maiden being deflowered." The old rumors of incestuous relations with his mother, Agrippina, are repeated, and "he so prostituted his own chastity that after defiling almost every part of his body [marked with spots and malodorous, adds Suetonius], he at last devised a kind of game, in which, covered with the skin of some wild animal, he was let loose from a cage and attacked the private parts of men and women who were bound to stakes."

Of the Golden House: "Its vestibule was high enough to contain a colossal statue of the Emperor a hundred and twenty feet high. So large was this house that it had a triple colonnade a mile long. There was a lake in it too, like a sea [where the Colosseum now stands] surrounded with buildings to represent cities, besides tracts of country, varied by tilled fields, vineyards, pastures, and woods, with great numbers of wild and domestic animals. In the rest of the house all parts were overlaid with gold and adorned with jewels and mother-of-pearl. There were dining rooms with fretted ceilings of ivory, whose panels could turn and shower down flowers and were fitted with pipes for sprinkling the guests with perfumes. The main banquet hall was circular and constantly revolved day and night, like the heavens. He had baths supplied with sea water and sulfur water. When the edifice was finished in this style and he dedicated it, he deigned to say nothing more in the way of approval than that he was at last beginning to be housed like a human being"—although the house was not yet finished when he died, forced to commit suicide. Nero was prepared to cover the costs for this kingdom from the immeasurable riches of Dido hidden in African caves and easily recovered, he was told. Dido's treasury was never unearthed, and the Emperor paid his building, decorating, and landscaping bills by forcing more than the usual number of wills to be made in his favor (already a common practice), ruling that death duties which came to the throne be multiplied several times over and that rewards given various cities where he earned prizes for his athletic prowess and artistic accomplishments be returned to him. Finally, he stripped the treasuries of temples and had those images of precious metals not already destroyed by the great fire melted down.

His house did not last very long. Another fire damaged it seriously, and Trajan later stripped off its marbles to build his baths. Little remains that is visible aboveground, merely a low rounded area next to the box that sells admission tickets and post cards and serves as shelter for the guides. The guides try to liven things up as they trot through the subterranean chambers—an incomprehensible collection of immensely tall painted passages, large ceremonial rooms, low rooms, rooms with niches for statues and possibly books—with leering side glances and sighing, envious reflections on Nero's hot-stuff habits. Your leader says there are 140 known rooms and many yet to be explored, and one wonders how it is decided what was a room after Trajan broke down walls to destroy the memory of Nero and filled spaces with rubble to support his own elaborations of baths hot, cold, and tepid among massage and dressing rooms, a gymnasium, a library, a theater and salons.

There, right there in the temple of Minerva (invisible), says the guide, was where the Laocoön was found, bought to adorn his house by Nero. The group may have stood there as part of Nero's collection of art and luxury but was moved some short distance away by Vespasian and his son Titus, who lived for a brief while in the Golden House and used a number of its treasures to enrich Vespasian's Temple of Peace. Or, Trajan may have placed the Laocoön in his baths. Although the Vandals invented the term, vandalism was an old Imperial habit.

One is shown an altar over a groove for the sacrificial blood, the tarred rock left by the fire, and a pause in a large octagonal room for more delicious vice: "Men, women, everything—you know how Nero was—and on those ledges above he had an orchestra, their backs turned so they couldn't see and be distracted by what was going on." The guide's fancy does not stop for an interesting architectural possibility: the opening in the ceiling that shed perfumes and flowers on guests (if this were the dining hall) may have been a model for Hadrian's Pantheon vault. "Right here," he continues in his imaginative tour of enviable excesses, "is where Poppaea, his second wife—after he had had that poor Octavia steamed to death and while he was still keeping his faithful ex-slave, Acte—took her bath of asses' milk in the big porphyry basin they moved to the Vatican museums."

For several reasons that might involve restoration, preservation, or the guard's understandable reluctance to linger in the damp, eccentric, limitless tomb, he does not always stop for the room of the Gilded Vault, the masterwork of the most fashionable painter of his time, Fabullus, who gilded, painted, and stuccoed the ceiling with mythological scenes emphasizing the erotic. Their delicacy, seepage, and erosion have clouded them, but with the help of those handy companions the opera glasses, you may make out traces of the figures. All else that remains is sketches of mosaic, quite modern in their pop-illusion conceits, and wall paintings. The paintings are rather limited and timid for the amount of space they might have filled, restricted to neat boxes that bind vaguely seen figures, small landscapes, or the birds, foliage, and misshapen creatures labeled "Pompeian." They are given importance by being divided into four periods: Pompeian I, quite primitive; II, regular, carefully spaced ornaments; III tries for perspective; and IV improves the perspectives by painting in window ledges revealing landscapes. The most appealing remnant of this narrow art is a trompe l'oeil window that opens on a distant view of a lake and a jolly boating party.

Your escort tells you that Raphael risked his life, dangling by a rope, to study the "grotesques" and to scratch his initials into the walls. Raphael's initials are missing, but he and Michelangelo and Romano and their contemporaries did come to examine and sketch the weird little figures in constant change and motion. One immediate result was Raphael's Pompeian loggia in the Vatican, and the style continued (and continues) in profligate use, at times engaging fancies, at times monstrously swollen. Cellini has his usual goodly number of instructive words on the then newly discovered "grotesques." "They have got this name in modern times from having been found by antiquaries in certain underground caves in Rome, these caves having been in ancient times chambers, bath-houses, studies, halls, and such like. The antiquaries finding them in those cavernous places—for while the ground has been raised in the course of time, these chambers have remained below, and in Rome are called grottos—hence has sprung the term 'grotesques.' But it is not their right name. The ancients delighted in drawing creatures, for the different parts of which they took hints from goats and cows and horses, and they called these curious mixtures by the name of monsters; so do our craftsmen compose from their medley of leaves another sort of monster. Therefore, monsters, not grotesques, is their real name."

The gaunt brick accusers of time and destruction, colossal crumbs left of Trajan's baths, still betray their gigantic size and the style of coffering that became the classic for vaulted Roman space. The rest is invisible, recorded fact-legend. Trajan's spa, they say, was the first to admit women and was, as well, the source of several important works of art now in collections of antiquities. Compendiums of saints' lives tell us that, for refusing to worship in a temple of the baths, the saints of the Quattro Coronati church were martyred there.

The park, as park, demonstrates the common casualness of the Roman toward his past. An ambitious little boy tries to straddle an octagonal column that graced a royal chamber, a donkey cart full of babies trots merrily between two broken arms of Roman brick, students take the sun and mathematical formulas leaning against a smooth granite pillar. Sweating boys kick a soccer ball through the magnificent Gardens of Maecenas (Orti di Mecenate), a children's playground supplants a Neronian playground.

For latter-day dreams of Empire, walk back into the park to the meeting of the Via degli Orti di Mecenate and the Viale Antonio Fibonacci, where Mussolini, whose image had disappeared more thoroughly than Nero's, is revived as a poorly stenciled deep helmet over prognathous jaws stamped on a traffic stanchion. Under the arch and inside a small cave manned by suspicious youths, there stands a heroic head of the Duce. The cave is the local branch of the crescent Fascist party which has placed its green, red, and white flames in niches and on columns of the park and in Hitlerian tones, with up-to-date variations, instructive symbols: the Communist hammer and sickle equals the Star of David equals the American dollar. The head inside the headquarters is certainly not new; it must have been pulled out of a cellar or shrine of old Fascists who now feel free to spill onto market stalls the records, songs, sheets, leaflets, books of poems and speeches, lauds for their submerged but unforgotten leader.

NOTE: The buses that go to the Colosseum, 16, 81, 30, 85, 88 (check for additions and changes in the first pages of the yellow telephone directory), should drop you near the Parco Oppio entrance diagonally across from the slashed side of the arena. A short slope leads up to the Domus, which should be open from 9 to twilight. So to be on the safe side try to make it by 5 P.M. The cost as of 1971 was 100 lire, and groups dashed through every half-hour. At least one of the guides will try to elicit an abnormally large tip by saying he is going more slowly, telling you more history, explaining more fully because you look so cultivated. Unless you are unusually susceptible to flattery, 100 lire will be enough.

Trajan's Forum

One hundred lire buys admission to a living Piranesi print, wide and close views, as wide as the Palatine, as close as the patterns of a shirt on a clothesline. This bargain is available in the formidable red tower that leans menacingly

on the stubs of Trajan's early-second-century expansion of
Rome, the Torre delle Milizie (entrance at 94 Via IV Novem-
bre). The tower was built specifically as a fortress in the
Middle Ages, probably because the Roman ruins that could
be adapted to the purpose—the Colosseum, the Theater of
Marcellus, the arch of Janus, the mausoleum of Augustus,
et cetera—had been preempted. Leaning on Roman support,
it incorporates flights and butts of wall and, as substructure
and grounds, Trajan's market, with which the visit (and
admission) to the tower is combined. The imposing entrance
hall was probably a suq or executive offices, or both, of the
market. The rest is remains of medieval vaulting and stone
steps that drop to a maze of Roman paths and platforms,
closed gates, and unexpected stairways to the upper stories
of the market.

Behind the tower you can peer into cages full of egg-and-
dart ledges, stand under a pair of Gothic eyes in a medieval
close, examine a sketch of Roman marble, and look up at
a smaller thirteenth-century tower wearing an eighteenth-
century cap. At the side of the tower facing the Forum there
is an approach to wooden stairs that go up and up and up
in the tower in a Kafkaesque, endless regularity. Unless
the challenge is irresistible, there is no need to climb; the
closer views from several vantage points are better for
exploring the compendium of periods and styles that spread
before and close behind you. Nor can you, from high in the
tower, worry with shapeless ladies about the care and feeding of a colony of tattered but well-fed cats and their swollen
concubines arcaded where once statues of noble Romans
stood. Leave detailed exploration of Trajan's remarkable
example of city planning for a while (hold on to your
ticket), and if you can—not always easy in these mazes—
find your way to the Salita del Grillo, named for a fictional
marchese credited with the pseudomedieval crenelations of
the Torre del Grillo. In his piazzetta, next to the sign that
announces the Forum of Augustus, another 100 lire will
admit you to that emperor's collection of massive iron-

clasped columns, mighty stairs that rise to a nonexistent temple and the house of the Knights of Rhodes, whose baronial hall, hung with magnificent banners, and high wooden ceilings stem from the thirteenth century. Other decorations are of the latter half of the fifteenth century and Renaissance discoveries of antiquity, a Silenus head held in a disk of stone embroidery and two hard-working caryatids who, as always, look like Daumier washerwomen, the trio dug out of the Forum below.

A twist of stairs reaches a coolly arched old loggia whose frescoes of trees parting for glimpses of distant landscape have been scored and blotted by time. The evocative charm of the high open salon for taking the air and sipping wine while admiring a recently discovered Greco-Roman head and glancing occasionally out to the trees on the Palatine and S. Sabina floating above the Aventine still lingers. The present-day vista is richer; around the side of the loggia, a gay outcropping of rococo house and zigzags of terrace; closer to, the miniature garden, laundry, and doorways of a tenant or housekeeper for the Knights. From the front of the loggia, St. Peter's dome and its numerous, lesser echoes all shining together. Through the trees and traffic, the red-brown brick of the Curia and the fingers of marble reaching up to the Capitoline Hill that was civic center (it still is) and religious center for century after century of Roman life.

The best direct approach to Trajan's Forum and market is by way of the stairs near the great column whose triumphal spirals trace the campaigns against the Dacians from the departure of ships that would cross the Danube to the display of conquered heads and spoils. (Flanked by two similar churches, the column completes an eminently photogenic trio, although a more interesting photo might be that of the sleek column accompanied only by the contrasting spurts of hortatory figures and Corinthian bushes on the church to the right.) Trajan's was the largest of the forums, and the last, but it has lost much area to the surrounding streets, and the limited square with its aligned temple pillars and beheaded statuary surrounding the extraordinary column (also Trajan's tomb) now seems insignificant. Contemporary reports were full of awe and wonder as they described the gilded equestrian statue of the Emperor, the splendidly decorated basilica, the Greek library and the Latin, and the market smoothed into a man-made hill as tall as the column.

The market is still to wonder at. An underpass at the far end of the Forum ends in big chunks of marble, fallen columns (notice one of fluted marble whose core is pressed rubble), a length of harsh wall that protects nothing and leads nowhere, and the tall semicircle of shops on several levels. The market was five stories high before later building consumed the upper levels, and it held 150 shops. At the lowest level, the vendors of produce and flowers, as one can see by climbing a set of Roman stairs at the southern end (and watch out for broken bottles) in balconied shops. Above a set of stairs at the northern end, the establishments were taller and larger, fronted by an arcade that shaded vats of oil and wine. Still mounting to a third level in the hill, one comes on an opening at the left to what looks like a prehistoric mound cut with rough stairs, actually the roof on a vault below. To the right, a twisting street of huge Roman cobbles and shop after shop framed in travertine, holding on to one balcony and the suggestion of others as remaining curved supports. As in Ostia, here is revival, life noisy and busy, buying and selling spices, a practice that continued into the Middle Ages when the street was called Biberatica for *pipera*, spices. A walk above the sunken street shows the shapes of taverns and shops and, possibly, of the fish market tanks supplied by aqueduct water and salt water from Ostia.

On the divided main avenue, an only-in-Rome scene— babies and their grandfathers, balls and prams, readers of newspapers on the benches beside the tree-shaded pebbled walk, unimpressed by, unaware of, the oldest forum behind and the grandest forum of all before them. All around, the medieval and Renaissance traces you saw intimately earlier, and below—with an urging of vision into lost times—scholars gathered around lecturing teachers, carts, slaves, merchants, and customers etching vigorous, swift lines to and from the market arc, and hordes massed in the forum to watch Hadrian burn the notes of debtors and Marcus Aurelius selling off his own treasures so that public funds might be augmented without recourse to increased taxation.

Grace Notes

To guard the spiritual life of the studios, galleries, and antique shops that fan out south of the Piazza del Popolo, the church of S. Giacomo at the end of the street of that name holds a Sunday Mass for artists. A velvet banner at the portal announces it for 12:15, an hour that shows knowledge of and consideration for *la vie bohème*. Those who prefer to have their spirits lifted by art spend their winter Sunday noons in gallery treks, rather like the Saturday afternoon pilgrimages on New York's Madison Avenue.

In the *bella figura* department: A menu of a trattoria may list more items than actually exist in the kitchen. The waiter will say it is finished, no matter what time of the day you arrive. A similar refuge is used by salesgirls who may not know where an object is, or whether the shop ever carried it; that, too, is *finito*.

The clean, careful dress of children on holidays in the most deprived neighborhoods is still another face, a moving one, of *bella figura*.

A maid out shopping will be embarrassed not to flash a 10,000-lire note before the other maids in the market. It makes her mistress seem poor and lowly, and by a persistent feudal osmosis she is debased.

A waiter, a barber, a parker of cars, will address any reasonably well-dressed man over thirty as *professore* or *dottore* and an older, portlier gentleman as *commendatore*. This enhances the *bella figura* of both the customer and the servitor, the haughty Count Almaviva and his shrewd Figaro.

The *sconto* game is not always for visitors. American residents play it but never with the haughty aplomb of a Roman lady. The woman stands at the counter, as if planted for centuries, her eyes fixed on the agitated salesgirl, who is saying that she has already arranged a 10 percent discount. "Ah, true, but I always get more; I'm an agent who shops for Americans, and I always come here" (not true, usually). "But I don't know you and I'm not authorized to allow more than ten percent. Please don't ask, I'll get into trouble." They both stand immobile, the customer calm, the girl struggling with uncertainty and fear. After a few burdened moments, the woman pulls a slip of paper out of her purse. "This is my friend, the Principessa X, who sent me here and said I would get a good discount." The ploy works. In spite of the several vociferous "left" political parties that step on one another's toes, the feudal awe of the mighty in their high towers lingers. Foreigners find *sconto* a word that opens no sesame except for young Japanese whose Italian is a steady flutter of *sconto, sconto* uttered as they assault one astonished shopkeeper after another, and it takes a great deal to discomfit a Roman shopkeeper.

.   .   .

There are few cities so indulgent of or so threatened by cats as Rome. The Teatro Argentina, which had a glamorous opera past and fell into decay, was slowly and at great cost refurbished to a honey-gold splendor. The season opened with an Italian version of Shakespeare's *Julius Caesar* in honor of the fact that the great man was assassinated on a spot in or near the theater. The run was short and the theater again unused through the spring and summer. In that interval the cats from the Largo Argentina ruins found a way into the theater (no one has, to date, discovered their private entrance) and soiled and sexed and bred and invited clouds of fleas, scratching and staining the amber seats and littering the well-polished floors. There is desperate talk of fumigating, cleaning and reopening, but no one says when.

"Only in Rome" items: A wig shop called Giotto and Cimabue; a hairdresser whose sign says "Messalina"; after the lights behind the statues, in the fountains, and on the façade of St. Peter's begin to fade, having done their devotions to St. Peter and St. Paul on the night of June 29, the Vatican pours out music from the *Messiah* and a Bach Mass. One result of ecumenical meetings, perhaps?

Nostalgia for his *paese* impels a worldling of the Pincio to keep a rooster whose raw, early challenge pierces through the Via Margutta and into Babuino.

Young nuns play ball—none of your light diaphanous float of veils and hands in a ladylike game; this is more like soccer—and then, at the sound of a bell, run back into the church next door to pray. One of them might tear down the hill on a motorbike after the Mass.

S.P.Q.R.—Senatus Populusque Romanus—is now translated

by Romans as *sono porci* (dirty) *questi Romani* and *sono pigri* (lazy) *questi Romani.*

The city has a large supply of garden-variety beggars, old bent crones with sad eyes and with glaring baleful eyes, wavering watery little old men and the staring blind. There is one gentleman who elevates the pathos of a curved empty palm to high drama. He is often to be found on the Piazza Navona leaning against a lamp or doorway, clutching his chest and breathing in harsh, rasping gulps. The man is suffering a heart attack, and you run to help. He gasps his story in excellent Continental English. He is a French artist (he gives a startlingly famous name and distinguished Paris address) in Rome on a grant from the French government. He is due to return home shortly but has not received his last check. The attack? Don't be alarmed, Madame. He has lived with heart disease and these spasms for some time, but this one is intensified by the fact that he hasn't eaten for three days. You are shocked, worried, and give generously and find him at it again two days later.

The beggars of Rome are as multifaced as the city itself and as varied in mood and impact. The first, and an engaging group, are the impromptus and the shameless fakes. The impromptus are those who carry the notion of begging lightly in mind, without sodden concentration, who will catch a pleased, open tourist face and turn to it with a hard-luck story of a lost purse or train ticket, and who take a refusal nonchalantly and politely. Another variety of the impromptus is the cat-feeders, ruined haunters of ruins, who enlist you in spoiling with gleaming, viscous tidbits their battle-torn kings, should you be in the vicinity of their distribution centers. One tall thin faker in black glasses, with cane and rattling cup, may approach you from a new corner after you have given him a few coins, proffer the cup again, and then withdraw it: "You've already given me something, Madame. Thank you again."

Gypsies come in a wide assortment, the lowest form a listless lolling on sidewalks, borrowed baby on one skinny arm, the other extended in dirty, begging claws. Larger, more vigorous gypsies, with the usual barnacles of babies clinging to their skirts, often have an enviable insouciance. Give one of them a coin and they march the kids into the nearest bar for gelati. Their little boys of seven or eight hang around not too central tour-bus stops. As the bus sighs to a halt they begin to wail, cascades of tears streaking down their cheeks. "Our mother is in the hospital, she's very sick, maybe she'll die, and our father went away and we don't know where he is and nobody feeds us and we're hungry"—rubbing their stomachs and pointing to open mouths to make the message unmistakably concrete. They extend a rather carefully made box covered with lettering: "mamma in ospedale, siamo orfani, papà non c'è." When the bus leaves, the tears stop instantly, and in the course of conversation, bought with a few extra coins, one finds that papa has made the box, that mamma is not exactly in the hospital, she is having another baby, and that the instant wailing, hungry gestures, quivering lips, and brimming eyes were well-taught lessons that the boys are proud to have mastered. Their older sister of sixteen, who works the isolated bus stops on the Aventine, is a frightening, brutal force who zooms in like a bird of prey, pouncing, turning, croaking, threatening. She is not begging; it is her right to beat it out of you.

On the other end of the scale is a very thin, small old woman whose summer costume is a long outsized gray coat and hat to match, the winter outfit a heavy dark coat, also much too large, and a woolen cap, who stands always in the same place at the entrance to the main post office. She looks distinctly like an American or English gentlewoman fallen into unjust, shriveled old age to be endured in silent dignity. Her hand is never out; she simply stands at the side of a wall. The shopgirls next door bring her lunch, a local caffè will give her an occasional cup of coffee, people who fre-

quent the post office will press a coin in her hand. She
rarely says "thank you," as if she must not notice that anything unseemly is happening to her.

Then, there are the ambulant patients of an imaginary
hospital always given a real name—S. Giacomo, S. Giovanni
—to create authenticity. The showpiece is usually a clumsily
wrapped grimy bandage on an outstretched leg attached to
an old woman sitting on a shop or house ledge. The shrewd,
practiced instinct for picking out responsive foreign faces
evokes mewling sounds and a pull on the bandage to reveal
livid spots and swellings accompanied by a nonstop recital
of disaster, woe, and malpractice.

Although few Romans could be called shy, there is often
a degree of aggressiveness in these afflicted that is sicken-
ingly violent. A woman obviously walking with difficulty on
a cane approaches another woman (always a foreigner; the
eye is sharp but not the mind, which insists that everyone
understands Italian) to say, "Help me to the corner, the bus
stop." She hooks her arm firmly in that of her victim, bearing down in total dependency. "I've been walking for three
hours from the Policlinico. I fell and my face was full of
blood"—you see no sign of bruise—"and my hand was
scratched and now it's swollen" (you are lost in admiration
of the blatant lie; the hand is quite normal). With hardly
a pause for breath: "It's better to die than live such a
cursed poverty-stricken life. I fell last year on the street
and one of my legs was crushed by a bus up to here"—indicating a line as high as her navel. You know what's coming,
and you try to free your arm. But she clings with iron
strength and will, and you, timid, well-brought-up foreigner,
are afraid to jerk your arm away lest she topple in the
street. Sensing the feeble resistance, suddenly, in full indifferent view of passers-by, she lifts her skirt, releases her
stocking, and shows you a plastic leg of morbid pink with
a perfect circle of hole in it, neatly bound in black. You
are a character in a Tennessee Williams play, and unbeliev-
ing, mesmerized, you stare at the hideous object, waiting

to be killed and cannibalized. Having fixed you in horror she whips out a coin purse and poking it, empty and tattered, at your glazed eyes, says, "I need a taxi, I can't get on a bus, I live far away, I've been walking for hours." No begging, no wheedling; these are hard facts for which you are responsible. She commands you to give her money. Fortunately, you are carrying only coins in your pocket and give her a handful. "I need more than that. You have more." "No, I haven't." "That's not the truth; you have more in your purse." "No, I swear," you blubber defensively. "Where are you going? We'll go there together and you'll get me some money." "I'm going to the station for some information," you find yourself explaining apologetically to the malevolent force. She finds the response unpromising, releases your arm from her vise, and clumps away, muttering the meaningless automatic incantation of a beggar's farewell blessing. The ugly moral is to understand no Italian, not even the most explicit of gestures, when you are offered an arm to support.

The noblest of the poor in Rome are a Jack Sprat couple, she four blowsy times his gnarled size. Always dirty, always attached to plastic bags that pop out from under their arms like water wings, they ply the narrow area between the Piazza Navona and the Campo dei Fiori, their favorite salon, winter or summer, the caffè at the side of the Museo Barracco. They never seem to beg and yet find enough money to keep themselves full of wine, so full that it heats their bodies and guards their sensibilities—if such remain— against the winter cold, and it is an admirable thing, as you are slanting hurriedly through the swords of winter rains, to see them chatting comfortably as if on a beach in July.

While he is foraging around for old bottles to sell or swiping a meagerly profitable object off a market stall, she sits in sole splendor, in her summer garb of big raincoat and awkward cap, at a table outside her caffè. Her face and

hands are crusted with filth, her toothless gums roll ceaselessly on each other, her small misted eyes stare into nothing, while she holds her bundles tightly. The waiter,
obviously new and not acquainted with the old clochard,
approaches briskly: "What do you want, you?" She throws
200 lire on the table: "Gelato," imperiously. He soon brings
her a heaped cone of mixed flavors, takes 100 lire off the
table, and says, roughly, "Put the rest away, don't forget."
She slips the coin into some subterranean fold of her many
wrappings. He could have taken the second coin or at
least have been tempted to, particularly since a waiter's
earnings depend heavily on tips and since Rome is not the
most honest of towns. But the satisfaction of being a little
crooked involves being clever, outwitting your victim, and
it is too easy to outwit an old sot. Furthermore, there is
something sacrosanct for Romans in the old, poor, and
witless, a superstitious placating of the gods with such
offerings, to keep the donor safe from a similar fate.

Womb and cradle of Catholicism or no, Roman workmen
find it convenient to tuck their newspapers under the arms
of saints and hang their coats on papal keys of outdoor
monuments. In some rioni every street has its votive box,
and often exhortations to admire and worship: "O you who
pass through this street, don't forget to do obeisance to
Mary." The man who lives in the apartment above the sign
tells scurrilous stories about the Pope, defines him as a
Fascist, and blames Rome's apparently insoluble traffic
problem on nuns and priests. "They have such big, beautiful
properties for monasteries and nunneries. Why don't they
stay in them instead of jamming the streets with their
cars?" And touching on another problem, housing, "If they
prefer to run around in the city, why don't they give their
lands to the poor people living in shacks and ruins?"

.   .   .

Some of the most enchanting bits of interior decoration in Rome—one cannot resist calling them "volutes" for their succulent baroque charms and their sole function as adornments—are the American, Canadian, French, English, German, Dutch girls who come to Rome as visitors or aspiring movie starlets and stay as Romaphiles, lolling on terraces and local beaches and particularly at bachelor parties, as easily garnered as bouquets of field flowers. Each says, "Oh, I give lessons," which might be language lessons or the types described in inviting ads posted in London's Soho. They are lovely, chic, and, in time, curdle a bit: "I loathe Italian men." The usual advance payment for a small part in a film didn't pay off; the loving brown eye turned with undiminished fervor to another face; the curly-headed Apollo with the outrageously long lashes whipped out pictures, at some crucial point, of his four bambini or of his particularly beloved, girlish amico. And they don't know where to go. Home and to a job? Ugh. And where will they find the sun and the flowered terraces and the turnover of visiting men, one of whom might be carrying the Holy Grail heaped with gold and a marriage ring?

Young working-class Romans, messengers, bar boys, apprentices, sing as they work or stroll through the streets, particularly when the winter sun begins to show a spring blush, when minute buds cloud the branches of trees, and the wisteria streaks across a terrace. It is a common, easy, natural thing for young people who love the aria—as operatic, as bleated or raucously intoned popular song or sweetly mournful tune of bygone days—to let the throat swell and spill sound. It is always a charming surprise, this fresh tune that joins the chorus of splashing sun on golden walls and the burble of sun-stroked domes. But is it the simple trilling of a happy bird or not so simple treaty with sadness? How is singing explained when it comes with the tap of a blind man's cane feeling its way among wet cobbles on a dark, rain-lashed street?

. . .

The Trasteverini complain, with cause, of the bizarrely dressed foreigners ("Why do they wear those rags when they're so rich?") who are displacing them at rentals beyond the local imagination. The resulting anger can express itself in burning looks of contempt, muttered obscenities, the comfortable method of overcharging, and impromptu explosions. Scene: Caffè on the Piazza di S. Maria in Trastevere. A girl reading an old copy of a New York underground paper has decided not to button the front of her dress and, being intransigently "Lib," is braless. A fat old woman, shocked by the seminude breasts, charges up to her and spits a stream of insults: "Why don't you close your dress, you slob? Haven't you any shame, you whore? Cover yourself, slut, or I'll denounce you to the police!" The fact that the girl understands not a word of Italian and calmly continues reading doesn't affect the woman. She has herself a fine, long, repetitious purge and trundles home to tell her neighbors about the foreign *troia*.

When a taxi driver has played the *spiccioli* (no change) game at night, in a neighborhood where there are no shops or bars to make change, and your Italian is not up to arguing, and the result is a forced tip almost as large as the fare, and you have decided to be resentful and wary, someone or other may twist you and your attitudes around. A chic watch shop which has made a minor repair and overlooked an even lesser fault will not charge you at all: they made an error and, consequently, kept you divided from your watch too long. Very sorry and, per carità, let us not discuss the cost, please. A small hole digs itself into a sweater. The lady who is in charge of darning in a cuff-turning, reweaving, elderly-clothing-recovery establishment advises: "Don't bother with reweaving; it's expensive and maybe won't work too well. We'll take a stitch in it. Have a seat." The hole returns magically invisible. The cost? Nothing, three stitches, a minute, what's to charge for? And you have to press a couple of hundred lire into the pocket of the black-smocked magician.

A Japanese painting in the "antiques" market of the Fontanella di Borghese insists you take it home with you to keep and love forever. In your pocket, no documents, no checkbook and 1,000 lire. Would the gentleman hold it until tomorrow? Unfortunately you cannot leave a deposit but will be back with the full sum in the morning. He rolls up the painting and insists you take it. "But you don't know my name, my address, my passport number—what if I just disappeared with your painting?" "You won't disappear. You'll be back, I know, and because you like the picture so much you should have the pleasure of it right away, tonight, and not have to wait until tomorrow." Moral: Never feel victimized; one Roman always redeems another.

RENDER UNTO GOD

Navicella, S. Stefano Rotondo, S. Gregorio Magno

In Nero's time it was part of a meat market that bellowed and hacked on the high green of the Caelian Hill. Now it is a piazza centered on and named for the Navicella, a marble galleon in the piazza fountain. Whether it is ancient Roman or a copy of a monument dedicated to Isis by sailors who lived on the rise of the hill or—completely unlikely—a creation of Raphael as some Romans insist, hardly matters to the amateur charmed by a sturdy little ship which tapers to a boar's-head prow.

If it is Sunday morning and a wedding is going on in the church called the Navicella (its formal name is S. Maria in Domnica)—as there usually is—while away a bit of time by examining the medieval elements of the building that lead toward the arch which once supported a Claudian-Neronian aqueduct and have a look at the figures that conduct to the park of the Villa Celimontana at the other side of the church. One is pregnant, the other seems neuter, both are dreadfully embarrassed, victims of fountain art grotesquery.

The wedding is over and one may enter through the calm, cadenced, almost unadorned early Renaissance arches to the portico (this may have been Raphael's contribution) of S. Maria in Domnica, which went through numerous transformations from the fourth century through the nineteenth century. The sixteenth century lent the interesting wooden ceiling on which have been imposed a big navicella and a small among a variety of tempietti. The prize of the church is the mosaics ordered by Pascal I in the ninth century. Here the traditional orderly Byzantine lengthening of figures—their gestures restrained and hypnotically repetitious, the heads small to maintain the undisturbed narrow line that darts from earth to heaven. In its time it was a novelty for the enthroned Virgin, surrounded by, but untouched by and unaware of, her hosts of angels, to sit in mystical isolation in the apse. The sainted become an infinity as a perspective of innumerable blue halos, receding scallops that merge into a boundless background. Pascal, in the square blue halo of the living, kneels at the Virgin's feet, the humble gesture countered by large, glistening letters to tell posterity that he rebuilt the church. The apostles, accompanied by Moses and Elijah, walk briskly toward Christ, their mantles thrust back in precisely the same parallel swing, the books in their covered hands at precisely the same level. Only the flowers that brush their feet are released from the mesmeric, intense strictness of design.

The adjoining park is dusky, deep green groves that open to straight classical paths and close again in bowers over a Roman stump, an egg-and-dart ledge. A Roman altar stops a child's red ball, a pedestal serves for the serious baby job of piling up leaves and mounds of earth. At one turn, an obelisk from a shrine to Isis that stood on the Capitoline Hill; at another, a vista over depths of trees and into smooth, hilled distances.

A gigantic reproving finger of broken aqueduct points to the street of S. Stefano Rotondo and its church. Old photographs and reports describe a round church which consisted of three concentric colonnaded rings, reputedly based on a building of Nero's time. In the center a broad altar held an elaborate tabernacle and the walls bore marbles, mosaic panels, and other riches that belong to a great church.

Scholars refute the Roman origins theory; they say the church was built in the late fifth century after the Vandals had stormed Rome and that it was designed to reproduce the church of the Holy Sepulcher in Jerusalem, imitating very closely the dimensions of that shrine.

For a number of years S. Stefano Rotondo has been a derelict, closed for *restauro*. However, a sign marked "custode" points to a bell whose ringing usually rouses a young woman's head out of an upper window. She will tell you she is quite busy, she is cooking dinner and her mother is out and her brother and his family are expected, and so on, in the companionable Roman window-to-street talk for some time. Be patient and look expectant. She descends and for a couple of hundred lire opens the portal that leads into the present and, for some years, the future S. Stefano Rotondo. The tabernacle tower of Babel on the central altar is gone; the altar itself, a broad, handsome structure, is closed off by ropes. The outer colonnades are gone; the inner still remain on their antique columns. Columns and wooden ceiling are supported by a strange invention of arches that cut across the round space in a unique mode of buttressing. The rest is dust, pits, ropes to keep you out of excavations and weak soil, boxes of stones and bones, a crude coffin covered with a piece of canvas. The only decorations are thirty-four frescoes in several states of decomposition that deal in exquisite detail with martyrdom, each martyr identified by name and the name of the emperor culprit. St. John in his oil cauldron, S. Cecilia in her steambath, S. Lorenzo on his grill, St. Catherine racked on her wheel, a saint with hands cut off and dangling from a thread of skin, wells of blood pouring out of torn breasts, a saint carrying his mitered head, a field of chopped bodies and a close-up of exactly how the chopping was done. Were the frescoes better, the sadistic encyclopedia of gore and agony would be unbearable. The excess and ineptness fortunately reshape the effect, which turns into an early version of black humor.

Late in the sixth century, the scion of a leading Roman
family who was to remain in history as St. Gregory the
Great divested himself of all his properties except a house
on the Caelian Hill. He converted the house into a monastery dedicated to St. Andrew, and here he lived in poverty,
charity, and chastity, writing forceful tracts and praying
for the soul of Trajan, a just, good man who did not deserve
purgatory. As if time were a sarcophagus adorned with
images factual and legendary, the saint-pope has become
encased in a sizable number of ornaments. The facts point
to his changes in church ceremonies and procedures, in his
use of the already existent chants which now bear his name,
in the vigorous campaigns against schisms in the Church
throughout Europe. The romanticism of the Middle Ages
would have us see him in conversation with the Virgin, his
constant guide and mentor, and with a shipwrecked sailor
to whom he had once given his mother's silver basin. The
sailor's spirit assured him again and again that he would
someday be pope. The most familiar of all Gregory's medieval images is the Venerable Bede's description of Gregory
standing in the marketplace in Rome, watching the sale of
white-skinned, blond young men. On inquiring, he was told
that they were Anglos of Britain and though fair of looks
were pagan black inside. (This experience is also attributed
to St. Augustine.) Carried away by their beauty and his own
missionary zeal, the monk Gregory set out to convert the
Anglos but was stopped by the pope. When he became pope
he sent St. Augustine on the mission, with some regret that
he hadn't the opportunity to convert the Angli who looked
like angeli.

    St. Gregory's angels were always especially attached to his
church which sits among ponderous artifacts of Imperial
Rome, across from the crumbling luxuries of the Palatine,
flanked at some short distance by the Colosseum and that

spa-city, the Baths of Caracalla. Sheltered in the atrium lie two sixteenth-century Englishmen, Robert Peckham and Edward Carne, both gentlemen of the court of Henry VIII. Sir Edward Carne was sent by Henry to see what he could do about arranging a divorce from Catherine of Aragon. Watching the development of events in England, the fate of unsuccessful emissaries, the wholesale execution of Catholics, the confiscation of Church lands and wealth, the gentlemen obviously decided to await more peaceable deaths in Catholic Rome. Three hundred years and more later, another English gentleman came on a different sort of mission, equally unsuccessful. Cardinal Manning, interested in excavating the underpinnings of the church with the possibility of finding the house of the saint, offered a substantial sum of money for the work. Because he was not Italian, although titular cardinal of S. Gregorio, his offer was rejected. The Elizabethan gentlemen kept stimulating company; their atrium is shared by "Imperia, a Roman courtesan, who worthy of so great a name offered an example of beauty rare among mankind." Imitating Periclean Greeks, the Renaissance sought out beautiful, intelligent women, and for a while Imperia reigned above them, as the mistress of the powerful Agostino Chigi, who kept her in a house next door to his villa in Trastevere.

The minute chapel for St. Andrew grew gradually into a full-sized church of the seventeenth and eighteenth centuries, with little to show of its antiquity except restored Cosmatesque designs in the pavement and old statues found in the attached cemetery, one of them believed to be of St. Gregory as pope. A fifteenth-century altarpiece of carved marble in high relief combines medieval images with Renaissance technique. The panels describe a literal twelfth-century purgatory complete with bodies boiling in cauldrons as for a cannibal feast, the primitivism belied, however, by the finish and grace of Donatellesque figures. Above the dark mind and enlightened hand of the marble piece, well-drawn, substantial saints harmoniously arranged by a Renaissance eye.

The pomp and magic of older religiosity return in the small chapel selected by tradition for the cell of St. Gregory. It holds a bishop's chair that might have been that of a Roman dignitary, its marble seems so venerably antique, and the elderly winged angel carved into the back of the chair needn't make it Christian, either. The Assyrians had winged gods, and so did the Greeks and the Romans, but this is a Christian shrine, so we convert it all. Still carrying the urn full of the far past, one crosses (with the permission and help of an elderly attendant which will cost a couple of hundred lire) a small yard bound by a portico on four ancient columns, to three chapels gathered together winsomely, like a trio of women gossiping, under a giant pine tree. The chapel to the right is that of S. Silvia, the mother of St. Gregory, and as painted by Guido Reni, she lives in the midst of an amiable angel choir who play lutes, harps, and recorders while God the bearded Father listens, too.

The central chapel (St. Andrew's) may have been the original sixth-century church whose seventeenth-century revision features the frescoed figures of St. Paul and St. Peter as painted by Reni and, by the same artist, a panel of St. Andrew kneeling to worship the cross that brings him martyrdom. A fresco by Domenichino deals with the flagellation of St. Andrew. A flagellation scene crowded with curious or appalled mobs and brutal soldiers, centered on a tortured body and rivulets of blood flowing under apocalyptic skies, was an attractive painterly subject, and Domenichino treats it as well as many of his contemporaries and infinitely better than most of his descendants. Possibly bored with the repetitious central material, like many painters who earned their money in the Church—and what other sources of income besides an occasional portrait commission were there?—the artist put his best skill and imagination into obscure, common figures, making a singularly beautiful thing, for instance, of the figure of a little girl hiding from the terrifying sight in the folds of her mother's skirt.

A naturalistic statue of St. Gregory and his companion dove stands in the chapel of St. Barbara, the third of the trio. At the stone table that rests on griffons the saint fed twelve poor pilgrims daily after washing their feet, the traditional Christian gesture of humility. Inevitably, the presence of twelve—the number of the apostles—asked for completion and the inevitable happened: a thirteenth presence, an angelic being, appeared among the others. Thus, the table became a sacred object, like innumerable others that gave to the devout concrete, unassailable evidence of mysteries often too difficult to absorb as abstractions.

SS. Giovanni e Paolo

At a negligible distance from the Navicella, five minutes by car and centuries of quiet from central Rome, one finds the endearing, irregular piazza of SS. Giovanni e Paolo, its medieval hush broken by the clanging brashness of weighty Roman arches and conspicuous keystones of a temple of the deified Claudius. The usual triumphant gesture of crushing paganism by enclosing or surmounting it with holiness is accomplished here by a monastery, buttressed and supported by the temple, and over that a soaring twelfth-century campanile restored as recently as 1951. A keen eye or binoculars will reveal that the ceramic plates, interspersed among the rounds of green and red stone, show Islamic designs, as well they might, since they are copies of plates that came from southern Spain. The exterior of the church is a collage of Roman portico translated into medieval terms, an early-thirteenth-century gallery, a repetition of baby arches under an eaved roof, a section of fourth-century church, a Cosmatesque doorway, a pair of thoroughly worn-out lions guarding the entrance. The interior, redone early in the eighteenth century, is quite irrelevant to the mood, history and dedication of the enclave. SS. Giovanni e Paolo is as multilayered as S. Clemente, but where the latter is orderly, contained in logical space, the former sprawls, bounces around in time, throws out arches like gigantic petals, and swells high on its hill a resplendent billow of apse. The church is not dedicated, as some suppose, to the major saints John and Paul, who are grandly remembered in their own basilicas, but to two officers attached to the household of Roman Christians, perhaps members of the court of Constantine, whose house stood here. The legend goes on to say that when Julian the Apostate came to power he called the officers John and Paul to serve in his army and, in the service, to participate in Julian's revival of pagan rites. The men refused, and were dragged back to their house for execution and burial, an extraordinary event not of itself but because, as mentioned elsewhere, burials within the city walls were usually forbidden. An explanation frequently offered is that John and Paul were well known and well loved, and it was thought best not to attract attention to their deaths, to kill and bury them quickly in their own remote house. That people soon became aware of their martyrdom seems to be indicated by the presence of five tombs, those of the saints and three of Christians killed while praying at their graves.

The first church over the tombs was built in the last years of the fourth century and had hardly begun to function when Alaric destroyed it, to be remade in time for an earthquake and, late in the eleventh century, for burning by the Norman Guiscard. Rebuilt, expanded, the convent and campanile soon added, it maintained its medieval face until the eighteenth century. That veiling was ripped off in the study and excavations sponsored by New York's Cardinal Spellman some twenty years ago to continue the underground explorations begun by the local Passionist fathers.

What should concern a visitor in the upper church is the space marked out for the actual spot of the murder of John and Paul; then, conducted by an official guide or one of the fathers (the hours are the usual Roman visiting and

shopping hours), plunge down into the subterranean building. Several stories below, the descent accompanied by a
chute for ancient tombs, one comes to a hamlet which lacks
precise definition but obviously includes a Roman house of
considerable size or several Roman houses, pagan, Christian, and transitional. It is an absorbing, erratic voyage into
the bowels of the earth and time. Paving stones, arranged in
slanting lines to surround a piece of black and white mosaic
bordered by a wall of network-patterned brick, point to the
first and second centuries A.D. A thermal room is sybaritic
Imperial, complete with a huge basin for baths and showers,
hot water and heating supplied by a sound, workable
arrangement of flues and stack. A nymphaeum was lovingly
painted as a calm sea cradling cuddly putti in boats that
glide among playful gods and nymphs. At the side of this
joysome scene, a gay blue and white mosaic floral design.
The walls of another room, designated a dining room (triclinium) because of its décor, are loosely designed swinging
vines, birds, and cupids playing among ducks, peacocks,
pheasants, and garlands held by youths.

The rich good life changes, in other rooms, to dour,
strongly marked geometric Christian painting of the
eleventh and twelfth centuries, to return to a curious mixture. A bearded, grinning Silenus leers at a landscape of
sheep, palm trees and meadow, and an orant, a female figure with arms outstretched in prayer, meant to symbolize
the cross, or the faithful dead, or a link between earthlings
and heaven, or all three. If the fresco is Christian, the sheep
an early representation of the Lamb of God and the palms
a corner of paradise, what is a coarse, hairy Silenus doing
there? If the scene is pagan, why the Christian orant? But
she may not be Christian; the figure appears in Greek art, on
Carthaginian stelai, and the birds and the trees are antique
symbols adapted into paleo-Christian art. On the other hand,
the pagan scene may have existed, and, on conversion, the
inhabitants of the house painted in an orant. (Paleo-
Christian puzzles are one of the quieter divertissements of

the city and not in great favor with rushed guides, who don't like the studied lingering they require or the difficult questions they evoke.) Farther along appears the fresco that echoes the martyrdom of the three saints—Crispo, Crispiano, Benedetto—one of whom, in spite of the names, seems to be a woman, all praying as they are about to be beheaded. Certainly Christian, and accompanied by a figure who is often identified as a young, beardless Christ, the painting is still quite Roman in style; the long, loose lines, the color, the placement of figures, an air of the supernatural, revive recollections of the House of Mysteries in Pompeii.

Out on the piazza watch the light touch the ceramics on the campanile and slip across the granite poles that hold up the portico. Imagine the stammering, embarrassed Claudius (not altogether the fool he seemed to be) staring at the temple built for him by Agrippina, his wife and Nero's mother. Let your eye slide over the apsidal paunch once again and slip down the Clivo di Scauro (an Italianized version of a Latin street name), whose narrow sky is painted with a series of arches that join walls cut with windows and doors of Roman houses. The shock, then, of an opening into the anachronistic lot which imprisons cars towed away by traffic police, and, turning back, the high apse and its modest lace riding the green slope and, immediately to the left, the gardens back of S. Gregorio Magno.

S. Clemente

Given the choice of only one church to see in Rome (we exclude St. Peter's, which fits the definition only technically; it is rather the showroom for the Universal Church), the church might be S. Clemente. It has conveniently placed itself between the Colosseum and the antique papal center, S. Giovanni in Laterano, for visitors; and for legend, in the path of the papal procession of the female Pope Joan, who was able to conceal a pregnancy under stiff ceremonial gowns but couldn't prevent the delivery of the baby near the portal of S. Clemente before she was crowned with the papal tiara.

The entrances, one of them of a plain, pinched medievalism, say nothing, in no way prepare you for the sparkling upper church and its less dazzling yet engrossing supporting structures. The glories of the upper level of the church are its restored twelfth-century form, the medieval mosaics and marbles and the frescoed chapel by Masolini, the pupil and assistant of Masaccio, to whom the chapel was earlier attributed. S. Clemente needs slow, bit-by-bit doing, and a logical place to begin is the Masolini chapel near the portal dedicated to St. Catherine of Alexandria, she of the famous wheel. Scraped here, retouched there, they are infinitely patrician frescoes. The lovely blond saint, whether disputing with the philosophers or converting the empress, whose size and serenity recall the virtues of Ambrogio Lorenzetti's *Good Government,* or threatened with being torn on the wheel, or slain by a lithe Florentine pageboy executioner, never loses her cool. The *Annunciation* in the chapel imposes arch on arch, classical columns, and patterned ceiling in so involved an exercise in perspectives that the bewildered Virgin retreats from it, leaving the golden angel isolated with his two lilies. The massiveness of Masaccio's example (or actual work) shows in the weighty body and sturdy legs of one man turning the wheel and in the extraordinary crucifixion that stresses the sagging heaviness of women filled with mourning, the full bodies of Roman soldiers, and the perturbed bearded faces of the elders in the crowds. As you leave, or enter, the chapel, you cannot miss St. Christopher, who in spite of his size is less substantial in mass and impact than the crucifixion figures. The scratches near the bottom of the panel were made by pilgrims who inscribed their names to commend them to the patron saint of travelers.

Moving toward the apse over the Cosmatesque floor,

one is stopped by the singular inlaid marble box of the schola cantorum and its floor patterns of porphyry roundels interlaced with mosaic bands. At either side, a pulpit with a double lectern and a twisted paschal candleholder. These are of the twelfth century with sizable sections of sixth-century work, a sure date proven by a monogram of John II (533–535) carved into the marble. The iconostasis of pierced marble is also of this earlier time, the oldest of its kind in Rome and a survivor of the earlier basilica under your feet. Above you, in the vault of the apse, an endless, golden magnificence of acanthus stretching, coiling, intertwining, closing around baskets of fruit, flowers of all shapes and colors, flaming oil vases, strutting peacocks, gleaming stags, birds flying and pecking at fruit, vintners, shepherds and their flocks, and where the tendrils coil back on themselves, framed mosaic figures of soldiers and holy scribes. The splendor centers on a crucifix decorated with twelve doves who represent the apostles and, on either side of the Cross Triumphant, the figures of Mary and St. John. Above, the hand of God holding a wreath of glory; below, a large acanthus in whose tangles a tiny deer struggles with the serpent of evil, and from the roots of the plant the four rivers that represent the Four Gospels or the rivers of the blessed life at which deer drink as eagerly as those who drink the words of the Faith. Pagan as its symbols are—the peacock was a pre-Christian symbol of immortality; certainly deer, doves, and acanthus were common pagan adornment—this is the Christian's paradise, as alluring a picture as there is, and it wisely includes, for the first time in this genre, as many commoners as saints, inviting all men to the heavenly kingdom.

From the blazing dome of heaven one descends to the chill of buried centuries. Briefly, there was a church built on this site, dedicated in the late fourth century to St. Clement, the fourth pope of Rome. The habitual changes went on under a number of popes, and then the church was utterly demolished in 1084 by Guiscard and his Norman-

Saracenic troops. Fifteen years later a new church was
erected on the heaped debris, and what could be rescued
of the early bits of mosaic, marble screen, and column
were put in their proper places. During rebuilding in the
seventeenth century the church was turned over to Irish
Dominicans, and it was a rector of the Irish Dominican
College, the Reverend Joseph Mullooly, who began to
explore the underpinnings of S. Clemente in 1857.

The altered lower basilica and its nineteenth-century
corridors act as a museum of antiquities of several periods,
classical columns, pagan sarcophagi marked with DM (which
commends them to the Dii Manibus, the gods of the underworld), those of Christians scored with DOM (an adroit
change meant for Deo Optimo Maximo), and a slab which
takes no chances, DM on one side and DOM on the other.
One finds brickwork of the fourth century, of the eleventh,
and the remains, some of them still vivid, of early frescoes.
A Virgin in a jeweled headdress with two courtly, equally
smart ladies at her side, of the eighth to ninth centuries
clearly stems from the mosaics of Ravenna and may, according to experts, be improvisations on an early version of the
ineffably haughty, beautiful Empress Theodora and her
jewel-laden ladies of the church of S. Vitale in the Adriatic
city. In spite of fading, cracking and loss of many sections,
there is an *Ascension* with Mary as an orant and a portrait
of Leo IV in a square halo (which sets the time of the
painting in the mid-ninth century) which has powerful
movement and emotion that force their way through the
strictures of their time. You will have noticed that the
fresco is built around a niche which probably held a reliquary for a thorn from Christ's crown or one of the ubiquitously common and numerous slivers of the True Cross, or
barring such choice relics, a handful of sand brought from
the Holy Land.

A group of frescoes of the late eleventh or early twelfth
century are less restrained, less "artistic," and much more
entertaining. Surrounded by floral borders, bright lettering

and decorated frames that might be stage wings, S. Clemente's adventures in the Black Sea are enacted in a room whose white drawn curtains look like elephant tusks. As in comic strips and much didactic early church painting—the only books for the masses—we find here, too, the main protagonists appearing in several attitudes in the same panel. The altar surmounted by the elephant-tusk curtains and surrounded by fish swimming through pale waters is the sepulcher of St. Clement, whose tomb, according to legend, was thrown into the sea, from which it rose miraculously once a year. The child in the painting represents a boy lost near the submerged tomb and found hale and happy when it rose to sight a year later. A highly ornamental panel describes the transportation, in a high pomp of banners and crosiers, of the body of St. Clement to Rome, the aureole of sainthood already on his pale head. Brilliantly colored and richly framed in a diversity of borders derived from the Roman, the Carolingian, and tapestry art, the saint's story continues. Wearing his white pallium and in the orant gesture of the Mass, the saint receives the Christian wife of Sisinnius, a brutish, low heathen who had been struck blind because he suspected his wife's fidelity. The wife pleads for him, and his sight is restored. Ungrateful *mascalzone* that he is, we find him, in a lower panel, trying to have Clement imprisoned. But his slaves drag futilely at immovable columns which have been miraculously substituted for the bodies of Clement and his followers. And here, a singular, truly comic book event rare in Christian art: in the vulgate lettering—not Latin—the coarse brute yells at his slaves, "Pull, you sons of whores, pull," exactly as you might hear it now in the workshops of the Via dei Cappellari or from furniture movers on the polished streets of Parioli.

Down, down one goes into a sourness of cellar and sewer smell into the rooms of a Roman house or group of houses of two or three stories. At the end of the corridor on this level, subtly and dramatically illuminated, a Mithraic altar. Mithras, wearing the Phrygian cap of foreigners and his windswept cloak, turns from the bull he is slaying to stare up at his mentor, the sun-god. The room in which he stands has ledges for the seating of the initiates and for ritual meals of bread and wine, certainly an echo of the Eucharist —or was the Eucharist borrowed from Mithras and the libations of the Romans? The spaces in the ceiling were probably scored with signs of the zodiac, and a niche at the back may have held sacred scrolls as well as images like the disturbing, squat Oriental figure at the top of the altar.

Still downward, to the narrow Roman streets with the herringbone pattern of pavement that was used at about the time of Christ, the network walls of a century later, and symptoms of prosperity as marble strips that once covered lengths of these walls. As you scrape your way through the houses and streets, consider the possibility that here Clement, probably the freed slave of a Consul Clemens whose name he took (as slaves in the American South were called by their masters' names), may have held church services and for the forbidden act was arrested and sent into the mines of the Black Sea, the background of the murals you have already seen. His meeting place in a Roman-Christian house was filled and covered to support the fourth-century church, which in turn was used as the base of a medieval church, which in its turn later buttressed a frescoed baroque church. Several ecclesiastical layers, Roman apartments, Mithraic temple, a branch of the Cloaca Maxima bounding toward the Tiber through a sewage system devised by the Etruscans, make an enclave of layered art, legends, and history that is no novelty in Rome. In S. Clemente, though, the layers of the strudel have been neatly arranged for us, thanks to the Irish Dominicans, and one is grateful for the relief from picking up a trace here, a stone there, a forgotten chapel elsewhere, a half-remembered fact, to try to put together in some reasonable order—an almost impossible task at times.

SS. Quattro Coronati

Religious matter of quite another sort lies in a street lost in the shadows of the Colosseum. Street and church are called Quattro Coronati in honor of four saints. Actually the name should be Nove Coronati to include four painters, or soldiers, or generals (versions vary), who would not worship Roman idols and were consequently martyred by order of Diocletian—always a safe bet for dating mass oppression of Christians—or Nero, who had uses for Christians as fanciful as Hitler's for Jews. The remaining five were sculptors and masons who refused to carve the images. One of the charms of the supernaturally long Roman memory is that the names are remembered: the soldier-painters were SS. Severo, Severiano, Carpoforo, and Vittorino; the stoneworkers were Claudius, Nicostratus, Sincorianus, Castorius, and Simplicius, and to do them honor and ask for their protection the adjoining chapel of S. Silvestro was used, in times gone, for a special monthly Mass attended by the guild of marble cutters.

The church is not much used now—marble cutters and masons would rather spend their Sunday mornings discussing union affairs or taking their kids to the Borghese gardens or the beach at Ostia. It looks unused and like a number of half-forgotten Roman churches acts timid and unseen, not unwilling to hide behind its wall on a steep path that seems to go nowhere. The craftsmen's church was already known to exist in the fifth century and expanded in the ninth to a fair size. In 1084 the same Robert Guiscard responsible for the destruction of S. Clemente and much of that section of the city burned Quattro Coronati as well. Guiscard, already deeply entrenched in southern Italy, did not come altogether on his own. The constant struggle of power between the pope and the Holy Roman Empire had taken a desperate turn. The mighty Gregory VII had excommunicated the equally mighty German prince Henry IV and cursed him with anathema, denying him Christian rites and comforts, removing him from the mass of European humanity and guaranteeing eternal damnation. Henry bowed to Gregory in the famous wintry vigil at Canossa when he stood dressed only in the light gown of a penitent and fasted for three days and three nights before the Pope, ensconced in the fortress of his friend the Countess Matilda, would permit him to enter and beg for absolution. The Pope relented, to a degree. A few years later the positions were reversed. Henry marched on Rome, camped outside the besieged city, and continued to do so in several successive years. By 1084 the Romans, rarely too eager to defend their popes for long or enthusiastically, opened the city to Henry and the Pope took the traditional scurrying route to the safety of the Castel S. Angelo. Henry created his own antipope and arranged his own coronation as emperor. Up from the south, as ally of the Pope—this time —and worried also about the threatened penetration of northern power into southern Italy, came Robert Guiscard to teach dissident Romans not to abandon their pope or ease the way of invaders. Having taught them, he took the no longer mighty Gregory to the protection of his kingdom in the south, lush with palm trees and mosquelike churches.

The seriously damaged church was rebuilt early in the twelfth century with no respect for its former grandeur. Narrowed and shortened, part of the nave left as second courtyard and portico, the matroneum (an Eastern church accessory that may imitate the synagogue) suspended in small, round arches, it is a disconcerting, inhospitable church, in spite of the Cosmati work in the floor, the incongruously noble ceiling, the billowy, Veronese-like frescoes in one of the porticoes. The heart of the matter here is in the adjoining cloister of the early thirteenth century, part of a nunnery which was, in its medieval days, the shelter of kings and high dignitaries and is now a school for deaf-mutes. It is a modest piece of antique jewelry, worked patches of formal garden edged by archlets painted in green and red triangles and droplets, sustained by slender double columns.

Find the entrance to the chapel of S. Silvestro and ring the bell near a wooden tube; wait for the tube to turn and return carrying a key which opens a marvel of murals that describe the conversion of the Emperor Constantine. Painted in the mid-thirteenth century at a time when Italian art elsewhere was tearing off the fetters of the Byzantine and beginning to fly, these frescoes outdo the Byzantine in rigidity but not awe. Though stiff, they are naïve, eagerly literal, and full of miraculous, carefully recorded detail. We begin with Constantine and his mother, St. Helena, as imperious Byzantine rulers, and go on to St. Helena and the sick man miraculously cured because he helped her identify the True Cross from those of the two thieves (a particularly pertinent panel here because the chapel, as any self-respecting holy enclosure must, contained a fragment of the cross). Constantine reappears, mottled with a most virulent case of measles in full Technicolor (actually leprosy, the disease of pagan sinners). Mothers offer him the blood of their babies to cure his affliction, but the first intimations of the noble Christian spirit he will soon become force him to refuse. The Emperor, very, very ill and still hideously stippled, dreams of Peter and Paul, who tell him that the bath of baptism is all he needs. St. Silvester makes his appearance in a cave on Monte Soracte, searched out by the Emperor's messengers. The saint shows Constantine icons of Peter and Paul, and he recognizes them as the faces in his dream. Against a background of peculiar houses, the Emperor is baptized in an uncomfortably small font. His spots have disappeared in the panel that shows him offering a tiara, shielded by a parasol, to the saint in his bishop's miter. Finale: Pope Silvester in tiara and under his umbrella, like an Oriental potentate, rides to the Lateran, leading an entourage that includes the happy, humbled Constantine on foot among mounted ecclesiasts.

The frescoes in short are a microcosmic medieval world of disease, sin, and redemption, and its detailed, painstaking translation to these walls is very amusing and worth the search for the secluded street and the waiting at the portals for admission.

SS. Cosma e Damiano

When Vespasian and his son Titus brought back the slaves and treasures of conquered Jerusalem—vividly portrayed in the arch of Titus erected some years after the event—the father built with the riches a forum and Temple of Peace, which meant another trouble spot hacked to inert bits. The area of peace would now roughly reach into the opening of the Via Cavour across the broad avenue of the Fori Imperiali and into the large, central forum. In the western section stood Vespasian's library, now the church of SS. Cosma e Damiano.

The church of the two Eastern physicians who treated the poor gratis, consequently suspect and slated for martyrdom, was consecrated by Felix IV in 527, rearranged, and again rearranged in the course of time, made baroque (there is a sketch by Turner that shows ripe curves fronted by freestanding Roman columns), and de-baroqued a century ago. Old stories tell of remarkable relics here, like a small flask of Mary's milk, widely advertised in the Middle Ages. They tell also miracle tales of the venerated healers who left the temples of Aesculapius to work in Christ's name and to perform such remarkable feats—precursors of today's transplants—as the substitution for the cancerous leg of a Christian that of a recently dead Moor. The Christian walked; the diseased leg attached itself to the corpse of the Moor and decayed with him. During Diocletian's rout of the Christians, the doctors went through the usual trials by fire, water, stoning, all of which they transcendentally survived, but, as usual, beheading finally worked. For their goodness, holiness, and suffering, and as examples, they were incorporated in the apse and arch mosaics, originally—with some additions and restoration—of the sixth century, to remain personae of remarkable examples of early Christian art. We see Peter and Paul presenting the saints, holding the crowns of martyrdom, to Christ. At the sides, the traditional palm trees that are heaven, the phoenix of immortality, and below, the apostolic sheep moving toward the four rivers of heaven and the Lamb isolated on a rise. The subject is in the convention, but treated with Roman naturalism not yet frozen in remote, untouchable Byzantine. Peter and Paul, who wear no halos because those were considered at an early time in Christianity the property of pagan gods, are the convincing portraits which will become prototypes for centuries of religious art, and Christ, holding a scroll as a teacher and doctor of the church, is a superb portrait of a dignified, compassionate, living man. The warm coloring in the heavenly clouds and the cloaks of the saints, the tonalities on drapery folds set in matte gold against a deep blue field, the freedom of drawing, all of it is high art which turns naïve and stiff only in restored later sections.

NOTE: Following a path at the side of the church, one reaches a famous Neapolitan crèche, open all year round.

Fuori le Mura—S. Paolo, S. Agnese

Why "outside the walls"? Because burials were not permitted inside the ancient walls for many centuries. This accounts for miles and miles of catacombs, also used for shelter and religious celebrations, and an infinity of tombs beneath the outer regions of the city. St. Paul was beheaded, tradition has it, in the Abbey of the Three Fountains (for the three spurts of water that rose where the head struck as it bounced) several miles south of his basilica. The martyr's body was taken to the cemetery closer to the city gate, that opened the roadway to Ostia, the Via Ostiense, which was for centuries the border for many burial places legally outside yet not far from the city. On that street, north of St. Paul's church one comes on clayey yellowed soil cut as niches for urns whose covers could be lifted for libations of wine and oil. Across the broad avenue, almost in front of the church, there is a shed which shelters a more complex group of niches and a stairway to a terrace where the family sat with its dead, a custom still followed in Mexico, for example, on All Saints' Eve.

Since the style of bricklaying places much of the communal tomb in the first and early second centuries, there would hardly have been many Christians buried there. It was, nevertheless, in this cluster of vaults that St. Paul was interred, and over his tomb the emperor Constantine built the saint's basilica almost simultaneously with that of St. Peter, late in 324. Enlarged some sixty years later, no longer facing the main road as it originally did, the church took on the luxuriance of broad aisles, glistening mosaics, and arcades that repeated the architecture of Byzantium.

Until the Renaissance version of St. Peter's was built, St. Paul's was the largest church in Christendom. Its landholdings were enormous, the accumulated treasures many and priceless. It was a glorious, awesome shelter for pilgrims and refugees from the Aventine when Alaric and his Goths sacked the prosperous homes of Christians on that hill. Having escaped Alaric, the basilica was devastated by the Lombards in the eighth century and again, in spite of the spiritual protection of Charlemagne, sacked a century later by the Saracens. Finally the vulnerable church, isolated monastery, and adjoining hamlet were surrounded by their own walls, which managed to withstand several later assaults. Whether exhausted by attacks and the efforts of rebuilding or in the natural course of slow slide from importance in a decayed time, the basilica of the eleventh century was almost entirely unused except for grazing cattle which wandered in and out of its aisles. The nunnery and monastery which had succoured hordes of pilgrims now held a few monks and the women who served them, living in a prophecy of hip commune. When Hildebrand, later Pope Gregory II, the scourge of Holy Roman emperors, became the abbot of St. Paul's he chased out the livestock, established rigid discipline, and refurbished the church, which suffered later disasters and finally, in 1823, a devastating fire.

The destruction by flames was immense, and almost equal to it, according to some authorities, was the destruction by rebuilders. The critics insist that more was ripped out than was necessary, that sizable sections of ancient mosaic and murals might have been saved. Whatever the truth, much of what you will see has been restored, and some of it several times. The knowledge that few objects in the vastness are authentically what they might have been, the close examination which reveals awkward retouchings, the pristine neatness and unlived-in newness, diminish very little the nobility of the basilica, in some ways more awe-inspiring, because it is less cluttered, than St. Peter's.

Avoid the campanile, an incoherent mess of the nineteenth century, and don't linger on the mosaics of the façade whose subjects are traditional and traditionally arranged but executed in a nineteenth-century realism that saps the figures of emotion. The courtyard is another matter—formal greens, several carefully placed palm trees, and above all, the rows of massive columns that shape an atrium for an awed pause before approaching the inner sanctum. Under the portico, a closed door marked with a large cross, one of the four Holy Doors (the others are in St. Peter's, S. Maria Maggiore, and S. Giovanni in Laterano) opened every twenty-five years and occasionally in the thirty-third year of the century to remember Christ's age at his death. It was a practice that began in the fourteenth century to invite pilgrims to do honor to and join with Christ, in theory. To enter the Holy Door, open throughout the Holy Year, was to heal wounds in the balm of religious solace. In practice the pilgrimage bought indulgences that erased a long catalog of sins, a much abused practice, as we all know from Chaucer and Martin Luther.

The ample calm of St. Paul's Outside the Walls with its broad nave and flanking double aisles, supported by eighty tall neoclassic pillars (a number of them said to be of the stone discarded in the building of the Simplon pass, contemporaneous with the reconstruction of the church), the breadth of the transept, its atrium like that of a Roman house, more resemble a mighty Roman basilica than the humbler ecstasy- and mystery-filled small basilicas of the Middle Ages. The early-fourteenth-century frescoes of Cavallini which may have been a milestone in Roman art history are gone; in their place nineteenth-century paintings of the life of St. Paul, slickly mediocre for the most part. The portraits of popes, beginning with St. Peter, painted as early as the fifth century, repainted in the ninth, were replaced by glistening mosaic portraits of interest now as iconography and curiosity as to what faces may fill the empty spaces in future years.

The mosaic of the Triumphal Arch, of Christ in glory blessing in the Eastern manner, surrounded by the symbols of the Four Evangelists, elders, angels, Peter and Paul, was made in the fifth century and paid for by the fascinating Galla Placidia, whose tomb in Ravenna is one of the pinnacles of mosaic art. The apse mosaic shows Christ enthroned as Teacher of the Church, again accompanied by the apostles and, in the close patterns that resemble those of Oriental rugs, a minute dovelike white figure. The dove is Honorius III, who had replaced an earlier mosaic in the thirteenth century and in this new one had himself portrayed as small and humble in the company of the Most Holy.

A chapel to the left of the apse encloses a contorted,

primitive Christ and the shadows of St. Brigid of Sweden, who came here often to pray, and of St. Ignatius of Loyola, who dedicated himself and his company to their mission here in 1541. Enlivening the cool horizontal spaces is the tabernacle designed by Arnolfo di Cambio, a warm, glistening cluster of small Gothic spires, angels embracing pretty archlets, Tuscan charm in the animal and bird figures of the inner spaces, and in the outer niches small but solid figures that show the influence of those masters of early Italian sculpture, the Pisano, with whom Arnolfo had worked. It surmounts the Confessio built over the tomb of St. Paul, walled up for many centuries but now partially visible and covered with a slab found in the nineteenth century which identifies "Paulo, Mart" in lettering that has been traced to the fourth century. The Confessio, under the altar, contains the remains or relics of a saint protected by grillwork through which the faithful lower a piece of cloth to touch the sacred object and thus accrue blessing and holiness. It served, additionally, for the confessions—hence the name—of those who denied Christianity in times of persecution and later, tormented with remorse and fear, confessed their *massima colpa* and dedicated themselves to the Faith once more; sometimes several times over, depending on how bad times were and how attractive or appalling they found the prospect of martyrdom.

In the right arm of the transept an extraordinary structure of creamy marble leaps up among the classic alabasters and panels of dark porphyry and serpentine. It is the famous Easter candleholder, and one must envision it during a ceremony on the eve of Easter Sunday. The church is entirely dark until one lighted candle is brought in to express Christ's spirit rising. From that candle the celebrants on the aisle light theirs and in turn give light to the candles of their neighbors, and they to theirs and so on until the church is a blaze of Resurrection. Then the original large taper is placed in the Easter candelabrum. St. Paul's immense paschal holder of the late twelfth century is a gem of intricacies and arabesques, of grotesque animals

and fruits, of flowers and leaves that fill enchantingly the
space above and below three bands of scenes from the life
of Christ. Look for the rough, serious peasant face of a
foreshortened Christ in the act of blessing; the faces and
attitudes of the men surrounding the high priest, and his
doubting, searching face; the fully armored soldiers sleeping at the tomb, and the crucifixion with the diminished
figures of the two thieves under Christ's outstretched arms.
Though it is crude, especially when one considers church
sculpture of the same time in other parts of Europe, it has
a simple, sincere, forceful beauty. Unfortunately, what was
reputed to be an equally notable work of an earlier century,
a bronze door made in Constantinople, is too battered to
show more than traces of its incised art.

Given the not impossible eventuality that a big basilica
means little to you, the cloister alone merits the effort of a
visit outside the Ostiense-St. Paul gate. Since no Italian cloister arcades are complete without them, St. Paul's also holds
sarcophagi pagan and Christian, and some of mixed usage,
as when a rich medieval Christian ennobled his remains
with burial in a large, elaborately carved Roman sarcophagus. One of the fourth century, for example, that of Pietro
di Leone, is carved in a crowd of cherubs playing on sailboats and at the corners Medusa masks which may have
been meant to ward off evil spirits or signified that the
originally entombed was connected with the theater. Less
luxurious sarcophagi were often fully made in repetitious
numbers, only the section for the memorial portrait to be
filled in later. The future occupant usually bought his own
tomb, hoping that his loved ones would pay for the portrait.
Some did, some didn't, as you will see.

The cloisters, once the scene of foul jollity, are now pristine and incandescent, a gem of gems fashioned over the
course of thirty years by members of the Vasselletto family,
who must have greatly enjoyed twisting little double columns, embedding sparkling mosaic patterns in them, carving fantastic leaves and animals into the capitals, topping
the ingenious diversity with a tra-la-la of small arches that

enclose the green and flowering patches of garden, and the craftsman's joy sings through the centuries to meld with one's own delight in his work.

The St. Agnes of the miracles in the Piazza Navona was buried near a major highway (Via Nomentana) north of the city walls in an already existent tunnel of catacombs. In the fourth century Costanza, the daughter of Constantine, had a church erected on the hill above her tomb. In spite of centuries of change the church maintains its basic form of small, early basilica whose pagan columns help support a matroneum. The pagan-into-Christian note repeats in the porphyry strips from Roman monuments used in the first church and still visible in the apse and altar, in the paschal candle which may once have served an Imperial chamber, and most strikingly in the altar figure of the saint. She is an alabaster classic who was given, in the early seventeenth century, bronze hands and head (the head seems recently silvered) and named S. Agnese. And, possibly, the bishop's seat extended to marble benches may have been that of a Roman judge and his assisting notables.

Unfortunately, brightly glittering restoration has somewhat distorted the apse mosaic, which follows strictly the Byzantine style of the seventh century, St. Agnes in jeweled court robes surrounded by the flames that did not burn her, the dedication of the church symbolized by a model held in a covered hand and, at the peak of the apsidal curve, bright-colored clouds that open for the hand of God, who offers the wreath of sainthood to Agnes. The church, not much used except as museum piece of early Christian art, is the scene of an ancient ceremony on the twenty-first of January, when a group of nuns bring two lambs (Agnes derives from *agnello*, lamb) to be blessed in the church over her tomb. Their wool is shorn, spun, and woven by the nuns to make the pallium (a neckpiece that takes its name from a woolen Roman cloak) worn by the pope.

There is an entrance from the church to the catacombs

that skirts—in the stimulating Roman tumblings of time
and purpose—a bocce court. For those, and there are many,
who suffer from claustrophobia or a simpler distaste for
convoluted underground strolls with the dead, there is a
rise, walled with ornaments and inscriptions both Roman
and Christian, that leads to ruins of a larger basilica, a faceless area that is cover for the catacombs, most importantly,
and to the mausoleum of Costanza. It is a round system of
double columns, the arches so perfectly shaped and placed
as to give the effect of an infinity of niches, an endless expansion of rounded space suffused in pale, even light. Not only
an architectural marvel (one often sees architecture students
measuring its proportions), the mausoleum is a treasury of
fourth-century mosaics celebrating the joys of wine and
food. Bullocks and carts wait for the grapes gathered by
boys climbing along the dancing vines, while their friends
rest to eat bunches of grapes or trample them with the
gleeful faces and light, leaping step of satyrs. The wine has
reached beakers and drinking horns in another section that
describes a dining hall, or its floor, appetizingly littered with
fruit, pheasants, nuts picked up with frail touches of gold
against the white background. Lovely borders separate the
scenes that are repeated (and each repetition welcome) and
frame portraits. In the seventh century things of the flesh
were partially removed to make way for the spirit. Christ
appears as a beardless young man standing with St. Peter,
St. Paul, and their lambs at the four rivers of Paradise and,
again, in a purple toga and bearded as a Teacher of the
Church. Midpoint in the circle, the wine harvest reappears
on the dark red sarcophagus of Costanza, a copy of the
enormous casket now in the Vatican museums.

Although it seems a fair way out, linked with nothing you
might want to see except possibly the catacombs of St.
Priscilla, not too far off, several bus routes follow the Via
Nomentana from central places. The ride takes no more than
15 or 20 minutes, no great journey even if you have to
stand, to see one of the most distinguished and beautiful
works of early Christian art.

Watch Your Tongue— and Theirs

You've studied Italian verb endings and hope some immi-nent moment for the triumph of matching the conditional with its nervous, coy partner, the subjunctive. You've had occasional surprising success sprinkling sentences with the redundant melodic notes that make arias of paragraphs, "ce," "ne," "la," and your vowels are distinct. You have mastered, to one degree or other, the language professors, radio announcers, and masters of governmental oratory speak, the Mandarin Italian taught in schools. Others, in-cluding the professors, announcers, and orators in their tieless minutes, often speak a quite other language which has the elisions and slurs of Romanesco attributed to Tras-tevere, but widespread throughout the city as indigenously working-class speech or affectation by the bourgeoisie.

Noantri for *noi altri, annam* for *andiamo, mo* for *adesso,* and a reversal of double and single consonants, where *burro* becomes *buro, pera* is spoken as *perra,* and as Belli shows in his sonnets and Trastevere restaurants like to repeat, *l* is changed to *r: soldi* to *sordi, altro* to *artro,* etc. With an attentive ear these mannerisms are not too difficult to absorb.

No school and certainly no phrase book interested in the problems of finding dentists and lost baggage will prepare you for the fact that much of the Italian spoken in Rome (true of Naples and the rest of the south as well) derives from fertility rites as few languages so directly do. There is almost nothing you can say, in innocent error, that cannot be turned into a sexual reference. Some expressions are not seemly for ladies, and yet well-spoken women are free to call a nag a *rompiscatola,* a box (balls) breaker. Should you order pasta *in bianco,* which also means "broke" —in a white sauce—an Italian neighbor will not snicker but look significantly at his friend; you have confessed to venereal disease. Should you say that someone, or yourself, went in white (*è andato in bianco*), you're really talking about an unconsummated sexual venture. A kind acquaintance will warn you never to order mussels, *cozze.* Many uncertain tourists have missed out on the delicious mollusks in sheer terror of ordering penises (*cazzi*), and denied themselves the bursting figs of late July because they had been warned, with light, Italian malice, to be sure to say *fico* and never, never *fica,* the word for vulva. Take the waiter by the hand and point to the object on the fruit table, or look for *cozze* on the menu and study the pronunciation carefully.

Someone *incazzato* is not turgid with sexual excitement and ready for rape; he is turgid with anger, and the whole furious man is symbolized by the engorged organ. Should you wish to say a woman is kind, make sure she is a *donna buona;* reversing the phrase makes her a prostitute. The errors come frighteningly close to the unaccustomed ear and particularly to the mouth that doesn't round on vowels distinctly: *scoraggiante* is "discouraging," *scorreggiante* is "to be flatulent"; *mannaggia* is "damn it," *magniaccio* is a pimp; a *casino* is a brothel, but if you are speaking only of gambling, it must be *casinò*; *cornetto* is a croissant, *cornuto* a cuckold. And thus perilously on. Watch it carefully or, better still, enmesh yourself in no conversations that require more than a knowledge of numbers and the usual politeness and greetings, and resign yourself, even then, to the likelihood of falling into one little obscene trap or another.

Tripping carefully among the dirty-mouth traps, you may fall into holes of embarrassment because you think a familiar word wearing a tail-plume of vowel must mean the same in Italian as it does in English. Not necessarily so. *Drogheria* is not a drugstore. It is a general food, bread, soap, and toilet paper dispenser, its repertoire broader than the specialized pizzicheria, a delicatessen. A drugstore is a pharmacy, *farmacia*, and, unlike ours, strictly that. If you are referred to as a *mostro* don't take offense. It may mean that you are prodigiously knowledgeable or gifted. *Morbido* is soft, and simply that, with no sinister shadows. *Assurdo* can mean absurd, and also grotesque and terrible. *Fastidioso* means boring, annoying, not fastidious. A palazzo is, by virtue of being a multiple dwelling, any apartment house.

There are certain phrases that must be valued at their inner, rather than their overt, dictionary meaning. *Subito* is "right away," only by flexible, Mediterranean time, not necessarily yours. *Ci penso io* should be reassuring: "I'll take care of it, don't worry." In reality, it says, "I'll take care of it sometime maybe, maybe never," or, worse still, expresses the beaming optimism of someone who hasn't a flake of knowledge related to the problem at hand.

Final note: Before you bother to learn "hot," "cold," "toilet," "where is," etc., memorize the essential word *sciopero*, for "strike."

Via Maschera d'Oro
Via dell'Arco di Parma
Tor di Nona
Castel S. Angelo
Piazza Ponte S. Angelo
S. Spirito
Ospedale di S. Spirito
Lungotevere in Sassia
Via Arco dei Banchi
Via dei Coronari
Via dei Banchi Nuovi
Via del Governo Vecchio

Museo Napoleonico

Via Zanardelli
Via dell'Orso
Via dei Portoghesi
Via di S. Apollinare
Via dei Tre Archi
Pantheon
Piazza Navona
Chiesa Nuova
Via del Corallo

Walk 2

Borgo Santo Spirito and Castel Sant'Angelo to Pantheon

The bend of the river immediately south of Mussolini's broad Via della Conciliazione, which crushed a most picturesque medieval neighborhood, is called the Lungotevere in Sassia; the church a short distance from the river is S. Spirito in Sassia; the hospital between river and church is the Ospedale di S. Spirito. Obviously, an important melding of two entities, one of them the name seen frequently on banks and mistaken, since its name means Holy Spirit, for a bank of the Vatican. The other, "Sassia," means Saxon. It was here that pilgrims from the British Isles, inspired by the art, culture, and fervor that poured out of the monasteries, founded their hostels to form the largest foreign settlement. The pilgrims were frequently among the entourages of Saxon kings, a more churchly breed in those days than later. First came the West Saxon king Caedwalla, in the mid-seventh century, who died and was buried in Rome. Next came two Saxon barons who adopted the monastic life in an enclave of their Borgo, a word they brought (burg, borough) with them. King Ine came with his wife shortly after (720), and he, too, taking vows of poverty, died as a monk in Rome. King Alfred made the pilgrimage as a little boy and King Canute came, and Macbeth seeking absolution for his orgiastic bloodletting. Where the church now stands, Ine had established a school and a hospice for the English, Irish, and Welsh pilgrims who emerged from the Aurelian road nearby, a number of them ill, a good number of them stripped of goods and money by the thieves who preyed on pilgrims. When the mighty Offa made *his* pilgrimage he established the tax of Peter's pence to help support the hospice and school.

Where there were thieves to victimize pilgrims there were also moneylenders, the primitive beginnings of banking, which took on the present name in the twelfth century. At about that time King John, in disfavor with his barons and greatly with the Pope, who had excommunicated him, fearfully offered his crown to the papacy and promised large sums of annual tribute. The money was used for a hospital, claimed to be the first in Europe and served by the Crusader Knights Hospitalers of the Holy Spirit. A foundling home was soon incorporated into the hospital, and the bank became guardian and accountant of the moneys received and spent. To this day the Bank of the Holy Spirit controls the hospital finances, and the hospital acknowledged the beneficences of Ine, Offa, and John by treating Anglo-Saxons at no charge, and may still do so.

In one of the meeting rooms of the large present hospital, a hamlet of various periods—one need hardly say—there is a set of murals that explains the need for a foundling home. In Innocent III's time (twelfth into thirteenth century) the papacy reached a pinnacle of power. Right and left, north and south, the Pope excommunicated princes and kings, for leaving their wives, for not accepting papal appointees as bishops, for being slow about gathering Crusade forces. His baleful eye turned on the delinquency of French and

English princes, but overlooked for a time the derelict condition of his own city. Constant warfare among the city's robber barons, waves of plague and indigenous malaria, sieges, sackings and burnings, the destruction of aqueducts, decimated the city which in Roman times numbered more than two million inhabitants. Its population in the Middle Ages was two large handfuls reduced to jungle living. If the frescoes are based on valid testimony, barbaric men fished and cloud-faced women earned their meager keep by sleeping with them, then throwing their get into the river. The infants' bodies were hooked out by the terrified, superstitious fishermen, their fathers, who according to the fresco brought the spongy little bodies to the equally horrified Pope. Hence, the foundling home, of which there are engaging and exceedingly sentimental stories told. Near the fine octagon traced with medieval forms which stood over an early entrance to the church there is visible still the turntable on which anonymous babies were placed to be taken into the hospital-orphanage. Next to it an exceedingly old slot; some say it was a place for offerings, some say it was meant for wet nurses to peer into, to judge whether they might enjoy feeding a particular baby or not. One feeling legend has it that there were no wet nurses, that the women who put their infants on the revolving disk waited a short while and later appeared to say they had lost a child, had anyone turned it in, and thus were given back their own child to nurse and care for. The rules for admission were lax for the time: the women were to leave forever the restless, promiscuous wilderness of their past and never to discuss it. To help them to silence—difficult for Italian women —there was almost constantly music. Experts say that music was especially written for the hospital and further specialized for particular situations. Like our "music to read by," "music to dream by," etc., there was music to nurse by, to accompany labor pains, and, it is said, music for the birth of boys which differed from that for girls. When the boys came of age they were sent out to learn crafts or help farmers, while the girls were taught household arts, modest manners, and devout thoughts and were later supervised through courtships into marriage and a dowry supplied by the governors of the hospital.

The earliest banking—an Italian invention which gave Italian capital great power in the Middle Ages and the Renaissance (London's Lombard Street in the banking district reflects the old webs of financial controls)—the earliest hospital and its first use of the microscope in Italy are distinctions enough for one area of a city. Not yet enough, however. Adjoining the hospital and its church there was a Jesuit mission building which had sent some of its members to Peru. There the fathers observed that sick Indians recovered after drinking at a pool unclean with the bark of trees. They brought home several bottles of the water, with bits of the bark and strips of tree. The Pope sent for large quantities of the bark, had it pulverized in the pharmacy of the hospital, and administered it to the numerous victims of malaria in the city. Quinine has since become known in several parts of the world as "the Pope's medicine" or "the medicine of the Jesuits."

Late some morning is a good time to go. Italian hospitals rarely limit visiting hours. It is assumed, as in Latin American countries, among gypsies (and in some American hospitals which are rediscovering primitive truths), that the sick become sicker if they are not cosseted and fed by their own, so you can attach yourself to any group carrying life-giving pasta and cooked greens to wander almost at will. Roaming in and out of the courts, one of them plastered with a huge clock and an immense cardinal's hat, and in and out of a maze of hospital chambers, you may come to an ancient section with extremely high walls that fly toward invisible murals and a decorative wooden ceiling; far below, the horizontality of beds reduced by the great height to very low, very small, very flat. In the court, two gentlemen in pajamas well enough to babble at length, to bring friends a drink or joke, act as hosts, offering the kidding, incomprehensible Romanesco welcome that looks and sounds courtly but may carry a subtle sting. (It is not always an advantage, as in dealing with opera libretti, to understand too much of the language and, particularly, Romanesco.)

The library is usually open near noon and supervised by a gentlemanly guardian who likes one to be impressed by the size and antiquity of the tomes and the illuminated medical manuscripts, part of a highly prized collection, in the cases. The meeting room next to the library is painted with the scenes already mentioned and a stupendous large fresco, a subject of the elder Brueghel as interpreted in the loose gestures of Venetian painting, of abundant women nursing fat babies while, from a corner, a flutist tootles and beams at them.

If one thinks of the Forum as the wrinkles, stubble, and warts on the ancient face of Rome, the Castel S. Angelo might be its entrails, an image enforced by the Roman colon and intestines of tunnel and stairway, Roman and stitched into the lacerated body in later centuries, which a visitor must follow from the depths of antique blocks and rocks up to the pinnacle where St. Michael sheathes his sword to signal the end of *his* plague in the time of St. Gregory the Great.

Hadrian designed his tomb, built like that of Augustus on the Etruscan mound style (exemplified, for instance, in the necropolis of Cerveteri, a short distance northwest of Rome). This was the most splendid of tombs, a broad, tall cylinder ringed by the choicest of Roman and Greek statuary among bands of marble frieze from which rose a cloud of cypresses surmounted by a bronze Hadrian as sun-god drawn by the mythical horses of Apollo's chariot. Hadrian died before his mausoleum was completed, but his successor, Antoninus Pius, took over, and it was finished in A.D. 139. Not much more than a century passed before the tomb was fortified as a section of Aurelian wall. As fortress, some of the marbled space was stripped, cut, and walled to make dungeons that remained in use for centuries, enclosing a singular list of prisoners: the Cenci, Cellini, Cagliostro, Giordano Bruno, among the many. The mazelike fortress with its lost curves and hidden angles was a comfortable place for assassinations, and the Borgias silenced a good number of their enemies in its dark folds. The Fortress of the Angel was equally useful for flight, particularly for besieged popes who rushed across the high ramp from the the Vatican to questionable safety inside the bastions. And through the ages, the battles raged. During the sixth-century Gothic invasion some of the invaluable works collected by Hadrian were torn from their pedestals and thrown from the walls to crush the invaders. Henry IV attacked, and Barbarossa and Charles V; the poisonings and strangulations continued; walls were destroyed and strengthened; remaining marbles were taken elsewhere or crushed, and yet the Castel remains not a bruised, bloodstained ruin but one of the most alluring of Rome's monuments, a golden ring that rides buoyantly in the night sky and, in spite of its turrets, crenelations, and bastions, a welcoming place by day.

The broad Roman ramp that coils up and up inside the mausoleum stops at models of Hadrian's monument and later elaborations, at gratings that cover worn mosaics and cuts of lower level, keeps coiling steeply to niches for Roman funerary urns and a plaque that quotes Hadrian's strange little poem, addressing his own fading life or the lost spirit of Antinous: "Little soul, gentle, drifting, guest and companion of my body, now you will dwell below in pallid places, stark and bare; there you will abandon your play of yore." Slender vases in the niches of a broadened area lead into a mad sight: a St. Michael with modern wings of metal strips standing over pyramids of cannonballs in granite and marble, tidily mounded in many square marble boxes. Off the court the rooms of Clement VIII, which are used as a museum of the castle's past (closed at this writing), and, across the court, an interesting, well-arranged collection of arms from archaic wooden mallets joined to their sharp-stoned heads by cords and Iron Age hatchets, early helmets like bowls, and small shields of the seventh century B.C. to bronze-winged gladiator helmets, to armor that develops through the years to become a complete metal skin tattooed with fine designs. Long, unwieldy swords, lances and pikes, harquebuses and guns, and for private combat, poniards as sharp as needles and distinctively sheathed. One ingenious device makes space in the cover of a parent knife for two smaller knives, the sort of expensive toy carried by a Tybalt or a Medici.

A few armored figures and bellicose instruments find themselves in the Sala di Apollo surrounded by filmy "grotesques" on ceilings and walls. Another turn or two (the areas are numbered so that all the ups and downs and arounds can be made without much backtracking) to the semicircular courtyard of Alexander VI, used for theatrical performances whose backdrops were worn murals of mythological figures. Immediately to the right is the smaller court of Leo X and the sight of people above and people below as they come out into the sunlight from one tube section to enter another. A few stairs upward on the return toward the larger court should reveal the large Pompeian bath chamber of Clement VII and, out of the court itself, the descent into the long coils of low, minute prison cells. One of the cells is said to show a sketch by Cellini. Whether in existence or not, it is invisible; the corridors are as dark and narrow as dungeon corridors should be, and the cells gated against entrance. About halfway between two long lengths of cell there is a roomful of concrete structures in which are embedded large urns of the oil to be boiled and cascaded onto the heads of the enemy.

One returns to the same court and ascends to upper arcades built by sixteenth-century popes that open to full circular views of bridges, river, and city and the comforts of a trellised snack bar. An arc of the arcade marked "Loggia di Giulio II" designed by Bramante leads to the papal apartment arranged for Paul III. The first salon is stuffed to explosion point with frescoes, grotesque decorations, marbles—everything the High Renaissance could throw on walls, ceilings, and pavements. The next tall narrow room ("Perseus," for a frieze along the upper walls) makes do with tapestries, a few paintings one cannot look at closely, and an old parchment tome of music on a slender leggio. A gate closes one altogether off from the next room, whose sole completely visible treasure is an intricately carved, gilded bed shaded by a sadly worn red velvet canopy. From the first room (del Consiglio) there is access to the library (Biblioteca), the most appealing salon of small painted and gossamer plasterwork panels on a sweetly rounded ceiling. Off the library (continuing rooms exist but have been closed for some time) the astounding iron casks that held the secret archives and treasures of the Vatican. A steep Roman run of stairs and, finally, the top, and benches from which to admire the city and St. Michael, who is surprisingly well and carefully made, especially for a monument that is to be seen from a goodly distance. One fault—his wings are set too low and seem to be sagging, no attitude for a victorious angel.

The considerate "Uscita" (exit) sign guides one down to a ramp at the left, the quickest way to the main portal. Turning to the right means following turreted wall, spiked with ready cannons and, inside, the layers of stone, brick, and granite that were the base of the mausoleum. A lower level, at the very bottom of the mausoleum, shows pathetic remains—a pair of heads, a scrap of lovely frieze, a butt of architectonic detail—of the majestic tomb. Hadrian, gifted, melancholy, a curiously "modern" man—or was it that his restlessness and controlled neuroses, his uneasy sense of a world too rapidly changing, seem familiar and therefore modern?—sits enniched high over the portal, a courtly gesture of welcome and farewell.

· · ·

NOTE: What is formally called the Museo Nazionale di Castel S. Angelo is closed on Mondays; open weekdays from 9 to 2, but no one is admitted after 1, and Sundays from 9 to 1; get there an hour earlier, at the latest. And for the contrast of immortal design, in beauty and durability, and short-lived, dismaying brutishness glance at the neighboring Palace of Justice, collapsing and unusable after a lifetime of sixty years.

Cross the river to the Piazza Ponte S. Angelo, erase the cars, the embankment, the angels from Bernini's studio on the bridge, the buses trundling out of the Corso Vittorio Emanuele, and replace them with a great triple arch of the late Empire and the travertine-covered bridge built by Hadrian to reach his mausoleum. Searching under the edges of the river, try to sniff the fumes that emanated from an entrance to the lower regions of pagan mythology and, near the noxious cave, an altar dedicated to those luminaries of the underworld, Pluto and Persephone, part of a complex which extended inland and produced, during the excavations of the late nineteenth century, a large, deeply carved section of altar now part of the collection of the Campidoglio museums.

Move your mind up several centuries to watch the crowding on this bridge, divided into "coming" and "going" sections for the jubilee year of 1300. Several other Roman bridges that might have carried pilgrims and visitors to St. Peter's had been washed away; thus Hadrian's bridge was forced to bear a dangerous load. During one surge of pilgrims across the bridge in the Christmas season of the Holy Year of 1450, the nervous mule of a cardinal began to turn and kick, forcing the crowd against the sides of the structure, which gave way, causing the death of 172 pilgrims trampled to death or drowned.

For many medieval and Renaissance years the sedate piazza where St. Peter and St. Paul now look sternly at a Protestant Institution was one of the most entertaining of open-air theaters. There were endless converging lines of pilgrims speaking strange tongues, fine-clothed gentleman bankers going to and from the contiguous *banchi,* periodic visits of the town crier to blare out news, clowns and acrobats, fruit and vegetable vendors, peddlers calling their wares—sandals, rosaries, headcloths, and, undoubtedly, "souvenirs of Rome"!—the rowdy fishmarket and its noisy wholesale bidding before retail sales could begin. The piazza bore elaborate adornments erected for papal and royal processions, great wheels of fireworks from time to time, and that finest of all spectacles, executions of the condemned brought from the adjacent Tor di Nona prison and the opportunity to examine at leisure the impaled heads and hands, the torsos lying below. Among the celebrities killed here was Beatrice Cenci in 1599; less illustrious criminals continued to finish their lives on the piazza until the mid-nineteenth century.

Cellini, when he isn't busy speaking of his amours and his glorious military career, during which he saved the life of a besieged pope single-handedly, often mentions his work as minter and goldsmith (and shops and houses of friends and foes) on the "Banchi," the stretch of street considerably altered when the Corso Vittorio Emanuele was cut through the area, but still called Banco di S. Spirito, curving into the Via dei Banchi Nuovi and the Banchi Vecchi, à spur now cut off by the Corso.

Palaces, big warehouses, efficient wharfs and their own rich church around their bend of the river, the Lungotevere dei Fiorentini, resulted from an influx of Florentine money and astuteness which established counting houses in the Banchi, and further strengthened its financial ties with the papacy. Flourishing and flourishing, particularly during the reign of the Medici popes (Leo X and Clement VII) in the early sixteenth century, the Florentine bankers, their families, and their employees became an independent, prosperous village within the city, ruled by no one because they held the money bags. The Genovese and the Senese Chigis, among other Tuscan bankers, pushed their way in to bargain for the concessions for mining and minting, for controlling customs receipts and the treasury of the Vatican. Things went opulently well until they went badly, and it was found necessary to open a public bank, backed by the immense funds of the Hospital of S. Spirito, in 1603. Adjoining the banks were the goldsmith shops, which were in several places (London is a particularly conspicuous example) the early beginnings of banks. Where there was money and gold there was easy betting, and the Banchi was the neighborhood where one could pick up a bet on the possibility of rain, the exact weight of a local whore, or play the lottery numbers—a passion that persists among Romans. Naturally, there were also countless money exchange places, quick at manipulations—a tax here, a service charge there, the threatened collapse of foreign currency—that left the traveler with the short end of the stick, hazards by no means gone.

Facing the piazza from the portion of the Tiber named for that family stood the imposing palazzo of the Altoviti, one of the richest of the Florentine banking families and patrons of the arts. Cellini sculptured a head of Bindo Altoviti as a serene patriarch which, according to one historian, so moved the Pope that he ordered it chained to the wall, that it might not be sold, given away, or stolen. The chain was obviously not strong enough, since the portrait bust made its way across the sea to the Gardner Museum in Boston. From photographs made before the demolitions and reconstructions of 1888, the river front of the palace was an impressive sight, six or seven stories tall with a loggia and balconies supported by arches that descended to the river, lofty semiopen terraces at the irregular top.

The summer stench may have been dreadful, but the view of the river traffic across to the Castel and St. Peter's must have been worth a few noisome fumes, particularly when the distractions included discourse with Raphael, who probably designed the loggia, Vasari, who frescoed it, Michelangelo, the mercurial Cellini.

The Via Arco dei Banchi, where the "magnificent" Chigi, Agostino, kept his money offices, leads into a tunnel whose vault is studded with stars gathered around a Virgin. Immediately inside the tunnel there is a slab of stone carved in rounded medieval letters that tells of the flooding of the Tiber in 1277 and an iron bar to mark the exact level, the oldest such marker of the many in this low part of the city. The vicoli that stem from the main street are gray, narrow, and very poor, but each has its once showy palace or church building. The Vicolo del Curato surprises with the **Palazzo Alberini**, an extraordinary Renaissance building with rustication around the noble main entrance and street opening, flat pilasters countered by the horizontals of ledges above the long *piano nobile* windows; under the cornice, a band of coffered roses and, between the bulging stones of the lower half of the building and the smooth levels of the upper, a band of shells. Quite a beauty, enormously photogenic, and worth seeking out.

Back on the Bank of the Holy Spirit Street and a bit down, passing groceries, plastics, detergents, and junk striving to be "antiques," you should find (number 41) a less imaginative palazzo of nice proportions and rhythms neatly boxed in a frame of heavy stone that runs down the edges, built in the sixteenth century for the Gaddi, a family of Florentine bankers and, like many of their breed, patrons of the arts and collectors of antiquities. Very little of the collection, if it exists at all, is open to visitors, but some vague idea of the Gaddi taste can be sensed in the court, entered through the deep tunnel this neighborhood favors. The arcaded area is niched to hold classic statuary, terms shoved into stone needles, and Bacchic types leering fruitily.

The more unusual objects, however, are the plasterwork garlands binding together cherubim and masks and an early Christian sarcophagus bearing a third-century representation of the Good Shepherd.

Keep poking into courts and their detritus of ancient elements—a column, a piece of Roman cornice, friezes of animals, putti and flowers, papal shields. Look up for arched or columned loggias, ornamented wooden ceilings, decorative ironwork, and become acquainted with the portieres, all of whom claim Sangallo the Younger as the architect of their buildings. It is true that he was highly respected, fashionable, and efficient, but not to such a superhuman degree. Then it comes to you like a ship in sail, the mint building in which Cellini probably worked, now a seat of the Banco di S. Spirito at the truncated angle of the opening of Banchi Nuovi. When Julius II decided in 1504 to change the extant monetary system, he had Bramante remake an old building. Later, the Medici Clement VII commissioned a new façade of the ubiquitous Sangallo when the mint moved elsewhere, and a major portion of the building was taken over by the Hospital of S. Spirito for its bank. Remove some of the anachronistic ornaments (later additions) and enjoy the subtle curve and the bold design gathered around a triumphal arch filled with symbols of papal might and splendor; it is like half of Rome, a stage-set, a testament to power; a lesson in Renaissance architecture with a prophetic glance at the Borrominesque.

Continue on past the shops of ironwork, the one-room *bassi* that hold sewing machine, table, stove, closet, semiconcealed bed, and too many bambini pressed into regal doorways. Say hello to Aretino, who lived here, and Cellini as he dashes from his studio. Watch the papal procession, all banners and bold-embroidered satins, as it emerges from one of the side streets. See what you think of the early-twentieth-century graffiti on the house at number 15, and turn toward the scraping and rubbing sounds on the Vicolo della Campanella to observe how working-class Rome lives, in venerable houses decorated with insubstantial kitchen balconies, appendages of toilet enclosures, and no central heating.

At this point of the Via Banchi Nuovi you should be able to see the huge clock which gives the Piazza dell'Orologio its name and the Borromini tower with a lovely iron lantern that encases it. Changes are going on quickly here— new bookshops, remade houses, "now" clothing, antique shops, exotic imports—which haven't quite yet canceled out the occasional small courtyard hung with bird cages and fragments of venerable stone, nor surging cornices and friezes of masks and shells, nor paled heraldic compositions, nor votive enclosures at street angles, or diminished the aristocratic piazza itself. With so much rebuilding in the area it is difficult to promise that festoons will still swing and Bacchic masks grin and fifteenth- and sixteenth-century houses still keep some of their integrity, but one can hope.

Governo Vecchio is one of the few streets that smells strongly of cat in the summertime, although there are not an extraordinary number visible. Should that displease you, there are the beauties of the Chiesa Nuova to your left, ahead of you the smorgasbord of pleasures which is the Piazza Navona, the church and coffee of S. Eustachio and the Pantheon. And, as you go, look on the corner with the Via del Corallo for the eighteenth-century tablets which tell you, on one side, that you are leaving the Fifth Rione, called Ponte. The rioni were and are the boroughs of Rome, as the contrade are neighborhoods of Siena and the barrios the divisions of Latin American cities. There are twenty-one or twenty-two (Roman facts have a tendency to fall into opinions), and the newer areas are called *quartieri* of this or that dominant hill or road. Each rione has its shield; Ponte shows a condensed bridge and tower straddling the river, and Parione, Rione VI, welcomes on the other side of Corallo with a curly-tongued and tailed griffon.

· · ·

This group of meanders can be shortened, lengthened, combined; they hang on to and cut across each other like their vicoli and need not be taken consecutively. They are intended merely to indicate streets and edifices that might be of interest, indigenously Roman, and often neglected in strictly designed tours. As brisk walk, they may, in toto, not require more than an hour. A slow relishing of architectural and historic memories, of resemblances and diversities of detail, may absorb much more time in this quarter of the "old" city whose every stone has something to tell.

For instance, the crossing from St. Peter's or the Castel might continue at a street that hides behind the embankment called Tor di Nona. The long narrow alley, pebbled by spots of sun that drift through the embankment trees, is inhabited by parked cars, slum-palazzi supported by heavy wooden crutches, a humble trattoria where the secondhand dealers and restorers of furniture from the tangent vicoli take their wine, and a few elementary workshops. One must pull away the gray scrim and erect a Roman tower built in the fourteenth century by the Orsini to protect their nearby holdings and for storing foodstuffs against the constant menace of siege. For two ducats of gold it was later sold to the functionary who rode in papal processions distributing coins to the populace, the papal translation of the Roman "bread and circuses." The same strewer of coins was in charge of the prison torture chambers which filled the Tor di Nona for several centuries. After the prison was transferred to the Via Giulia, Tor di Nona became the site of the first public theater in Rome, opened in 1671, built entirely and perilously of wood. After several remodelings it was consumed by fire late in the eighteenth century, again reconstructed as the Teatro Apollo (designed by Napoleon's architect, Valadier), and later, more elaborately embellished, it became the theater of Rome where Verdi's Trovatore and Ballo in Maschera opened to gleaming, rustling audiences. The ruthless and necessary rebuilding of the local streets to limit the river and its frequent

inundations, late in the nineteenth century, battered down
the theater, leaving no witnesses of its existence except old
photographs of the tall building with outer stairs which
stood, like its neighbors, ankle-deep in the shallows of the
river and on the embankment a marble lyre flanked by
masks to commemorate the Theater of Apollo and Verdi.

The Via dell'Arco di Parma seems to have lost its arch
and the use of its church, S. Simeone Profeta, whose façade
was a background for clowns, acrobats, and deep-bonneted
laughing ladies in prints of the early nineteenth century. The
door is now shut forever and the only opening is a broken
oval window which gives onto wooden beams that support
unused palazzi with brick-blinded windows and doorways,
the only breath of life betrayed by the swing and lilt of rags
and socks on a clothesline, probably those of squatters, not
uncommon in Rome. If you haven't followed some of the
capillaries that flow out of the vein of Coronari, this would
be the time to look for the Vicolo S. Trifone and the Via
dei Tre Archi and whatever other vicoli you step into. In
spite of work noises they have an ancient stillness contained
in deep arches that support pairs of houses across medieval
space. They are very private places; the cavelike ateliers,
the clotheslines, the geranium pots, the cats, the inept votive
paintings screened by heavy wire, and the blackened doorways are their own small, securely walled village, and if
you snoop too slowly or too thoroughly you may experience
a walled, xenophobic response. (As always, watch out for
swinging wood overhead and small trucks mashing their
fenders against gray stone.)

The mask of gold that gave the street called Maschera
d'Oro its name was once part of the glorious, much-admired
façade of number 7, painted in the sixteenth century to tell
classical stories—the sorrows of Niobe, the rape of the
Sabine women—and glorify Roman heroes and their conquests; in the intervening spaces, an ornament, a festoon
draped over the shoulders of overfed putti, one of whom
held the golden mask. Concentrated searching, the willing

of an element or two of the grandeur to appear, may reward you with a few traces. The house at number 9, recently restored, was luckier in having a few of its graffiti patterns dimly stay, as well as its ancient corner column of slanted incisions. One can still make out the shapes of knights, horses, a castle, and on the upper stretches, female graces and putti in blowy veilings. It must have been a brilliant street, a museum of architectural ornaments, in the sixteenth century, with its sharp, frenetic, heroic façades all done, according to contemporary judgments, with high skill. Adjoining these palaces, there were in the sixteenth and seventeenth centuries botanical gardens of an extensive collection of rare plants, and it was here that the first Accademia dei Lincei was founded (1603) by the Cesi family, who harbored and stood by Galileo.

The Cesi palace had, as had all buildings in old Rome, an eventful history which included ownership by a duke of Northumberland in the nineteenth century. His was a short stay, and the palace is now inhabited by the Supremo Tribunale Militare, a name that translates itself. The Tribunale is reached by the minute Arco degli Acquasparta (named for a dukedom of the enlightened family), which acts as partial support for a charming small fourteenth-century house, porticoed, terraced, balconied, intimate, and called the "house of Fiammetta" for the famous Florentine courtesan whose extravagant bills were paid by Cesare Borgia. Its attribution to the hetaera is doubtful, but given the choice of whether to believe or not, it is always better to believe, at least in Rome, where actual threads of facts are often impossible to pull out, and should they be, might show duller color than those tinted with hearsay. In any case, it is difficult to trace ownership when addresses were vague as they were in medieval and Renaissance years. Cellini, for instance, who had a passion for detail in his work and his prolix autobiography identified his homes and workshops as "standing near the palace of X, behind the buildings of Y, not far from the river."

Choose a site in your present vicinity for rebuilding a house whose façade Raphael helped decorate, demolished in the remaking of the river streets, and from the corner of the Piazza Fiammetta at the Via Zanardelli enjoy a Roman skyline of the tower of the church of S. Apollinare and one small pyramid on the crest of an imposing palazzo. On the piazza itself, the Palazzo Sampieri and the Palazzo Ruiz face each other like knights in full armor, ready for combat. Across the long triangles and converging traffic on the Via Zanardelli, and into the Via di S. Apollinare, one comes to the piazza of the same name and a full view of the four pyramids at the crest of the roof loggia of the Palazzo Altemps. Its restless story and kaleidoscopic changes of name and purpose, too long to recount fully here, began in the late fifteenth century as the showplace of a Sforza heiress married to a nephew of the della Rovere Pope Sixtus IV. The present name (although the palazzo is now inhabited by the Spanish Pontifical College) is an accommodation of the Italian to the German Hohenems, a noble family married to Medicis and collectors of rare books and manuscripts now cherished by the Vatican Library. The best way to see the unity of the general scheme, the marble-framed windows and the rams, roses, and crosses under the cornice, is to start at the broad portal on the Via di S. Apollinare and follow the Via dei Soldati for the best of the early sections and round back on the Vicolo dei Soldati and the Via dei Gigli d'Oro to the gracious entrance of a later time. The courtyard is uniquely rich in its classics of enniched statues, bearded terms, grotto fountain, and arcades stunningly arranged by Peruzzi or a gifted follower. The courtyard fountain of the palace attached to the church of S. Apollinare is shadowed by heavy mosses and ferns from which surge the heads of dolphin-dragons with big eyes and angry crests among lowering rock effects that prophesy the fountain colossi of a later period. The church of S. Agostino is a much more serene neighbor, with the Isaiah of Raphael, guided by the spirit of Michelangelo, to show and, immediately inside the entrance, a staggering number of silver-heart ex-votos. Best is the slow-moving grandeur of volutes and economy of ornaments on the calm, generous space of the façade, set bold and high, and unexpected inside its street arch.

This might be the time to visit the Napoleonic Museum at the river end of Via Zanardelli. If it is closed or you don't care to spend Roman time on the large Italian branch of his family, wander the streets of Cancello and Palomba, the Vicolo del Leuto (named for inns) and look for grand windows, with stylized Greek wave patterns on their ledges, staring down on brooklets of garbage; fine portals dissolving, fine portals in restoration, courtyards that are battered, courtyards whose ancient stables or servants' quarters hold small workshops; basic groceries and the entrances to backyard tenement flats, bulging sixteenth-century stones, half-erased Latin lettering, faded shields, a flower-bearing balcony or two, always laundry, and always, under the voices of people, machines, and motorbikes, that sunless, airless silence.

A dip down below the embankment finds the Via Monte Brianzo, a major pilgrimage route from the north, which no longer shows the painted façades that flashed on the river. One vestige of prosperous days is a fountain, across from number 74, whose waters pour from the mouth of a bear, a reminder that the Orsini lived here. The Orsini bear brings us to a famous landmark on his street (dell'Orso), the Hostaria dell'Orso, a picturesque and heavily advertised dining place. It has so often been described as a "medieval inn" that there are those disinclined to believe it. Face liftings and the introduction of gorgeous "period" fittings notwithstanding, it was an inn of the fourteenth century almost concealed by the river wall, the narrowness of its own street, and the patchy deletions and additions it was subjected to. It is best seen from above, standing on the Piazza di Ponte Umberto, which shows a minute loggia, a portico that incorporates Roman and later elements dimly painted with a large papal escutcheon. There is a persistent, erroneous legend that Dante slept here; quite impossible, although Goethe did, and Montaigne. Like other Roman hotels the Albergo dell'Orso had its ups and downs, and photos taken a hundred years ago show the dismayed face of cheap shelter for transients with thin pockets. Now their cubbies have been opened and converted to velvet hangings, glistening candelabra, and breathlessly attentive service at a sizable price.

The Via dell'Orso, centuries ago an "antiques" street, is now a path of whirring saws, shrieking planes, and thundering hammers, the odor of glues and enamels, working for the antiques shops on the Via dei Coronari. If your Italian and the resonance of your voice are up to it you might engage one of the restorers in conversation. He very probably will tell you, "We restore, remake, supply, and depend on the Via dei Coronari. In short, we are their feudal holding." Make your peace with the noise, amble through courtyards, peer into the metalwork shops and the collections of secondhand furniture that sit behind or next to heavy wooden doors or traces of low arches. A telling example of the improvisations worked on old courtyards appears next to number 26. A deep arcaded entrance with doors and stairways at its side leads into a crowded township of small houses, a one-man printing plant, a photoengraver, a gilder, a polisher, cars, motorbikes. Crisscrossed by laundry, the enterprising living, working, and cleaning space revolves around a fountain protected by grillwork so that no one may harm or steal the goldfish that play in its waters. Are the fish community property? Hardly likely; the Roman will have little to do with the meekest symbol of community living. Is the lock on the grille held by one man who feeds and guards the fish? Probably. Who is he and by what right has he taken the fountain? The answer must be that he is old and eccentric, categories freely indulged by the otherwise contentious Roman. A less lovable fountain—if your appetite for fountains is not yet sated—sits in all its eccentricity inside number 74, a series of big, bigger, and biggest basins topped by a Medusa head.

The impersonal tower attached to the Palazzo Scapucci where the Via dell'Orso becomes the Via dei Portoghesi bears under its high crenelations a stone Virgin and Child surrounded by metal rays as if to sweeten the bloody memory of the Frangipani who used the tower as one of their numerous fortresses. Since almost any tower was a fortress, the fame of this one rests primarily on a legend which gives it the name of the "Tower of the Monkey." The legend, used by Nathaniel Hawthorne, tells of a pet monkey who picked up the newborn baby of the family and scrambled with it to the top of the tower. The baby's howling brought the family and servants running, but how to save the infant without frightening the monkey, who might send it crashing to the street? With fervent praying on all sides the father made his usual sharp signaling call to the monkey, who climbed down the pipes and returned the baby safely to the family. Thus, the votive box for the Virgin so unusually high on the building and the light that burns before her in eternal gratitude.

The seductive Piazza Navona sings its siren song, and there is no reason for resisting it, at least long enough for *tartufo* or coffee (the time for concentration comes later) and a spot of dog, baby, people, and fountain watching before you plunge into the backyard of the big piazza.

PALAZZO MASSIMO

South of the Piazza Navona, there is a small, ghostly piazza, de' Massimi, a mustiness gathered around a crippled marble column and draped in a long, rusted wall which reveals, as from a dim distance, the figures of monochrome frescoes painted in the sixteenth century. The scaffolds that supported the painter and his assistants must have throbbed with the steady thump of a printing press, the first in Rome, established (1467) by two Germans at the invitation of the heads of the Massimo family, a family that traces its ancestry back to prominence in Republican Rome. Their invitation to the German printers accords well with the Massimo reputation for cultivation, the sponsorship of learning, and the collecting of choice pieces of antiquity, among them one of the better reproductions of Myron's *Discobolus*. So ancient a family and rich and Roman must, like the rest, have had a colorful history, the predominant color the usual blood red. One historian with a taste for gory detail in wholesale disasters tells us that in the sixteenth century the palace housed the lord, his lady, and six sons. On the death of his wife, the lord married a former mistress of one of the mighty Colonnas, who had taken the woman from her first husband by the simple expedient of killing him. The sons objected to the marriage and shot their new stepmother the day after the wedding. The father died shortly after of a broken heart, heaping curses on his sons as he breathed his last. Thus, all the sons, except one who refused to enter the conspiracy, died unnatural violent deaths.

A gentler death is commemorated once a year in the Palazzo Massimo alle Colonne. Paolo Massimo, aged fourteen, died on March 16, 1584, and S. Filippo Neri, come to console the family, put his hand on the child's head and spoke to him. The boy was restored to life, answered him, and died again, especially blessed. As miracles go this is not a monumental effort, but it is cherished by the family, which opens parts of the palace and the chapel of the miracle to the public each March 16. The back entrance (near the column) opens into the small, remarkably inventive courts of the palace designed by Baldassarre Peruzzi to replace the building demolished in the sack of Rome, 1527, five years before. The *piano nobile,* now business premises, remains invisible, but the frescoes of the loggia, the rich darkly patterned stamped leather on the walls of an upper room, an intricately patterned floor, a curious series of paintings either of minor Dutch masters or of Italians working in the Dutch manner, may be viewed this one day of the year. Coffered ceilings, a number of heroic busts, and portraits bring one to the chapel glowing with fine candelabra and medallions, miniature towers and spires, and boxes that hold relics. Almost any saint you can name has left a shred of bone, all painstakingly labeled, even those—maybe an eyelash—that are too small or fine to be seen.

The loggia affords intimate proximity with a deep cornice, pretty windows, the trompe l'oeil used to give symmetry to the irregular, limited courts, and the tired wheels, like those of an old well, that drag an elevator through a chute attached to the side of the building. The first court, whose horizontals are delicately emphasized by short runs of the simplest patterns, makes room for carefully selected Roman sarcophagi panels—one or two of them among the best of their numerous kind—a grotto whose enchanting nymph and fauns are equally authentic, and to give the objects and space enough light, one wall is cut short and the others are pierced by well-proportioned rectangles. A dramatically narrowed and heightened arch leads to the second court and out under the back façade.

Return to the main entrance on the Corso Vittorio Emanuele and cross the street for a slow look at the subtle curve designed to conform with a disappeared street, and notice the ingenuity that saved one smooth long gesture from monotony by variations in window shapes and frames and the densely columned portico. The main entrance drapes itself in red velvet, gold fringe, and a painting of the miracle on its day of welcoming the public, the public including a fat old lady who has wedged her broad pasta- and wine-fed bottom between two columns and fallen fast asleep in spite of the groaning buses, the whining motor- cycles, the yelps of horns, the voices and feet of passers-by on the busy avenue. She has a right to shelter here; it has long been a Massimo tradition that anyone may use the protection of the portico. After admiring the obdurate sleeper, have a second look at Peruzzi's portico, whose dec- orated vaulting and statues in niches give the small area a monumentality much beyond its actual size and which pro- vides a theatrical effect of dark hinting at a burst of light beyond. Call it a jest of the High Renaissance, as some people do, or of Mannerism or the Baroque; or better still take it out of all categories and place it—and its courts and façade—with the masterworks of architecture.

NOTE: Since March 16 is not on everyone's travel schedule, you should know that the portiere will try to keep you out of the courts, saying this is a private palace, which it no longer altogether is. Disregard him or, if you find it easier, ask his young grandson to show you around. The boy is well practiced in spilling dates and names and will be very pleased with your one or two hundred lire, which he duti- fully hands to grandpa.

SANTA MARIA SOPRA MINERVA

Once in a while the pebbles that were Roman marbles, the sandaled footsteps, the echoes of age-old voices, the shadows of togaed or mitered power, encapsulate themselves —rather like a cyst that contains a bit of hair, a nail, a rudimentary tooth—to become one harmonious entity, or an unlikely bundle like S. Maria sopra Minerva.

The earliest S. M. sopra Minerva may not have grown precisely on top of a temple for that goddess, but it shared the immense pillared space, the fields of lions and sphinxes, with Minerva in her guise as Isis, an adaptation that was reasonable in Pompey's victorious, permissive metropolis. On the ruins of temple grounds the Dominicans built their church, the only authentically Gothic structure in Rome, they say, an anomaly in a city committed through the centuries to versions of the Roman basilica. But Romans were rarely comfortable with the tall, narrow, troublingly mystical, tight-pressed Gothic of the thirteenth century. They—the popes, cardinals, mighty families—managed, over a long period of time, to bring it toward earth, closing it down to dimness, slapping baroque elements, like plasters, on the tired, ailing body. In the nineteenth century, a time that loved the dark mysteries of the Gothic, there was an attempt to restore the original style in terms of the later era, and thus the church vaults ineptly decorated, the painted bands along the ribs trying to be both cheerful and Gothic—and quite dull—combine to resemble a Victorian Gothic borough hall in a hidden section of London.

With the help of a pocketful of 50- and 100-lire coins to

feed the boxes that control a minute or two of light, one comes on a number of oddities and beauties. A respectable number of popes and members of their families are entombed here—all with resounding names: Medici, Aldobrandini, for example, bedded in an edifying diversity of monument art. The earliest is a Roman sarcophagus that depicts with high skill the straining foot of Hercules, the bulge of his arm muscles as he pushes at one paw of the enraged lion and jams his head into an upraised back paw, forcing the animal to immobility. The Renaissance surrounded its dead in a cheerfulness of delicately cut marble flowers and fronds and handsome marble ribbons, the color light and airy, restricted to touches of gold on white marble. The tomb arches dedicated to the Medici popes, for all the Michelangelesque figures, papal tiara, and holy gesture, might easily be a model for one of the Roman victory structures were it not for the fact that the side arches are too low for the large figures; no classic Roman would permit his gods or heroes to be squeezed into such mean space. Later still, freed from the judicious (usually) taste of the Renaissance, enamored of movement, its rendering, and its capacity to attract and disturb, the Baroque has its dead start up—rather in the Etruscan style—staring brightly into their new worlds. Or their heads surge out of marble circles, or they stand dourly in storm-tossed ceremonial gowns as designed by Bernini and his atelier. For true serenity and the absolute stillness of holy death, one must return to the late-thirteenth-century tomb built by Giovanni di Cosma, an invention of Gothic angels, arched little chapel, and gold mosaic to glorify a Byzantine Madonna Enthroned.

The mid-nineteenth century treated poor Catherine of Siena, a hysteric, a firebrand, a political force, a fighter for the purity and unity of the church, badly. Her sanctified remains were covered by a large insignificant figure, a plaster saint without the pink cheeks and sweet smile that makes those occasionally bearable. Not far from the mis-

treated Catherine lies a lesser, happier religious, the blessed
Fra Angelico, who lived and worked contentedly as a
Dominican friar and died in the convent attached to the
church. A third type of religiosity stands nearby, the young
Michelangelo's view of a young Christ, strong, muscular,
militant, who holds his cross as if it were a banner of war.
(There are expert doubters of the attribution, you should
be warned.) Michelangelo or not, he was created nude, too
nude for the Dominican fathers, who probably considered
it a lack of respect to make Christ so completely man and
therefore had him draped and a sandal put on the foot that,
like St. Peter's, had been kissed into near-obliteration.

A fourth expression of religious devotion is yet another
triumphal arch breaking into scored pilasters and acanthus
to frame frescoes by Filippino Lippi. Working with the extraordinary skill that was an ingredient of the Tuscan air in
the fifteenth century, playing with perspectives that make
gowns and ribbons dance in and out of the background, and
having shown this aspect of his virtuosity, the painter settles on portraiture and details of court dress on the personae of the holy story. The angel of the Annunciation has
just flown in, a creature of a fresh, newborn world, sandaled feet barely touching the ground. The Virgin, distracted
by the angel in her moment of blessing the cardinal Caraffa
(for whom this tomb was made) as he is presented to her
by St. Thomas Aquinas, is a real, pale woman who seems
already touched by morning sickness; and very real the
cardinal, with deep-set long-lidded eyes and a prominent
"Roman nose." Above, playing lutes and harps, dancing,
flying, infinitely happy in their softly colored airborne
draperies, a chorus of angels entertains a more contented
Virgin. In another section, a squat St. Thomas is stamping
out the shaggy brutal figure of "Error." Two pairs of ladies
appear on the platform with the saint, their Botticellian
features and gossamer drapery not altogether appropriate
to their roles as Grammar, Dialectics, Philosophy, and
Theology, the basics of early learning. In the background,

the statue of Marcus Aurelius at the Lateran, where he stood before Michelangelo had him moved to the Campidoglio. In the foreground, two exquisite young men dressed in a splendor of furs, satins, and gold ornament, the young Medicis later to be the Leo X and Clement VII of the triumphal arch tomb.

This is hardly devoutness at all, the greatest devotion shown to technique in rendering distance, figures, and faces, with a brushful of flattery where it might be helpful. However, it was commissioned by church fathers for the chapel of an extremely churchly man, which brings us to another facet of religion, bigotry. In spite of the presence of the intellectual, searching St. Thomas surrounded by symbols of scholasticism, the Caraffa Pope Paul IV who lies at the side of the chapel was an enthusiast of the Inquisition, and so antihuman that the Roman populace took great pleasure in destroying his effigy when he died. The Dominicans had the privilege of conducting the Inquisition, and it was in their convent at S. Maria sopra Minerva that Giordano Bruno was condemned to imprisonment and the stake and Galileo was forced to recant his revolutionary theory that the earth moved.

To add to the mélange of Inquisition, Medicis as golden princes and popes, the contemplative Thomas Aquinas, the fervent Catherine of Siena, a virile young Christ, and lissome Maypole angels, one must add the elephant on the piazza carrying a small obelisk found in Isis' terrain. He is one of the fancies of Rome, like peculiar fountains shaped of books or easels, of houses whose door and windows are grotesque mouth and eyes, of lost, solitary Roman columns and dozens of etceteras. It is said that the elephant was chosen by Urban VIII to show that a solid, healthy mind is needed to sustain wisdom and knowledge. Be that as it may, and one can think of better symbols for a solid mind than the patient plodding elephant, he is distinctly "cute," a baroque cousin of a Walt Disney elephant and very fetching in a rug that covers the legs supported by a large inner core of plaster. How could Bernini have done such a thing? Not left the legs freestanding, covering the defect with an Oriental drape? The fact is that Bernini didn't do it; he liked the idea, turned it over to someone else for execution, and probably in the press of turning out papal busts and tombs, architectural and theatrical projects, did not supervise closely. (There are reports that a troop of wine-filled American soldiers of the occupying army found the elephant so irresistible that they tried to uproot him, obelisk and all, to take home. The indignant locals stopped that quickly.)

An immutable of the city, the rising of the river, is charted through several centuries on the right of the façade of the church. Sometimes it is a line with a date, sometimes three fingers from which waters flow followed by a date, sometimes a sailboat, etched out to show where the usually sluggish river could rise in its wrath. It rose high in this area, the lowest part of Rome, periodically washed out, periodically rebuilt, and tagged with many such signs of hands, boats, and wavy waters on the neighborhood streets.

Immediately to the right of the plaques a reminder that Rome was a goal not only for pilgrims but for sun and antiquities worshipers, refugees, and the restless as well. The Hotel Minerva lauds Stendhal, who stayed there (1834–36) when it was the Palazzo Conti, and speaks of him as "worthy to be called a Roman" for his *Promenades in Rome*—written on someone else's notes, the marker omits to say. A legend on the other side of the hotel façade tells us in Spanish that in February 1845, Don José de San Martín, the liberator of Argentina, Chile, and Peru, lived here.

Restaurants

One of the explanations given for the passion that surrounds food in Italy is the fact that the country has been for centuries, and still is in many areas, an underfed place. But there are poorer countries, much poorer, which eat to live and not the vice versa that seems to motivate Italian life. The preoccupation may stem from riches, as witness the mosaic art dedicated to foods, and descriptions of feasts in Roman palaces (Trimalchio's feast in the *Satyricon*, for one) and lists of imported delicacies that enlivened the bored gullets of the Empire. A concomitant preoccupation with food arose from envy of the rich, who ate so conspicuously well, and the unspoken vow to do at least as well if Fortune turned a brighter cheek. The bitter Juvenal, whose patrons were rarely generous enough, feasts his angry eye, constantly, on platters not offered him: "My lord will have his mullet, imported from Corsica or from the rocks below Taormina." "Virro is served with a lamprey: no finer specimen ever came from Sicilian waters." "What comes in next? Himself is served with a force-fed goose's liver, a capon as big as the goose itself, and a spit-roast boar, all piping hot, well worthy of fair-haired Meleager's steel. Afterward, if it's springtime, and there's been sufficient thunder to bring them on, truffles appear. 'Ah, Africa!' cries the gourmet. 'You can keep your grain supply, unyoke your oxen, so long as you send us truffles!' "

Inspired by the Roman's enthusiasm, the tourist, too, is carried away, traduced by the steamy, noisy, orgiastic pleasure into feeling that a plate of spaghetti, a slice of veal, and a salad are several species of manna. But one often has the impression, more deeply incised as time in Rome prolongs itself, that there is somewhere, maybe in a broadened colon of catacomb, an endless kitchen of rows of cauldrons, vats of oil, frying pans the size of major fountains, and, dipping, frying, ladling, dashing, shouting, creating stimulating little emergencies, troops of robust Italian mammas with strong voices. Their handiwork, *la cucina Romana*, appears on the menus and tables of countless trattorie and restaurants whose dishes and prices are so much alike—the same pasta sauces, same pieces of chicken with small splinters of bone attached (watch it), same bits of veal, same sausages—as to make the fantasy food factory seem almost real, in spite of the tearing in and out of busy, crowded, actual restaurant kitchens.

This sameness in more basic restaurants does not and should not affect the traveler, who will find enough to please him, including the pleasure of eating copiously for three dollars or less and the latent carnival atmosphere carried by every arriving group. The most explosive bonhomie is the specialty of Trastevere and vicoli in the old city, at its fireworks best in obscure places marked anonymously "trattoria" and commonly a family enterprise of mamma at the stove, papa setting tables and washing dishes, a son or two as waiters. The restaurant is an undistinguished room whose walls give space to uniquely bad paintings, not naïve, just bad and proudly signed. If you get in at all, usually by going near eight o'clock and not too much later, or very much later, you may find yourself near a long table of boy soldiers in fresh uniforms and new, spruce haircuts, their faces flushed with country color and wine and the excitement of a free evening in Rome before they are reassigned to the listless dullness of a small town far from home. Shouts leap over shouts, the faces glisten pink and hot; one boy shows off his English by repeating loudly, "One, two, three, four," and the rest take up the chant for your benefit and welcome. Bill time is good-natured wrangling, young, full voices playing leapfrog, a scrabbling for wallets, elaborate exchanges of currency held up by careful peasant counting of each coin, and an exodus of beaming goodnights all around. The five minutes of abnormal quiet is erased by a crowd of students who occupy three long tables, but not immediately, since there must be a discussion, in which everyone takes part, as to who sits where. The wine is placed, the orders given, and they turn out to be a succession of several kinds of pasta, served in wholesale heapings. Huge dishes are handed around from table to table, a large forkful lifted and swallowed, and the platter moves on. The more eager and agile jump up to follow a plate, catch a forkful here, there, running around tables, reaching over the shoulder of her and under the elbow of him. The wine, the Dionysian elixir, inspires the running and thrusting and laughing and poking and counterpoking. As almost always in Rome, where "happenings" are an ancient and necessary punctuation of life, you are in the theater or, when the young athleticism runs high, in the circus.

Another side of bonhomie, and this is true of a number of working-class trattorie, is intense fidelity to old friends. The old friends of the proprietor, who is both cook and waiter, occupy several tables for long hours, taking only cheap carafe wine, and they *are* old, wearing shapeless caps and old coats and the vague, defeated silence of slow, constant drinkers. It is touching to be turned back by the owner who says he has no food or space for you, nor any interest in your money, while his old charges, ancient, toothless babies with unfocused eyes, choose to grace his house. Were you to find a table and the dishes well prepared and very inexpensive, the ambience might lower your spirits; it is rather like eating in a saloon or pub of a depressed area whose habitués seem to have been trapped in their chairs years ago or, worse still, painted on the faded walls.

Both circus and dusty wax museum atmosphere fade in places designed for American tastes and pockets, though they always maintain a waiter or two who pirouette, cast beams of charm, and mesmerize with their dancing hands, actors acting "Italian." No traveler with one friend in the world is without a list of restaurants in Rome recommended as "best," a word of vague definition. You will find high on that list Passetto (14 Via Zanardelli, behind the Piazza Navona), consistently reliable in every department, from the exquisite flakiness of its pizza, through the freshness of its seafood, to the flavor of out-of-season fruits and the wine which is exclusively of the house. Outdoor summer tables are shared with the noise and exhaust of traffic, the common fate of even the most exclusive outdoor restaurants, except the Casino Valadier (on the Pincio, overlooking the Piazza del Popolo), a Frenchy prettiness of salons and terraces designed by Napoleon's architect for whom the villetta is named. It is a source of international delicacies, including a Parisian manner with beef (usually not worth bothering with in Rome), cool, aristocratic service, and a wide view of the city, including St. Peter's.

On your list, among "high-moderate to expensive" and "English spoken," there will probably be George's, 7 Via Marche; Hostaria dell'Orso, 94 Via Monte Brianzo; Piccolo Mondo, 39D Via Aurora; Caesarina, 209 Via Sicilia; the two fettuccine Alfredos—Alla Scrofa at 104 Via della

Scrofa, whose lift, flash, and twist of fettuccine are accomplished by golden flatware, and the Alfredo at 30 Piazza Augusto Imperatore, which claims to be the original emperor of Italian noodles. Although it has slipped in quality, Tre Scalini on the Piazza Navona is, for its position and its endless outdoor caffè, still quite popular.

The list will probably include, also, Sabatini, 45 Arco di S. Calisto in Trastevere, and Galeassi, on the Piazza of S. Maria in Trastevere, both noted for seafood—which, keep in mind, comes fairly high in Rome. The "hoopla" group will undoubtedly include Meo Patacca and its adjoining Ciceruacchio, on the Piazza dei Mercanti, rambling, noisy, winey, untiring. If you don't hate people who must travel in packs, who become tipsy on a glass of wine, whose women blush under the forthright stare of an Italian eye, who naïvely, sincerely feel—their gain and your skeptical loss—that they are deep inside Italian life and the well-springs of its gaiety, go. It is fun, and the musicians at Ciceruacchio, especially if they are primed by the Italian friend you may be lucky enough to have, alternate lovely old songs with scurrilous impromptu couplets. The same sort of games on a less gargantuan scale are played in and around the Cisterna, 10-13 Via della Cisterna, also in Trastevere.

To add to the "international" group, all quite high in price: El Toulà di Roma, 29 B Via Lupa; Al Vicario at 31 Uffici del Vicario; Sans Souci at 20 Via Sicilia; People, 40 S. Lorenzo in Lucina; L'Escargot, 46 Via Appia Antica, particularly attractive when its fireplace gives out warmth and welcome on a winter day; Ippocampo II or Chez Marcel, 10 Passeggiata di Ripetta; Giggi Fazzi, 22 Via Lucullo, a big place, big portions, big sounds—more indigenous than truly international.

(At this point you should be informed that "high" designates a cost of more than $6 or $7 per person, "moderate" straddles the area below, to $3 or $4, and "modest" takes care of the rest.)

Descending in the price scale but steadily satisfactory: Piperno on Monte Cenci. Try not to be shunted into one of the back rooms, in spite of the diverting art, but share the opening salon with other knowing eaters who engulf impressive numbers of the best *carciofi alla giudea* (artichokes Jewish style, pared to their tender centers and fried, and when well made an extraordinary dish), fried sticks of codfish, also considered a Roman-Jewish specialty, and for dessert, bombe, frothy balls of nectar concocted of sweetened ricotta strengthened with chocolate. The same repertoire (with the exception of the bombe) on a slightly diminished scale of price and quality is to be had at Gigetto's at 21A on the Via di Portico d'Ottavia, whose summer tables sit next to the gate Augustus built for his sister. Considerably cheaper, smaller, and a return to the pattern of family enterprise: da Costanza, off the Campo dei Fiori, 65 Piazza del Paradiso. They, too, prepare *carciofi alla giudea* and fried cod, but their specialty is a diversity of hors d'oeuvres not found elsewhere. You may not like all of them, but give it a try; the cost will be negligible.

There is an infinity of others to consider, a selection grouped here according to neighborhood.

Trastevere

Carlo's on the Piazza Mastai, long and well established, not yet tourist-ridden and generous enough to leave a section of its outdoor tables for the rione's ancients who eat at home and sip their cheap wine here, as they have done for years. High-moderate.

La Tana de Noantri, Via della Paglia, at the side of S. Maria in Trastevere, is the usual large ebullience that rushes thousands of pizze as well as other classics to its eager mobs. Decent, friendly, moderate in price, its great charm an outdoor annex—a sloping, tiny piazza at the back of the venerable church, at one side an abundantly stocked antipasti and greens table and at the others, a surviving Romanesque bit, a forgotten Renaissance stone frame and a small, decayed, rococo villa. Nowhere else in the world can you struggle with stringy pizza cheese in so picturesque a setting.

Manuai, 56 Vicolo del Cinque (reserve, 587-016). At this writing the restaurant is fairly new, a chummy club for a group of Rome's young "beautiful people" of several sexes. The whitewashed brick walls and unsurprising paintings will remind New Yorkers of places in the Village and the Upper East Side; so will the customers dressed, coiffed, or uncoiffed in the current *carnevale* style. The waiters, long-haired and bearded, wear tie-dyed or embroidered Oriental shirts and collections of amulets; a waitress in dungarees or hot pants serves you with a cigarette dangling from her lips, the ash ready to season your salad. One customer lady is all gold—wild golden mane, chains, rings, golden silk caftan; another is wrapped from chin to ankle in giraffe stripes tight enough to be a glaze rather than silk. Other members of the club drop in for a moment of greeting friends and being admired. One very slender boy, tossing his dark locks and shark's tooth earring, pirouettes from table to table to show the lovely, colorful, and expensive outfit he bought of Mr. Fish in London, where he had a faaaaabulous time. He is everyone's darling and makes a pretty, triumphant progress from table to table. A girl brings in a sackful of Indian shirts and does a brisk trade in them. Everyone carries a sack, in fact, for a bit of selling or because the look of the nomad—achieved at considerable expense here—is the fashion. It is and hopefully may remain quite a kermis. Hopefully, too, the limited menu will stay at its present quality. No Roman restaurant dare deprive anyone of a few Italian basics, here mingled with several French specialties: a respectable, coarse pâté, an entrecôte dressed in a subtle mustard sauce, veal in a Norman sauce of wine, cream, and mushrooms. The French dishes are convincingly authentic, the house wine thoroughly palatable, one waiter speaks good English, and the cost for all this and the changing show comes to no more than four or five dollars apiece, including wine and tip. Reserve for about 9:30 and linger to enjoy the gathering of the clan which begins at about 11.

Where Trastevere prepares to become dour wall, at the Porta Settimiana, in a house where Raphael's Fornarina was domiciled in legend, is Romolo a Porta Settimiana, which feeds its customers in an attractive garden, at prices that might be considered high-moderate.

No gardens, no décor, no striving; limited, fresh supplies for home-style cooking, and amiability at Vincenzo's at Lungaretta 173, Enzo's and two or three others on the Via di S. Cecilia, and still others on the streets leading off the Viale Trastevere. On the viale itself, an unending spread of pizza, porchetta, stuffed tomatoes, antipasti and pasta, roast chicken, to eat at counters or tables, or on the lively, combative sidewalk. The mineral water is often tastier, certainly purer, than the wine, but what is one to expect for a meal that costs little more than 1,000 lire? At not too much more, the wine a shade better, the pleasure of eating under a thatched roof at La Villetta, Vicolo del Buco 2. Highly spiced dishes and customers at Gino's (seafood, largely) at Lungaretta 85. Spicy, passive, local, foreign, beat, and respectably working class, they all converge on Ivo's for pizza and *bruschetta* (garlicked and oiled toasted bread), on the Via S. Francesco a Ripa, at 158.

Not exactly in Trastevere but on the island that links the two ancient ghettos, Sora Lella, 16 Via di Ponte Quattro Capi. The stout proprietress, the sister of the famous comic whose photos line the walls, is a worrisome ad for the earthy dishes of a Roman oiliness that is not to everyone's taste. The location is delightful, however, particularly if you can find a table—or reserve one (656-9907)—at the little, leaded windows that give you the river and the ancient bridge.

Absolutely basic Trastevere is a wineshop at the corner
of Fienaroli and Fratte di Trastevere and, next door, the
Trattoria dal Facochio and Ottavio, also a pizzeria. Gianna
all'Angoletto, 44 Via della Luce, serves Sardinian specialties:
suckling pig (*maiellino*), and a good, grainy short pasta
with a distinguished Latin name, *Maloredus Sardus*, all
served in a triangular garden on a quiet street. Modest.

Piazza Navona—Pantheon

Responsible, solid—never stolid—often ceremonial centers
for celebrations by the well dressed and well packed, and,
as the evening slips toward 11, the sleek people of television and theater:

La Maiella, Piazza S. Apollinare 45 (reserve, 564-174). A
good way with meats, fondues, and anything you choose of
the long menu. The outdoor area charges into major traffic;
that discourages no one from trying for a table in the frenzied air, while the interior remains calmly empty. Moderate
to high. Same clientele, quality, and crush of outdoor tables,
though no fondue, at L'Angoletto, Piazza Rondanini 51.

La Campana, 18 Vicolo della Campana. The descendant
of an old posting inn whose neat, noncommittal decor offers
no distraction from the most *arrabbiate* ("angry," ergo
spicy) *penne* in Rome and viewing the parade of trayfuls
of *abbacchio* (young roast lamb), chickens, veal, and pork
roasts carried high, like imperial trophies, over the admiring heads of customers. Women should be pleased to know
that the service is old-fashioned. That is, solicitude laced
with flirtatiousness and lingering Valentino glances. Moderate.

On the Piazza Navona proper, the reliable Mastrostefano
(moderate) and in the trattoria-pizzeria class, Quattro
Fiume. The area abounds in inexpensive trattorie from
charming to bleary: the tree-capped, raised set of tables on

the engaging triangle of Largo di Febo; the toothless winos, male and female, who share with the international hippie young the tables on the secluded medieval piazza of Monte-vecchio. Try Da Francesco at 29 Piazza del Fico or the Fiammetta on its piazza, Fabi on Tor di Millina, or any of the trattorie that call themselves simply *osteria* or *cucina Romana* on the web of streets and vicoli that spreads east of Navona.

A most interesting restaurant in the Pantheon vicinity is one established and conducted by the Church, L'Eau Vive, 85 Via Monterone (reserve, 651-095). The novices, or initi-ates, are a bevy of charmers, from the delicate Indonesian blade in her native silk trousers and tunic to a large, round, brown girl, cheeks marked with cicatrices and a turban soar-ing on her head. The menu is French classics and, each evening, an additional list of Asian, African, or French regional dishes. Necessary compromises must be made now and then, and thus an "Oriental" dessert becomes Italian ice cream in a sauce of canned litchis. There is, however, a serious attempt at authenticity, and the cellar holds good French wines. High-moderate to expensive.

Less exotic, cheaper, and consistently satisfying: Papa Giovanni, a truffles fancier, 4 Via dei Sediari; Battaglia, whose dishes have a Venetian flavor, at 48 Via Colonna Antonina; La Pentola, consistently reliable with tables on its Piazza Firenze (20); Carmelo, whose flavors are Sicilian, particularly in the handling of fish, at 9 Via della Rosetta; Trattoria del Pantheon, 55 Via del Pantheon; Trattoria la Maddalena, on the Piazza Maddalena. Prices rise somewhat, not alarmingly, near the Piazza S. Ignazio: Il Buco, which emphasizes the Tuscan, Via S. Ignazio 8; and on the piazza, Le Cave, which adds pizze to its full repertoire, including soufflés. It is open fairly late and if you're early there may be a table on the beguiling square.

Hiding in the obscure Piazza della Pigna, the old-fashioned, full-of-integrity restaurant La Pigna. Good game and fish, polite, unhurried, and easy on the pocket.

Piccolo Roma, Via Uffici del Vicario. The more serious business of toasting *bruschetta* and grilling meats on an open hearth is usually a winter activity. Summertime serves the trenchermen from the government offices nearby for very good Roman chicken and peppers, piles of sliced mushrooms, artichokes, and brains dipped and fried together (one of several *fritto misto* dishes) and, to finish, one of the ineffable confections of Giolitti down the street. Moderate.

A trattoria in the old style—old waiter, old-fashioned manners, old, vaguely hunting-lodge décor and, best, old prices, at the Gatto Bianco, 8 Via della Stelletta. Modest.

Piazza di Spagna— Piazza del Popolo

Your list should mention Dal Bolognese, on the Piazza del Popolo, at the end of the Via Ripetta (reserve, 380-248), a polite, serious place with a talented kitchen. The pasta is remarkable even for pasta country; ask for one of the house specialties (the waiters all speak some brand of menu English) or, better still, have the dish that carries a few generous spoonfuls of four types of pasta (*quattro paste* should do it). The boiled meats and chicken, served out of a large, radiant cart, are invariably tender and served with a fine green sauce and, if you ask for *mostarda di frutta*, a bowl of semisweet, spiced preserved fruits. If you have been in Italy long enough to want a change from the national repertoire—no matter how consistently well prepared—order the pilaf, rice, and chicken that comes with a truly courageous curry sauce. The fruit is fresh, the salads very well dressed, and there are tables outdoors, always crowded and not worth the effort. The noise and exhaust of the traffic, enhanced by black-clad gangs of motorcyclists who convene and roar through the piazza, diminish the true excellence of a meal. Take a table indoors, eat in quiet dignity, watch the several kinds of enameled theatrical glamour that arrive at about 10:30, and have your coffee at Rosati's next door, if you can get a table, to take in the fumes and the piazza adornments of both stone and flesh. Bolognese is moderate unless you order imported delicacies.

The Buca di Ripetta at 36 Ripetta mashes its intellectual-artistic habitués closely together. They don't mind and you won't either, since the clientele that comes from the nearby galleries and studios are a colorful, companionable lot, the food good, the service sometimes slapdash, hasty (hold on to your dish until you've absolutely finished), or forgetful, but friendly, and the cost is negligible. Try to make it close to 8; otherwise, a longish wait for a table.

On the Via dell'Oca, a Roman version of "Village" street, La Lampara, at number 22, a large, well-designed fish restaurant which spreads an enormous hors d'oeuvres table of fish, clams, snails, herring, anchovies, baby octopus, mussels, and greens cooked and raw. Follow, if you dare, with rice in the ink of cuttlefish or, if you don't, the grilled *mazzancolle* (small crayfish), the rich *zuppa di pesce* (bouillabaisse) or any fish that catches your eye. Moderate to high-moderate, depending on the type of seafood you order.

The Largo dei Lombardi off the Corso gives itself entirely, in the summertime, to the Capricciosa. Too few waiters for a sea of tables makes slow service, particularly when a parade of itinerant musicians gets in the way. But the pizza is notable, the rest of the dishes thoroughly edible, the location convenient, the hours stretch into the night, and the price is modest to moderate, depending on whether pizza is beginning or both beginning and end.

The mood cools, space becomes easier, in the large, severe interior of the Augustea, 5 Via della Frezza. The customers, primarily dark-suited, prosperous businessmen and politicos, favor the seafood cooked in several styles and, occasionally, a fishy oddity in small supply, the sort of thing put aside for praetors in the old days. High-moderate to expensive, again depending on what and how much you order.

Back to noisy chumminess in the two small rooms of da Mario at 64 Via della Vite. You might try to reserve (683-818), but it may not do you much good: the family has a good many old friends, and the bright-clothed tables are comparatively few, often shared. A happy meal can be made from the endless procession of antipasto platters and cauldrons ushered out of the kitchen, followed by one of the homemade cakes, rarely pretty (which proves they are homemade), but delicious. Or control the antipasti and go on to the game in season, one of Mario's strengths, or the roast kid, *capretto*. Moderate.

In the same area, same financial category, less jollity, more English, and no *capretto*: Nino, 11 Via Borgognona and the plainer Vertecchi, 109 Via Frattina.

La Berninetta, small and obscure, at 57 Via Belsiana, is possibly the only silent, even sullen, restaurant in Rome. The waiters are sad, quiet, reluctant, and the men who shove the pizza in and out of the wood-burning oven (becoming an anachronism) look perennially bereaved. They do, however, produce the thinnest pizza, so delicate that the usual embarrassment which impedes engulfing two or even three at a sitting doesn't operate at all. It is the custom here to order in a series.

Hiding in the glamour streets and the crafts alleys that spray from them, there are a few modest, dependable trattorie. One or two of them, run by elderly ladies for steady, solitary boarders who share tables but not talk, may be a bit forbidding in their quiet and privacy for a foreigner. Less closed-off and seclusive are Toto at 9 Via della Carrozze; the Carlino, on the Via Canova near Ripetta (good spaghetti carbonara); a couple of trattorie on Mario dei Fiori, and the *tavola calda* in Angelino's on the Via della Croce. Da Peppino, Via dei Greci, is small and during the summer months trails a line of students waiting for inexpensive, filling meals.

And of course you know about Otello on the Via della

Croce, a short block in from the Piazza di Spagna. Its shaded yard surrounding a large still life of vegetables and fruits designed, placed, and put away each day by a gifted, tireless waiter, is a pleasant place to be, usually. But the younger waiters are easily rattled by demands on their meager English, become forgetful, and, once in a while, resentful. When the yard is crowded and it is later than 1:00 or 8:00, use a closed section or be patient and forgiving. The kitchen makes an occasional mistake, too, in the frantic season, but not often. Modest to moderate.

Fontana di Trevi— Piazza Barberini

Two old favorites, for solid reasons: Al Moro, 13 Vicolo delle Bollette and Da Necci, 50 Piazza dell'Oratorio, both of which treat their provender and their customers' palates with respect. Moderate.

Corsaro, 6 Via del Boccaccio, has that movie Marseilles look—vats of shellfish, mariner-waiters, and loops of fishnet. Order *spaghetti alle vongole* (clams) to begin with, and ask to see the menu and its prices for the rest. There is a tendency here—and in other restaurants—to steer the happy, guileless tourist with fast talk and big smiles to dishes he may not want. Hold your ground, in English if necessary. High-moderate.

If you'd rather wait for seafood in a coastal town and stay with the meat classics, examine the list posted (most restaurants display a menu one can examine before commitment) in the window of Sergio e Ada at 1 Via del Boccaccio.

Tullio, 26 Via di S. Nicola da Tolentino, is easy, roomy, dependable, located on a short hill off the Piazza Barberini and modest to moderate.

The Fontana di Trevi sprays into a good number of trattorie which vary comparatively little in décor and price. Consider, also, the possibilities of the big, well-supplied *rosticceria* and *tavola calda* called Al Picchio at 38 on the Via Lavatore and two trattorie with sidewalk tables on the Piazza dell'Oratorio near the remarkably decorated Galleria Sciarra, and the Quirinetta Hostaria and Pizzeria (open late) on the Via dell ' Umiltà, off the piazza.

Colline Emiliane, 22 Via Avignonesi, keeps hidden behind its modest corners an endless supply of white truffles to be heaped on creamy fettuccine, embedded in cheese confections, piled around veal, and served in a delectable salad. Then, a crème caramel laced with chocolate. The owners and the waiter-relatives are fine hosts with the best of country courtesy, and the cost, in spite of the lashings of truffles, modest to moderate.

On the same street, nearer the Via del Tritone, a large, ebullient pizzeria called Gioia Mia, whose joy is to invent combinations of fillings for pizza and names to go with them. There is one called Giapponese, for instance, that bears at least six ingredients. Order one of the fancy variety to enjoy the sight and taste of a pizza that is so laden that it looks like an inverted hat with a dough brim. Modest. On the next street, Via Rasella (52), Gino's serves, more restrainedly, the polenta and risottos of Tuscany, and game, when it is in supply. Moderate.

Campo dei Fiori

La Carbonara, Campo dei Fiori 23, stretches almost to the feet of the heretic monk, Giordano Bruno, burned and then monumented on the big market piazza. The vaunted dish is spaghetti alla carbonara, which means bits of bacon and an egg whipped through the strands just before the dish is served. Whatever else is served—*abbacchio, porcini* (very large mushrooms), fish, and so on—is made with a

knowing hand. Go late (reserve, 564-783) to see the slick,
dark-clad gentlemen who, Romans say, make their living
by hanging around the airport looking prosperous and
businesslike, with portfolio under one arm and good raincoat on the other, casing the scene for promising luggage
to steal; to see the rich young who come down, in full
refulgent gear, from villas and new, balconied apartment
houses north of the city; especially to see ancient building
angles cut into the dark sky at the other end of the Campo.
Moderate to high.

Polese, 40 Piazza Sforza Cesarini, shares its shaded square
with two other restaurants, and on summer evenings their
combined lanterns and the waiters rushing disks of pizza
make a convivial Renoirish spot on dull, practical Corso
Vittorio Emanuele. Have the boar in season, or *cuscinetti*,
little cushions of veal stuffed with ham and mozzarella.
Other than the fact that prices are low for the satisfactory
quality, Polese's distinctions are dinner served as early as
6 P.M. and at least one waiter who speaks Spanish, English,
German, and some French.

The Campo is surrounded by inexpensive trattorie, small,
plain family holdings that will always have a group of
pastas, salads, and a couple of styles of veal on hand, usually freshly bought that day. Look in at the Hostaria
Farnese, on the Via Baullari, 109, at la Quercia across from
the Palazzo Spada on the Via Capo di Ferro. Pierluigi on the
Piazza Ricci lets you choose from an enormous table of
spicy antipasti well doused in oil, and occasionally over-
cooked, and lets you take it out to a table in the piazza.
Although the bean soup and the pasta, which must be served
to you, are often better, the service, accustomed to do-it-
yourself customers, is fairly disorganized. Best gather your
own antipasti or be prepared to wait in the company of
young customers escaped from Parioli, Scarsdale, and points
west.

More polite and efficient, La Pollarola, on Piazza Pollarola
25, and the Grappolo d'Oro, 80 Piazza della Cancelleria,

whose few street tables make fine loges from which to watch the burbling of Campo dei Fiori life. An *osteria* on the Via Monserrato near its meeting with the Via in Caterina refuses to give itself a name. The proprietor is cook and waiter, sometimes assisted in the latter capacity by an old, unforgiving anti-Fascist. Have any kind of pasta your host suggests and follow it with rabbit or chicken cacciatore style (which does not mean, as it does in the States, garlic and tomatoes, but spices and a light dousing with vinegar —extremely tasty). Go at about 9 or 9:30 to make part of the welcoming committee for a group of students celebrating graduations and the slow seepage from the street of a local drunken *conte*, an old musician who cannot carry through a tune largely because he cannot hear it, a singer of sad prison songs full of farewells to mothers, children, and beloved girls, one or two "antiquarians," which can mean anything from broken chairs to Etruscan finds.

Colosseum

La Tana del Grillo, 6B Salita del Grillo, shows what the Ferrarese can do. For one, the proprietress, whose wonderfully classical face sits on a monumental pedestal, and for another, a curio called *salame da sugo* which goes back to Byzantium. A section of pork intestine is stuffed with meat, spices, and potassium, tied into a ball, and hung for months. When matured it is steamed for seven hours and, when cut, tastes like spicy hamburger with a fizz. (The round dark roots that hang on a beam above are the dainties, seething silently.) If this is too daring, order the *lombatina* (veal steak) *alla salvia* in a milky sage sauce and the zucca (yellow squash) cooked with lemon rind, mashed macaroons, and beet sugar. The Tana adds to its assorted exotica the virtue of late hours. High-moderate.

Sante, a trattoria and pizzeria on the Via del Buoncon-
siglio off the Via Cavour. The wise saws in Romanesco and
the frescoed landscapes try too hard; concentrate instead
on the food, which is good and inexpensive. Or, the less
verbal Trattoria d'Albanese, Via dei Serpente 148; garden,
and inexpensive. Good crayfish (*mazzancolle*) at Al Gladi-
atore, 5 Piazza del Coliseo.

The Scattered and Miscellaneous

Pizza? Always available. Rome is practically paved with it,
in several degrees of coarseness, from heavily bubbled to
paper thin, in disks or squares. The major tourist lures—
the Vatican museums, the Colosseum, the Pantheon, etc.—
are ringed with snack bars that serve pizza and another
indigenous snack, *supplì*, a hot croquette of rice and mozzarella cheese. There is hardly a bar that does not stuff
several sorts of sandwich, and baked pizza base, golden
and dimpled, is available in most bakeries, to be eaten as
is or to serve as platform for prosciutto or cheese from a
neighboring pizzicheria.

Should your shape and seams be suffering from too much
pasta, and summer fruits be in full supply, lunch on a
frullato di frutta, milk and fruits whipped and spun around
together to make a liquid nectar. Among the most reputable: Pascucci across from the big bar and *tavola calda*
called Delfino, on the side of the Largo Argentina approaching the Pantheon; a place that prides itself on the wholesome ingredients of its cakes and juices, the Ristoro della
Salute, at the western side of the Colosseum. The resplendent Alemagna caffè and tea shop on the Corso and Via Con-
vertite so heaps its *frullati* counters with perfect grapes
and peaches and nectarines in overflowing big urns as to
make the drink irresistible. A sharp contrast to the light,

sweet, and wholesome is *coppie,* two bits of raw horsemeat aged in lively spices, tied together (*coppie* = couples) and sold out of baskets by itinerant vendors on the Campo dei Fiori.

Porchetta, roast pork in a sandwich, is a favorite dish of fairs and country markets. Rome sports large, crackled, brown torsos around the church of S. Giovanni on his day, along with custard-filled *bigné* to celebrate S. Giuseppe's day in the Trionfale area, and during the festival of Noantri in Trastevere (late July). One of the few places where *porchetta* is constantly found is near the entrance of a *tavola calda* on the Viale Trastevere, a block or two from the river among the cheek-by-jowl food dispensaries on the south side of the street. The old hands do not buy ready-made sandwiches, apt to be laden with fat. They select a few slices critically, and buy their bread elsewhere.

The secret of the superiority of Italian ice cream is not that it is creamier but that the flavors one orders actually meet the anticipated tastes. Chocolate is deep, dark, and rich, peach tastes of peaches, pistachio has its unique green flavor. Although a lady of size, packed with respectability, would rather die of hunger than eat a sandwich or cookie on the street, a dripping little papery cone heaped with multicolored ice cream is perfectly acceptable. Pretty pictures outside bars advertise inventive packaged goods in assorted sizes and prices. Larger bars keep vats of ice cream from which to fill cones and cups. Tre Scalini on the Piazza Navona stocks an inexhaustible supply of *tartufo,* chocolate bits embedded in rich chocolate ice cream. *Mela stregata* (bewitched apple) is an apple of thin chocolate enclosing layers of ice cream and frozen mousse wrapped around a core of sponge cake soaked in sweet liqueur. Its home is naturally Bianca Neve (Snow White), a caffè that sits on the Piazza Paola across from the Castel S. Angelo. Giolitti draws a long thread of tables on its street, Uffici del Vicario. There is no sidewalk, the street is narrow and well trafficked, and you will be charged a considerable sum for the privilege of eating ice cream in close intimacy with door handles and fenders. But not to worry: no car has yet been known to plow into a set of tables, and, in any case, a mixed order of melon, raspberry, date, and watermelon ice cream, or *torrone*, full of bits of dried fruit, plus nut, chocolate, mocha, and banana, makes too satisfying a mélange to leave attention for menacing cars. For simpler tastes: the *affogato*, chocolate ice cream topped with a syrup of cherries, or combinations of fruit ices, or a cup of mixed flavors to carry away. Less lustrous and equally serious about fruit ices, including the famous *granita di caffè*, and ice cream, is the establishment in a northern area of the city, Parioli, at 8 Via di Villa San Filippo. You'll find it not far from the large Piazza Ungheria, always mobbed with the young and matrons who order (as you may, too, by phoning 879-314) beautiful party confections. The name? Most Romans, being Roman, call the gelateria "I Froci"— pronounced "frosci"—which means "pansy," based on fact or fancy. It is a common, mild expletive in Rome, and who cares as long as the customers keep coming? On the way to or from the magic portal stop in at Fassi on the Via Principe Eugenio for a mixture of their monumental assortment.

For one of the capitals of the world—let us say provincial capital, reluctantly, but capital nevertheless—Rome has remarkably few restaurants of other nationalities. A number of restaurants mentioned above serve French dishes; the few Chinese restaurants that exist at this writing are not worth the effort of seeking out. The Japanese restaurant at the corner of the Via della Vite and Propaganda, where Japanese tour buses stop to disgorge hundreds of camera-hung co-nationals, is consistently reliable for its tempura.

De Alfonso, 23 Via Brescia, states its motif by way of a scimitar-shaped door handle under Moresque curves, to set the mood for Tunisian dishes. Have the delicate, perilous *bourik* (pronounced "brick," more or less), a thin, crisp crêpe into which an egg has been cooked. It must be eaten with head and hand well over the dish, napkin tucked under chin, so that the mischievous yellow spurts of egg which love white shirts can do as little damage as possible. Couscous, which can be a variation of cooked flannel, is given its full flavors here, particularly when accompanied by zesty meatballs and a hot sauce on the side for those who like to eat fire. While you wait, there are carrots marinated in lemon and spices to nibble on. Dessert is of the baklava type, honey and nuts folded into papery pastry, and, to finish, almonds floating in mint tea. Moderate.

Da Rosa, 141 Via della Scrofa. Rose is a plump, white-haired Hungarian lady whose restaurant is as plain as—and cleaner than—a tenement kitchen. The chicken soup with liver dumplings is not quite as rich as mother used to make. Settle for the goulash soup instead, the chicken paprikash and stuffed cabbage doused with yogurt as substitute for sour cream.

Placed in this grab-bag category because, although it serves indifferent Roman food, the main dish is *parolaccie* —obscenities—in words, music, and gestures. Take an Italian friend to translate, no great burden since the repetitions are so frequent and many. The address is 3 Vicolo del Cinque (Trastevere), and the décor heavy lashings of trellises and rose-filled baskets sprawling along the walls and up into the ceiling. To keep the Saturnalia spirit going, a constant din of sound from a tall, big-nosed, saturnine guitarist and a short Sancho Panza accordionist. A greeter's welcoming phrases run the small gamut of *finocchi* or *froci* (fairies), *cornuto*, cuckold, for men with or without women, who are *mignote, zoccole, troie*—all words for whore. Any short exchange between entertainers who cannot, must not, stop in this all-night marathon quickly comes to *fa in culo*, which translates as "up yours." It makes a good rapid lesson, especially when one or other of the musicians chooses to translate each obscenity into several languages and, when the wine has released the last few reluctant psyches, everyone sings obscene parodies of popular songs. As one release leads, wine-inspired, to another, someone dances on a table, waiters and musicians fall on the necks of good-looking young men, who then fall into each other's laps. All this nonstop fun and games, plus insults, decent, plentiful carafe wine, and a forgettable meal should cost no more than 4,000 lire and a mild hangover or sourish stomach the next morning.

Vecchio Falcone, 60 Via Trionfale. An old coaching inn, supervised by a stuffed falcon and several work-worn, amiable ladies at the cash desk and the stove. The ravioli—little balls of spinach and ricotta (the Italian equivalent of cottage cheese)—are a specialty of the house, as is, in season, *puntarelle*, a long, slightly bitter leaf happily married to an anchovy sauce. Have anything, in fact; the ladies guard their reputations carefully. And yours may be the fortunate evening when a plump TV tenor, dressed in black velvet, fringed by an adoring entourage, sings out and sings and sings, his voice bounding and bouncing off the raw brick walls. If he were an ill-tuned, itinerant musician who went on too long, he would be given his coins and a waiter would usher him out discreetly. In this situation the clientele takes over with shouts of "Basta, basta," and the golden boy shuts up only after rising above the vulgar noise with a few thunderous, triumphant tones. Moderate.

Mirabella, Via Ripetta, near the Piazza del Popolo. A late cellar for wine, cheese, hamburgers, and sausage. High-moderate. On the Via della Croce, a pizzeria and a bierstube that keep late hours at less cost to you.

Al Fogher, 13B Via Tevere. Roomy, cleverly decorated without straining for too much atmosphere, the service alert though unhurried, and the specialties the cuisine of the Veneto-Friuli district. This far north in Italy means central European influences—goulash and cream sauces over meats. The bean soup (*crema di fagioli*), treated with cream, herbs, and cheese, is distinctly regional and tasty, as is the sliced suckling pig, the pot roast (*stufato all'erba*), and the puddings doused with cooked fruits. The regional wines are excellent; let the waiter guide you through them or show your knowing stuff by ordering one of the Pinots.

Cecilia Metella, near that monument on the Appica Antica. For inordinate Sunday eating: *scrigno*, green and yellow noodles known as "straw and hay" baked under a crust of cheese; an *arrosto misto* of veal, lamb, chicken, and quail; or the house treatment of breast of chicken; rich cakes, plus gardens for the children and rooms set aside for wedding parties. All for about 6,000 lire, including wine and tip, for two. Closer to the Baths of Caracalla and also favored by Romans, the Horti Galateae, 5 Via di Porta S. Sebastiano. Moderate.

Nardi, Via S. Vito 11. Courtly, elderly waiters, an unusually full menu, and the delight of sitting in a tiny piazza inside an unexpected and elegant arch in an obscure neighborhood. Modest.

Osteria Campidoglio, Via dei Fienili, near S. Maria della Consolazione, behind the Forum and below the Palatine. The menu decent, undistinguished; the location superb. Modest to moderate. Also enchantingly positioned and in the same price category, Angelino's on the Piazza Margana.

The trattorie near the Vatican museums are very inviting after the long culture safaris. They know their greatest asset is proximity and consequently are not always meticulous about the quality of their cooking. The prices tend to be a shade too high, but not inordinately. However, the local caffès are merciless: 350 for a lemonade, 500 for a small dish of ice cream. Contain your craving for refreshment until you reach caffès farther along Cola di Rienzo.

The Grand Hotel near the station has brightened up its snack bar to serve up good cheeseburgers, among other homey items. More homey still, the restaurant bar on the Via Nazionale, at the corner with Torino, which feeds the homesick appetite apple pie, poached eggs, waffles, pancakes, hamburgers, cornflakes, and "percolator coffee."

Picnicking is possible anywhere in a green patch of the city. Supplied with an etto (100 grams) of this and that out of a pizzicheria and rolls from a bakeshop, you can picnic in privacy among the trees above the Via de Teatro Marcello, or on the Palatine or at its base, by walking southwestward in the Forum toward the remains of the Palatine walls, which shape private dining rooms marked off by columns and pieces of cornice, and altars to serve as tables and chairs.

A latteria-bar on Bocca di Leone, near Carrozze, serves fresh sweet rolls and cappuccino as early as 6 A.M.

A lady in Breton headdress used to make French waffles in a caffè-"drugstore" at the corner of the Corso and S. Giacomo; she may still be at it.

Two popular seafood houses in neighborhoods you might not normally visit are Loreto, 19 Via Valenziana (near the Piazza Fiume), long-established, responsible, and moderate, and the Costa Balena, 5-7 Via Messina, near the Porta Pia, whose pride is giant shrimp at prices in the high-moderate category.

Up the Spanish Steps and north, there is a lunch-snack-caffè almost entirely sheltered by hedges that cascade toward the Via Margutta; goldfish in a flower-bordered pool, seclusion, banners of Roman sunset for the price of a gelato or coffee.

Hardly a restaurant and mentioned because it would be too bad to miss: Buccone, a wineshop at 19 Via Ripetta, as close as Rome comes to the leisured, quiet conviviality of a good pub. The handsome shelves are laden with bottles of domestic and imported wines from which you may choose your slow glassful or two.

Not everyone's taste, but there must be enough Romans who like dried codfish soaked and fried to support a restaurant on the Largo dei Librari (Campo dei Fiori) that serves nothing but, calling the delicacy *filetto di baccalà*.

The slaughterhouse neighborhood, Testaccio, feeds well on steaks, chops, sweetbreads, and mounds of spicy pasta. The choicest dish, however, is intestines of newborn calves still full of milk, *pagliata,* available at Turiddu, Via Galvani 64, and at Perilli, Via Marmorata 39.

Rough, boisterous, loving care at the Consolato d'Abruzzo, Piazza Elio Callistio, 15-16 (Parioli), expressed in platterfuls of salami and friendly, inexact estimates of how many inches of the several kinds you have consumed. And at Armando Zanni (Romans call the place "Baffi"), Corso Francia 115-7, near the Ponte Milvio, a baronial hearth that issues forth hot, crusty *bruschetta* and, among the good broiled meats, a distinguished confection called "Mexicana." Both moderate, both mobbed by 9 o'clock.

Finally, to close arbitrarily an endless subject, remember that all restaurants are closed one day each week. Telephone or arrange a list of alternates.

ROME SOUTH

Testaccio, Pyramid,
Protestant Cemetery

For a change from taxis and buses take Rome's subway
system, which is hardly yet a system, since it runs only
from the main railroad station to Mussolini's show city
EUR and on to the Ostias old and new on the sea. Attempts
at expansion have cut large holes in the city, shaken up
rows of houses, pierced water mains, bumped into buried
Roman streets, and, suffering from the usual work stop-
pages and "where will we get the money," are not making
spectacular progress. The Metropolitana will not take you
at present to most places you would like to see but does
serve for a few points south of the center. Having paid
your 50 lire and held on to your ticket, get off at the Pira-
mide Station (also available to many buses), walk through
the gate of S. Paolo and, some few hundred meters on, look
back to a stunning composition. The eye is caught by a
long stretch of Aurelian (late third century) wall that still
rings parts of the city, rises to medieval turrets and then
turns to the surprising presence of a white pyramid—small
compared to Egyptian pyramids but unmistakably an
Egyptian tomb—that sits in the wall, the monument of an
important government official (praetor) and high priest who
died shortly before the birth of Christ. As you approach the
gate, you may observe that a corner of the pyramid extends
beyond the wall; it was in this corner that the tomb was
placed to keep it *fuori le mura,* outside the walls. The rest is
within legitimately tombless walls. Still moving closer and
into the gate, vestiges of a shrine of the fifth century and,

back of the pyramid, the austere spires of cypresses, the mourning trees that rise not for the Roman Gaius Cestius, who might have wanted his tomb bold and unshaded, a thing of Egypt, but for the non-Catholics who lie in the cemetery near him.

It is a curious and moving juxtaposition, this African sepulcher of a power who wished to be buried in rich robes, swaddled luxuriously like an Egyptian pharaoh (his descendants denied him that afterlife pleasure); the legendary shadow of Remus, who, the medieval storymaking mind decided, was buried in this grand oddity in spite of the clear Latin attribution on one of the slopes; the famous and obscure British buried in the cemetery, and the ghostly presence of St. Paul beheaded and buried a short distance from the non-Catholic tombs. The combination inspired in English visitors to Rome spates of Protestant prose, as, for example, a paragraph quoted by Augustus Hare: "St. Paul was led to execution along the road to Ostia. As he went his eyes must have rested for a moment on the sepulchral pyramid which stood beside the road; and still stands unshattered, amidst the wreck of many centuries; upon the same spot. . . . Among the works of man, that pyramid is the only surviving witness of the martyrdom of St. Paul; and we may thus regard it with yet deeper interest, as a monument unconsciously erected by a Pagan to the memory of a martyr. Nor let us think those who lie beneath its shadow are indeed resting (as degenerate Italians fancy) in unconsecrated ground. Rather let us say, that a spot where the disciples of Paul's faith now sleep in Christ, so near the soil once watered by his blood, is doubly hallowed. . . ."

A more recent martyrdom, that of citizens and soldiers killed in resisting the Germans in 1943, is remembered by a plaque at the far side of the pyramid and, beside it, the entrance to the Museum of the Via Ostiense (closed Mondays, open 9 to 1 on other days), where it is unlikely you will find anyone else; your only company will be the guardian, who tags along not because there is anything to steal but because he is lonely. By no means among the major museums, much of its matter told in photographs and models, it is, however, an evocative experience to walk under the old brick arches, on ancient stairways into low vaults connected by crenelated walks and, beyond them, the mélange of antiquity and modernity.

Though the name that appears on maps and buses is Porta S. Paolo, a name that goes back to the Middle Ages, the gate is still called by its Latin name, the Porta Ostiense, which opened the road to the prosperous port of Ostia. It is this road, the Via Ostiense, one of the oldest Roman roads, and the majestic shade of St. Paul in his martyrdom, tomb, and church and the port, that concern the small museum. Here you will find models, maps, sketches, and photos of the road and the port in its several stages of growth. Here and there, Roman road markers, pagan altars, sarcophagi found in the area, tomb slabs crudely scored and attributed to the sepulchers of a saint or two, the most notable that of "Paolo Apostolomart," a copy of the tomb cover of his church. Look for the reproductions of the fine patterns and pretty goddesses who danced on the inner walls of Gaius Cestius' tomb, publicly viewable up to about ten years ago; try to find a print of the church of S. Paolo immediately after the nineteenth-century fire which shows the cruel devastation and some of the decorations and paintings that might have been restored, but weren't. Awkward recent paintings of the nearby tombs help fill the halls and, in compensation, attractive old prints of the pyramid and gate, two of them superb and in the Italian sense "terrible," by Piranesi.

Some of the material of the museum you may have seen or will see in Ostia Antica itself, and sarcophagi are ubiquitously in good supply, so save time for the best of the museum, the charming little marble column wreathed with grapes and leaves on the high open walk and, from a balcony on the upper floor, a view directly into a looming side of the pyramid, a corner of the cemetery beyond, frenetic traffic directly below, a minor railroad station, knots of buses and, not too far off, a high ash-gray mound, ragged in contour and texture, the third of this oddly assorted company of burial places, Monte Testaccio.

Back of his pyramid, on the street named for the Egyptophile Roman which trails off into auto repair shops and anonymity, stands the entrance gate to the "new" section of the cemetery. Its orderly, flower-bordered paths, the carpets of ivy, the gentle rise to the ancient wall at whose base lie plain amphorae lacking a handle, a neck, a bulge, the presence of artists, writers, and historians of a number of countries and their young, all resting in dappled light that slips through the trees, make it a gently rueful place, though a bit too crowded for total serenity. That mood belongs to the "old" cemetery, a smooth, broad stretch of lawn, a few pomegranate trees standing over sparsely scattered graves, and the protective white presence of the solemn pyramid.

Like all cemeteries, it has the look of "forever," a place frozen in immobile, untouched silence of centuries gone and centuries to come, an effect belied by its struggling history. The neighborhood, Testaccio, was from medieval days until early in the nineteenth century a place of public spectacles called the Greens of the Roman People. Early shows were at times religious processions, frequently the enactment of the Stations of the Cross, which may account for the slender cross at the top of Monte Testaccio. Altogether irreligious were the jousting meets which often involved resounding ducal names and those of the papal hierarchy, occasionally including a *sportif* pope himself. The populace, not admitted to these noble games, invented their own, baiting animals, chasing them to a chaotic, screaming kill, then taking what meat they could wrest home for cooking and eating. Who paid for the jousting and the hunting? The Jewish community, whose role it was to underwrite much of Rome's public amusements.

When Paul II, the Venetian, moved to his new Palazzo Venezia late in the fifteenth century, he took the tourneys

to its courts, but the people kept their ancient grounds and
continued amusing themselves in the wine cellars dug into
the base of the hill, eating, drinking, dancing, and welcoming the prostitutes attracted to the gaiety. No one was awed
by the stern, white pyramid, or the ghost of St. Paul, nor
concerned about the non-Catholic dead until they began to
arrive in numbers. Earlier, Protestants were interred in the
company of prostitutes, in unconsecrated ground at the foot
of the winding wall (Muro Torto) that runs into the Piazzale
Flaminio. In the eighteenth century, two young men, one
English and the other German, were buried at the foot of
the pyramid. Others—German, Scandinavian, American, and
many English—followed surreptitiously by torchlight, since
no daytime burials were permitted in this unhallowed earth,
open to wandering animals and the citizens of a pugnacious,
superstitious neighborhood. The papacy was equally uncoop-
erative; it would not permit a wall or lines of trees to mark
off the cemetery, nor Christian symbols—not even a simple
cross—to be carved on the tombstones. The church fathers
conceded to digging a moat, which responded as Roman
moats do: it revealed a cobbled Roman road and began to
fill with refuse, including enough animals to earn it the
name "dogs' cemetery," a poor double-edged local joke. The
unification of Rome with the rest of Italy in 1870 changed
all that; gravestones were permitted to appear Christian
and devout, a protective wall was erected, and control was
ultimately given to committees from the non-Catholic
communities.

The English graves of the nineteenth century make good
prosy reading. One Britisher wanted it known that he came
from a village in Sussex, that he was a professor of classical
studies and a stalwart English gentleman even in death. The
wife of another Englishman, unwilling to let death erase his
identity, achievements, and virtues, caused a substantial
stone to be carved with precise information of his lineage,
his places of birth and work, his travels, his love of knowledge, his marriage to her and her lineage, his many virtues,

and how much she misses him. On the other hand, the stone of Antonio Gramsci, one of the fathers of Italian communism, is surprisingly taciturn for an Italian statement: his name, dates, and the fact that his ashes rest here. A large, undecorated stone box commemorates Swedes who died in Rome; a temple-like structure engraved with an angel lifting a young girl heavenward is that of an English girl who died at sixteen; a section of classic torso and drapery, a lovely bit of antiquity, whether genuine or not, is the monument to a young woman who died more recently. It is as if Rome demanded too much, as if she burned them out too quickly, these many young from more orderly, less feverish places. At the top of the slope, embedded in severe classical style, the profile of Goethe's only and illegitimate son, August, whose tombstone glorifies father rather than son, who is identified as "Goethe filius."

For most English and American visitors there are two famous lodestones. Against the wall almost adjoining the moat, the plaque that covers the ashes of Percy Bysshe Shelley with the words "Cor Cordium" engraved on it and, from *The Tempest*, "Nothing of him that doth fade/But doth suffer a sea-change/Into something rich and strange." As in life, so in death Shelley's body wandered. Everyone knows about the drowning at sea in 1822, the body washed up in Lerici, the beach cremation, the heart snatched from the flames; it is a famously dramatic, romantic event. The episodes that followed took on unfortunate Gothic grotesquery. Mary Shelley wanted the ashes buried near the grave of their child William in the Roman cemetery. When they reached the British Consul, it was discovered that the Roman Church would permit no new burials in the section where the child lay. The box of Shelley's ashes was placed in the consulate cellar to await rescue. Less than a year after he had buried Keats, Joseph Severn was sought out for help. He and the consul decided to exhume William and place him in the grave ultimately allocated for his father's ashes. But it was not William who lay under his stone but an adult's skeleton, so the grave was covered and Shelley's ashes rested alone until, some short time later, that devoted romancer Trelawney bought another plot and had the ashes moved there. Many years later, in 1881, he was himself placed in an adjoining plot. At the other side of Shelley lies someone with the unbelievable name of Bertie Bertie Mathewarm, straight out of Wodehouse, although he died in 1844, and an incongruous note on which to leave a great poet and nonconformist who may have been hounded out of England by just such Bertie Berties.

The "old" cemetery has space for benches on its open paths among the pines and pomegranate trees and oleanders. The few scattered graves—a small plinth, a wreathed column—scarcely disturb the grass and patches of wildflower that creep through the green matting which runs back to a full unobstructed face of Gaius Cestius' tomb and medieval turrets of the wall. In the course of leveling the earth at the side of the pyramid, excavators found the remains of three bodies lying close to its base, one of them under a lead shield inscribed "Gorgius Ludovicus Langton, Nobilis Anglus Oxoniensum," the young Oxford gentleman who, according to imperfect records, was the first non-Catholic buried in Testaccio.

The bench at the far corner of the old grounds is rarely empty, although the cemetery is hardly a crowded tourist lure. One frequently finds a young couple, fresh from university and youth hostels, reading from a volume of Keats near his grave or, hand in hand, sitting quietly, looking, thinking. Unlike the sweet, gentle sadness or the calm Latin directness that speaks from other young graves, Keats's voice is anguished defeat. No name, no date of birth, simply a lyre and below: "This grave contains all that was mortal of a young English poet who, on his deathbed, in the bitterness of his heart, at the malicious power of his enemies, desired the words to be engraved on his tombstone," and in larger letters, Keats's words, "Here lies One Whose Name was writ on Water." One of the terrible ironies of his brief life was the fact that the Italian sun, which was to cure, betrayed him and gave him instead an agonized wintry death far from his woman and his friends, except one whose grave stands next to that of the poet. Of the same size and shape, its symbol is a palette and brushes, since Joseph Severn was a painter both in and out of fashion in the course of his long life and, as the tombstone informs us, "British Consul of Rome and Officer of the Crown of Italy in recognition of his services to Freedom and Humanity." To posterity, the most important words are: "devoted friend and deathbed companion of JOHN KEATS." Although he was a prolific painter, one sees little and cares less about his work, other than sketches he made of Keats. He was a conscientious and at times courageous representative of the British Crown but hardly a potent figure in British history. Severn's immortality rests on his talent—genius—for sympathy and friendship, which impelled him to care for a friend whom he loved as man and poet through weeks after sleepless exhausted weeks which were nightmares of shared agony. After the death he saw to the burial, accompanied by very few mourners, wrote the necessary letters, and continued, all his busy life, to keep the memory of Keats alive, to have his poetry collected and published, to stimulate and cooperate in the writing of a biography. By the time Severn died, at eighty-five, he had a large family, most of them in the arts or married into the arts, and money was tight. His monument was raised on funds from donors listed on the reverse side of the stone, an extraordinary roster of artists and writers: H. W. Longfellow, J. E. Millais, Dante and William Rossetti, Frederick Leighton, His Excellency the Honorable James Lowell, homage paid him in large part for his unceasing devotion to Keats.

One always leaves the cemetery slowly, haunted by Keats, inspired by Severn, and reluctant to take off the cloak of funerary balm. But *tempus fugit,* a phrase invented by a Roman and particularly applicable to tourist time in bottomless, endless Rome.

At the corner of the Vie Zabaglia and Galvani, under the
tall, broad chalky mound of Testaccio, there is a gate to the
stairway that climbs the hill. It skirts a minute, unexpected
house complete with unambitious dog, a flurry of cats, barefoot children, and a wizened grandmother hanging clothing in the spot of yard. Beyond the stairway you will climb
toward the peak and its old cross over millions of pieces
of old amphorae of which the hill entirely consists. From
the flattened crest one can see the cemetery, the pyramid
and wall, the glitter of tin roofs immediately below, and
in another direction, the cross-hatching of the pens attached
to the abattoir and the river. Immediately below, along the
stretch of the river now called Lungotevere Testaccio, there
was, as early as the second century before Christ, an enormous set of government warehouses which controlled the
storing and distribution of the oil and wine, grains, fruits,
and delicacies from Africa, the East, and the North, brought
to Ostia by large ships and transferred to rivercraft. According to one theory, the shards of containers broken by acci-
dent were dumped immediately behind the storage buildings. Another theory has it that accidents couldn't account
for the height and width of the hill; it must have been that
amphorae were cheap and not worth reshipping empty, and
so they were smashed after the transfer of goods to storage
vats. A third theory is more ingenious and colorful. Having
observed that the hill consists of an extraordinary number
of handles among its myriad bits and pieces, knowing that
a tablet near the warehouses defined taxable as opposed to
nontaxable imports, knowing also that the word for "tax"
derived from the word for "handle," one scholar concluded
that the collectors would simply batter off one handle to
identify a container of taxable goods. An imaginative theory,
and more vivid than endless lines of weary Roman steve-
dores dragging amphorae up uncertain, slithering paths of
broken amphorae to smash more amphorae.

The only way down is by the same stairs. Walking to your
right toward the abattoir, you will shortly come on a village

with its own isolated smells and flavors—vestiges of the wine cellars that once existed more abundantly, ramshackle cottages that run into and flap on each other, a horse or two picking at a few blades of grass that spring from the shards, unkempt children sliding on loose pieces of pottery, and as the sun slips off the corrugated tin roofs, a number of the city's least successful prostitutes stationed in the abandoned, unused alleys.

Roman version of an Egyptian tomb, a hill built of Roman commercial conquest, the martyred St. Paul, walls built against barbarian invasions surmounted by small medieval fortress, mementos of the port of Ostia, jousting, passion plays, robust fun and games, an enormous brilliant and noisy present-day market, the cemetery full of Romantic northerners who came to paint, to write, to study and breathe the classical sun-struck air of Rome—a multi-textured collage unique to this city.

NOTE: St. Paul's Outside the Walls is a five- or ten-minute bus ride to the south. A short climb diagonally across from the pyramid reaches S. Sabina. The Metropolitana goes on to Ostia Antica or drops you at EUR, which has the biggest assembly hall in Europe and the coldest museum, the Museo della Civiltà Romana. Sober, exhaustive studies of types of temples and arenas, instruments, arts, sciences, music and letters, feeding and accounting, dress and jewelry, and, inescapably, the busts of ancient Rome lead to an immense sunken model of the Imperial City—too much of it, say some experts, since a number of the miniature buildings never existed at all. Should you feel impelled to see the Colosseum before it was stripped and the racing shape of Piazza Navona and the bleachers of the Circus Maximus, get off at the second EUR Metropolitana station, Esposizione.

Martyrs Forgotten and Remembered: SS. Nereo ed Achilleo, S. Cesario, Casa del Cardinale Bessarione

Almost lost in the massive shadow of the Baths of Caracalla is the church of SS. Nereo e Achilleo, the fourth-
century *titulus fasciola*, "the church of the bandage," built
on the spot where St. Peter dropped the wrapping that
protected the leg sores made by his prison chains. The
basilica one sees now is certainly not the original monument, nor the eighth- into ninth-century version dedicated
to two eunuch martyrs who had been in the service of members of the Imperial family and exiled by Domitian, but it is
a tasteful attempt by a sixteenth-century cardinal to revive
and maintain wherever possible the antique contours and
details. The eaves usher one into a dark glow of marble,
the frail glitter of Cosmatesque work on reading desks, in
the swirls of candelabra, the inlaid marble screen of the
schola cantorum and the altar. Several centuries after the
Cosmati, Renaissance craftsmen carved lyres, wreaths, and
cadenced classical motifs on the graceful swell of a paschal
candlestick. The eighth-century mosaics of the Annunciation
and the Transfiguration are not the best of their kind,
though they are unique for the fact that this is one of the
earliest Transfigurations known and that a large gemmed
double cross takes the place that would become the more
literal Crucifixion. Too near the time when crucifixion was
the common death of slaves and riffraff (St. Paul, S. Eustachio, St. Cecilia, St. Agnes, all Roman citizens, were offered
the dignity of beheading), a crucifixion wouldn't do as
symbol of victorious Christianity. Instead, the glorious, blazing cross of the Church Triumphant.

A large bishop's seat, its back shaped like a Gothic church and supported by the lions who bear patiently so much Romanesque weight, is etched in the fine, careful lettering of a homily by St. Gregory. The lettering and parts of the carving are attributed to a Vassalletto, a family whose name is often joined with that of the Cosmati in "Cosmatesque." There are authorities who think the Christian carver may have used the seat of a judge from a Roman basilica, as Roman columns and slabs of colored marble from the nearby baths were used in the corpus of the church. Nor is the altar 100 percent Christian: one side shows a pagan block of stone bearing a breezy nymph who died with the triumph of Christianity, not to reappear until Renaissance art needed her.

Across the large piazza of Numa Pompilio—we are in the Rome of Imperial green vistas and parks of Renaissance villas—and a short distance southward, along the Via di Porta S. Sebastiano, is another basilica that has retained its primitive form and early art, S. Cesario, like its companion church restored with respect in the sixteenth century. The decorations follow the style of SS. Nereo e Achilleo, though with greater delicacy and gaiety. Little birds, griffins, and strange animals skitter along the winking tiles; a piece of dragon (the rest either stayed in another church or was discarded in remodeling) tries to hide around the corner of the altar. The reading desks are held up by smiling angels rather than the usual dour eagles; the bishop's throne, bound in fragile patterns of gleaming color, substitutes for homily a lion, a rooster, and two kissing turtledoves.

A Roman bestiary and its world live below the church, originally set into baths. In large blocks of black and white mosaic, fish, naiads, and sea-gods sport on the floor of the pool designed in the second or third century A.D. In techniques that vary from minute bits of stone to big coarse tiles, wonderful sea horses rear their foaming heads, and

sea-goddesses loosen their billowing veils to show breasts
and ample curves deftly delineated in white mosaic lines.
One sea-god rears a commanding face, another whirls and
coils his great tailed body in luxuriant laziness, and in
swarms of octopi, big fish, little fish, broad and arrow-like
fish ride Europa and her bull. (The source of the water to
support this thermal playground is still visible as a deep,
functioning well.)

The villa next door (number 8) was that of Cardinal
Bessarione, a humanist and art lover of the fifteenth century. Though the house is now used by the city for recep-
tions, it has been painstakingly kept as it was, the home
of a cultivated Renaissance gentleman, a prosperous villa
of its time with a typical loggia whose painted landscapes
are bordered by bands of grotesques. Similar decorations,
replete with fruits, columns, curlicues, continue into the
reception room to set off the stamped leather furniture of
the period. A bedroom shows off a bold flower design and,
where the Cardinal's bed no longer is, a crucifix and an unfortunate portrait of the Cardinal as if he were the Merchant
of Venice in caricature makeup. He collected good ceramics
and silken Eastern rugs, a rare gilded wood Virgin, fine
cabinets, classic heads, one or two early paintings, and very
likely not the too much retouched and doubtful "Raphael."
There are very few people who can readily set themselves,
easy with pipe, slippers, and book in the Palazzo Doria or
the Farnese or a dozen other overstately mansions. This old
bluestocking of a house, in spite of its august age, still
manages to welcome and warm.

.   .   .

S. Giovanni a Porta Latina,
S. Sebastiano

A not too long walk along the Via di Porta Latina, a secretive street that opens meager grilles at the sides of obdurate gates to allow a glimpse of villas and gardens will bring you to S. Giovanni a Porta Latina. In a city where layers of time and fierce history have arranged to make dramatic compositions, the medieval piazze like that of SS. Giovanni e Paolo, for instance, and particularly that of S. Giovanni a Porta Latina, offer a soothing pause in the insistently rhetorical. It is hardly a piazza, simply the exactly proper placing of an enormous cypress to hang over a tall, light Romanesque tower and, below the bower of sunlit shaft and shadowy black-green tree, an arcaded portico held on a diversity of marble columns. Before it, two timeless columns that support a medieval well traced with intertwining bands that might be Celtic or Carolingian. Stripped of accretions of recent years, the church shows what it might have been when it was young, more than a thousand years ago, when it repeated church patterns of the East: the apsidal windows, the flanking smaller apsidal curves which take on angles as their exterior aspect, very much like churches on the Adriatic coast. In the course of restoration a set of twelfth-century frescoes dealing with the Old and New Testaments were uncovered. They are not all easily visible, or worth deep regret if you can't see them, except for a sworded guardian angel who watched Eden with dozens of eyes set in his halo and his double pair of wings.

If it is permitted, and it usually is, ask to see the private chapel attached to the church, a plain, modern structure which displays six remarkable icons of considerable antiquity, a white shrouded Virgin holding a Byzantine elderly Babe, a taut Peter and Paul, and a figure in a black and

white patterned robe like those often seen in Yugoslav
monasteries. Above the altar, an effective painting of a parting of Peter and Paul. The rectory leads into a large well-
ordered garden kept by a minute elderly gentleman in socks,
sandals, and very short shorts, all probably bought in the
children's clothing stalls of a market. His precise rows run
back to a section of Aurelian wall, a glimpse of a white
Roman arch and, through small openings, the traces of
other curves and pieces of mosaic and statuary that date
from the third century, when the wall was arcaded for
sheltering from rain and sun. Immediately inside the Porta
Latina, a stone flower called the oratorio of S. Giovanni in
Oleo, to mark the place where John the Baptist emerged
from a cauldron of boiling oil, miraculously untouched. The
chapel, a tempietto attributed to Bramante and restored by
Borromini, carries a frieze of roses and acanthus leaves
tripping harmoniously together toward a crest of stone bouquet and the motto "au plaisir de Dieu," caused to be placed
there by the French prelate who subsidized the oratory.

A break in the wall near the Porta Latina opens to a park
whose caretaker conducts people to depths behind his house
(medieval rooms over Roman) where there are several types
of burial structures, two columbaria—urn niches that resemble dovecotes—a Christian catacomb with the usual slots
for bodies in several layers, and, most notable, rooms of a
Roman house that retain strips of floor mosaic and a ceremonial entrance to the tombs of the Scipio family, built
into a slope near a Roman road, now a wilderness path.
The tomb slabs in the complex, low space speak several
names of the powerful family. There are praetors, consuls,
triumphant generals who expanded the empire, and their
wives and children, but *the* great Scipio Africanus, who
defeated the Carthaginians in the Second Punic War and
became the virtual dictator of Rome in the second century
B.C., thus the main target of Cato's accusations of corrup-

tion, died in exile. Had he lived three hundred years later there might have been erected triumphal arches and spiraling columns carved with mighty deeds, but he lived in a plainer time, and no carved column or plaque remembers him.

Walking venerable Roman walls seems a more exciting idea than it actually is, but nothing in Rome is a total loss of time or effort. If you happen to be in the area on Sunday morning, a good time for the local small churches, make your way westward—noticing the shards of vases and tile under foot and the buttressing, the stone and brick work of several epochs in the wall—past the Porta Ardeatina for the sturdy bastions built by Sangallo the Younger at the behest of Pope Paul III, and turn back to a grassy close behind the Porta Ardeatina. A sign informs that groups go through at 9:30, 10:30, and noon, but you don't have to wait. Tip the attendant and follow his instructions to walk the short distance westward to a locked gate and then back toward the Porta S. Sebastiano, the ancient Porta Appia of the Appian Way that led to the Adriatic. Like many walks in ancient Rome, the wall, too, is arcaded. It looks on one side over surprising wastes of green high enough, in comparison with the low auto roads at the other side, to suggest that there might still be much Roman structure under the weeds. A city wall, by its very nature a long, rambling fortress, would necessarily have apertures for weapons or jets of oil or whatever was being used for holding off enemies at any given time, and here they are too. At one stage of its history some of the space was expanded as a chapel or, as one of the attendants insists, the cell of a hermit. That it was some sort of religious enclave is affirmed by a crude, faded painting of the Virgin.

An authoritative Italian guidebook places a museum at the gate of S. Sebastiano. There may some day be a museum; it doesn't exist at this writing. If the door has not been shut, to force you all the way back to the original entrance, you will find a man who uses fascinating Romanesco to point out that the black horseman on the white ground of a broad mosaic looks like Mussolini. The mosaic is modern, made in honor of the Duce, who must have been pleased to see himself in his favorite role of emperor executed in a favorite art form of the Empire, by a high Fascist functionary who lived in the rooms above the gate and built for himself, like his praetor ancestors, a pool surrounded by gardens in one turret. The attractive, irregularly shaped rooms in reconstruction and the capricious flights of stairs ultimately reach an open height that shows again the unexpected barren land and traffic on the via named for Christopher Columbus, heading for the pristine exposition city, EUR. Inside the wall, the pool and reflectors of an attractive old house owned by a movie star, separated by protective stands of shrub, tree, and wall from a school in the fireworks red of Naples, and in every direction a snooper's view of the villas, pools, and gardens which, at street level, remain hidden behind inscrutable blanks of stone and clouds of tree.

Stop for a moment at street level to look at the Porta S. Sebastiano and its huge blocks and gold crenellated turrets, at the accompanying misnamed Arch of Drusus (it was of Trajan's time). Arches, turrets, massive stone, and the marble columns that held an aqueduct built by Caracalla, make an unmistakable "Roman" entity, almost forbidding in its hauteur and indomitability. And indomitable it still is, still imperious, although the gateway lost its ceremonial processions in the sixteenth century. The last march of conqueror, nobles, distinguished family, and friends followed Marc Antony Colonna after the Battle of Lepanto, and thereafter the gate remained silent but undefeated by man or time. Who knows, however, what the automobile and its greed for wider, swifter space may do?

. . .

NOTES: The 89 bus starts at the side of the Palazzo Venezia and goes to the Baths of Caracalla. The 118 should, if bus routes haven't been rescrambled, return you to the baths or the terminal point, the Colosseum. It may be difficult to see SS. Nereo ed Achilleo and S. Cesario. As a rule, a not immutable rule, they are open from 12 to 1 except on holidays or when they are used for weddings, frequently on Saturday and Sunday late mornings. The safest time for the Casa Bessarione is 10 to 1. If S. Giovanni a Porta Latina is closed, ring at number 17.

Fosse Ardeatine, Museum of the Resistance

Near Raphael's house at the end of the Via Coronari, a marble plaque identifies the home of a fighter for liberty buried in the Fosse Ardeatine; the Via della Stellata carries several others. Mark with these Via Tasso near S. Giovanni in Laterano, the seat of the German SS Command and its prisons, and later a museum dedicated to documents of their stay and of the liberation. Mark the street called Rasella that slopes from the Palazzo Barberini. Mark a vast pit a short distance south of the church at which, according to the legend quoted in the Sienkiewicz novel, St. Peter, fleeing Rome, met Christ and asked him, "Domine, quo vadis?" When Christ answered that he was on his way to be crucified for the second time, the shamed Peter returned to Rome and martyrdom.

To pull the various points together: On March 23 of 1944, a bitterly short time before liberation, thirty-two members of the SS were killed by a bomb which exploded at the top of the Via Rasella. Immediately the Germans began rounding up men of all ages from fourteen to eighty-one and of all professions. They picked them up on the streets, dragged them out of the houses and prisons, until the total of three hundred and fifty—ten men for each German plus a few extra—was taken, to be charged with political crimes and, in the case of the Jews, who comprised a full third of the number, violation of "racial" laws. As far as is known not one of the three hundred and fifty had had any part in the bombing very probably planned by the Resistance. The carpenters, teachers, students, a priest or two, tailors, plumbers, writers, were told they were being taken to work the quarries south of the city. When they reached the pits on March 24 they were shot in the back of the neck and buried by an explosion. They did not remain hidden, as the Germans supposed; someone was always aware of German movements. At first, a sudden gush of traffic and at 10 and again at 11 o'clock in the morning a detonation of mines, heard but not seen because no one was permitted to approach the place. Later a German soldier speaking to a French and German guide was heard to say that ten were killed for one. His comrade felt the proportion wasn't high enough. They also said that there would be another explosion, and there was. The next day both guides found only the wire used in the detonation, but whispers had begun to circulate. Someone reported having heard screams; another spoke of a boy shot four times who dragged himself to a nearby inhabited area. In the meantime the site began to give off a strong stench, not strong enough to discourage a group of street urchins bent on pillage. Following the wire which led to a blocked hole, they came upon a long gallery of the heaped dead, each with his hands tied behind his back. The clandestine radio had picked up the course of events, and eight young listeners came to search for their fathers. In the course of the nightmare investigation, they found an older corpse, proof that the pit had been used before, and discovered that the dead were arranged in four layers with caustic matter between to accelerate disintegration. Aware of Italian awareness, the Germans returned and in three powerful explosions covered the gallery. After the Germans left, the bodies were exhumed to await final burial in one of the most moving of World War II memorials, the mausoleum of the Fosse Ardeatine, opened to the public exactly five years after the massacre, March 24, 1949.

Driving, or riding the 218 bus from S. Giovanni in Laterano, one wonders about the unconscious force that made the Germans bury their victims in this vast ancient burial ground of Christians and pagans, tunneled with endless catacombs and studded with tombs. Possibly it was not a sense of the fitness of Roman things, an atavistic response to antique tradition, but the knowledge, which diggers of the catacombs had come to centuries before, that tufa, the stone of the area, was easy to extract and that it spread when blasted as dense powdery cover.

In the long wall of worked tufa dug from the same local quarry, a bronze gate of intertwined sharp, angular forms speaks of torment. Under an outcropping of cave quarry, a few discreet memorials to others who died as Resistance leaders or innocent victims—the son of a famous poet, all the men of a northern town taken and destroyed by the Nazis—marked with the cross or the Star of David. Standing high and monumental, three figures with their arms linked to represent the young boy, the middle-aged intellectual, and the elderly worker entombed together. Walking quietly through the catacomb-like alleys of dark, ponderous tufa, past dignified Jewish and Christian chapels cut into the stone, one comes to a deep pit, the rough, gouged earth of the actual explosion and burial. A smaller bronze gate stands before the pit, repeating the bitter motifs of a larger gate, and soon the essential monument itself, an enormous stone casket with a raised lid that encloses rows of identical sepulchers of the murdered men, each identified by a photo, name, age, and profession. One coarse stone box is marked "Ignoto" (unknown) in honor of "all martyrs for liberty and the dignity and independence of labor." Emerging from the strict, silent rows in the cool light sifting into the raised cover of the enormous coffin brings one to a serenity of

undisturbed space sweetened by modest greens that flow
toward the blind, innocent tufa mounds.

No souvenirs are sold, although an attendant may give you
a post card or two. There are no drink and food stands, nor
benches for picnicking, as there are above the catacombs
across the road. A short distance along the road a one-armed
man will sell you a drink, but if you ask him whether he
has post cards he will say politely, "No. Never. We carry the
picture in our hearts."

The 218 bus which returns to S. Giovanni stops within a
short distance of 145 Via Tasso, a nondescript middle-class
apartment house where the German SS command made its
dispositions, kept its meticulous records, tortured and
walled up choice prisoners. They may have used the whole
house, but the Museum of the Resistance now occupies
several small apartments one above the other and, like the
Fosse Ardeatine, makes no overtly dramatic show. The
objects speak for themselves. The bloodstained shirt of a
professor of philosophy hangs near his photo and a testament that he was tortured in the Via Tasso without betray-
ing any person or plans of the Resistance, then taken out
to the Fosse in the roundup. The rope that bound wrists; a
piece of shirt in whose hem a strip of cloth bearing a farewell message was hidden; varicolored cards that sent Italians to concentration camps, to slavery in German factories,
to the torture chambers of Regina Coeli prison, to execution,
to solitary months of total cell darkness, to months in cells
whose light was never extinguished; charts of the organization of the Resistance and the links between the many centers marked on large maps. One room is given over to the
Jews—8,000 as hostages, 2,900 deported, 1,000 or more hidden in churches, nunneries, and monasteries, and there is a
document of thanks by the Jewish community to Roman
priests, a good number of them Resistance fighters.

One section is hung with the public orders that rained
down on the Roman populace and clung to their walls. In

German and Italian there were warnings that all strikes, sabotage, the carrying of arms, were forbidden. The punishment was execution. Phones were monitored, and anyone who spoke more than the briefest greeting was subject to charges of plotting and subsequent execution. The warnings did not altogether take; several posters offer large rewards for the disclosure of caches of arms and parachutes. The cooperative Italian government issued calls for *calma e disciplina* after reiterating German warnings and posting the order that turned citizens into soldiers between the fifteenth and thirtieth of November 1943.

Another section displays underground propaganda, several issues of the clandestine press, and leaflets occasionally stamped with cartoons. Mussolini declaims from the Palazzo Venezia; above, the gigantic head and arms of Hitler controlling the strings of his puppet dictator; below, soldiers marching toward a sign that points to Russia, Libya, and Death and a caption that repeats the greeting and farewell of gladiators: "Ave, Caesar! Morituri te salutamus."

What will haunt you, and possibly ruin your carefree Roman holiday, at least for a while, are not the documents necessarily but the men who still live in the cells—the man who wrote a lullaby for the expected child of a fellow prisoner, the diary of an eighteen-year-old too hungry and tired to move from the plank on which he sat day after day thinking only of not thinking, a signature scored into a wall before execution. One prisoner in an isolation cell sought distraction by incising Greek words in the wall; another scratched a poem of aspirations for the free Italy that would come after his death. Yet another dug out of the plaster a letter of farewell to his family. Perhaps the most desolate of the mementos, an object that lives in dreadful vividness, is a thesis written by an eighteen-year-old with a slender scholar's face, the thesis finished and neatly bound shortly before his execution.

NOTE: Open on Saturdays from 1 to 2 P.M. and Sundays from 10 A.M. to 1 P.M.

Borgata

Monumental Rome, palazzi Rome, churchly Rome, hooded medieval Rome, free-swinging baroque Rome, plashing, chortling, trickling, fountain Rome. Yet most of the three million Romans do not live in overgrown gardens of history. The prosperous like the space, the chic boutiques, and the swift roads that lead to EUR and the sea. Others prefer the meandering treed dips and rises of Parioli or the community swimming pools of modern apartment blocks in Vigna Clara or the Farnesina area, or along the Cassia to the north. The very poor do what they can, many of them immigrants from the south who feel as isolated and shut out of the city as New York's Puerto Ricans and London's West Indians and Pakistanis. The desperate find empty houses waiting for demolition or vaguely future reconstruction and settle in as bathless, toiletless, candle-lit squatters, or they collect discarded tin sheds and construction fencing to rear Bidonvilles, some of them blatantly in view at the side of one of the seaward roads, others hidden at the edges of slum quarters. And then there are the *borgate*, shown on detailed maps as irrational outcroppings of streets surrounded by emptiness, cheap land that has lost its identity as country and not yet city, frequently used for government housing and more frequently for speculation in instant slums. Modern Italian literature, the press, and films have drawn heavily, in a new *verismo*, on the violence and vice of the *borgate*, the gangs of thieves, the boundless promiscuity, the cheap purchase of young girls and boys who function as free-lancers or are kept imprisoned in shanty brothels.

There are larger enclaves at other edges of the city, but the Borgata del Trullo on the 96 bus route (from the Piazza Sonnino in Trastevere), because it is not too large, shows quickly the typical unease, the crumbling and insubstantial new, the equivocal position neither rural nor urban that trails into vacant lot, depths of tufa mine, and garbaged mounds. The oldest houses of mucky, scabrous mustard yellow in long blocks whose openings are thick cement prison bars were built by the Fascist government to house a handful of the southern poor who paid for the favor by crowding government trucks to become additional noise and mass in souped-up monster demonstrations of fidelity to Mussolini. The newer houses, optimistically hung with ivy and sprouts of geranium, stand like soldiers in stiff rows, promising to take on the poverty-stricken look of cheap housing at any moment.

The public entertainment facilities consist of a bocce court for the old men, a movie house notorious for pickups of nymphets and faunlets, an abandoned central piazza of bare green in a fence of indifferent trees, and a bar or two which are the permanent habitats of a few men with rough, scarred faces and brown, pitted teeth. On Sundays, wine and cards on tables in the streets and the kids hanging around, waiting for excitement. Playgrounds are the empty lots on muddy, unpaved streets and the underpinnings of new, papery building. Women shop, children go to the schools growing in the area, there is laundry flapping in courts and on balconies, and, nevertheless, a sense of emptiness, of homelessness, of people beating their way through life on an alienated, threatened island.

Potpourri of Advice

Carry a compact pair of opera glasses to bring the view of the Forum from the Campidoglio closer, to peer at the mosaics high on the walls of churches, to see more closely the minute figure of the Pope on his balcony when he makes his Sunday appearance or delivers his Christmas and Easter messages and blessings.

Unless you have the time to make repeat visits, be prepared to see almost any Roman museum only partially or not at all. The large treasure troves are often shrunken. A sign which says *in restauro* means a museum has been closed and may never reopen. Other than the Vatican museums, which belong to their own government, the museums of Rome were closed through the entire tourist month of August 1970, and from mid-March to Easter in 1971, and that included the Pantheon, which one might consider the property of the world. The strikes were called and maintained because the guards were not paid enough and because of the lack of personnel, which made guarding art objects, especially in a period when there were many thefts, a nervous job. There was also objection to the shabby condition of many museums, a justified complaint. When there is no strike, rooms of galleries are open and closed on erratic schedules—afternoon hours are often shortened or don't exist at all. It has been suggested that all travelers and art lovers form an international organization, headed by devoted, hawk-eyed functionaries, that would tax them ten dollars a year for cleaning, guarding, and maintaining buildings and collections in Italy and elsewhere. Until that day, and while Rome is distraughtly, unhappily, carelessly stuck with its abundance, the best a visitor can do is to phone before he ventures, using the list of monuments and museums that appears in the early pages of the yellow phone directory. The only Italian it requires is a knowledge of numbers, recognition that 16 is the number for 4 o'clock in the afternoon, and the phrase, "È aperto oggi il museo e fino a che ora?" If the answer includes *sciopero*, you should recognize it as the word for "strike." Or, look at your map and make alternate plans for the chosen neighborhood, keeping in mind that many churches are closed from 1 to 4, a few from 12 to 3. Or, walk the streets and indulge in people-watching, a prime Italian entertainment for actor and spectator.

By law, there is a service charge of about 15 percent added to every restaurant bill or concealed in the prices of items. A tip is nevertheless expected and universally left; in a simple place it might be 100 lire per person, and where the atmosphere is more luxurious twice that.

· · ·

Be careful of cameos, particularly if they are the products of Cameo Joe, an amiable fellow who shows pictures of himself with friends and clients in several American cities. His terrain is the Colosseum, where several souvenir and booklet counters display the same composition cameos that Joe claims he makes by hand.

Black-market cigarettes, at two-thirds the normal price, can be had from dealers at the Porta Portese market, women on the Vicolo del Cinque in Trastevere, one on the Via Frattina at the corner with Belsiana, men who ply the Piazza Navona district greeting passers-by with a polite "Tabacchi," as if it were "Buona sera."

People who have had to make their own beds in hotels, who couldn't find a taxi at night, who had been barred from museums, been obliged to crawl into the bellies of planes for their luggage and carry it to customs and out under their own steam, all because of strikes, have been known to speak wisely on their return of a "left" turnover. Those who witnessed a mobbed Fascist rally and saw the Fascist "Viva la Gioventù" streaked all over the city think it will be a "right" coup. Both groups may be wrong. There is a constant, amoeboid fission and fusion in the left which keeps it volatile and essentially uncoordinated. The right, should it attract enough adherents, may vitiate itself by turning into splinters. In short, the basic tendency is toward anarchy, for the pleasures of dissent rather than cooperation, and the restless, centrifugal movement maintains an uneasy balance. In other words, don't worry.

The bargain in guided tours is those conducted by the Ladies of Bethany of the Foyer Unitas. They are informed, energetic, and enthusiastic, use public transport, and ask only 100 lire for their services. Tours usually start at 9:30 at the Foyer, 30 Via dell'Anima, and continue to about 12:30. For the week's program call 651-618.

Every hotel desk has information about quick city tours (Cityrama conducted by Appian Lines on the Via Veneto is rated high by tourists). For slower, more informative guiding, the hotel concierge may be helpful; the American Women's Association of Rome arranges tours for its members and may be willing to supply you with the names of its experts; also the American Embassy. For meeting Roman arts and artists *in situ*, phone 345-1352 or 304-382.

Avoid raw seafood except in the most reputable, busy seafood houses, and then hesitate.

Spectacular shoe cleaning and shining, an act of resurrection, goes on at the shop marked Lustrascarpe, 19 Via Belsiana.

The auto club in your area provides Italian museum passes to members at a small charge. The offices of Antichità e Belle Arti, Piazza del Popolo 18 (take your passport), issues free museum passes. A membership in Italia Nostra, 287 Corso Vittorio Emanuele II, which costs about 3,000 lire per year, buys a card for free admission to national museums, Sunday trips to little-known points of interest, and the virtue of helping maintain the natural beauties and to members at a small charge. The offices of Antichità arts of the country. For a complication of greedy reasons, "saving" Italy is a dying battle, and support is desperately needed and deserved.

· · ·

The Falk map, with a careful index and diverting folds that obviate the necessity of struggling with an outstretched sheet, is the most complete, noting almost all of the innumerable vicoli and bus lines that lead toward them.

Except *in extremis* of desperation, the toilets in bars of the old city are to be avoided. They are usually situated in a cellar redolent of medievalism, there is no paper, the chain will not pull, and bowl and sink are usually brown with ages of neglect.

It cannot be repeated too often that one must be very alert in Rome's traffic. The time to be at the peak of wariness is when a station wagon full of nuns, driven by a middle-aged nun in full old-fashioned habit, comes bounding at you. This is Women's Liberation at its most happy, careless extreme.

Castel S. Angelo
Piazza della Rovere
Borgo S. Spirito
Città
dei
Vaticano
Via della Lungara
Farnesina
Via S. Francesco di Sales
Via Corsini
Piazza Moroni
Via di S. Dorotea
Vicolo di Bologna
Via della Scala
Via Garibaldi
Vicolo del Cinque
Vicolo della Paglia

Via Giulia
Ponte Sisto
Ponte Garibaldi

Gianicolo

Pantheon
Largo Argentina
Piazza Paganica
Lungotevere Anguillara
Ponte Fabricio
S. Bartolomeo
Ponte Cestio
Via dei Genovesi
S. Cecilia
Aventine
S. Crisogono
S. Francesco a Ripa

Viale Trastevere

Via di Lungaretta
Piazza di S. Cosimato
S. Maria in Trastevere

Walk 3
Trastevere to Pantheon

The Trastevere of tourist hoopla, drug raids in its most
venerable piazza, a neighborhood festa of blazing ugliness,
the Trastevere of bursting resturants, of fat, tough ladies
in full-voiced, ceaseless conversation, of cheap wine on
rough board tables, the Trastevere of working-class snob-
bishness that insists it has its own dialect (it once truly
did), of the humility of rich, apologetic newcomers, of
innumerable summer trattorie that send their white tentacles into adjoining alleys, the Trastevere of shrewd, con-
versational shopping, puts on fine faces at its bridges. From
the Isola Tiberina, it shows an amiable irregularity of well-
maintained prosperous medieval houses; from the Ponte
Sisto, a triumphal-arch fountain and the gesticulating vivid
form of the Trasteverino satirist and poet, Trilussa. His monument quotes a poem which ends with the lines: "I mean to
speak of things as they are without fear, even of prison,"
and he spoke out and was not imprisoned; Mussolini could
neither silence nor touch him.

The Ponte Garibaldi meets the Torre dell'Anguillara, a reconstruction of a thirteenth-century house and tower in which, the neighbors tell you, Dante lived. Although it is a seat of Dante studies, the palace-fortress was the river-guarding stronghold of the Orsini, too busy for dour hell-visioned poets. A much-loved, more recent poet, Giuseppe Gioacchino Belli, who wrote in the course of his seventy-two years, ended in 1863, more than a thousand sonnets in the local dialect, acts as host for this gateway to Traste-vere. There was nothing in Roman life that wasn't caught by his mordant eye and pen: the abuses of the clergy, quar-rels of market women, the pouter-pigeon strut of a lady *per bene*, the zesty comments of her maids, bitter howls about the human condition, lyrics to the freshness of a Roman morning. He sits now in his comfortable paunch and top hat, reciting to his loved, pitied, and hated neigh-bors, on the clearing named for him behind the books on Dante.

The Viale Trastevere, the Main Street of the neighbor-hood, hides one of its relics behind fruit stalls, newspaper stands, and the exigencies of crowds of shoppers, possibly the heirs of the English, Corsican, and Genoese sailors who maintained hospices in the shadow of the church of S. Cri-sogono and the many Jews who settled here among other freed slaves, refugees, and merchants from the East. In spite of neglect—except for a sodality of elderly ladies who dress its columns in red velvet on festa days—the church owns matter for pride. The floor was designed and placed by the Cosmati in the thirteenth century, the apse mosaic, no longer clearly defined, is often attributed to Cavallini of the same time, and the ancient porphyry columns that rise to the triumphal arch are among the largest you will see in Rome. Not far from the church, a slender head pokes out of a wall to remind passers-by that here lived Pinelli, the artist who painted views of his Rome as prolifically as did Belli.

If you've wondered where the horses that pull Rome's

carrozze settle their withered flesh at night, look into the stalls on the Vicolo di S. Rufina and, while you are at it, up to the small Romanesque campanile of its church. A number of dusty little churches may delay you, if you choose, but ahead, westward on the Via della Lungaretta, sits Trastevere's justly renowned showpiece, the broad piazza, the grand fountain barnacled with the determinedly tattered young and the church of S. Maria in Trastevere, the first church in Rome dedicated to Mary. The place that preceded the church was a retired sailors' home, an early ancestor of the numerous hospices and hospitals for the old and infirm in modern Trastevere. A Roman church needs a miracle; the local version was a spurt of oil that leaped up here to trickle into the Tiber, its appearance predicting the coming of Christ in an obscure churchly way. The church was forced to wait two centuries after His birth for its founding stones and was not finished until one hundred years later. Since nothing stays unchanged for sixteen centuries, particularly Roman churches, S. Maria in Trastevere is the expected amalgam of styles. The façade owes its regal beauty to the thirteenth-century mosaics which may have been the work of Cavallini, or more probably his reworking of twelfth-century mosaics that were added to the church contemporaneously with the bell tower. The portico, built five hundred years later, protects the common and always attractive antiques-shop display of sarcophagi, lettering, and carved stones discarded by an older church. The interior is less rewarding, although the *fons olei* under the main altar still bears its sign, and mosaics by Cavallini and a group thought to be earlier still shimmer in the apse.

The back of the church shapes a minuscule piazza with a mellifluous, swollen name, Largo Maria Domenica Fumasoni Biondi, that gathers several styles around the outdoor annex of a restaurant and then sprays into the Vicolo della Paglia, which specializes in English-language films, punctuated by repetitions of *Woodstock*, an all-time favorite with Rome's non-Italian youth. The Vicolo della Frusta retires from the "with it" to take care of garages and repair shops that peer out from cascades of ivy. From the picturesqueness of the Vicolo del Piede (foot), del Cedro and Cipresso (cedar and cypress), turn into the Piazza Renzi, an irritated piazza hung with laundry, cluttered with a few wine-stained tables and chairs. Neither piazza nor chairs, nor inhabitants, nor smell of poverty, wants you; there is no welcome and no seats for *stranieri*, a word that might mean people who live on the next block. The next block, the Vicolo del Cinque, spreads its arms wide open to embrace and carry you to a number of restaurants and "antique" shops and digs deep under wide pannier-like aprons stretched over seat-crates for black-market cigarettes. Much *allegria* of several kinds on Cinque. Turn the page, back to grimness on the Vicolo Bologna, reputedly a prostitutes' street, a very poor one where the family must clear out of the one street-level room that serves as kitchen, dining room, bedroom, and business quarters. The Vicolo del Moro, something of an improvement, ends near the Piazza Trilussa. Take the alleys immediately behind the Piazza Moroni; the street of S. Dorotea, distinguished by an attractive church façade and the ghost of Raphael's Fornarina who may have lived there; the bizarre, slap-dash Piazza di S. Giovanni della Malva. Observe that the women of Trastevere are almost as fat as those of Naples, and for the same reasons, a working-class diet based on bread, pasta, and wine, and the Mediterranean taste for women as bountiful as counterpanes. And look closely at the men outside the bar that hangs on the Porta Settimiana to decide whether they really look like the thieves they are reputed to be. To the inexperienced they resemble thousands of men who chat the day away, or play cards or *morra* in other working-class caffès, but you are told frequently that these men have two addresses maintained on a fairly even alternation, one on the Vicolo Bologna or Moro or Scala and the other Regina Coeli, the prison a short distance northward.

Now choices, as too frequently. Beyond the gate lie two

palazzi, one a dream, the other full of paintings of several degrees of excellence. South, returning from the gate, a good deal more—not extensive though fully and raucously packed—of Trastevere. Leaving the palazzi or having taken them, find the street named for Garibaldi. The Via Garibaldi, a steep street that curves into the Janiculum, is worth the climbing and down again, for a glimpse of the overgrown bosky dell, the Bosco Parrasio, an early eighteenth-century continuation of the "Academy" founded by Christina of Sweden. Like its counterparts in France and England, the society chose Arcadian names ("Parrasio" refers to the sacred grove of Apollo) and seriously endeavored—successfully—to improve the quality of learning and literature. Immediately below, at number 27, a bare yard and building that might be a warehouse designed by Louis Sullivan. The nude brick swells, is flattened back to broad areas cut by niches obviously meant for chiaroscuro effects and not statues; in the niches are shapes that rise to cut additional intricacies of light and dark. It is a puzzling building, lost in time and space, totally undecorated except for tones of sunlight and shadow in sophisticated abstractions. No cross, no saint, marks this as the church of S. Maria dei Sette Dolori (Seven Sorrows), though the prophetic design and the characteristic singularity and isolation identify it as Borromini's. The monastery and the cloister gardens have been converted to a coeducational, nonsectarian pensione, and you are free to admire the gardens, the satin woods of doors and armoires in a long arcade and, disregarding the trompe l'oeil angels and gloppy paintings, enjoy the fluidity of space in arches and vaults.

As you descend into lower Trastevere, watch for a curve of restored medieval houses and stop for a view downward to an Italian version of a Meistersinger set, constructed of irregular roof angles lapping at each other and shattered light in sunstruck windows.

On the Via della Scala and its knots of vicoli, keep an eye open for the many medieval shards Trasteverini inhabit, the scrap-iron bits, cheap trunks, the "sterilized" rags that earn their pasta and uncertain wines. The church of S. Maria della Scala protects itself from its parishioners by a tall gate that encloses façade and stairs, afraid of damage to or theft of its glittering stalactites of chandelier. The square, like its immediate neighbors, is indigenous, poverty-stricken, maimed, its tones and textures made for painting, not living. The piazza is more authentically Old Trastevere than the streets to the south, but the invasion is coming; an art gallery predicts transformations, slowly, stubbornly resisted, but, as long as foreign and Milanese money seeps into Trastevere, inevitable.

The old monks' pharmacy next to the church is in several ways threatened; the Benedictine monks cannot act as certified pharmacists; their role is window dressing and a timid, impotent watchfulness, a hand-wringing worry about their imminently collapsible future. The street-level pharmacy seems new as of the turn of the century, stained glass in its ceiling, small paintings of medicinal plants in the arches and pale plasterwork ornaments shaped of retorts and beakers. Gentle decorative art is overshadowed by a conspicuous, doomsday sign that proffers analyses of blood, urine, feces, sputum. An elderly sad-faced Benedictine with not much else to do conducts one up to the original pharmacy of the seventeenth century. While the visitor covets the beguiling vases and vials locked in a glass cabinet, examines an old hand-lettered album of dried medicinal plants (the book is kept open at a sprig that eases parturition), the flowers painted on the ceiling, and the stern portrait of the founding father, the old monk drones through his litany of complaints and fears: "Look at that broken window. Our Communist neighbors threw stones at it one night, and there is no money to repair it, and anyhow, they will break it again. We have lost the respect and faith of the neighborhood. Boys now don't become monks, and monks don't study pharmacy. Most of the monastery grounds have been taken by the government and they make us pay rent and maybe they will confiscate this place altogether." A back room layered with dust holds handsomely lettered spice boxes and piles of ancient books which might be invaluable if they weren't eaten by worms and disuse. "I'd like to sell the books, the boxes, and the vases before the government takes them. Are you interested, maybe, in old pharmacology books? Do you know anyone who might want to buy them? Maybe the little bottles? They're very old and pretty."

The obvious answer is that he call in antiquarians. He must know they exist, and where, but the *brutta figura* of defeat he and his confraternity will make repels him, and so he prays, hoping for a miracle while the ceiling broadens its cracked gulches and pours dusty flakes over vials, books, counters, cabinets, and fallen pride.

The piazza of S. Cosimato is Trastevere's equivalent to the Campo dei Fiori market, not quite as large or laden with so eventful a history, though equally explosive and multi-colored. Where the market trails off to the south the attractive façade of the church of S. Cosimato, attached to a pair of cloisters, one Romanesque, the other of the early Renaissance, and both shedding their charms, flowers, and cool fountain droplets on the old people for whom they are now a hospice.

Alert for ghosts of medievalism, as narrow, hooded houses frilled with precarious flights of outdoor stairs (the streets of Montefiore, Luce, Lungaretta, for instance), amble which-ever irregular path suits you across the Viale Trastevere and, skirting low motorbikes driven by child demons, con-versational groups as firmly planted as oaks, the embattled drunk fighting the inimical air with his stick, make your way to the Piazza in Piscinula, arranged by that capable designer, time, to become a significant and winning collection of Trasteveriana. Ahead, the Roman bridge—in considerable part still Roman, though it required help in later years—that links with the Isola Tiberina and takes a second short, Roman leap into the ghetto. On the river's edge, the twin

openings and winsome loggie of the house that once belonged to the Mattei family. Across from that a decrepit
aristocratic palazzo, a lantern-hung outdoor restaurant
aswarm with tourists, a sprawl of bar that drinks and talks
all night, and the retiring churchlet of S. Benedetto, whose
timid Romanesque campanile is said to hold the oldest
working church bell in Rome. The name of the piazza?
"Piscinula" probably refers to a pond on lands owned by
the Anici, for whom a nondescript street a short distance
back of the river is named. Back of the street that shares
the piazza's name and across Salumi, an almost untouched
relic of medievalism, the Vicolo dell'Atleta, a slot on two
levels and a recently restored thirteenth-century house
which appears in some annals as a synagogue—a reasonable supposition for a good house in an area that held,
among its other polyglots, large numbers of Jews. The
statement is often improved by appointing Anacletus II,
the Jewish antipope, builder of the synagogue. Unfortunately
the neat conjunction of semifacts will not work; Anacletus
II died in the twelfth century. The synagogue street owed
its unsuitable name to the marble copy of a Greek athlete,
now in the Vatican collection, found under its uneven
stones.

On a street that serves as parking lot for the automobiles
of customers of a discount house and the gusty restaurants
which wrap tourists in becks and wreaths and smiles,
stands the church of S. Cecilia, the patron saint of music.
  S. Cecilia's church is rich in miracles, numbering three.
She was a daughter of a wealthy Roman family of the
third century and a Christian who lived a white marriage
with the heathen Valerian. As a result of either desperation
or conviction, he and his brothers were converted and soon
beheaded for their refusal to participate in pagan rites.
Cecilia was imprisoned in the bath chambers of her house

to suffocate of steam, a common form of execution in
Roman times. Cool showers came through miraculously to
allay the heat, and it was necessary for the axman to cut
her head off. Though he hacked vigorously he didn't succeed, and for three days, lying in her own blood, she
preached so beautifully and convincingly that she made
hundreds of converts. After offering her house as a church
to the pope, she blissfully died.

Miracle two: Pope Pascal I of the ninth century, a builder
of three distinguished early basilicas (the others are S. Prassede and S. Maria in Domnica) and much occupied with
finding the relics of the saint to put in her church, had a
vision in his sleep. S. Cecilia revealed to him that she, her
husband, and friends and relatives were lying in the catacombs of S. Callisto and designated the exact spot. There
the Pope found them and had them brought to the church.

Miracle number three: When the tomb was opened in the
late sixteenth century S. Cecilia had not deteriorated at all
but lay as if in sleep ("upon the right side like a virgin in
her bed, with her knees drawn modestly together"), only her
axed neck turned at an abnormal angle. Stefano Maderno
was called in to make a marble copy of the body, and it
lies today under the altar, enclosed in marbles, bronzes, and
silver too heavy for the exquisite, frail figure. It might have
been more fitting and aesthetic to leave her unadorned
under the Gothic grace of the Arnolfo di Cambio tabernacle.

Behind an enormous antique marble vase in the orderly
ample courtyard, the church presents the usual stimulating
mixtures of rebuilt basilicas. Baroque volutes and finials
and a large ecclesiastical shield of the eighteenth century
stand over a portico of the twelfth century, adorned with
strips of mosaic, supported by antique marbles, and accompanied by a bell tower of the same period. A section of wall
on your left, as you enter, was placed there in the sixteenth
century; at the right, a wall of the 1200's; behind you a
stretch of twentieth-century socks on a clothesline. Considerably distorted, the church deserves patience and explor-

ing for its several strata of darkened or concealed treasures.
The apse, for instance, retains the mosaics ordered by Pascal I in the ninth century. The Pope, from the East, probably
used Greek monk-artisan-refugees (Saracens, Eastern emperors, and ecclesiasts were making life difficult for those
who were of dissident schisms), and the Byzantine shows
conspicuously in the apse mosaic. Christ is imperial and has
the long staring icon eye. His blessing gesture of third finger
meeting thumb (said to be a shaping of the first letter of
his name) is particularly a sign of the East. You will notice
that the halo worn by the pope who is presenting his
church is a blue square which signifies that he was alive
when the mosaic was placed. Here, too, the symbols you
may have seen in many early mosaics: the tree that signifies eternal life; the phoenix, a symbol of immortality borrowed from the Romans; and the inexhaustibly beguiling
flocks of sheep emerging from their minute cities, those
from Jerusalem the converted Jews led by St. Peter, those
of Bethlehem the non-Jews converted and led by St. Paul.

Wandering among the tombs of several centuries, under
areas that were, in the original basilica, the matroneum
(women's gallery), you should find a corridor to the right
that takes you to paintings by Guido Reni of Cecilia and
Valerian and, in a corner behind a metal plate and grille,
the tubes that conducted the murdering steam. Their resemblance to organ pipes may be the saint's link to music;
there seems to be no other unless it was her mellifluous,
nonstop preaching. The crypt, a place of nineteenth-century
mosaics that try for the Byzantine and layered tombs, opens
to a maze of rooms of the prosperous Cecilian family and
a few of its original fittings: a pagan figure, a shrine for
Minerva, a broken vase, shadows of mosaic floor, and
plain floors in smaller rooms which may have been storage
bins and slave quarters.

A sequestered treasure in the nunnery attached to the
church is visible only on Tuesdays and Thursdays from
10 to 11 and Sundays from 11 to 12. Conducted by one nun

while the others have fled, you are taken to the marred and greatly imposing *Last Judgment* and *Annunciation* of the late thirteenth or early fourteenth century by Pietro Cavallini. Once in places of honor in the basilica, they had been covered in rebuilding and disfigured by a floor that hides the lower sections of the frescoes. Noble and hieratic, the *Last Judgment* is an extraordinary work, especially for a city very much behind Tuscany, with its Duccio and Giotto, in the early development of painting. It merits arranging your Trastevere hours to accord with those of the cloistered nuns.

North of the church dedicated to Cecilia one comes to the street where the Genoese of the community built their church, S. Giovanni dei Genovesi. Its interest rests entirely in a ravishing cloister of the fifteenth century, gathered around a central fountain vaulted by a leafy, flowered arch, a beguiling disorder of garden and citrus trees held in rows of slender octagonal columns, typical of their time and symbolic of the Week of Creation—six days for earth, waters, animals, and man and the seventh day for resting.

Isolated at the end of the silent Via dei Genovesi (you may have sensed by this time the indigenous Trastevere alternation of gaunt, empty, taciturn streets with the overcrowded ebullient) there is the shy, homely, little S. Maria in Cappella, whose modesty evokes a firm image of a poor parish church of the eleventh century. The church is not generally open, but one of the women in charge of the adjoining old people's home is usually pleased to open it to visitors for a small contribution, to help keep the pensioners—among whom there must be a number of redoubtable gardeners, to judge from the height of the corn and the wilderness of tomato plants hiding behind the street wall.

An interminable stretch of building that resembles a prison absorbs the banks of the river below the almshouse and garden. Once a hostel and crafts school for poor boys, much later a refugee center, it is now as completely unemployed as the once crowded port that bustled below its windows. The church of S. Francesco a Ripa, at the end of the street that runs sharply toward the piazza of S. Maria in Trastevere, has its miraculous touchstone, the rock on which St. Francis of Assisi laid his cloak, a portrait of the saint that imitates a famous painting by Margaritone d'Arezzo, and a relation of St. Teresa by Bernini. The Blessed Ludovica Albertoni is not pierced by religious ecstasy; she is dying of fever. No Eros smiles at Ludovica; her audience is merely sympathetic putti, her face is sweeter and gentler than St. Teresa's and yet the distorted thrust of the head, the hand clutching a breast, the breathless mouth, and the agitated drapery are obvious repetition. Howard Hibbard tells us that one of Bernini's brothers was involved in a conspicuous scandal, and in order to hush it up, the sculptor carved the Blessed Ludovica at no charge. How a tomb figure hushes up a scandal can be understood only by an Italian and particularly a Roman of the seventeenth century. However, Bernini must have been in rather a rush and returned to one of his most brilliant works for, shall we say, inspiration.

Trastevere is not a place to leave on a religious note in spite of its many and splendid churches. Walk back along the Via di S. Francesco a Ripa, have a pizza at Ivo's, or a *porchetta* sandwich on the viale and a gelato on the great S. Maria square, while you watch the bambini watching the hippies, and be comforted when the rest of the city pours out to the beaches on Sundays, leaving its streets tongueless and bloodless, to know that Trastevere stays at home, arms folded, guarding its shambles, drinking its wine, rumbling its big-voiced greetings and arguments.

The name Farnesina, "little Farnese" (north of the Porta Settimiana), merely indicates the fact that the Farnese owned the villa for a while, long before it passed through several hands to become the seat of a learned society and

a fine collection of engravings, taken out of hiding for public exhibitions from time to time. The Farnese acquired
the airy, happy small palace from the heirs of Agostino
Chigi, whose rise from a degree above rags to untold riches
is an oft-told Renaissance tale that parallels the biographies
of the Fricks, Morgans, and Onassises: ownership of mines,
of an immense network of shipping, of banks in Italy that
controlled finance all over Europe, and the support of and
influence on the papacy. As symptomatic of Chigi's wealth
is the popular story, documented by a sixteenth-century
historian, of a feast given in honor of his friend Pope Leo
X, the Florentine Medici who bore none of his city's grudges
against his Sienese host. The banquet was held in a cool
loggia on the banks of the Tiber and served in plates and
beakers of gold which, when emptied, were tossed into the
river as things of little worth, one of history's most memorable gestures of *bella figura* and conspicuous consumption,
worthy of a Nero. But since that is hardly the way shrewd
rich men stay rich, Agostino had a net and men to tend it
placed in the river to recover the gold. In spite of precautions, gold plates and flatware disappeared from time to
time, and not necessarily into the murky depths of the
river. But Chigi was too sensitive a host and debonair a
Maecenas to question anyone or even mention the loss.

After the manipulations of power and commerce, Agostino loved best the arts and learning and to entertain
scholars and artists, witty, beautiful, cultivated hetaerae,
learned men and distinguished cardinals. As the proper
setting for wit, talent, learning and beauty, he had his com-
paesano, Baldassarre Peruzzi, design a small, radiant house
with an elegant loggia and then called in Raphael and his
assistants, del Piombo and the brilliant, eccentric Sodoma,
to help decorate it. Sobered as it has been by the presence
of learning and carefully kept archives, it is still a hymn to
Renaissance gaiety free from tormented saints, sorrowing
Virgins, and apocalyptic threats. Classical mythology, with
special emphasis on love among the gods, swings in aban-

doned joyousness from loggia to hall, from room to room.

The majestically proportioned loggia side, now unfortunately glassed in, thus losing the original scheme which welcomed visitors from the outdoor gardens directly into the painted gardens of Olympic love, uses marble for its floor inlays and for the frames of its doors. Gaps in unfinished work provided entertainment for later decorators who invented columns, doors, and niches in cheeky trompe l'oeil. Across the ceiling, down the wall, in imitation of tapestries and as direct painting, interlaced with bands of fruits and vegetables too hard in color and literal in shape to let the festoons sing as festoons should, fly Cupid and Psyche on their wedding day, Venus ascending in her shell for a conversation with Jove, the gods gossiping about the marriage, and so, buoyantly, on. They carry with them their accustomed accouterments of winged putti bearing pipes of Pan, arrows, and shields, all seriously occupied and very cute. A large baby Mercury flies off one wall, quite startled to find himself airborne. Goddesses and graces have opulent, shining bodies like baroque pearls, daughters of Michelangelo out of Botticelli or vice versa, and although the painting is generally attributed to Raphael, he did little of it, torn between work in the Vatican, the well-known exigencies of his love life, and the clamor of too many commissions.

An adjoining room features strong bands of plasterwork frieze concerned with other aspects of mythology by Peruzzi and soon the renowned Raphael *Galatea*, a poised, lovely creature riding her shell pulled by dolphins and surrounded by amorini playfully threatening her with arrows. Here, too, Raphael probably left a more complex project unfinished, since the rest of the room seems improvised and disconnected from the mural: the ceiling of sharp, vigorous constellation figures by Peruzzi; scenes from Ovid's *Metamorphoses* by del Piombo; a monumental chiaroscuro head by the same painter, sufficiently accomplished to have been mistaken at one time for a work of Michelangelo.

Peruzzi again shows his manifold skills in an upper room

whose walls are covered with trompe l'oeil marble balconies that frame views of his Rome, delightful scenes that record a city of towers and arches, green hills, and valleys of medieval huddling. And then we approach Sodoma ("the Sodomite"), a collector of exotic animals, lissome boys, and extravagant costumes whose work was as uneven as his temperament. His *Marriage of Roxanna and Alexander* may appear too thickly populated, too restless at first glance. It should be taken passage by passage to enjoy the virtuosity inherent in the churning mass of putti, the alluring faces of the couple and their attendants, the caressing brush strokes that form the full rump of a white horse and the cheek of a black slave, a massive kneeling figure reminiscent of Masaccio, the deep perspectives into a classical city of a distant landscape and, returning, the consummate handling of veils, feet, folds, and the subtle luster of skin.

The garden is of the same moderate size as the house, providing a short stroll among clipped hedges and flowering shrubs under trees that also shelter a fountain pool sprinkled with red buds of goldfish heads rising for their usual astonished look at the world and a bubble of air.

The gardens would undoubtedly have been more imposing if the Farnese had completed their scheme, represented by one extant arch on the Via Giulia, to bridge the Tiber between their palaces. The park was probably larger and more varied in Agostino Chigi's day when leaves dappled marble statuary, and one rather regrets that it wasn't he and his artist friends who discovered the treasures of antiquity that lay under the roots of his trees. Three and a half centuries after his death the city opened, in the course of remodeling the river embankment, an imperial palace uncertainly identified as belonging either to Cleopatra or to Geta, the brother whom Caracalla murdered; its frescoes and fragile plasterwork, as well as the marbles found in a tomb nearby, are now in the museum of the Baths of Diocletian. It seems unjust that the first eyes to look on these long-buried, choice objects should have been those of

a dredger or digger rather than the eyes of Raphael,
Peruzzi, Sodoma, Michelangelo, and the connoisseur Chigi.

NOTE: Open only mornings; closed Sundays and August.

Across the street from the Farnesina is the collection of the
Palazzo Corsini, known also as the Galleria Nazionale
d'Arte Antica, a title it shares with the Palazzo Barberini.
Before entering 10 Via della Lungara, look down the street
named for the Corsini. Dead center, a huge cloud of dark
leaves embracing waxy magnolias, and on the right side of
the street a procession of scooped iron barriers held at
frequent intervals by a long row of rococo pillars, badly
treated by time and their own frangible material. The
gnawed pillars walk toward a broad mat of green that rises
to the Janiculum; this is the Botanical Gardens to which
access is a now-and-then thing, rarely now.

The dreaming palace, a prop for *Last Year in Marienbad*,
housed lively visitors and events in its time. The present
building, of the early eighteenth century, was the French
Embassy with Joseph Bonaparte as ambassador in 1797.
His future brother-in-law, affianced to the showy Pauline,
was shot in a local skirmish between the French and the
Italians, an event that provoked the entry of French forces.
Less bloody but no less interesting were the visitors in an
earlier palace. The annals include the presence of the beautiful, talented Catherine Sforza (married to a Riario, the
founding family), whose eventful life included battle and
defeat by the forces of Cesare Borgia. He brought her back
to Rome in chains that, suitable to her valor, beauty, and
station, were made of gold. Michelangelo stayed awhile
trying to interest the resident cardinal in art projects with
no known success, and in the seventeenth century came the
incredible Christina of Sweden, who died in the palace in
1689. Here she busied herself in the arts and sciences, estab-

lishing her academy, subsidizing experiments in the sciences —including dabbling in alchemy, collecting *objets d'art*, manuscripts, and famous men, and giving no little trouble to the Church with her curiosity, zest, and a lack of queenly, pious decorum which constantly embarrassed and worried the Vatican. Her zeal for learning and the arts leaves vestiges as the scholarly library in the palazzo, related to the Accademia Nazionale dei Lincei across the road, and the presence of paintings, none of them her property, however.

The present collection is that of the Corsini, who had the palace rebuilt (and, in the process, found a heap of dead who had fallen or been pushed through a trapdoor), and a number from the Torlonia collection. The galleries concentrate on Italian works of the seventeenth and eighteenth centuries and some of their Flemish contemporaries in an undeviating palazzo painting menu: Holy Family singly, together, with and without saints, at least one St. Jerome, several other paintable saints, a couple of dramatic Old Testament characters at the apogee of their careers, a number of portraits and landscapes, and always bouncy satyrs and languid Venuses. Why spend the time in this palazzo gallery, or any other for that matter? The answer is simple: for the person who enjoys paintings, there is always a rewarding surprise that abandons the clichés. The first sala, for instance, is absorbed in "classical" landscapes which place the Teatro di Marcello next door to the Pantheon or linger lovingly in a pale romantic light on one desolate temple near the Pyramid of Cestus, where soldiers approach a persuasive St. Paul, the sort of painting that economically combines the romanticism of ruins with holiness. Among these Italian paintings, however, your eye will be caught by light, unmuddied views of his Rome by the seventeenth-century Dutchman Gaspare van Wittel (Italianized as Vanvitelli), one of several northern painters whose training in clean lines and spare color frequently left the best portraits of the city.

Sala II continues to wander among Dutch paintings of

mediocre quality as genre pieces, big bumpy melons and flickers of light caught by beakers and wine glasses, big dogs surrounding a boar, the boar threatening the big dogs, all the high-light virtuosities and displays of dog anatomy surrounding a straightforward portrait of a young man by Paul Moreelse. Among the scenes of battles and carousing on the canals, and the hungry canvases that are Adorations of sausage, fruit, vegetables, wine, coffee, lobsters, and fish, try to find an appealing winter scene by Lucas Van Uden and a keenly observed study of a zooful of contented animals, an *Earthly Paradise* whose Adam and Eve are faint shadows back of a brilliant red cockatoo.

The gallery makes a turn at this point (Sala III) to show a Teniers inn scene, more brooding ruins, two small, highly enameled paintings by Jacques Callot, several portraits by Sustermans, one of them a royal petulant child, already frighteningly secure in her power. Rubens shows a Madonna and Child as a peasant woman leaning over her baby, the milk spurting from the abundant breast and, of an earlier time, a St. Sebastian who, for a grateful change, is not his usual, poised, pincushioned Renaissance image, but a young man who was wounded and is suffering. A winter scene of thin icy white and pale blue, relieved by spots of colors on wagons and riders, is the work of Jan Brueghel the Younger. The place of honor, an easel of its own and the end of the gallery, is given to a Murillo *Madonna and Child*, interesting to compare with an unsentimental, truly tender *Rest in Egypt* by Van Dyck.

There is a portrait of Bernini in Sala IV and three works by the fascinating Magnasco of the seventeenth and eighteenth centuries. One, in a palette reduced to greenish browns, is of three hermits in a cave; the other two are fantasies of intense highlights on weird figures in ruined landscapes. A frenzied faun whips the air and earth with his hooves and tail; a chained figure lies among a Walpurgisnacht of demons—or are they satyrs?—preparing to pounce.

Air and candid light return with Tiepolo (Sala V), whose

fat, lazy faun plays patiently with a winged baby satyr. Judith, who runs close to St. Jerome as a favored subject, is a cool girl indifferent to the head she has just lopped off, which is almost entirely lost in the "scuro" of the careful chiaroscuro. The rule reads, for that painting era, that ladies who chop off gentlemen's heads must have no sense of guilt and an easy tolerance for runnels of blood—or perhaps, like Lady Macbeth, they reacted slowly. Guido Reni's *Salome,* for instance, serves forth John the Baptist's head with the aplomb of a good cook offering a choice creation. Reni's *Beatrice Cenci* moved him—and us—considerably more. The painter might possibly have seen her; she was beheaded in 1599 when he was twenty-four, and although his work in Rome dates from a later time, he may have been in the city and near the Ponte S. Angelo when she met her death. (There exists a painting that shows Beatrice in prison, in the company of a friar and Reni, who is sketching her face, almost surely an apocryphal event.) She is supremely beautiful. The white cloak and headcloth from which a few wisps of light hair escape set off a young sorrowing virginal face whose innocence and suffering one must believe. It is inescapably the face to launch legends of trusting youth maltreated and wronged, the pure white of virtue tormented by the black of evil. Shelley, seduced by her legend and face, describes her at loving length, lingering on each feature and its spirit, summing up with, "In the whole mien there is a simplicity and dignity which, united with her exquisite loveliness and deep sorrow is inexpressibly pathetic."

The room in which Queen Christina died (VII) bears a plaque that spells out her credo: "I was born free, I lived free and shall die free." In the same room, among large canvases dipped in syrup, the superb young *John the Baptist* with a rude, warm peasant face painted by Caravaggio; by the same painter, the masterly *Narcissus* and an earthy affectionate *Mother and Child,* not certainly by Caravaggio but clearly in his style. And to turn to another master, a bust of Pope Alexander VII by Bernini, not one of his most spectacular achievements, Bernini nevertheless.

Among the ensuing bright colors and exaggerations of form, an ascetic face by Cavallucci, a few adroit genre pieces, a good male portrait by Luca Giordano and, by the same painter, an animated *Christ Among the Doctors.* Salvatore Rosa's profile portrait of his wife, a face of fire and earth, needs no pointing out; it will call to you with its power. And so will the portraits of the seventeenth-century Sicilian Pietro Novelli.

By way of grotesque games of perspective perpetrated by French painters on several faces that seem to have been flattened paper-thin and wrapped around distortion-glass bottles, you will reach hymns in praise of food as only the Neapolitans could do it. Odes to sharks, oysters, inkfish, lobsters, a skate dripping entrails, conches—everything that shines of scales and fins and carapaces; sonnets of paint laud exhibitionistic pomegranates and grapes and figs of ruby and jade.

NOTE: Slowly, the gallery is acquiring new material, sometimes—as in the case of Reni's *Beatrice* and Caravaggio's *Narcissus*—moved back from the companion gallery in the Palazzo Barberini or, like the Bernini bust, simply marked "new acquisition," although one should like to know where it was acquired, from what heretofore sealed palace. Nothing to do with painting at all: should you be in the gallery at noon, you may feel your eardrums shattered by a cannon blast. Don't be alarmed. It is neither the Communist nor the Fascist revolution, simply Rome's anachronistic announcement of midday, a job performed by an old man and an older cannon surrounded by the entranced young on the crest of the Janiculum.

The time to visit the gallery is before 1 P.M., never on Tuesdays.

.   .   .

The Via della Lungara, in spite of a beckoning court fountain or two, takes on the bleakness of unwanted churches
and blank walls. A ray of light breaks through on the Via
S. Francesco di Sales as a row of small bright houses and
disappears again in the long, sulphur-yellow walls of Regina
Coeli (the Queen of Heaven) prison. The Institute of Divine
Love, behind a dignified fence, adds another touch of ironic
holiness to the formidable prison-fortress and then points
you down the stairs into the Via delle Mantellate, once the
women's wing of the prison and now studio and gallery
center of high, broad spaces and patches of garden intelligently, often luxuriously, planned.

From the doorway of one studio or other, pity the bored,
sun-struck guards who make the rounds of the prison roof,
and if it is Monday, the women carrying canisters and
baskets of food and fresh linens for their men. The place
is not for lingering, no more than is any prison block, but
take a moment at the embankment to look back at the play
of angles and shadows on the prison walls. Beyond? The
embankment grows taller and taller, providing a strip of
roller coaster for gleeful motorcycles. At the end of the
run, Borgo S. Spirito, the Vatican, the Castel S. Angelo,
or closer by, the bridge that runs from the Piazza della
Rovere into the bulge of the old city. Or, back into the
unprivate life of Trastevere and its companion island.

The acquiescent Tiber thrashes and rumbles protest as the
point of the Isola Tiberina cuts into the smoky waters
below the Ponte Cestio, the bridge that ties the island to
Trastevere. From the Lungotevere Anguillara, one looks
down at the sudden anger and at the bars that hold pre-
Christian, late-Empire, and modern bridge stone together;
southward to the embellishments and broken arches of the

Ponte Rotto and the sewage dashing out of the Cloaca Maxima; above, the rise of the Aventine. Directly ahead, from the bridge, a large wedge of green that shades the hospital, for centuries and at present controlled by a medical confraternity. In the center of the island, the diminished tower from which the Pierleoni surveyed their segment of river and the approach to Trastevere and, next to it, a refurbished medieval structure that from time to time houses English nobility and, steadily, the aged sick of the ghetto, east of the island.

The church of S. Bartolomeo should not keep you long with its conventional seventeenth-century extravagances except for one chapel ceiling painted in deep, rich colors, a Romanesque font or well on the steps that lead to the altar, and a broad, shallow basin in which St. Bartholomew's body was transported from Benevento in the south to Rome. The rest may be worthy, but one cannot say; the church, whose business is not thriving, keeps its art in permanent dusk.

In the atrium there is a marker that indicates a frightening rise of the river in 1937, and near the atrium, theoretically, there should be an entrance to the medieval church and access to the walk around the island. It is closed, and one descends to the river's edge on a stairway near the hospital to take one of the most peaceable passeggiatas in Rome—no traffic, a polite nod from silent fishermen, a shy glance from a pair of lovers, a greeting from another solitary walker, and the turbulence of dropped waters at the far end of the hospital. The heavy foliage of the court at the back of the hospital half-reveals—one is never quite sure—the form and color of a piece of worked marble, the hint of an ancient column.

The only uncomfortable moment of the walk is a narrowing under a support of the bridge whose shoe of damp garbage makes slippery footing, and no railing to hold. In the clear, again, the freedom to examine the irregularities of slapped-together medieval remains that house the ghetto infirm. From this short distance the griffons on the Ponte Rotto threaten to fly off their impotent bridge to sit on the Romanesque arches of a former S. Bartolomeo's or join the Roman stone below the church. These layers of substructure wrinkle and take shape as the hair, neck, and shoulder of a god and, near the other shoulder, a snake coiled on a stick. A rough, unmistakable bull's head makes a third figure.

There seems to be no explanation for the bull, which may have been, like the dark, mottled marble column at the entrance to the hospital, a piece of temple decoration. The snake on the baton and his curly-haired master tie up satisfactorily the presence of modern hospital grown of old roots, the Jewish hospice, the discovery, during the building of the adjoining embankment, of terra-cotta ex-votos of parts of bodies and life-sized clay torsos cut to show vital organs, with the island's legend. On the island which grew, according to tradition, from grain of the Tarquins, thrown into the river when they were routed, a temple to Aesculapius was erected. The site was chosen by the snake of the god who sped before the ship which carried Aesculapius' image (therefore, the boat shape of the island) to curl up where the church is now. Later the physician-martyrs Cosma and Damiano cured and preached among the temples, probably attending sick slaves abandoned on the island. There was a late Roman period when the island held prisons, but the almost continuous uses of the area remained within the province of Aesculapius.

A debatable appendage to the medical entity lies below a chapel under the old people's home. Guided by a knowledgeable friend of the friend, one rouses a plump friar—as merry-eyed and full-bellied as an old pub sign—who emerges from his chirping garden full of canary cages and crosses the piazza to find that he cannot work the three keys in the three locks on the door. Someone runs for the sacristan, who arrives grumbling and sweaty, shouting at the friar, "I have no time for your nonsense. What do you want now?" The friar beams and obliquely apologizes for the sacristan by telling what a real tough he was before he came to the friars. At the back of the chapel, finally opened, a stairway that goes down to a glass door with a red glass cross as center. No key for that lock. Everyone looks into chest drawers in the chapel, and another friar is sent for. He, too, is busy and doesn't know anything about any keys. One of the visitors notices a bunch of keys hanging from a chest. The largest, rustiest key works, and the open door frames a long bench of skulls and bones in orderly arrangements and, around a corner, niches that contain one skull and two crossbones each. The cellar smells of murky river, mold, airlessness, and the cobwebs hang like low tree traps. The dankness produces a certain unease, but not the bones and skulls, too long dead to matter. The macabre rises from a chilling wigless figure lying in a corner, a discarded saint whose red robe has faded to long blotches like bloodstains, and from a dead-white mourning figure, lifted from a cemetery monument, who is bent in a farewell kiss with a skull.

The friars say that in this building, where once missionary priests were taught Oriental languages, there was until recent years a confraternity that made a vocation of burying suicides and the corpses of the unknown and unclaimed in fields and woods. The gossip, persistent and loud, is that their skulls and bones are discreetly sold out of the ossuary for medical study. The friars deny any knowledge of such trade in their precincts. Whether true or not, the story circles back to Aesculapius, his staff and snake.

The Ponte Fabricio, commonly called Quattro Capi because of the four-headed herms that stand on it, is older by a few years than its partner and thus the oldest bridge in Rome. A step to the right off the bridge brings a church façade painted with a big crucifixion and, in Latin and Hebrew, an Old Testament lament about "this disobedient people," an introduction and gateway to the ghetto.

Beyond the moaning church, a fresh reconstruction of a medieval palace that serves as a government center for the preservation of antiquities and, according to a marker, the gathering place in October 1943, from which Roman Jews were sent to extermination camps by the Germans. The pillars of Ottavia's portico continue to march down the street of that name, slit by the Via di S. Ambrogio, which begins with a minute, orderly buttons, lace, and edgings shop supervised by the gentle old lady whose natural, limited domain—in any country or language—is this sort of shop. The short street stops at the portal of a church atrium, a hidden box of space that hides, in turn, a waterless grotto fountain and on the steps of the unused church, converted to ramshackle housing, a local citizen making besoms, tying the bunch of twigs together, then thumping them on the church ledge to discard loose bits, as he might have a thousand years ago.

From S. Ambrogio's former church, a view back onto a quintessential symbol of the Middle Ages composed of a tumble of varicolored tiles on meager houses clinging to and supporting each other in a patchwork of varying levels. The street turns to the Piazza Mattei and its joyful fountain, past an isolated triangle of building (Piazza Paganica) crusted with a strip of alley which has seen neither sun nor change for five hundred years, and you are in the oceanic space and roar of the Largo Argentina and *a due passi* from the Pantheon.

Hotels: A Sampling

Rome's tourist season is nonstop throughout the year, and the gay insouciance of "we'll find someplace when we get there" may result in a consumption of dreary time while you might be strolling on the Aventine. If you are planning your trip with the help of a travel agent he will offer hotel choices in several categories and arrange reservations well in advance. The independent traveler should take the same precautions, aware of the fact that hotels in the highest categories are sometimes fully booked for months on end.

The royalty, whose rates (rising, like all other costs) start at about $25 and soar, depending on type of accommodations: the Hassler-Villa Medici, Trinità dei Monti (Spanish Steps); Grand Hotel, Via Vittorio Emanuele Orlando (Central Station); Excelsior on the Via Veneto at 125; Cavalieri Hilton, Via Cadlolo (out of the center, but they maintain a schedule of rides to shopping and sightseeing).

The peerage, the rates a shade lower: Ambasciatori Palace, Via Veneto 70; Eden, Via Ludovisi 49 (Veneto area);

Raphael, Largo di Febo (Piazza Navona); Boston, Via Lombardia 47 (Veneto); Victoria, Via Campania 41 (Veneto); Quirinale, Via Nazionale 7; Mediterraneo, Via Cavour 15; Massimo D'Azeglio, Via Cavour 18. (The latter three in the area between the Colosseum and the railroad station.) De la Ville, Via Sistina near the Hassler. In this category, several that require a few extra minutes of transportation to travelers' goals: Hotel Parioli on Bruno Buozzi; the Fleming on the Piazza Monteleone di Spoleto; the Panama, Via Salaria 336. Back in town, the Forum, Via Tor de' Conti 25 (Colosseum).

Downward on the price scale but not necessarily quality: the Inghilterra, Bocca di Leone 14 (Piazza di Spagna); Albergo Nazionale, Piazza Montecitorio 131 (Corso); Genio, Via Zanardelli 28 (Piazza Navona); the Viminale, Cesare Balbo (opera); Hotel Columbus, Via della Conciliazione (St. Peter's); Victoria, Via Campania 41 (Veneto); President Hotel, Emanuele Filiberto 173 (Station).

Moderate to modest—$5 to $12, roughly: Adriano, Via di Pallacorda 2; Portoghesi, Via dei Portoghesi 1; Hotel Minerva on the Piazza Minerva; Albergo Bologna on the Piazza dei Caprettari; S. Chiara on the Piazza S. Chiara; Albergo del Sole, Piazza della Rotonda. (All the above close to the Pantheon.) Also the Hotel Ivanhoe, Via de' Ciancaleoni 49, in the lost and vivid Suburra; the Condotti and the Albergo Piazza di Spagna, both on Mario dei Fiori; the Homs on della Vite; the Margutta on Via Laurina; the Hotel Carriage on Via della Carrozze may have priced itself out of this group, all near the Piazza di Spagna. Near the Piazza Barberini, the Hotel d'Italia, the Albergo Anglo-Americano, the Albergo Quattro Fontane, on Quattro Fontane, and the Memphis, Via degli Avignonesi 36. On the quiet Aventine, the S. Anselmo, on the Piazza S. Anselmo.

There is an inclination to think that *pensione* means lower prices than *albergo*. Not always, though pensione prices include, as a general rule, breakfast and one major meal. Unless they have changed their style, the top of this category might include the Pensione Villa Borghese, Via

Sgambati 4, Dinesen, Porta Pinciana (both Pincian Gate–
Veneto); La Residenza, Via Emilia 22 (Veneto); Pensione
Maria Adelaide, Via Maria Adelaide 6 (Popolo); Pensione
Trinità dei Monti, Trinità dei Monti (Piazza di Spagna);
Pensione Steiner, Lungotevere Prati 22; Pensione Orsini, Via
V. Orsini 4 (Prati). Prices range from $6 to over $15, the
highest usually in the Veneto area. Somewhat cheaper: the
Pensione Hotel Daria, Via Sicilia 24 (Veneto); Pensione
Erdarelli and Pensione Riviera on Due Macelli; Pensione
Suisse, Via Gregoriana (Piazza di Spagna). Cheaper still:
Pensione Manfredi, Pensione Forte, both on the Via Margutta
(Piazza di Spagna); the Metropolitan, Via del Corso 4
(Popolo). For the flattest pockets: Pensione Sette Dolori,
top of the Via Garibaldi (Trastevere), three meals and no
English for under $4.00 a day. No meals, no English, and
interesting neighbors at the Albergo del Sole and the Al-
bergo della Lunetta on the Piazza del Paradiso (Campo dei
Fiori); the Hotel Fulvio on Frangipane (Colosseum); the
Nettuno on the Via Lavatore (Trevi), several small busy
hotels where the Via Francesco Crispi meets the Via Sistina.

Nuns' orders supervise a number of pensiones. A few serve
full board; others do not. Some insist that you be inside
their locked doors by 10 or 11; others give guests doorkeys
and the right to keep their own hours. The Foyer Unitas,
30 Via dell'Anima (Piazza Navona), serves only breakfast
and a lively program of lectures and socials for about $5 to
$6 per day. It is booked almost solid by the same faithful
clientele that returns year after year. Write well ahead of
arrival time. Others like that attached to S. Stefano Rotondo
and several on the Aventine should be visited and examined
before a commitment is made. Cleanliness sitting close to
godliness is a vision dreamed by the Puritan north, not the
lands lapped by the Mediterranean. For a long-term stay
without the bother of apartment hunting investigate the
Velabro, an apartment hotel with full service in one of the
most gracious situations the city offers, the rise from the
gate of Janus and S. Giorgio in Velabro above the Via del
Teatro di Marcello. Quite—predictably—expensive.

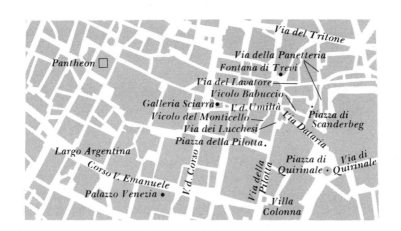

Walk 4

Trevi to Pantheon

The Trevi fountain which grew and grew and grew and might have continued growing were it not for the limiting size of the piazza, already reduced to flat borders that timidly contain a berserk outbaroquing of the Baroque. The first fountain, in the nearby Piazza de' Crociferi, was a simple composition of marble bowl and masks designed by Leon Battista Alberti in the mid-fifteenth century. Urban VIII brought the basin to its present spot in the seventeenth century, but it was not until 1730 that Pope Clement announced a competition for its embellishment. Nicolò Salvi won the contest, but the amassing of arches, niches, seagods, horses galloping toward rocks and into breaking waters that gush and splash and crash, went on for some thirty years until the piazza could stand no more. In Hawthorne's day the piazza was "filled with stalls of vegetable and fruit dealers, chest-nut roasters, cigar-vendors, and other people whose petty and wondering traffic is transacted in the open air. It is likewise thronged with idlers, lounging over the iron railing and with *forestieri* who come hither to see the famous fountains." The loungers are still there, and the stunned visitors, but the fruits and vegetables have moved eastward as a tangy street market, and the old men and boys with buckets and the girls with pitchers balanced on their heads no longer dip into the Trevi water, "in request far and wide, as the most refreshing draught for feverish lips, the pleasantest to mingle with wine, the wholesomest to drink, in its native purity, that can be found anywhere." The feet of coin-searching boys and of young travelers have changed all that, and the old custom of drinking from the fountain to seal a future appointment with the city has perforce become the newer tradition of dropping coins.

The clamor of waters, visitors, ice cream vendors, shops, is silenced in neighboring mute hollows, one of the many dark honeycombs where the city hides from its own extravagant gestures. The shopping street of Lavatore is stilled by the bald mountain that holds the Quirinale palaces. Scale the hill of the Via della Panetteria, up past gross buttress, parked cars, a red tabby with shocking green eyes spread like an odalisque on a pallid gray Fiat near a span of gnawed red wall and black shutters, an amalgam that belongs only to Rome. To complete the Roman blend, an immobilized gate and a tall white tempietto pissoir. The path at the top should, if it hasn't been closed off, drop to the Vicolo and Piazza di Scanderbeg, named for an Albanian hero whose intrepid image rides on the Piazza Albania, on the lower Aventine. A year or two ago the vicolo was an annex of Travestere or Naples, though more peaceful than either place, hoping not to be noticed in its cloaks and blankets of wet wash. Prosperity has bustled in, refitted doors and windows, splashed paint around, and opened a smart gift shop, a sure symptom of greater changes about to happen. Before they do—or it may already be too late by the time these words reach your eye—follow the Vicolo de' Modelli, once the nest of models who postured on the Spanish Steps, now an alley of steamy laundries and shops where cross-legged, humpbacked tailors sit under reluctant light bulbs; the Vicolo Babuccio, the Vicolo del Puttarello, the Vicolo del Monticello, whose yellow walls curve around one car, one old man, toward a yoke of bells, and gather at a medieval hush. The arch at the top of Scanderbeg announces the Via Dataria, a bewildered rise that was until a hundred years ago the sole slope from the Corso and the Via dell' Umiltà to the Quirinal. It is a street of worn palaces left with faint etchings of poised shapeliness in a doorway, a plaster arabesque, and divested by a non-descript wall and set of stairs of its role as fanfare to the display of papal palace above.

Guards as polished as toy soldiers police the government —once papal—palace that entertains such diverse notables as Nixon and Tito. Babies try their collapsible legs on the stairway, girls spread their furbelowed carnival costumes for Babbo's camera to catch against a view of lower Rome, automobiles swing wide and fast through the boundless Quirinal piazza, using the central obelisk as a spina for their chariots. Nevertheless, babies, cars, little girls, pal-aces, monuments are shadowy, sunken, erased in a seductive desolation that might be the work of de Chirico. Or, vice versa: the boundless space flowing from white, white in-different giants, the edgy entrancement, may have designed the work of de Chirico.

The obelisk was brought from the mausoleum of Augus-tus in 1775 and the fountain dragged up from the Forum fifty years later to join the mammoth horses and the colossi, *Castor* and *Pollux,* dug out of the ruins of the local Baths of Constantine and erected on the hill in 1585 by Sixtus V. The palace which stands immediately at the top of the stairs from the Via Dataria was built over a long period, 1574 to 1870, though it was inhabitable and inhabited by popes from the end of the sixteenth century until, in 1870, it became the royal palace and, after World War II, the White House of Italy. Sir Rennell Rodd tells a story of French control of the city. The palace, already sacked by the French, was the prison of Pius VII, who "on his refusal [1809] to renounce the temporal power at the demand of Napoleon, [was] seized by the French General Radet and sent to France. Thereafter for five years Rome became a French city, reluctantly subject to a process of Gallicisation so thorough that the intendent Martial Duru represented it to the imperial government as intolerable that the clocks of the Quirinal should be an hour different in time from those in Paris." Pius IX had trouble, too. When the republic of Rome (1848) placed the palace under siege, "the pontiff disguised as a simple priest escaped in the French Ambassador's carriage by a back door" to make his way to loyal Naples.

The Via dei Lucchesi angles down from Dataria into its irregular piazza whose church which seems pushed back by a rude hand affords—if the church is no longer *in restauro*—sweet chanting by nuns after 4 in the wintertime and after 5 in other seasons. At 32, an unreconstructed nineteenth-century shoplet of glass and dark wood, divided as screens that show medals and printed reproductions of medals in arrangements that are as charmingly unfashionable as the shop itself. The Piazza della Pilotta, named for a game that may have resembled the Spanish pelota (jai alai), is a weighty stage-set, ready for operatic tragedy. Its warm red-gold walls slip under arches of the Via Pilotta at one side, disappear into a narrow street behind the other side of the wings and, in the center, a palazzo equipped with arches, forceful window frames, and ledges.

As one very quickly finds out, if only by scanning an allover map, the city is full of villas surrounded by large parks, a few open to the public, many closed behind indomitable gates and iron spears. The same is true of longwalled palazzi which, one hears, are crammed with orderly or heaped gems of antiquities and painting. A few of them, like the great houses of England, permit their galleries to be viewed at set times in the week.

The gallery of the Villa Colonna follows the pattern: from 9 to 1 on Saturday mornings, the entrance at 17 Via della Pilotta, a blank street whose walls carry posters of musical events and, above, the short bridges that link the gallery with the gardens of the villa.

Although the Colonna, whose might was sung by Petrarch, mark with splendor and blood centuries of Roman history, the gallery does homage principally to two personages comparatively late in the family's endless history. The first is Martin V, the Colonna pope (1417–1431) who established the family palace with the commanding position of a fortress on the Quirinal Hill, where he lived and held papal court out of mistrust of the safety of the Vatican and from the practical habit of living in a high, closed place, protected by one's relatives and their cohorts. The second, who postures on the ceilings of the gallery, was Marc Antonio Colonna, who with Don John of Austria defeated the Turks in the Battle of Lepanto (1571) and, like Trimalchio in the *Satyricon*, covered his rooms with his glory. The cultivated generous lady Vittoria Colonna, who was a close friend to Michelangelo, appears in an insignificant painting among the many family portraits.

Like other costs, the price of admission has been raised, from 500 to 520, and the first immediate discouraging sight is of your seven-thousandth sarcophagus in an anteroom. Pass it by, and in the second small room look out the window to one or two bridges that run to the long rows of hedge surrounding the gardens of the villa.

Before you now lie the marble halls of the seventeenth-century gallery (some of it restored or completely renewed), glowing marbles of several colors in ingenious geometric designs, flashing Venetian chandeliers, extravagantly framed Venetian mirrors painted with amoretti peeping through frames of flowers, marble tabletops sustained by convolutions of gilt painted on cannons, sea-goddesses, shells, anything that can thicken intricacy.

The ceiling of the first salon leaves a surprising amount of sky for its space, isolating the Virgin who waits to be presented to Marc Antonio Colonna, not by the customary saint but by a nude Hercules. At the sides, St. Peter in chains, trumpet-playing angels, recording angels side by jowl with the god Tiber, and Indians complete with bows and arrows; bursting out of the corner, the Colonna emblems triumphant over a wrecked heap of war machines crushing terrified Turks. Standing free in the center of the room, a red marble column (the "colonna" of the family name) spiraled as triumphal columns must be, with bellicose figures marching or mourning and topped by a family patroness, Pallas Athena.

Some of the paintings are placed too high to see properly, others are courtly family portraits, one large and extremely serious attributed to Van Dyck (51), another by Carracci (57), and still another by Lotto (64). The rest are a mixed bag of bouncy, warmly colored classical romps like the juicy Angiolo Bronzino (56) composition of a satyr with his tongue poking licentiously out of his sensuous mouth, a little callipygian Cupid, Venus just about covered, teasing Cupid by holding his bow away from him. She is a succession of pink and white rotundities except in strategic places. Her arms are quite muscular and the position of her breasts anatomically uncertain, implying a common Renaissance practice of using boys—as the Elizabethan theater did—for women, making adjustments where absolutely necessary. Tintoretto returns us to quiet holiness (59) in a group of four masterfully painted heads in prayer as they observe the faint golden angel's heads that surround the illumined dove of the Holy Spirit.

On the stairs leading down the grand sala, a reminder of the time when the French attacked and laid siege to the city in 1849. One of their cannonballs landed on the steps and chopped a large chunk out of the marble, and there they still sit, hole and cannonball. The ceiling of the next sala concerns itself with several panels that show the Lepanto hero entering, full-panoplied, a southern gate of Rome for the last such triumphal welcome in Rome and the placing of a statue of the conqueror, as in Roman times, on the Campidoglio. The center is an explosion of smoke, crosses, ships, dashing seas in a riot of movement that is the battle itself. Under such ceilings and in such shine—this is the most magnificent of the salons—it is sometimes difficult to look at paintings, but you might make the effort and enjoy the subdued lusters of a painting said to be by Jacopo Bassano (75); a dignified, muted double portrait by Jacopo Tintoretto (79); a stylish portrait of a Colonna whose hat plumes almost tickle the nose of his protecting angel, maybe or not by Van Dyck but certainly in his style (84). Several family portraits, in the ermines, brocades, and jewels suited to kingly wealth and power, will lead you to a convincing, ascetic, muscular St. Jerome as painted by Ribera (102), and (104) a display of the remarkable skills of the young Rubens in a painting of the *Assumption of the Virgin.*

Terrified Turks, harem odalisques, a victorious Venetian lion, ships, waves, banners, masts, and the irresistible perspective bravura of painting a high balcony for spectators of the Battle of Lepanto busy the next ceiling. Below, the extraordinary jewel chests, one worked in ebony and ivory that reproduces, among other paintings, the *Last Judgment* of Michelangelo as a painstaking ivory miniature, and the other of inlaid semiprecious stones, both tall caskets held by exotic Moors or Indians, the indispensable caryatids of the High Baroque. The paintings are largely landscapes and interesting mainly for their range of styles, including the unmistakable manner of Canaletto in one of his innumerable Venetian snapshots.

The next small sala honors the churchly member of the family with reduced brilliance and noise, as suits the apotheosis of Pope Martin V. The paintings he floats above include a dramatic Mola work in Mannerist *verismo* of Cain fleeing the dead Abel (142), two distinguished portraits by Tintoretto (143 and 144), another by Titian

(156), a genre piece, *The Eater of Beans* (164), which might have been painted by Franz Hals, so light and dashing is its style. For even greater dash, observe the lightning-like highlights in the silks of a portrait by Veronese (170).

The Sala of the Throne was the room common to important palaces where the pope was received. The ancient cut-velvet chairs, quite ample and comfortably designed for elderly bodies (the chair alone and facing the wall was reserved for the pope), the brocade silk on the walls, the cut velvet of a canopy, the scintillating crystals in the chandeliers, and the columns, crowns, volutes, and shells of colored marbles in the floor, urge one to complete the salon with the rustle of churchly red and purple silks, the flash of jeweled rings and clasps, and the murmurs of ceremonious voices.

The room that belonged to Maria Mancini, a Colonna wife, is justly French, since she was a niece of the powerful Cardinal Mazarin and, through him, connected with the French court and an admirer of its fashions. The paintings remain, as in the other salons, the work of Italians of the sixteenth and seventeenth centuries and of a few Flemish painters. Number 203 is a sycophantic oddity that shows the Colonna rising out of their sarcophagi and coffins along with Christ on Resurrection Day in an inept imitation of Signorelli's stunning mural in the cathedral of Orvieto. The popular Renaissance profile portrait—red cap, pageboy haircut, and arrogant expression—shows us a young Duke of Urbino (216) and, slipping back in time, the decorative, unreal, engagingly semiprimitive work (221) of an early painter of Verona. Painting 224 treats with flattery the biggish nose and large mouth of Maria Colonna Mancini, all dressed up in furs, pearls, and a pleasant expression. The expression doesn't altogether hide shrewdness, nor does it betray her taste for variety in lovers, a smorgasbord wiped out by her husband when he enclosed her in a Spanish convent. After Maria, stay for a moment or two with a small

Rubens (226), *The Farewell of Jacob and Esau.* Its fine composition and free, flowing line give deep satisfaction, a fine mood in which to leave a gallery.

Make your way back toward Tritone by way of Via di S. Vincenzo and try to spot (on your right) a miniature chapel deep in from a slit in the street. The small church on the Piazza dell' Oratorio once upon a time celebrated Lent by giving parishioners whips and, while they took off their coats and shirts, promised them hellfire and damnation with the vividness and passion described in Joyce's *Portrait of the Artist as a Young Man.* The action was lively enough to belie the claim that flagellation—for one reason or another—was "the English vice." Relief from masochism rears its diversions immediately northward as the Galleria Sciarra. Tall and narrow, washed in shallow gallery light, it unfurls the immortal Pompeian ribbons, arches, and acanthus blooms in dissolving colors to surround Belle Epoque paintings of Proustian ladies in full, elegant, decadent bloom. Odette Swann is being laced into her corset, a mature Albertine bends in gracious discourse with a gentleman who strongly resembles Marcel. Each set off by bands of Pompeian red—a color that refuses to pale—several Virtues show off their pinched waists between full skirts and flossy bodices as they stare blandly at banquet scenes of gentlemen lifting glasses to deep bosoms and puffy hair. The big dinners, the little intimate dinners *à deux*, and significant fireside chats rise toward a finale of watery, Japanesy lily patterns entwined in the style of Whistler amended by Beardsley. One hopes, in spite of the fact that the gallery is inhabited by indifferent business offices, that the discreetly sexy Ceres and their slender, gallantly mustachioed friends will not be permitted to melt further into the walls. Restoration can do no harm to this art, and Roman walls are in need of jollity more recent than Greek-born satyrs and cupids.

NOTE: The Palazzo Venezia is close, and that leads to the Largo Argentina, and that is no distance from the Pantheon. Or, you can pick up the Piazza del Popolo walk at the Corso.

Entertainment

Theater

Not quite within the embrace of Bernini's colonnade at St. Peter's piazza sits the Teatro Borgo S. Spirito, the home of La Compagnia di Prosa d'Origlia-Palmi, located on Via dei Penitenzieri, a few paces from the corner with Borgo S. Spirito.

As if in collaboration with its street the theater devotes some of its efforts to plays about penitents. *Smarrita e Ritrovata* (Lost and Found Again) deals with the life of Mary Magdalene, for example. Other saints—St. Agnes, St. Teresa, Catherine of Siena—who trod unflinching paths to sainthood also tread these meager boards, their turns interspersed with performances of less holy matters: *Il Poeta e la Ballerina* and, a constant favorite, *La Nemica* (The Enemy), another version of *Smarrita e Ritrovata*, which, come to think of it, might be the basic theme of most tear-jerkers.

The theater is small, bare, and unheated, seats sold on a first-come, first-served basis by polite old women wrapped in shaggy coats of unidentifiable pelts. The cashier might be a leading lady, the solicitous bundle who is the ticket collector a wardrobe mistress or a prompter. The price scale for the performances that take place at 4:30 on Saturdays, Sundays, and either Tuesdays or Thursdays strongly favors the churchly. Members of religious orders pay only 100 lire, members of the Society of S. Spirito only 200 lire, the unaffiliated must part with 500. Go, with or without Italian, at about 4 o'clock, and watch the plain, middle-aged women in plain, dark coats, pale faces under home-washed, home-bobbed hair, struggle eagerly for seats center front, to relish and partake of the miseries that grip the protagonists, to weep for and with them more intimately. Farther back, a few priests and a good number of nuns for whom the indigenous ladies—cast and audience—respectfully find seats. Last to arrive, and consequently inhabitants of the far half of the hall, are the show and showy people—embroidered, fleece-lined coats from Hungary or Bulgaria, *outré* hairdos and Theda Bara makeup, pouting powdered boys and potato-shaped, close-cropped, strident girls—from the theater, television, art galleries, and boutiques. They have come, a few of them, to study this anachronistic art form, this urban equivalent of itinerant country shows and folk theater. The rest, usually the younger members of the intellectual cliques, come to laugh at the passé sentiments and the ardent, old-fashioned *verismo* acting and to be loftily amused by the tears that course down the middle-aged faces of the dowdy women in the front rows.

The audience is settled, as settled as an Italian audience can be. The last warning raps have been sounded, the lights dim, and the curtain rises on several chairs, a small table or two and, in the background, classical columns and bunches of roses, faded of age and overuse. To accommodate the small backdrop and avoid the necessity for too many props, the stage has been narrowed by several sets of curtains. Thus the personae appear, for a while, extraordinarily large, like the clanking puppets of Sicily on their minute stages, and some of the younger members of the company enhance the resemblance with their jerky, monotonous gestures, considerably less free than those of a well-manipulated puppet. The play, a series of duets, short trios, and only one overcrowded quartet, leaves no stops unpulled. The family is French and noble, headed by a grandmother complete with black lace head-veil, cane, and shrewd little observations; an icy, regal mamma (the enemy); a young son cherished by mamma but not by the girl he loves, who is in love with the older son, as is everyone except, and this is his crown of thorns, mamma. He speaks of her in classically Oedipal terms—the most beautiful, most regal, most desirable, most inaccessible woman and the only one whose love would satisfy him. Before you realize that this paean to Nefertiti and the Greek Helen, confided to the younger brother, describes their mother, the tears have already begun to course down the rough cheeks of the regulars. The cast also includes a self-sacrificing angel-girl, a shrewd devil-girl and her cool, diabolical father and, in a most salient scene, the Church, as represented by a cardinal—no ordinary priests serve this exalted ménage. The climactic scene in which the older son, on his knees, begs his mother to love him and her confession of his illegitimacy, leading to, "I tried not to love you in order"—you guessed it—"not to love you too much," brings laughter and derisive applause from the back. Two lights, like baleful eyes, suddenly shine from either side of the stage to shame the noise. No one obeys the lights, but an abashed silence sets in when one of the neighborhood women, her face wet under her disordered hair, stands up and with the long, pointed finger of a prophet shouts in her market voice, "Shut up! This is the most beautiful moment of the play, you fools. Be quiet!"

And they are, so that one wonders whether their derision is altogether genuine. They are, after all, Italian and suffer from a severe national case of momism; it must touch them, especially those who have been living with present-day arid arts too long and need more emotional nourishment than those arts furnish.

Not content with illegitimacy, several kinds of unrequited love, scheming, charged confrontations, the play rings in a mother's tortured waiting for news from her sons at the front. It comes. One son has died, and you must know who walks on stage—the magnetic, unloved bastard, of course, who delivers a message from his dead brother. "He spoke only one word, that word which makes flowers blossom in the desert, the word that brings the sun to a rainy sky, that word which eases pain and lightens black nights..." and on and on in the emotional striptease which has skeptics and weepers leaning forward, yearning for *the* word that finally, tremulously, comes: "Mamma!" A passionate embrace of long-parted lovers and the curtain goes down.

Between big scenes for which everyone waits as for favorite arias—and they have the same quality of framed, set pieces—you might concentrate on the stagecraft, the long earrings clanking to the floor and diamond collars slipping out of their clasps during moments of extreme hauteur, the boy who acts with one arm and a timid voice, the girl who stands planted in one spot. The elderly mamma (your neighbor, a knowing buff, has told you that the actress was quite ill this morning but the show must go on) supports herself on the backs of chairs, keeps moving her shawl up around her neck, lets it drop to her arms, adjusts and readjusts it to lend the role movement and vivacity which her body cannot manage. Between the purple patches have a look, also, at the plump young nun with a very light mustache lifted in a grimace of displeasure because of the cigarette smoke around her, at the absorbed faces of older nuns tasting vicariously the life they have relinquished, and at

Theater 265

some of your jazzy neighbors whom Inquisitional tortures wouldn't induce to say they were caught up in this anachronistic, absurd play. Nevertheless, some of their faces, now and then washed of scorn, seem as eager to be enfolded in the drama as children pleading for the life of Tinkerbell.

Ambra-Jovinelli Theater, at the corner of Giolitti and Guglielmo Pepe, at the far end of the railroad station, across from the government milk distribution station and a suddenly stopped run of aqueduct arches.

The woman who sells tickets for 300 lire and the ushers are graduates of the short chorus line in the vaudeville show that alternates with films. The movie, something you saw three years ago or would never think of seeing normally, flickers on a considerate schedule. It allows you to find a seat up front, if there are seats at all available in this always crowded theater, at about 6:40 P.M., to see twenty minutes or so of the film, on with the show at 7:00, and out in time for dinner. The *varietà* is fairly consistently scheduled to begin on the odd hour, but the best is the show at 7:00. The quality of song, dance, and jokes doesn't vary with the hour; the audience does. This is the time of masons, carpenters, porters, the semi- or altogether unemployed, men on strike who aren't ready yet to take the trams that leave from the Via Giolitti for the *borgate* (poor peripheral areas of cheap or impromptu housing) and pasta in a cramped kitchen. It is the time of local old ladies, not too many, who find this a diverting way of baby-sitting with their sleeping grandchildren, the time of country-visitors with raw hands and faces, in shabby suits, who will later search for a 500-lire bed in a dormitory room of a local pensione, the time of very young soldiers with a few hours off before the 200-lire cafeteria meal in their mess nearby.

The orchestra, making up in volume what it lacks in number, pounds out a rollicking Charleston, and a good-looking redhead in a dress cut down to there announces the opening number, by the Red Scotch Ballet. The ballet of three consists of one flaming-haired girl who might be Scottish and two fair girls who appear in bath towels (just out of the bath: naked, see?). Towels are removed, swung about in tight-elbowed burlesque style, and what is left of the costume, gold bra and miniskirt, dips, shakes, rises, and falls in high kicks and a pretty display of youthful, not especially sexy, energy.

They and a young girl singer who belts it out in a monotone of high decibels are frills for the heart of the matter, jokes broad, sharp, unceasing, about sex. Sex is the goal of several different scenes in an all-purpose set, acted—if that is the word—by a matinée-idol type, the décolleté redhead, a black-haired Ceres who is a cornucopia of extravagant mounds and curves, an older, "seen it all" blond, and an elderly comic who is genuinely funny in Chaplin's way. No matter where the situations start—a night club, a furrier's shop, a psychiatrist's office—they wind up in verbal and visual sockos of sex, hetero and homo. The only disturbing note is the comic, who moves one to pity, not as a fictional character but for himself, a man with a limp and a weak voice that has been used too coarsely, too hard, and too long, an old man who shouldn't have to make the effort of forcing his voice or his uneven legs in a buck and wing several times a day.

Whether your Italian can get the fairly basic messages or not, the theater deserves an hour of your time. You will be part of an audience too tired or too stunned by this big-city experience to laugh or applaud much, an audience whose dress and faces never come to tourist routes and, up in the balconies, the men and boys who wait and those who search them out for an hour's companionship or a short meeting in the men's room. Balconies in theaters all over the world make room for this sort of hunt, but here you see it in the context of a long continuum, from the time Augustus devised lures for men to leave their boys for marriage and breeding.

.   .   .

The Piazza Margana, a permissive place, accepts sculpture shows and, now and then, robust plays that use the whole piazza for their vigorous action. International theater and ballet, spread over several houses, comprise a "Premio Roma" festival in late May. Theater in English is listed in the *Rome Daily American* and *This Week in Rome*.

Some seasons yes, some no. Inquire about classical theater at Ostia Antica; the productions may lack but don't seriously hamper the extraordinary experience of sitting in the antique theater, particularly when the moon is full enough to shed light on the ruins of the ancient port.

Music

Concerts in the Basilica of Maxentius. Two thousand lire buys a reserved seat for a program of well-performed, unadventurous music. If you can manage to arrive fifteen or twenty minutes before 9:30, performance time, it is preferable to take an unreserved seat for 1,000 lire which will afford you a sweep of unforgettable night vista: the high, lit vaults of the basilica above the orchestra, light floating from the apertures of surrounding ruins, the baroque façade of S. Francesca Romana painted in muted night-gold, and an unreal, flat yellow cardboard slice of the Colosseum.

The Baths of Caracalla operas are universally cited for their *Aïda*, mainly because of the Triumphal Scene whose legend has expanded it to encompass every known tropical animal.

No, no elephants or tigers, only a tired camel or two, and masses and masses of people to charge through the monumental scenery. If *Aïda* is not being performed in your time take a chance on another opera. The casts and orchestra can be competent at times, and the stage of the baths is one of the Roman colossi one should experience. As a matter of fact, go early to absorb the bitter grandeur of the gigantic blocks of broken wall and to walk around in the immensity of the archaeological zone. In the early third century A.D. it was a large village of several types of luxurious baths, communal, private, and of varying degrees of temperature, surrounded by gymnasia, libraries, numerous public rooms and gardens resplendently decorated, and an area for spectacles. Its brilliance was extinguished with the coming of the Goths (537), who cut off the supplying aqueduct, and through the centuries since it has become an evocative wreck sung by poets, etched and painted by artists, and apostrophized by romantics. (There is, as you know, a famous portrait of Shelley composing in the ruins of Caracalla.)

The beguiling courtyard of the church of S. Giovanni dei Genovesi offers chamber music—a choral group, a pianist, classical guitarists—during the summer months.

The cortile of S. Giovanni in Laterano is frequently the site of concerts as well as plays of a religious nature selected and arranged with careful taste. You should have Italian to understand *Murder in the Cathedral* and a playlet based on the poems called "Fioretti" of St. Francis, but the direction and acting may be enough to sustain your interest. The church of S. Cecilia is, appropriately, the house for many concerts. S. Alessio on the Aventine sings Gregorian chants at 9:00 A.M. on Sundays, and there frequently are concerts of old music in many other churches. Watch church façades for information and the listings in the newspapers *Il Messaggero* or *Paese Sera*.

Truncated opera, unevenly performed, in June, at the Teatro
Eliseo.

Voyeurism

For the extremely courageous voyeur (in pairs, if possible)
there is the rich field of whore-watching in several categories, financial and sexual. A renowned area, used frequently in Italian films, is the Tor di Quinto, a road leading
north and spotted by night fires around which the prostitutes gather like gypsies or, if your vision is poor, like Girl
Scouts. It isn't necessary to go that far from the central
city, however. The girls, in tall white boots, sequined mini-
dresses, and fluffy, coquettish furs, parade the Via Veneto
down to the Piazza Barberini and up to Francesco Crispi,
which supplies them with hotel space. On a lower rung, by
a considerable sum, the women with the shapes of neglect
or pregnancy, no furs, and vicious makeup who patrol the
streets and arcades near the railroad station, the northern
façade of S. Maria Maggiore, the main streets of the
Suburra, taking shelter with their partners in the neighborhood pensioni. The Parco del Celio, south of the Colosseum,
offers cheap, wholesome bargains. One thousand or so lire
buys a contraceptive, sex *en plein air*, an illusion of privacy
in the cave darkness of buttresses or a twig hut as large as
a beehive and, for warmth and checking sums of money, a
fire. If there are no police in the vicinity—there rarely are
—the groups of waiting men relax on the park benches as
easy and conversational as if they were in a barber shop.
And talking with them are the pimps and the young homo-
sexuals who are the friends and messengers of the whores,
taking time off from their business in the Colosseum.

An expensive car stops at an entrance to the Colosseum.
Bracelets jingling, chains flashing, long blond hair tossing,
out steps The Queen and his affectionate, subtly painted
entourage. From the entrance there emerges a group of

unadorned poor boys standing at a distance, admiring, adoring. The dazzling creature may or may not be a pimp, but he has made it, proof that they, too, might. They return to the arena and, prowling in small packs, observe the lonely middle-aged man loitering in an arch, bending over a barrier as if examining the substructure, waiting to be approached, or a pair of timid foreigners clinging to each other, for the time being. A boy separates from his pack to talk of this and that with the man at the barrier; another moves toward the foreigners with a smile, ready to discuss the marvels of the Colosseum as a conversational starter. By midnight, when the illumination goes off, light conversation has already turned to arrangements, and inner arches and black corners become impromptu bedrooms.

You can quit at this point, or carry on the pursuit of a stimulating subject. Serious study will require a car to crisscross the city from the Colosseum to the Castel S. Angelo, the showcase of transvestites, and on to the Pincio, near the obelisk (on the Via del Obelisco) built by Hadrian to sing the charms of Antinous, which should be a romantic spot but is, actually, a meat rack. This quick survey, however, by no means exhausts the sex market; every slum and *borgata* is amply and busily supplied, recalling Petronius' statement that "every person . . . seems to be drunk on aphrodisiacs."

You might be ready for investigation of mixed bags such as the lushly green avenues that lead to and surround the Baths of Caracalla. The girl on a stone or bench, or cruising in a car, may be a girl or transvestite. A rough judgment can be made by heft; the girls incline to plumpness, the boys are painfully thin under their falsies. The car owners, casual jokers and bargainers, carry their customers back to an apartment or hotel or park the car in one of the undisturbed streets that fringe villas and cloisters to the south. The rest of the boys and girls enjoy the hospitality of trees and bushes. The Circo Massimo edges its emptiness with the densest greenery, thick, wide, and low to the ground, and yet high enough to make efficient screens from the upper roads. When the weather is favorable, this is, literally, exhibition grounds and, if the lure is sufficiently attractive, a plunge into the bushes. The Baths of Caracalla environs have a market joviality: the girls of both sexes hailing each other across the road and jocular bargaining through car windows. The Circo Massimo is a sinister place, to be viewed from above unless you are interested in participation. In that case you should be told that a woman was found murdered among the bushes not too long ago.

There are purists who are offended by these desecrations of antiquity which took on a look of false chastity as brightly colored temples and statues turned parchment yellow, like the skins of studious old men. *La Dolce Vita* is a vapid imitation, however, of the *Satyricon*: there were prostitutes of both sexes and combinations thereof everywhere in Imperial Rome, the most expensive professionals emperors themselves whose favors came high, an assassination or two or three the minimal fee for a Tiberius, a Caligula, and the most imaginative of them all, Nero.

Multisex, unisex, sex in twos and threes and more, a city full of Midnight Cowboys and Girls, but unlike our puritanical portrayals, they don't necessarily come to a bad end. Many of them find protectors or respectable jobs or marriages and live as happily or unhappily ever after as the rest of the world.

Miscellaneous

The prime entertainment is eating outdoors and being entertained—or plagued—by a universe of musicians, so to speak, who insist on being paid by everyone in the vicinity of their questionable sounds. Some are not bad, or only half bad, or bad and appealing; others, bad and unappealing. Be prepared with 50- and 100-lire pieces, many of them in the high greedy season.

English and American films in the original languages for 600 lire at the Pasquino on the Via della Paglia in Traste- vere. In Italian, always, international "oldies," at about 300 lire (plus slipping reels and blank pauses) in the Farnese on the Campo dei Fiori, the Nuovo Olimpia on the Via in Lucina off the Corso, the Planetario, Via Cernaia near the station. At considerably more for softer seats and well-kept space, look for new American and English films at the Fi- amma and the Fiammetta, joined together on a corner of the Via Bissolati, and the Archimede on the street of that name in Parioli. The serious student of the cinema on an extended visit might look into membership, neither expensive nor difficult, in the Filmstudio (Trastevere), which has eclectic tastes that embrace Laurel and Hardy, Garbo, Chinese documentaries, and American underground films.

Have a drink at the Caffè Greco on the Via Condotti and among the voices of the birds of brilliant plumage at the bar listen for Byron being Byronic, Joyce rasping criticism, Ibsen growling, and Mendelssohn humming. Then, watch the dress parade on the trafficless Via Frattina.

Always, at any hour of the day and into the night, people-watching on the Piazza Navona, whose contours and fur- nishings enhance the dark-mushroom beggar ladies eating grapes discarded by the Campo dei Fiori and the tempers of snappish little dogs and boys.

A slow-sliding gelato while one watches a big-chested, long-haired fire-eater, the portfolios of art opening and opening like an endless screen, the unisex in its expensive rags and patches, the gapers at the river fountain on the

Piazza Navona at night, is an essential experience. If time doesn't whip the opportunity away, try to see the piazza in the full early afternoon light of a summer's day. The cameras, art, balloons, and toy birds, and the aristocratic hip are gone. The sun blazes the contours of the big fountain into a swirling mass, erases the shapes of the accompanying fountains, drives sharp scratches into the texture of the houses and saps their flowers of color. There is no sound except the gush of waters.

A gentle evening of songs in several languages chastely accompanied at the Arciliuto on the Piazza Montevecchio. Go after dinner, and not in the summertime, when the owner-entertainers go off to the sea or mountains.

Watch for announcements of celebrations on the Campidoglio. On some of these occasions the flares are lit to flicker along the stairs and ledges of the buildings, a lovely example of lily-gilding.

People-watching on the Piazza S. Maria in Trastevere. The mosaics and proud fountain should ennoble its inhabitants, but they don't. The stateliness and pride seem to diminish the drooping young tendrils of human ivy. Gawking from the caffes of the Via Veneto has its Italian rewards and others, including mirror images and caricatures of yourself.

For a week in mid-May, the Via dei Coronari dresses up in lights and flowers and puts on an admirable antiques show, open late into the evening. No need to buy, no traffic, and a chance to enjoy a bright night passeggiata with a good-humored crowd.

. . .

The solitary might look for companionship at **Approdo Romano**, Via della Pilotta, 31A, which posts meetings of foreigners in several kinds of activity. The more adventuresome might try the Turkish baths, sauna, massage, and artificial sun dispenser—for men and women—called the *Terme Roma*, Via Poli 51, near the Trevi Fountain.

Entertainment and dancing exist in the center, in Parioli, in Trastevere, in the Campo dei Fiori area. Because their lives are often fleeting, the safest suggestion is that you ask the concierge at your hotel or a bellboy or buy a copy of *This Week in Rome*.

Archaeology, exercise, and fresh air, all gratis, on Monte Testaccio, searching for pieces of old vase to put together as a leaky ashtray.

Listen to the vendors near the walls that lead to the Vatican museums try their tongues in several languages. "Voulez-vous regarder, monsieur?"—pointing to booklets— and with no pause, "Barato, barato, muy linda," and as the Spanish group moves on, "Guten Tag, meine Herren." The gelato dispensers push their linguistic capacities only as far as "Aice cree. Verry goot, verry goot."

Not the most boisterous sort of entertainment, but much better than sitting alone wrapped in the gloom of hotel walls and lilting voices from the street, is a Saturday evening visit to the Campidoglio, a golden room at night. The museums there are open and afford, if not gaiety, the virtues of edification.

A CURIOUS
QUARTET

Fontana dell' Acqua Felice

The fountain that pours the Acqua Felice (Happy Water) of Sixtus V is thoroughly *infelice*. It is a serious mistake exaggerated by a vastness that encompasses sweet Egyptian lions who look like the elderly Toscanini in repose and a triplet of arches that hug Joshua, Aaron, and Moses in their peak moments. The mishmash adds up to one of the most appalling of Roman fountains, and there are, among the beauties, a fair number of beasts. The Moses, taken with a myopic eye from that of Michelangelo, repeats that unearthly sculpture as a squat caricature so insistently ridiculed that the master sculptor (the actual work was that of an assistant) committed suicide shortly after its construction.

S. Maria della Vittoria

The contrast in skill and conviction in sculpture is around the corner on the Via XX Settembre, in the church of S. Maria della Vittoria. The church is not particularly hospitable in spite of shining marbles and baroque rays that try to cheer up images and chapels. But Bernini's *St. Theresa Pierced by the Love of God*, more commonly known as her *Ecstasy*, lies here in a fall of marble folds that opens to a limp hand. Her head has fallen back, and her face (more clearly seen in the photographs at the back of the church) is utterly uncontrolled, loosened in unconsciousness, the mouth slightly opened as if in shallow, swift breathing, the eyelids dropped to an unseeing slit. She lies in a golden glory of light that seeps through concealed amber glass. At her side stands the messenger of God who had transfixed her with his arrow, his breezy drapery still in flight. He is just barely a Christian angel; his pagan beauty and gleeful mischievous smile are an edition of Eros. At either side of this intimate encounter Bernini has built two theater boxes for Venetian gentlemen who look on and comment animatedly. The whole ensemble, including the angels swirling in the vault, is a splendid architectonic-theatrical achievement, a compendium of the effects of scenery, dramatic personae, and clever indirect lighting that Bernini used for masques and theater performances in the palaces of his patrons.

Reactions to St. Theresa have been as vivid as the sculpture itself. An English woman quoted by Augustus Hare used the phrases, "a parody of Divine Love," "grossest," "most offensive, vileness," "the least destructive, the least prudish in matters of art would here willingly throw the first stone." Pointing out the "contrast between English and French taste," Hare also quotes Taine, whose phrases are "adorable," "évanouie d'amour," "de bonheur et d'extase," "l'angoisse voluptueuse," "délicieux," "corps charmant ardent," "si séduisant et si tendre." Basically, of course, both judgments agree, and one wonders how the church fathers viewed Bernini's interpretation of St. Theresa's ecstasy. Were they so innocent in their presumed celibacy that they did not recognize "l'angoisse voluptueuse"? There is every reason to doubt it. The luxuriant voluptuosities of the Renaissance had been tamped down considerably, but the church was still controlled by worldly men and art lovers untouched by northern puritanism. It was the cardinal Scipione Borghese, after all, who built for the Carmelite fathers of this church a new façade in exchange for a hermaphrodite they found in their earth which he wanted for his distinguished collection of antiquities.

See what you think of it, and keep in mind that Bernini

was a member of an order whose precepts included visualizing religious experience clearly and immediately, that the school of painting he studied and admired was that of Caravaggio and his followers. Most important to remember is that the figures are only in detail flights of the sculptor's imagination. The Spanish saint wrote fully and graphically of the "intolerable joys," the "delicious wounds," of the "sweetly-killing" dart.

S. Carlo alle Quattro Fontane

At one corner of Quattro Fontane, named for fountains in the sixteenth-century style of big river-gods pressed into the foliage and waters of low shallow grottoes, stands one of the most extraordinary of baroque churches. S. Carlo alle Quattro Fontane, usually referred to in the diminutive, S. Carlino, was the first church that was solely Borromini's and in a sense his last because he died before its completion. Works on architecture invariably add the word "eccentric" to Borromini's name, occasionally modified by "able," and in two or three instances "genius." Without fail he is coupled with Bernini as rival, although the rivalry was fairly short-lived. Essentially there could be no rivalry. The gods smiled on Bernini through most of his long fruitful life. They gave him a sculptor father who fostered his precocious talents; the limelight shone on him early and stayed long on his multiple activities as sculptor, architect, painter, supervisor of vast works like St. Peter's, imaginative designer of anything he attacked, whether it was colonnades, fountains, angels who swing on church ledges or gesture from bridges, and scenic design. (John Evelyn's diary reports that he "gave a public opera wherein he painted the scenes, cut the statues, invented the engines, composed the music, writ the comedy and built the theater.") He was a courtier, a man happily ensconced in his time.

Borromini started life as a stonemason and came to St. Peter's from the north to act as apprentice to his cousin Carlo Maderno, the designer of the façade, who assigned him a job of chipping out architectural details and ornaments. In spite of growing success and respected achievements he remained a morose, difficult, inward man obsessed with every detail of a work, unlike Bernini, who employed and trusted a good number of assistants. Borromini had no time, nor the temperament, for the embellishments of life. On the contrary, he was intensely, uncomfortably religious and died a suicide by lunging on the point of his own sword. He was not of his time, rather one of the geniuses who push the dimensions of their art beyond its accustomed limits. Although Bernini left models in sculpture and architecture that were followed for a long time to reach a dying halt, Borromini's followers were the fantasists, the innovators who opened new horizons. Bernini recognized, rather sourly, the difference in their attitudes when he spoke of the superiority of a poor Catholic (his own work) over that of a good heretic (Borromini), criticizing Borromini's radical abandonment of proportions based on the human body, a Renaissance concept to which Bernini adhered.

S. Carlino immediately betrays its singularity from the corner diagonally opposite its site, where one sees the play of curves within curves, shallow and deep, on the curiously shaped campanile and lantern. A frontal view of the façade hides them—a common difficulty with Borromini's structures—and one is left with the narrow dynamic front that is in constant motion, the motion of music rather than of restlessness. The size of the church was, of course, dictated by limited space, and Borromini, of his long experience at St. Peter's, chose the width of a pier that supports the dome for his measure. It is an interesting conceit but of no major importance; what matters is the flow of rhythms, the alternations of concave and convex immediately introduced by the façade, the brightening of a concave space by loose arabesques of stone around oval windows, and the deep portal that balances, in its turn, a convexity of steps. Sweet robust Borrominesque angel heads and wings frame superbly the niche for S. Carlo Borromeo (to whom the church is dedicated) and bring it into prominence at the fullest swell of the façade, although the niche itself describes an inward movement. The upper order both contradicts and parallels the lower section, answering the saint's niche with a windowed turret and deepening curves as balustrade.

The interior has been studied as a complexity of formulas based on a Greek cross cut through and reshaped by various geometric relationships. Yours may be the eye that can make them out, but it is hardly essential. Scan the spacing and placement of the columns, the alternating heights of niches, the counterpoised lines of direction in the coffered vaults, the unique meshwork of forms that diminish in size as they move toward the center of the dome, and the ingenious arrangement of almost hidden windows whose light suffuses the dome and filters down cool and clear on the shafts of columns.

The adjoining narrow cloister, made many years before the façade, which was not quite finished when the architect died in 1667, is deceptively simple. Stand in it for a while and observe the subtle broadening of massive wall between the arches at the ends of the court, the shape of the ledge below, the slightly disturbing design of the capitals on the upper wall, their way of meeting ledges and the sharply turned balustrade ornaments. Then return to the church to trace the flow of the entablature above the columns, the graceful band that acts as coda to repeat and hold together the musical forms. He was dry, taciturn, a dour man, but it isn't a Borromini work if it doesn't sing. If ever there was architecture that suited the definition "frozen music," it is Borromini's.

S. Andrea al Quirinale

A fortunate contrast between men and work arranges itself nearby on the Via del Quirinale with Bernini's church of S. Andrea al Quirinale, built for a nephew of Innocent X the Pamphili during the later years of S. Carlino's long making. There is nothing eccentric in it, or profound. It is a sheer delight of the jeweler's art of the High Baroque and, at the same time, a theater in which to set a religious experience. The severe façade rising over a semicircle of stairs leads startlingly into riches of deep-colored and pale marbles, dozens of angels and putti, fair and white against the gold coffering of the broad dome. Stucco babies swing on garlands, climb among the coffers, converse or stare down into the church from a circular opera loge at the base of the lantern. Larger stucco figures dangle from the ledges abandoned by the cherubim. Rich Corinthian columns at the high altar surround a painting of St. Andrew's martyrdom that leads heavenward in golden rays and creamy clouds and putti afloat in sensational lighting. Heavenly space rises and rises to meet a plaster figure of the saint sitting on a broken pediment above his altar, his eyes turned upward to the pinnacle of celestial heights inhabited by more bouquets of winged babies. The stucco figures are the work of a gifted assistant, Antonio Raggi, but their placement in the oval gem was sketched out by the master, the impresario and choreographer of this dazzling, captivating show.

AND CURIOUSER

The heads of St. Peter and St. Paul, the grill of St. Lawrence, the steam pipes that suffocated S. Cecilia, enough pieces of the True Cross to reforest the Sahara desert, hair and bits of sanctified bone, and a long list of etceteras are necessary equipment for a Holy City. To glorify the personages and their legends, the city developed extraordinary decorative skills, polishing marble to the shine and suppleness of silk, bending stones into ribbons, fitting together little glittering squares to make the waters and flowers of paradise, devising the trickiest trompe l'oeil to fake antique statues and perspective, and latterly reproducing anything from Roman sarcophagi to eighteenth-century French pews dangerously well.

S. Maria della Concezione

Yet another meeting of veneration for blessed bones and ingenious, appropriate decorating occurs in the cemetery of the church of S. Maria della Concezione on the Via Veneto. It stands immediately above Bernini's fan-shell fountain, whose waters appear to spill from the mouths of three Barberini bees under the grandiose lettering, lest you forget, of the donor: URBANUS VIII, PONTIFEX MAXIMUS, the Barberini pope whose monk-brother founded the church. One is ushered into the cemetery by a cordial Capuchin monk and urged toward an arched corridor at the side of several tombs of monks. As in life, they share in death and decay the sociability of togetherness, three, six, eight in each area, surrounded by ingenious adornments. A minute's examination of the fragile floral designs on the ceiling of the gallery, of latticework and slender lamps, reveals the stupefying fact that they are all made of human bones— vertebrae and lower arm bones as chandeliers, flowers, leaves, and curvaceous rococo bands created of ribs, large blossoms of scapulae petals, a delicate fancy made of jaw- bones, with teeth; a sturdy wreath depends on a painstaking arrangement of pelvic plates. Larger bones and skulls make the walls and niches that support drooping skeletons still in their hoods and habits. The skeletons too weak to stand rest on biers supported by skulls, one set protected by a layer of eaves of overlapping scapulae quite like roof tiles on Italian houses.

It must be an entertaining, creative, time-filling occupa- tion to polish and match one's confreres' bones so that they may replace a too-dry, fallen bit. When a monk dies, no accommodation is made for him among the others, nor can there be—in an area jammed with travel offices, bars, and tourist-purchase shops—expansion of the cemetery, which is considerably above the street level. Therefore, the most antique monk is taken out to be replaced by the latest, a just scheme, since the earth of the tombs came from the Holy Land and each monk must have his period of rest in sacred soil before he becomes lantern and bone-ivory flower.

Portal of the Alchemists

Roughly midway between S. Maria Maggiore and S. Gio- vanni in Laterano, a few streets from the endless line of related buildings that trail the railroad station, there is the Piazza Vittorio Emanuele II, a rectangle of shopping ar- cades, open markets, and long ripples of corrugated tin which mean a promised subway station or civic pride which hides heaps of garbage and a decayed fountain of the third century. The market is market—sheen of fresh-cut meat, red glow of tomatoes, greens from the pallor of delicate shoots to the hard old green of spinach, castles and turrets of cheese, the moist glitter of fish, and boisterous amiability. Several curios set the market apart from the many, small and large, in Rome. Should you approach the piazza by way of Via Carlo Alberto you may stumble on a marble slab fenced in and shaded with tin on which stretch and yawn in the sun the original cats on a hot tin roof. No local seems to know why the caged slabs are here and in the remains of park behind the market, or what they mean. They may be linked to the fountain and the high shafts of ruin and scattering of column one passes in search of the most provocative curiosity in the neighborhood.

At the northern end of the piazza, almost immediately opposite the crags of ruin, there is a doorway whose sentinels are two nude dwarfs with stylized curly beards that might be Chinese or Assyrian, the heads unusually large and stern, the stubby hands resting on short, thick thighs. Above the portal, a marble Star of David on which is imposed a circle ending in a cross, and within the cross another circle. On the upper and lower ledges and the sides of the door frame, legends in Latin, Greek, and Hebrew intersperse with incised symbols—the universal sperm and ovum symbols, circles, hooks, arrows, and crescents in several combinations. The symbols and cryptic messages in the various languages ("He who knows how to burn with water and wash with fire makes heaven of earth and heaven a splendid thing"; "If you make the earth fly above your head, with those plumes you can change torrent waters into rock") and the presence of the squat monsters inevitably produced legend: Queen Christina was in cahoots with cabalists and alchemists whose meetings took place in the villa of a magic-inebriated Roman nobleman, the builder of the eerie doorway to a laboratory for the black arts. Another tradition insists that an earlier owner of the villa found a formula for making gold of dross and spells. He called in all the magicians and occultists he could muster to help make the recipe a glittering reality, with no success. Therefore he left the formula, hidden in the signs and cryptic statements carved on his doorway for posterity to use. Posterity, as far as is known, never succeeded except for one mysterious figure who asked the nobleman for expense money and a secluded chamber and shortly thereafter disappeared, leaving traces of gold. And it was he, they say, who left the bewildering instructions on the doorway. Take it as you like, but take it if you possibly can.

St. Paul's (Protestant)

Rome, the city that has everything—including mosaics by the Pre-Raphaelite of the pale, auburn-haired medieval ladies, Edward Burne-Jones. The mosaics appear in and on the façade of the American Protestant church of St. Paul on the Via Nazionale at the corner with the Via Napoli. The church is not always open, but the misplaced Victorian Gothic form, complete with rose windows and trill of blind arches, and the façade mosaics might do. As if awed by the church commission, Burne-Jones forgot his art revolution and hewed to the traditional of the Four Evangels and, over the double-peaked portal, St. Paul preaching to a Roman soldier in shining armor.

Sacro Cuore del Suffragio

South of a marble panel that says here lived a Finnish translator of Dante's *Divine Comedy*, on the Lungotevere Prati, one bumps into the only overtly Gothic church in Rome, Sacro Cuore del Suffragio, a late nineteenth-century imitation of an authentically Gothic church in Pisa. A door to the right of the altar and a short corridor bring to view a minuscule museum of superstitions, or demonology, or however you choose to categorize the display. First, a long narrow painting of a half-closed door with a distorted evil face peering through the opening, a vague photo or print of the same subject, and a photo of a church altar with the demonic image at one side. A prayer book bearing the imprint of the fingers of a dead woman, footprints, and more fingerprints, all burned into cloth, wood, and paper are testaments of unhappy souls wrapped for a time in the flames of purgatory. Two plastic-bound sheets tell of the incidents that surround the appearance of the dead and their souvenirs. A Belgian testified that his mother, twenty-seven years dead, returned to haunt him noisily and nag-gingly, begging him to change his ways and devote himself to the church so that she might rest easy; to keep him aware, she burned her fingertip prints into a prayer book. A hand and cross on a table, a left hand on paper, a right hand on a sleeve, combined to burn their way, two hundred years after the death of their owner, through the tunic and onto a nether garment of an abbess in Umbria. A German woman dressed as a pilgrim appeared in the house of her daughter-in-law, who did not recognize her. The old woman moaned and stared sadly but would not speak for a discon-certing while. In time she revealed who she was to the daughter-in-law, who knew her to be dead for thirty years. The specter told of her intention to continue her pilgrimage for special Masses at a holy shrine and, having accom-plished her mission, returned to the house, announced that she had been liberated from Hellfire, burned the contours of her hand on a copy of the *Imitation of Christ,* and dis-appeared forever.

Another German (Germans seem to lead the field in this specialty) returned to his brother to ask that he pray him out of purgatory to make up for the lack of religion in his —the dead man's—life. And so the exhibition goes on, not extensively, in a primitive collection of lessons one might have thought abandoned centuries ago and smacking, more-

over, of a degree of Satanism that the modern church could
scarcely sanction. Yet here it is, not in an abandoned village
of Calabria but a short walk from the Vatican. (Go before
10 or after 5.)

SS. Vincenzo ed Anastasio

One of the rarer types of reliquaries and contents is a set
of urns, not ordinarily visible, in the church of SS. Vincenzo
ed Anastasio, across from the Trevi Fountain. They contain
the entrails of all the popes from the late sixteenth century
to the early twentieth, the period when the palace on the
Quirinal was papal property and this its parish church.

A Swift, Light
Survey of Shopping

The list of recommended restaurants carried by every well-equipped traveler bears on its reverse side the names of shops, usually headed by the triplets Gucci, Pucci, and Cucci. Then, following Cucci for men, Carlo Palazzi on the Via Borgognona, Battistoni on the Via Condotti, Brioni on the Via Barberini; for women, Eleanora Garnett on Via Sistina, Gattinoni on the Piazza di Spagna, Schubert on the Via Condotti, Fontana on the Salita S. Sebastianello, a sprig of the Piazza di Spagna. But there is hardly any point in going on; you have the names in their well-arranged categories.

It might be more helpful to mention the fact that the best shopping is done from the secretive address book of a resident friend who treasures a bootmaker, a dressmaker, a cutter and sewer of pocketbooks or ties or gloves. If you are not gifted with such a friend, be assured that each glamour name sits in a cluster of neighbors and peers on the Corso, the Piazza di Spagna, the Vias Condotti, Fontanella di Borghese, Borgognona, Frattina, delle Vite, Sistina, Gregoriana, Crispi, and on and off the Vie Veneto and Barberini. If their prices rock you back on your heels— you were sure everything was much cheaper in Italy—look in at the shops on Due Macelli, Tritone, Nazionale, around the Porta Pia, the Trevi Fountain, along the Appia Nuova and Cola di Rienzo, the Vie Campo Marzio, Leoncino, Ripetta, and della Scrofa. If you are willing to let high style, or any style, go to concentrate on the inexpensive, explore the arcades and stalls around the market of the Piazza Vittorio Emanuele II, the shops of the ghetto and the Campo dei Fiori, the Viale Trastevere, the Vie Arenula and Merulana, the Porta Portese market on Sunday morning, and every day on the Via Sanio south of S. Giovanni.

To deal with a few items your informative friends may have neglected:

Souvenirs. In great supply on and off the Piazza di Spagna, and this might include the handmade, inexpensive jewelry made and shown on the Spanish Steps; the Via Sistina immediately after it has crossed Francesco Crispi going down the hill; the Corso; the Via Nazionale and especially at Galeazzi, 203A; surrounding the Pantheon and the Trevi Fountain and, with a firmer religious note, shops on the Via della Conciliazione and the Borgo S. Spirito as they approach St. Peter's.

Antiques. Vie del Babuino, Margutta, Coronari, and Giulia are the leaders, with Monseratto and Governo Vecchio coming up. And keep your eyes peeled in the old city for affable, musty shops like those on the Salita dei Crescenzi (Pantheon), for example.

"Trendy." Should your native city lack them, and it hardly seems likely unless you normally hide in the Gobi Desert, you will be able to find Hungarian shepherd coats,

Afghanistani vests, Indian blouses, North African djella-bahs, caftans, jewelry, and amulets, Rumanian embroideries, and the rest of the popular ethnic requirements on the Via Margutta, the Vie Oca, Penna, and Orso, the Via dei Cestari, and in the company of a few good Persian antique pieces at Molayem, 111 Via del Seminario. Old clothing, still very stylish, as discarded uniforms, insignia, and boots and, since you are in Rome, an occasional nun's shawl or monk's hooded gown, on the Via Sanio, the Porta Portese market (Sunday morning), and a stand, afternoons only, at the corner of Serpente and Baccino. Confections made of cast-off clerical garments are invented in a boutique across from the Pasquino theater on the Via della Paglia.

Prints with and without old books. East side of the Pantheon; across from the church of S. Agostino on that saint's street; on the Largo di Febo; several shops on the Via del Babuino, where they are likely to be costly; less costly on the Largo Pietro di Brazza, and very cheap, for good reason, on the stalls near the central railroad station. Good reproductions of Italian classics flat or wrapped around handsome boxes at Alinari's on the Via del Babuino a few paces from the Piazza di Spagna. Modern prints are usually the business of galleries, but there are at least two ateliers of prints only, one on the Via dei Greci, and Il Grifo, 135 Via di Ripetta.

Galleries. Babuino, Margutta and its alleys and the short streets that run between the river and Babuino, south of the Piazza del Popolo (Vantaggio, Brunetti, Laurina, Frezza, etc.). An increasing number near the Campo dei Fiori, and in Trastevere one of the most splendid of all, Il Carpine, 30 Via Mantellate. Several of high repute in the Spanish Steps area—Marlborough at 5 and Il Collezionista at 36 Via Gregoriana; Schneider on the Steps, a gallery in the court of number 8 Piazza di Spagna. (A good boutique, as well, in this court.) And remember that there are strict rules about taking art out of the country which gallery owners will know.

Jewelry. Jewelry antique and modern, in Renaissance, Baroque, "Liberty," late Bauhaus, and Calder styles, flashes from many polished windows in the Condotti-Babuino streets. If lesser adornments will do, examine the windows on the Via del Pellegrino and the hundreds of medals and medallions at Cravanzola, 341 Corso. A gift for someone you love expensively might be their fine boxful of framed miniatures of Raphael paintings.

Frames. Many and in a staggering diversity of styles on Margutta, Brunetti, and other streets off the Piazza del Popolo, surrounding the Via Ripetta.

Crafts. Modern, as household objects, on the Piazza di Spagna, Vie Condotti, Babuino; at Living, 46 Piazza Scanderbeg. A large collection of Venetian glass at 36 Crociferi, and at 33 of the same street (Trevi area) crafts from provenances as disparate as Mexico and India. Varied Italian crafts at Artigiano Folklorico on the Via Campania off the Via Veneto; pottery of several famous craftsmen at Myricae, 35 Via Frattina; and Calabrian crafts as straw objects, embroideries, and ceramics on Via d'Ascanio, 16. Straw and cane can be found near the southern corner of the Piazza Navona, on the street of S. Eustachio as it meets its piazza, and at several shops between these locations. Also, on the Piazza di Montecitorio and near the river, off the Corso Vittorio Emanuele, at the Via Consolato.

Assorted Bargains. It takes a little time and the possible cost of overweight, but if you have a few significant books that are bursting their stitches, consider bringing them for fine, comparatively inexpensive binding to 30A Via del Falco, 43 Vicolo della Torretta, 25 Via dei Lucchesi, 55 Via della Scrofa. Other repair services also remain inexpensive and skillful. An establishment that takes on almost anything— a contrary umbrella, a reluctant purse clasp, a dented valise, lives opposite the Teatro Centrale off the Piazza del Gesù. For clothing repairs, cuffs turned, faded pants sewn inside out, darning, reweaving, shortening of trousers and skirts, consult with the Clinica del Vestito, off Tritone, near the mouth of the tunnel. The most centrally located of restorers of fine objects, of whom there are many, works at 21 Via Vittoria. Used paperbacks are sold at the Economy Book Center, 29 Piazza di Spagna, and inexpensive art books are available at newsstands. Mountains of inexpensive sweaters swell the Via Gambero, and smaller hills of inexpensive gloves rise on the Piazza di Spagna. Handmade belts with a fair choice of buckles can be had at very little cost from a shoemaker on the Via di S. Cecilia near its piazza (Trastevere). An impressive gift at no great price is a bronze nameplate made in one of several styles and sizes and available within a few days of ordering at shops whose signs say "Targhe." They exist in every neighborhood, and the hotel desk should be able to point you to the nearest one.

This and that. There is a tendency, blinded by the dazzle on conspicuous shopping streets, to overlook the varied charms of their neighbors. The Via delle Carrozze, for instance, a few paces from the Via Condotti, opens with a distinguished bookshop, goes on to "with it" clothing and Art Nouveau, in a shop all for its curvaceous self. The Via Vittoria is moving up and out of mending and dry cleaning and in its refurbishing has given room to a branch of Oxfam (14) where you might pick up, among the donated goods, an attractive gift. And don't neglect, for rewarding window shopping, the boutiques on Belsiana, Mario dei Fiori, and Bocca di Leone.

Yearning for a dashing plumed hat worn by one sector of the army or a drooping red combination of fez and stocking cap worn by another group? They can be bought, plus army belts, insignia, and inexpensive shirts at 24 Via Giolitti across from the soldiers' mess back of the airport terminal.

You may have no need for what they offer but might enjoy, nevertheless, some of the old shops in the Pantheon-Navona quarter. A specialist at the side of the Museo di Roma keeps its grains, chestnut flour, potato flour, and beans in burlap sacks with yawning hippo mouths. Next to the Palazzo Massimo on the Corso Vittorio Emanuele there is an ageless place that supplies fuel for flares and, among a broad, serious miscellany, attractive candles. Near the northern end of the Piazza Navona, at the end of the Corso del Rinascimento, a shop nicely decorated to imply monastery cellars and cloisters, Ai Monasteri, sells honey and liqueurs produced by monks while the nuns keep busy with soaps and face creams. On the Piazza Rondanini a venerable herbalist does well with medicinal herbs in spite of the modern hygienic splendors of *farmacie* all around. Yet another place for looking, not necessarily buying, is a crammed clothing market on Tritone which shows admirable flexibility in its use of English. One window bears a sign: "The store at love [low?] prices," while the other window says: "Lowest princos in Rome."

As mentioned, Romans and a few intrepid foreigners expect a discount of about 10 percent. No guarantees, but try asking for a *sconto* and see what happens. Bargain, bargain as hard as your Italian and fingers will permit, in markets, and don't plan to shop on Monday morning, because most stores are closed then in compliance with a recent ruling (which keeps them open on Saturday afternoon, however).

A closing caveat. Between faking and thievery the Italian art market, from Etruscan urns to modern prints, leads a punch-drunk life. Seals and documentation, the solid ground on which the buyer thinks he stands, are also stolen, copied, and forged. Deal only with the most reputable galleries and antiquarians, and even then, if you intend to spend a good deal of money, take an expert along or sharpen your own expertise.

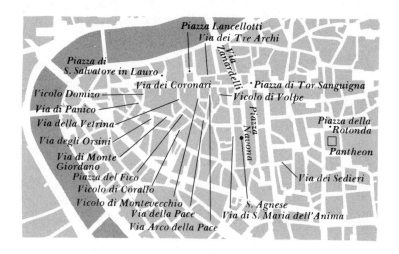

Piazza Lancellotti
Via dei Tre Archi
Piazza di
S. Salvatore in Lauro
Via dei Coronari
Via Zanardelli
Piazza di Tor Sanguigna
Vicolo Domizo
Vicolo di Volpe
Via di Panico
Via della Vetrina
Piazza della Rotonda
Via degli Orsini
Piazza Navona
Pantheon
Via di Monte Giordano
Piazza del Fico
Vicolo di Corallo
Via dei Sedieri
Vicolo di Montevecchio
Via della Pace
S. Agnese
Via di S. Maria dell'Anima
Via Arco della Pace

Walk 5

S. Maria della Pace to Pantheon

A long, buffeted life may distort an old face or create a carved ivory beauty, and so with churches. S. Sabina, for one, is the serene, perfect union of spirit and flesh that was the face of the old Einstein and that of Marie Curie. Other old faces and churches show as scored, pitted battlefields on which soothing transfigurations refuse to grow. Such, among a number, are S. Maria sopra Minerva and S. Maria della Pace, the latter more fortunate in its baroque theater-piazza bent into medieval alleys that run for breath to the sun-drenched, water-splashed air of the Piazza Navona. The church is an almost invisible octagon attributed to Bramante that holds in one of its obscured sides a fine unused Renaissance doorway. It is a semitemple on vigorous columns which stride forth to complete and balance wings of arch that answer the Mannerist need for flashing light beyond dark masses. It is also a dim, narrow set of rectangles breaking into chapels that gather what weak light they can find to display Renaissance pride and chapels retired to become collectors of the mold, scratches, and damp that gnaw at neglected churches.

Cats, girls, black-clad women appear and disappear into the piazza wings, and neighborhood boys play fervid games of soccer, scurrying for the ball among the pillars and under the bulging shopping bags of their aunts and neighbors who join to chorus anger. The boys play on, as they did in the fifteenth century, when a stone thrown by a boy hit the holy image of the Virgin which hung in the portico of a much earlier church, then called S. Andrea. The Virgin bled, attracting great miracle-hungry crowds, and the church was renamed in her honor S. Maria della Virtù by Sixtus IV; shortly after, to celebrate a peace pact—one of the numerous pacts that were constantly written and instantly forgotten—it was renamed S. Maria della Pace. A finer temple was needed for the changed dedication, and in 1482 work was begun on the new church. Though it went very slowly, shapes of chapels and altar changed in time, and ultimately in the mid-seventeenth century, under the Chigi Pope Alexander VII, Pietro da Cortona gilded and curled large areas of the interior and changed the face of the church and its compliant piazza completely. The piazza was required to keep its new design unaltered according to an order carved into an adjoining wall which prohibits the building or rebuilding or the introduction of any innovation under pain of punishment by papal authorities.

In spite of the machinery that welcomes to a church— the portico, the papal coats of arms, the papal portraits that have a Mephisthophelean cast in spite of the presence of angels, the neoclassic pilasters and pediment—there is no entrance to the church here. One must go through the arch of the Via Arco della Pace and enter the cloister at number 5. This work of Bramante, his first in Rome (early sixteenth century), is orderly, uncluttered, a Renaissance vision of a humanist's reasonable house yard. The purity of Bramante's

conception asks for little decoration except exceedingly
handsome lettering. The only other adornments are the shallow pilasters, a classical overhang, and the restrained elaborations of corner meetings of pilaster—and one wishes that
Bramante's solution of how to turn this sort of corner might
look less like a pair of cauliflower ears. The monuments in
the cloister are worth a little time; for one, the face of a
fashionable, smiling lady with a fresh roundness of cheek
and chin, a little curl and a flirtatious plume of hair escap-
ing from her coiled braid.

Achieving the church from the cloister requires some
exercise of Christian virtue: patience in waiting for its
attendants (a round portiere in black shawl and wary face
and her female relatives), charity in forgiving their crude
manners, and hope that, after you have paid the minimum
—underlined and stated in four languages—of 100 lire, they
will not bar the doors with their sturdy, intransigent bodies.
Traversing black passages, one comes into the light shed
by windows under the cupola of coffering in receding sizes
(another example of how Italian architecture was haunted
and supported by the Pantheon) bearing beguiling wreaths.
The ubiquitous Sangallo the Younger, who worked on the
cupola with Cortona, was responsible for one of the most
crowded of Renaissance tombs, surprising for a Florentine
who helped create the tasteful palaces of Montepulciano in
Tuscany. His heavy triumphal arch bearing excessive carvings, side niches overflowing with distorted figures of St.
Peter and St. Paul, and pensive tombal figures resting on
their elbows, wondering why they must lie on pseudo-
Egyptian sphinxes, is a bewildering too-muchness. It is
true that a major portion of the work was executed by a
pupil, but the master should have been supervising more
closely. But then, again, it was an exuberantly excessive
time.

The chapel near the locked portal is another, more subdued matter, the family chapel of the Ponzetti, *familiae
Partheonopae Romae* (a Roman family of Neapolitan ori-

gin), whose two little girls, Beatrice and Lavinia, died of the plague in 1505. The sad, plain small heads look balefully out of marble circles surrounded by exquisitely carved and wisely spaced frail ornaments. The designer of the monument, the Sienese Baldassarre Peruzzi, also painted the vault, a skillful boxing of curved space to hold several biblical scenes, one or two of them (especially the horizontal panel that deals with Noah and the Ark) reminiscent of the ethereal painting of his Sienese predecessors.

Other than the idealism of its cloister, the star of S. Maria della Pace is Raphael's paintings of the sibyls. The limited space is boundlessly opened by angels soaring forward and back of the large women and their messenger angels, the gestures of angels, sibyls, and putti creating a garland of suave movement. The sibyls, with their muscular arms and thrusting knees, bring one inevitably to Michelangelo, whose Sistine ceiling Raphael saw. Vasari: "Raphael, who was excellent in imitating, at once changed his style after seeing it [the Sistine Chapel] and to show his skill did the prophets and sibyls in la Pace." The younger man's sibyls (painted 1513–14) are less impassioned and overpowering; they prophesy and gently admonish, but their great eyes do not threaten and brood on apocalyptic visions. "After being dilated and spoiled by Michelangelo's great forms, my eye took no pleasure in the ingenious frivolities of Raphael's arabesques," said Goethe, too harshly. But he had a point.

Too close on, the stage set looks neglected, bathed in dusty weeping and hung with tattered posters of vanished concerts and pilgrimages. It must be seen at a distance that will restore its capacity to startle as one turns a corner. Searching for a more open view—not always easy because these crafty vicoli and via coil on each other like small gray burrowing animals, you should come to the Palazzo Gambirasi, which occupies the meeting of the Vicolo degli

Osti, the Via Arco della Pace, and the Via della Pace. The
original building of the fifteenth century has left only a
door on the Vicolo degli Osti. The rest submitted to the
urban planning that came with the rebuilding of S. Maria
della Pace in the seventeenth century, and it was during
that time that the original owners, a Spanish fraternity
dedicated to St. James, turned it over to a prelate of
Bergamo, a Gambirasi. The family shield over the main
door at 8 on Via della Pace is an interesting departure from
the lions, eagles, doves, and other fauna that announce and
protect noble Roman buildings; this one is a prawn (*gambero*) rampant—if a prawn ever can be so described—with
a cross rising from its claws. The devout, heraldic shrimp
leads upward to a row of windows decorated with masks
male and female. The prelate, or the artisan he hired, or
both, must have been fond of women—the male masks are
monstrously ugly, the women uniformly attractive. A few
paces along, the Vicolo degli Osti meets the Vicolo di
Montevecchio, whose meanders and those of its fellows are
like the venations of a leaf. You needn't examine anything
in particular to enjoy them, but a small palace of the sixteenth century (number 3) might be of interest. Peep into
the shops that occupy, as they were originally meant to, the
street openings, and if you are permitted to, go into the
courtyard—a polite smile and a hand in a pocket or purse
jingling a promise of coins will usually do it—for its pleasing proportions, the traces of a fifteenth-century door, and
good-looking antique column. As the Vicolo di Montevecchio
broadens into the piazza of its name, smell the smells and
listen to the sounds, if the time is appropriate, that pour
from the basic trattoria at the corner, and glance at the
appealing slight Renaissance house at number 4. The
crown of the piazza is a palazzo (number 6) attributed to
Peruzzi, denied by others who consider it too Palladian.
Leave it to the experts and feast on the harmonious duets
of window framed by triads of pilasters, the rays of rustication that spin out of the lower doors. The ensemble is

somewhat dimmed by age and the resigned air of its piazza, yet the bone structure holds. Again, as in many quarters of the city, a marble plaque warns of the penalties incurred by throwing garbage around, a warning that has never impressed Romans of any time, even as far back as the injunction of a very early king buried in the Forum. This particular call to civic pride is dated 1748 and bears the name of the king of all these twisted paths, Orsini—but more of him later.

Turn back into the Via della Pace and its adjoining Piazza del Fico, which enclose a small, gregarious market and a fair smattering of the foreign young who live in some of the unreconstructed, heatless apartments of the vicinity. The Vicolo del Fico and its neighbors, Corallo and Vacche, are in spite of rebuilding poor, poor streets, their former grandeur to be searched out carefully, like 8A on the Via delle Vacche with a fifteenth-century door and the scrappy remains of a frieze whose winged lions and putti have long stopped their gamboling. The erratic, narrow Via della Vetrina, lined with shops of lively meagerness, is dominated by the Palazzo Tanari (19–21), a tall seventeenth-century house whose rusticated corner doesn't seem to belong to the house at all. Nor does the minute piazza at the top of the stairs that run up the side of the house. Like many small working-class piazze, this is the communal fair-weather living room formed of several distressed houses, ill-lighted workshops, a strayed piece of marble column, prams, a few men going to or from lunch, a small, vocal population of children running up and down the stairs, and women, women, women of all ages and sizes who have something to say to each other every day, all day, and never weary of the conversation. Turning with the Via di Monte Giordano, looking for palazzi rescued and palazzi drowning, for heraldic symbols under cornices, you should reach the Vicolo del Montonaccio ("ugly big hill," neither ugly nor big), a modest rise that flattens into a handkerchief square with a couple of renewed houses, one of which might have been a Romanesque church.

You have about reached the heart of the extensive enclave that for five centuries bore the names of several branches of the powerful Orsini family. Like the Medici in Florence, the Visconti in Milan, and the Gonzaga in Mantua, the Orsini were for several centuries the history of their city. They made popes who were members of the family and others who were of the family's politics, which in the Middle Ages often meant agreement to destroy an enemy tribe. The overweening Boniface VIII, of whom it was said, "He got in like a fox, played the pontiff like a lion, went out like a dog," was imprisoned by an Orsini. Rather surprisingly, they aligned themselves with Cola di Rienzo, an opponent of the Colonnas, and an almost mystical figure of the late fourteenth century—a promise of Mussolini to some historians, a precocious egalitarian revolutionary to others —but managed to sustain his downfall and continued to fill the streets of Rome with their mercenaries. Occasionally, as a response to a papal curse on all their houses, several families formed an antipapal union and, the job of destroying or at least frightening a pope done, went back to snarling at each other.

As early as the twelfth century the Orsini were ensconced in a fortress built inside the Theater of Pompey in a strategic part of the city, near the Campo dei Fiori. In the thirteenth century the "monte" of Montegiordano, an artificial hill built on remains of older structures, already supported a fortress-tower that bore the Orsini name. Dante mentions it in describing the pilgrims on their way to and from St. Peter's in the jubilee year of 1300. The property ran down to the river, where there was a watchtower to guard the waters and the only access, which the family controlled, to the area of St. Peter's. As the family grew and proliferated so did the stronghold; towers and houses for various branches of the family abutted on each other, were demolished, added to, and remade to form a close, fortified village. It was a field for martial show and political conclaves, especially when Giordano Orsini, the head of the central line of the family, was a senator of

Rome (1341), and later the tapestried background for Renaissance princes, their cousin cardinals, their artists and writers, and their courtiers. The family fell into serious disfavor with the papal powers of the sixteenth century, partially because the mainline Giordano Orsini, Duke of Bracciano, fell in love, with the wife of one of Sixtus V's young relations. In the grand, feudal, king-of-all-I-survey manner, subject to no rule by pope or peers, Giordano strangled his wife in his castle on Lake Bracciano north of Rome, and his lady love saw to it that her husband was killed in the city streets. The couple were married, but Sixtus V banished the husband and confiscated his properties. The new wife was murdered by ex-relatives—some say of the first husband, some say of the second—perhaps for revenge, perhaps for the opportunity to pick up some ducal trinkets. The Orsini were not in a healthy condition, and in the seventeenth century, members of the collateral branches of the family began to leave out of choice or debt; the vast mound, after 500 years of being Orsini, was sold to a Gabrielli family whose lines became enmeshed in a later time with the Bonapartes. The intertwined Gabriellis and the families they married into dispersed and died, and late in the nineteenth century the hamlet was taken over by a Taverna family.

It is by that name that you now look for the shards of palazzi, a scramble of the medieval, blocks of the fifteenth century, a run of imitation medieval crenelations, a seignorial fountain that combines the seventeenth and eighteenth centuries. Walking around the walls—one is inclined to say "ramparts," prompted by the fortress faces of the palaces on the Via di Panico and the Via di Monte Giordano —gives some idea of the size of the holdings now let to workshops and, above, the choicest apartments in Rome, whose tenants must run a gauntlet, as they go through neighboring streets, of Communist party posters, blistered tenements over Renaissance doors, washing attached to ancient iron hooks, the sound of saws, and the smell of glue. The more rewarding view is from the courtyard, entered on the Via degli Orsini, which centers on a large frail fountain whose waters splash into four successive basins covered in the golden-green velvet of moss. At the left, a small inner court that recalls the fourteenth century. Back of the court, an ancient stairway, the remains of a tower and, to the right, a line of battlements. While you are trying to put it all together in its well-kept greens of vines and orange trees, look for a pair of bears (*orsini*—the family name) which once stood on either side of a set of walls and, holding the family shield before them, spat adroitly into the fountain. That was in the time of the proud Orsini; the bears now do nothing but sit.

A stairway at the back of the court will let you slip into the Via dei Coronari, another sort of King of the Hill, feeding as many retainers as the Monte did. With the Via Giulia, the Via del Babuino, and their tangents, it comprises the major antiques market of the city, an unrelenting row of patinas, gilt, bronze, curlicues gleaming and springing from polished windows. After following the engagingly turned clusters of local streets, the absolute straightness and length of the Via dei Coronari is disconcerting. There was purpose in it; with its adjuncts to the east and west it made the old Via Recta (straight) a wide direct pilgrimage route to the river and across to St. Peter's. Along the way pilgrims could buy rosaries whose makers and vendors gave the street its name—as the signs of inns that housed the pilgrims gave their streets the names of Volpe, Fico, Orso, to pick out a few.

The word "pilgrims" usually evokes a picture of barefoot, sackclothed, medieval dourness which, however, does not belong to the Via dei Coronari as it was cleared and remade by Pope Sixtus IV, in the late fifteenth century. In the freshened ground there spring up palaces of considerable luxury, and it proves rewarding to look up above the shop fronts of Etruscan vases, marble torsos, cut-velvet chairs, and ornaments wrested from defenseless churches, to the upper façades of the houses, glancing below, now and then, to catch a grand old portal. It doesn't much matter in which direction you go first from this central point of a web of colorful paths. Some paths of laundry, sawdust in the street, baskets that haul up groceries, bumping against frieze griffons and fantasy foliage, will lead you pleasurably back. You might be near the Via Gabrielli, at 156 Coronari, which is a restored fifteenth century house, insistently medieval under its low, distrustful cornice. A number of the houses you pass were once magnificently scored with skies full of birds, winged horses, and winged babies flying in a shower of fancies. Gone, gone, gone, and too bad. The house of Prospero Mochi (148 Coronari) has fared better. Designed by Pietro Rosselli, who worked with Sangallo the Younger and, possibly, with Michelangelo, it was built in 1516 on virile Renaissance-classic lines, the ornamentation low-keyed except for the lettering that affirms the name of the proprietor and his job with the Vatican and, above the windows, little bits of homily: "Only that which you make is yours"; "Keep your promises"; "We cannot all do everything." One sees the proprietor as a sententious bore, but the lettering is good-looking and the Latin rings sonorously. Next door, a less verbal house, equally attractive.

At its meeting with the Vicolo Domizio, the corner has been sliced down and flattened to leave a surface for a splendid tabernacle designed by the nonstop younger Sangallo. The immediate neighbors ask for some imagination: where there is a plaque to commemorate a martyr buried in the Fosse Ardeatine there was the house of a furrier to the pope, covered with paintings of horrifying mythological subjects which, fortunately and unfortunately, no longer shriek into the street, and at 122 a sixteenth-century house skirted in a painted band of weak terra cotta unworthy of its purported owner, Raphael. A family of high papal functionaries under Gregory XIII, the Vecchiarelli, built in the 1500's a grand house whose rusticated door, alternations of rounded and square window frames, and the white box of *altana* follow the orderly rules of their time. The small courtyard breaks no rules either but within them manages to achieve greater appeal with a spitting lion fountain, the essential sarcophagus that sprays greenery, and in the vaulted entrance two Renaissance pages, as poised and disdainful as hundreds of Renaissance paintings insisted they be.

Turning on the Via dei Coronari (with a look, from the Piazza dei Coronari, at the campanile of SS. Celso e Giuliano which looks like a broad velvet cap) in the direction of the Piazza Navona, one comes on a piece of "Roma Sparita" never entirely *sparita* (vanished), as no period of Rome ever is, totally. This time the anachronism is a pair of street musicians, both in rusty country black, the accordionist seemingly the father of the fifteen-year-old girl who sings in harsh rural shouts, demands payment sharply from shining store to store, and then retires to count the take on the piazza of S. Salvatore in Lauro. This shapeless piazza abandons rather than embraces its church, a result of ruthless demolition. In the seventeenth century the barracks of the Corsican Papal Guard stood on the piazza and, in front of it, a monument that told their shame in provoking the French court. The papal family, the Chigi, were out of favor with the French—and vice versa—in the late seventeenth century, and when the French ambassador arrived escorted by an impressive number of troops to settle into the Farnese palace, Mario Chigi, the pope's brother who was in charge of the Vatican army, called out the papal guard to surround the embassy. When a Corsican was killed by a French soldier, the pope's guard rushed the palace and, held off by the closed gates, turned on the ambassadress and her entourage, just then returning from an outing. The ambassadress escaped, but one of her company was killed. As a result, a full-sized French army was soon gathered to march on Italy. Before it could arrive, the Corsican guard was dissolved, the pope apologized, his general-brother apologized, and so did other members of the family. The story of the Corsicans' misbehavior was scratched into a pyramid on the piazza, removed when life with the French became easier some years later.

The piazza, named for a vanished laurel grove, was something of an academic center at various times. In the late eighteenth century, Pope Pius VI built a school for the education of poor boys of the rione here; the mid-nineteenth century saw the music academy of S. Cecilia housed in a pleasant seventeenth-century building (13). The most important scholastic entity was the great library of the Cardinal Latino Orsini. He set up a hostel for a group of learned Venetian canons to whom he bequeathed his invaluable collection of manuscripts, which were reduced to ashes in the 1527 sack of Rome. The church of S. Salvatore in Lauro leaves interest and charm to the convent (number 15). Practically all cloisters, their maidenly bashfulness dressed in embroidery of tiny arches and slender pilasters, please. This Renaissance cloister is in the usual attractive pattern and, in addition, holds by the hand a smaller courtlet whose bits of old church, good doorways, and round fountain add up to an engaging miniature.

On Coronari, under a tall loggia burred with ancient iron hooks for clothes poles, one comes on the sudden opening to the stairs that lead to the nonchurch of SS. Simone e Giuda. The disconsolate houses, one of them incongruously burdened with the hubris of the Orsini name and rose, narrow and narrow toward one another, their walls covered with drying laundry, the worn stairs hospitable to female tenants and their dogs—the small, snappish dogs of concierges, portieres, and janitors. The one old-fashioned lamp light near the top of the stairs illuminates vestiges of church color around a doorway that now gives out the sounds of a carpenter's shop. A city whose business was the papacy had necessarily to build churches for every confraternity, every group of citizens from other Italian cities and other countries, for guilds, for large numbers of monastic orders, to show devotion to a crowded hagiography of saints. It became equally necessary in times of diminished fervor that many of the smaller churches be abandoned. You will find them, dusty blanks, on a number of streets in the old city, not lucky enough to sustain life as carpenter shops, or better yet, the movie house that SS. Simone e Giuda had been before it began to measure and saw wood.

Almost next door, near the Vicolo di Montevecchio, is the nicely balanced Palazzo dell'Antico Monte di Pietà and, beyond, the worn Palazzetto Bonaventura, scraped down to brick but its once attractive details of pilasters and capitals still visible. The courtyard, with a leafy trickling fountain, rows of birdcages, window frames carved in a seashell design, and skillful plasterwork on a stairway, shows restoration by an affectionate hand.

Simultaneously watching traffic—particularly carts bearing credenzas like royal biers—and the tops of buildings to see what overhang protects a vestige of graffiti designs, searching for shields that sit like birds of prey at the corners of palazzi, for noseless Roman heads pressed into Renaissance walls, you should come on the Piazza Lancellotti and its palazzo, built in the late 1500's for a family of Sicilian origin who were doctors to Popes Julius II and Leo X. Other than its size and cool progression of windows, some of its distant allure derives from a roof cornice confected of egg-and-dart designs interlaced with floral patterns and an unusually elaborate doorway designed to show off a grotesque head whose long mustache and beard shape a cornucopia. At the corners, votive adjuncts charge out of the rusticated stone, not larger than others you will find in Rome but as large as any and certainly as animated. Some facts you might care to know about the Lancellotti. One prince (of the "black" papal aristocracy) closed his grand portal when Italy became unified under a king rather than a pope late in the nineteenth century, and it remained closed—a symbol of secession from the perfidious city—for fifty years, although minor doors were kept open for

business and subdued entertainment. Another prince was
the owner of one of the great works of antique art, the
Lancellotti Discus Thrower (now in the Museo delle Terme),
which came to rest in the family collection after its discovery on the Esquiline Hill in 1781. Third matter: you
cannot get into the court with main force or lire, but
try. You are in the city of miracles, and from the testimony
of old prints the stately columned and statued court would
appear to be worth the supplication of saints or major-
domos.

Among the contortions of alley that wait for release into
Coronari, look for the bridging of houses on the Via dei
Tre Archi and the entrance arch to the Vicolo S. Trifone,
which earns the distinction of being the narrowest street
in Rome among close competitors, its slice of sky blazoned
with a neighborhood signature, the strangely sharp high-
colored foreign spire of the church of S. Maria dell'Anima,
an early sixteenth-century curio from the north. A twentieth-
century curio inhabits 34 Coronari, where a playful hand
has painted vines and Rousseau flowers to trail over door-
bells and mailboxes.

On the street of S. Maria dell'Anima there was a rest
house and chapel for pilgrims from Germany and the Low
Countries. The early chapel became the national German
church (a sign advises of a *Sonntagsgottesdienst* in *deut-
scher Sprache*), which is a more peculiar mixture than
many in a city of distracted churches—strict Renaissance
façade whose upper lightless windows give it the look of a
granary, the interior in late Gothic style, the stained glass
and monuments largely kitsch of several eras. From the
ceiling at the right of the altar there hangs a red cardinal's
hat, perhaps that of the last non-Italian Pope, Adrian VI of
Utrecht. He was, according to all accounts, a reforming
pope from a no-nonsense country already touched by the
angry breath of Luther. The Church, he said, must be puri-
fied of corruption and luxury, the pouring of treasures into
already glittering temples; the processions and theatricals

must stop. The profligacy of a Medici, Leo X, who spent everything that he and the papacy had and to replenish the exchequer sold indulgences (which cost the Church a good number of adherents), must stop. Adrian unluckily followed not only the Medici pope but the erratic, energetic, artist-consuming Julius II, who was no more a holy country prelate than *his* predecessor, the Borgia Alexander VI. It was an unjust line for a reformer to follow. Ineffectual, thoroughly hated by the merry cardinals, he died after one year in the papacy (1522–23), mourned by no Italian. As if in apology, one of the most conspicuously Italianate tombs is, ironically, that of the dour pope. The body lies flat, like that of a medieval abbé, but all around him, clogging his gaunt aura, is a frenzy of symbolic figures and bas-reliefs designed by Peruzzi, whose taste could be impeccable but rarely austere. The kitsch returns at the side of the church with a sugary offering box whose Babe looks like a young Brendan Behan—big chin, potato nose, and swimming eyes.

Remaining for another moment in the Via dell'Anima, look up (from the shelter of a parked car, preferably, the viewer's best friend) at the vivacious cornice of lions and olive branches, at 61, and, at 66, the early sixteenth-century Casa Sander, the property of a functionary of the German hospice-church. Redone in the nineteenth century, it remains an interesting building where some attempt has been made to renew the bands of graffiti. Between the bands, plaques that quote the classics, offer up short prayers, and, near the overhang, two busts that might be Dante and Vergil, the latter claimed by the church because church fathers found, in one Eclogue, a prophecy of the coming of Christ.

At the place where the Via dei Coronari empties into the Piazza di Tor Sanguigna, near a palazzo that grows lilies and stars, a most stupendous *edicola* in honor of Mary and the Piazza Navona.

Behind the northern end of the piazza there is an open-

ing in a building (on the Via Zanardelli) which permits
one to view the glass-protected rutted and stepped blocks
of a "circus" (race course) of the end of the first century
A.D. The piazza was already a place for games in Caesar's
time and Augustus'. Nero remodeled it for imitations of
Greek Olympic games in which he often took part, to the
shame of the more respectable of the Roman citizenry, who
liked some minimal decorum in their emperors. The less
amusing Domitian changed the area into the marble lozenge
that held from 30,000 to 50,000 spectators and which gives
the piazza its present closed, salon-like shape. Like any
sporting center where the betting ran high, shops and eating stalls affixed themselves to the arches, and for the gam-
bler who couldn't tear himself away, a brothel or two.
Classical Rome's supply of prostitutes, according to contemporary reports—see Juvenal and Martial—was as popu-
lous then as later and today.

The Circo Agonale, for the Greek (as chic a language in
Rome as French was in pre-Soviet Russia) *agone*, which
means racing, leaves its name stamped on the church of
S. Agnese in Agone and less distinctly as a corruption which
became, in later dialect, Navona. The word *gogna*, fetters
or being deeply humiliated, may also have some bearing on
the name and enter into the story of the piazza with
particular reference to S. Agnese. The Christian girl of the
early fourth century ("of a good Roman family" must be
added to all legends of Roman lady martyrs) was seized and
pressed to deny her religion and to marry a heathen. The
alternative was to work in a circus brothel. She held to her
faith and was dragged stark naked to a local bordello
where, miraculously, her hair flowed down as a great golden
cloak to cover her completely. The soldiers tried to burn
her on a scaffold where her church stands, but the flames
turned to gentle rain for her while the fire consumed her
executioners. Although it was difficult to find small enough
fetters for her fine hands, they managed to drag her to
beheading outside the gates of the city where S. Agnese

fuori le Mura now stands. When the church was freed under Constantine, some few years later, a chapel was built over the scene of her miracle. The zealous feel impelled to say that the remains of mosaic flooring below the church were part of the brothel. There is no harm in believing so if it makes a convincing, concrete picture. Certainly, the young nuns visiting from the rural convents recoil in convinced horror as they tiptoe into the substructure of the church.

That there was an earlier church is recorded fact witnessed by scraps of medieval fresco. The present church is a billowing of marble ordered by the Pamphili Pope Innocent X, designed by Carlo Rainaldi, modified and finished by Borromini, who put his intricate balances of volume and space into the façade and the twin bell towers. As anyone who has ever read a book on Rome knows, two figures of Bernini's Four Rivers fountain make gestures of contempt for the rival's façade; one shields his eyes in horror while another seems frightened by the possibility that the church might fall on him. A good story, and it makes the brilliant, swirling, roaring baroque masterpiece of fountain art more intimate. However, the flat facts deny the story. The fountain was erected in 1651 and the church façade not finished until five or six years later. Confused chronology rarely stops an amusing story, however, and this one will go on merrily through generations of tourists, untainted by fact.

"Ah, how the piazza has been ruined, these beatniks and their crummy art and crappy jewelry, and I'm sure they're passing dope, and the noisy demonstrations on that side street," moans an "old Roman," usually an expatriate who fled Pittsburgh. It isn't what it used to be, they tell you. They are wrong; the piazza was always a place for crowds, games, buying and selling, at times the arena of the aristocracy, at others the property of hoi polloi. Through earthquakes, riots, political upheaval, the fortunes and misfortunes of popes, waves of plague and floods, the show went on, as tourneys, processions, races, the stage for raucous itinerant entertainers. In the late fifteenth century the big market that had from time immemorial lived on the fringes of the Capitoline Hill was moved, by order of the papacy, to the piazza. There it remained until Innocent X had it removed, but it returned and stayed until the late 1800's, when it went a short distance southward to the Campo dei Fiori. One historian records a magnificent pageant staged in the beginning of the 1500's for Cesare Borgia, very likely arranged by his doting father Alexander VI, when, with classical accouterments of appropriate magnificence, Cesare was not too subtly identified with the triumphant Julius Caesar. The piazza activity most often pictured in old engravings was that which took place on August weekends, on and off, from the mid-seventeenth to the mid-nineteenth centuries. The circus, more sharply sloped toward the center than it now is, was flooded by the waters which normally fed the fountains. The gentry took their Sunday passeggiata in carriages—the Pamphili vehicle was a golden gondola—hub-deep in water and poor children who waded in for fun and to gather up coins that occasionally spilled from vehicles. As for every festa, broad banners of silk and cut velvet fringed in gold hung from the windows of the palaces.

The only banner now visible is that of the Museo di Roma which hangs over the door of the Palazzo Braschi at the southern end of the magnificent piazza and its three fountains (only the stupefying Rivers fountain is actually by Bernini; he sketched out the fountain of the Moor, executed by others, and had nothing to do with the fountain of Neptune, which was begun by Della Porta in 1574 and not finished until three centuries later). The Braschi, built for the nephews of Pope Pius VI and the last of its nepotic kind, is overlarge and resolutely classical as a late-eighteenth-century revival of the Renaissance. Except for a noble stairway, the palace doesn't work, but your interest will, in any case, be concentrated on museum matter.

Rounding back into the piazza, one comes immediately

on the Palazzo Pamphili-Doria. Since it now houses the Brazilian Embassy, which opens its doors to the public on Sunday mornings, there is difficulty in sorting out the imported from the indigenous among the furnishings. Certainly a modern bar wagon, photographs, a jade collection placed in convolutions of trellis on the walls, the collection of china, and, above all, silver as tea and coffee ensembles set out in haut-bourgeois spreads are probably Brazilian. More difficult to place in time or provenance are the crystal chandeliers and the Venetian mirrors, the silk wall covers and the curios, which include bunches of alabaster grapes, a reminder of the Roman practice of presenting the best bunch off a vine as a gift, and the alabaster eggs used as precigarette, preworry-bead occupation for nervous hands. The grisailles in window and door frames are often games of endearing putti overshadowed by yards of biblical and mythical painting. Two works of unusual interest are the Borromini ceiling in the room before the gallery and the gallery itself planned by Borromini and painted by Pietro da Cortona as a billowy retelling of the adventures of the first Pamphili, Aeneas, surrounded by myriad Pamphili doves, in sharp contrast to the dour Roman faces below.

Give the Rainaldi façade, its family motifs, the dove with an olive branch in its mouth alternating with fleurs-de-lis, and the court some time while you consider the wealth and power of a family who owned and still does the whole of the piazza, who could put their dove on the Four Rivers obelisk while most other obelisks were required to wear crosses or saints. No one quite knows what the Greek-named Pamphilis were doing in the millennia after Aeneas founded the family (it was a practice of the powerful to choose a mythical hero as the first sprout of the family tree), but in the fifteenth century they were a noted Umbrian family who by ones and twos came to Rome to install themselves in houses near the piazza and improved their standing by marrying into princely Roman families. In the seventeenth century the family produced its pope, Innocent X, who ordered that church and palace be rebuilt and glorious fountains erected.

The superb Bernini portrait of Innocent X in the Doria palace on the Corso shows a shrewd face with an alert, slightly malicious gleam playing around the eyes. The equally masterly Velázquez portrait that shares the small room with Bernini betrays a tiredness that does not, however, erase the shrewdness. Innocent X appears to be a man not readily bested. He was: by a woman whose pugnacious face, carved under graceful veiling intended to soften—unsuccessfully—an implacable toughness, controls another section of the Doria galleries, as she controlled life on the Piazza Navona. Unlike the artists for whom he sat, his sister-in-law, Olimpia Maidalchini, found the Pope extremely biddable. There are historical hints of boudoir scandal and broader hints of the power she wielded, through her brother-in-law, over the papacy. According to biographers, no papal business went on without the knowledge and interference of Olimpia, and she saw to it that each transaction was profitable. All applicants for office had to pay her and heavily; no bishop could take a see without settling with Olimpia, often putting his family heavily in debt for the privilege. She stayed very close to Innocent and left him only, they say, one night a week, carrying off sacks of money and treasure to hide in her own palace. On these forays in the last months of Innocent's life she locked him into his bedroom so that he might do nothing, see no one, without her knowledge and control. Voracious even after his death, as she had been through the ten years of his reign, she refused to meet his funeral expenses—she was a poor widow, she said—and the dead pope lay in a rat-infested toolroom unclaimed by any Pamphili until a couple of minor officials supplied the coffin and funeral costs. An ironic end for a man who bought architects, painters, and sculptors of genius, who owned valuable tracts of Roman property and quarries of the choicest marble and, as the Vicar of Christ, was the head of a great kingdom.

A place of several moods and aspects, the piazza shows its most appealing face across from the church, which wears little balcony-aprons and large hats of spurting pink, yellow, blue flowers and green vines that set off the tonalities of old wall. As you walk under the balconies for still another view of the Rivers fountain, notice the plaque that marks the height to which the Tiber rose in 1870, bring back the market awnings that sloped from the tops of rusticated doorways and low balconies to shelter greens and oranges, bric-a-brac (through which John Evelyn rummaged in the seventeenth century), old books, and clothing. Almost entirely an act of the imagination is the viewing, at number 45, of a palazzetto believed to be of or by Vignola, enclosed in private property, a garage in fact. One can just make out, through the grillwork, a fine arch and a strip of frieze above it. Kneeling will bring more of the plasterwork to view and three distinguished windows. From the Via Tor Sanguigna, only arches, two handsome lamps, and a river-god fountain are visible, rare furnishings for a garage. A few of the houses at the northern curve of the piazza, fairly new additions to restore the curve of the oval after demolition in the 1930's, look like clowns in their fake painted rustication and patchy plaster. Take your eye quickly to the wooden baldacchino that imitates brocade panels and tassels on a neighboring house and, to return more closely to the antique flavors of the piazza, stop in at the turned-around church of Nostra Signora del Sacro Cuore, once upon a time the Spanish national church, still sparsely sprinkled with the shells symbolic of St. James of Compostella. Like S. Maria sopra Minerva it smells faintly Gothic and is more attractive because its vaults have not been freighted with poor décor. Glance at the odd pair of angels, one skillfully worked, the other lumpish, over the portal, and at the austere chapel for St. James designed by Antonio Sangallo the Younger.

The Via dei Sedieri, named for the makers of chairs who worked and work at the trade on this street, should take you to the best coffee in Rome, in the caffè S. Eustachio on the piazza of that name. Before you take a seat, station yourself near the facing newsstand and look back at the glorious swells of Borromini's S. Ivo hidden in the Sapienza Palace and the ardent, coiling, flaming spire much admired and copied in northern countries. Seated and sipping of the nectar, gazing around the quiet space, you will come on the deer's head and cross that are the emblem of the piazza church. The head is the replica of a vision that appeared to one of Trajan's generals. As he gazed at the moving face he heard a voice commanding him to be baptized in the Christian faith. He obeyed, taking the name of Eustachius, and saw to it that members of his family were converted as well. As if cursed rather than blessed, he soon suffered every sort of loss—possessions gone, his wife carried off by marauders in Egypt, where the family had migrated, his children killed by fierce animals. Reduced to poverty and ignominy, he was sought out by Rome to lead troops in a new campaign in the east, this time under Hadrian. He conducted his campaign gloriously; his wife and a number of his children reappeared; all went well until he was asked to participate in the sacrificial ceremonies to celebrate the victory. He refused, and the whole family was killed. There is something wrong with the story; the punishments and rewards fall out of and into incongruous slots. The only possible explanation may be that S. Eustachio was appointed the role of Christian parallel to the Hebrew Job.

A step under the deer, a turn on a street that sells old books, a few cane chairs and baskets, and there it is, the Piazza della Rotonda, the starting point of the 94 bus pausing for its flight to the Aventine, the 87 which picks up its load to carry it to S. Giovanni and beyond; where a curvaceous fountain holds up yet another obelisk dug out of the vast local temple grounds for Isis; a piazza ringed with trattorie, caffès, stuffed with taxis when you don't want them, crammed with behemoth tourist buses from Easter into the fall; a pool of beefy, Nordic sweat in August; the Pantheon.

ROME CENTRAL

S. Giovanni

Long before St. Peter's was a chapel built by the frightened
Constantine (busily building shrines but not converted until
death stared into his face), the site of S. Giovanni in Laterano was famous in Rome. Here were the gardens of the
Lateranus family, extensive, ennobled with marble and
statuary, enviable enough for Messalina the wife of Claudius
to grab the way much Roman property was taken. Accuse
a man of anything that suggested disrespect or remote
menace to the Emperor and have his properties confiscated,
quite in the manner of Henry VIII in his gathering of
church property 1,400 years later.

Constantine gave the land to the pope, who built a church,
destroyed and rebuilt, destroyed and expanded, in the common experience of Roman churches, from the fourth to the
nineteenth centuries. Unlike St. Peter's, it has no unifying
gesture of colonnades or walls to hide its irregularities and is
less populated and more popular, in the Italian sense of "common people," than St. Peter's. Buses etch their intransigent
paths across its buildings, disgorging visitors to the wandering, many-aged hospital nearby. On S. Giovanni's Day
porchetta and caramel-nut sweets stands waft their succulent odors up to the frenzied holy men who threaten like
Old Testament prophets (at a distance they are subdued
to a pale-golden wreath over the city), and rattan baskets
fill the space where Holy Roman emperors and popes trod
in their silken shoes. Standing on one of the perilous islands
that make the vast shapeless piazza just about possible to
cross, one sees outcroppings of aged wall and aqueduct
supporting houses where they can, the tallest and oldest
Egyptian obelisk in the city, the glitter of mosaics in an

unexpected concavity, stretches of flowered green that lead
to a modern version of St. Francis and to the side and
southward the Porta Asinaria, almost winsome for a Roman
gate, that provides descent into a prosperous shopping row,
astonished at the gaping pits and angular metals of subway
construction. Immediately to the right, the restless market
of Via Sannio. Infinitely less demanding than St. Peter's,
the gathering must still be taken section for section, bearing
the knowledge that this was once the core of the papacy.
Here kings were anointed and at the climax of solemn
magnificent processions the tiara placed on the heads of
new popes, a ceremony repeated for nearly 200 popes who
lived in the palace attached to the cathedral until Avignon
became the papal seat in the early fourteenth century. The
papacy never returned to S. Giovanni but established its
ceremonies and offices, after the Avignon exile, at St. Peter's.

The octagonal baptistry built by Constantine, its shape
and a few interior details recalling his time, stands off by
itself, to the west of the church and palace. A double row of
marble and porphyry columns circles an enormous green
bowl used for total immersion, the practice in earlier bap-
tisms. Led by a tall, elderly gentleman in a black smock
with the significant face of a Dante or Savonarola, one is
admitted to several chapels that reveal mosaics of the
fifth and seventh centuries, vestiges of early structure, and
a Virgin among saints in a royal purple robe extending her
arms in the gesture of an orant. The chapel Dante treats
with the greatest respect (his hands do not touch the door;
he uses a black cloth) is that of the fifth century whose
bronze doors, taken from a pagan structure, sing an eerie
polyphonic tune, an air of buried stone and centuries.

The red granite obelisk adorned a temple of Thebes 3,500
years ago. Try to visualize the size of the Roman boat which
carried it across the seas, the vehicles that wheeled it to
the Circus Maximus, the number of slaves and the rope
required to pull it erect and embed it in the race course.
Then the slow, careful lowering in the sixteenth century
and cartage to S. Giovanni to replace Marcus Aurelius,

who had ridden off to the Campidoglio. Diagonally across the piazza, a reconstruction that includes original elements of a triclinium of the papal palace of the eighth into ninth centuries. The message of its mosaics is missionary, Christ instructing the Apostles to carry his word throughout the world. Charlemagne and Pope Leo III are both present, wearing the square halos of the living. Romantic historians like to see Charlemagne, a determinedly Christian king unlike some of his successors, sitting at table under the invocations, celebrating his coronation at the Lateran and, later, St. Francis asking that his order be accepted by the church.

Nearby, another vestige of the old palace, the Sancta Sanctorum, the private chapel of the popes, moved into a building of the late sixteenth century as was the stairway, the Scala Santa, attributed by persistent legend to the fortress-castle of Pontius Pilate, of which there is a model near the stairs. On these treads which supposedly knew the feet of Christ and were consequently sent back to be venerated in Rome by the mother of Constantine, St. Helena, thousands of pilgrims have toiled up on their knees to peer into the heavily barred Sancta Sanctorum, which holds almost invisible relics of superior holiness and an image of Christ not made by human hands. Steps for normal access flank the sacred stairs, and don't try ordinary locomotion among the kneeling devout pressed close to each other during Holy Week. The results would be troublesome, and in any case, not all of us have the courage of Martin Luther, who is reported to have risen to his feet midway up the stairs and walked down among the kneeling.

Only the courtyard of the papal palace is now visible, often used for concerts or plays with a devotional tinge. The façade of the church proper rises portentously, like the side of a mountain, on colossal columns, and speaks its meaning for all the world to know: "The cathedral of Rome and the world."

The last of the five entrances under the portico is closed and blank, except for its cross, to mark it as a door opened only during Holy Year. The bronze of the central door once closed a portal of the Roman court, the Curia, which still stands in the Forum. Inside, as in St. Peter's, the eye doesn't know where to rest and looks for a haven in the long Borromini arcades that seem bare, unfinished, offering few distractions from the ingenious shifts of light and shade that come to rest in the long folded wings of young angels.

In the center of the transept, a soaring Gothic tabernacle whose lacework gathers around two silver busts, the reliquaries for the heads of St. Peter and St. Paul and, below, the much restored papal altar which incorporates remains of the altar used in the first church. Tombs and tombs and tombs of popes and cardinals and their families stud chapel walls in styles from the Cosmatesque to the "classic" of the nineteenth century, from the appeal of Arnolfo di Cambio to later dull, and more church painting than any but the expert or the obsessed might care to examine. You may come across a fragment of fresco that is timidly accredited to Giotto, and a relief copy of Leonardo da Vinci's *Last Supper* with a piece of The Table included in its boundaries. There are many bits of holy wood in many churches, so let it go if it isn't immediately visible, and head for the cloister. (Closed, keep in mind, between noon and 3, like the baptistry.) It resembles the cloister of S. Paolo fuori le Mura, made by the same Vassalletto family in the same period (early thirteenth century) with the same twisted, straight, turned, glittering little columns and the strange fauna and flora in their capitals, a repetition of a miniature, enchanted world whose ordered fancies and fragile charms never pall.

S. Maria Maggiore

A straight indifferent arrow of street, Merulana, whose pieces of exoticism are a tank of ferocious tropical fish at the corner of the Via Machiavelli and an on-and-off, in at least two senses, burlesque house, the Teatro Brancaccio, shoots to the top of the Esquiline Hill, where in broad, "here I am and here I'll stay" baroque indomitably sits S. Maria Maggiore, another of the major pilgrimage goals. Improvements of many epochs, worth your time if you are devoted to church art of several centuries, fill the great space, the prime lure the mosaics that depict Old Testament events as they were visualized in the fifth century, strong, direct, and difficult to see because of the height at which they are placed; they require binoculars and the cooperation of Roman sunlight. The mosaics of the same period in the triumphal arch dealing with New Testament events are somewhat more available, as are the large thirteenth-century figures in the apse, under the fairly unique—for Rome— Gothic windows.

S. Prassede

Near S. Maria Maggiore there is a yellow sign which points to S. Prassede, hidden in a dim street of the same name. You will not enter the main entrance, but the most easily accessible, the result of distracted changes since the ninth century and the density of working-class houses that crowd and cover the church. In spite of Robert Browning's "The Bishop Orders His Tomb at S. Praxed's," which suggests a male saint, S. Prassede was a woman, the sister of S. Pudenziana, whose martyrdom was honored in a fifth-century church. The indispensable necrophilia of Roman churches has its counterpart here in the shape of a porphyry disk in the center of the floor, the cover of a well in which the saint collected the blood and remains of earlier martyrs. A coin in a box buys a short period of light for viewing the sisters in gemmed Byzantine costumes standing with Christ and saints who hold the crowns of sainthood in their covered hands, worked in ninth-century mosaic along the triumphal arch and in the apse vault. Very-old-often-equals-very-modern in art is exemplified by three rows of white-haired, white-bearded figures, all of the same height and age, all making the same gesture in a singularly abstract, hypnotizing distribution of verticals, horizontals, and circles which might, with minor changes, have been painted in this century.

The breathtaking chapel of S. Zenone, of the same period and style and justly called the Garden of Paradise, was closed to women except on Sundays during Lent—according to Augustus Hare—at one time. It may have been a vengeful act on all women because of Eve's conduct in Paradise, although the stated reason for barring women was the presence of an extremely holy relic, a section of the pillar to which Christ was bound. That doesn't make much sense either.

Now women, like men, can drop a coin in the light box and be readmitted to the Garden, first passing through an arch of sternly handsome icon-like holy portraits. The vault of the chapel, centered on Christ, is supported by a serene flight of four attenuated, exquisitely drawn angels. The same unearthly slenderness forms the apostles, saints, and symbols that take their perfect places in the small, golden box. Remarkable as they are, they do not make Paradise; that is achieved by deep, full-colored bands and sprays of floral design in reds and blues and small bursts of yellow and orange, giving and taking luminosity from the golden glistening fragments they bind. This, like all versions of Paradise, is hard to leave, but one must at some time gaze respectfully at the flagellation column brought from Jerusalem in the thirteenth century, at the immortal colored stones in the pavement, at the columns, pieces of architectural ornament, and the marble urn that introduce the chapel. The original main entrance looks into a dark yard draped with laundry, nothing left of façade but the white abstract patterns of sectioned windows and a much later portal. The exit to the street is a brick funnel, its pride lost centuries ago, as long ago as the flight of the papacy to

Avignon, which left many churches impoverished and ready
for decay.

A short distance away the unexpected presence must be
noted—in this area of shops, bars, buses, and busy, practical here-and-now moving toward the railroad station—of a
remarkably well-preserved Roman arch that makes a picturesque corner of Via S. Vito. The Arco di Gallieno, for
the emperor Gallienus of the third century, served as the
gate of a wall that protected this section of the Esquiline,
and its distinction, other than its good proportions, is the
fact that it was built to honor the emperor by a man of no
particular distinction or fame, "a simple citizen," a guidebook says. But it seems unlikely, from what one knows of
late Imperial Rome, that he was truly, innocently simple
and not buying at least a genial atmosphere for a future
favor.

Suburra and S. Martino ai Monti

You are now on the eastern border of the Suburra, not a
rione (its parent body is Rione—from the Roman city
divisions, regiones—Monti) or a quartiere. The name appears only on a sunken piazza behind a Metropolitana station and as an alternate name for a church dedicated to
S. Agata, and it is still referred to in guidebooks as the
"ancient quarter of ill fame," quite ancient, judging from
Juvenal's reference to "the cesspools underlying the slums of
the Suburra." Conveniently close to the imperial forums, the
slimy well on whose crests stood the gardens, palaces, and
baths of the exceedingly rich and the villas of lesser though
prosperous luminaries, it was a Hell's Kitchen of cheap
brothels, of thieves' dens, of beggars' hovels, of the disso-
lute poor and the destitute. It remained a tough neighborhood, as rough and varicolored as Trastevere, with which it
did battle regularly, in centuries past, among the sheep and

cows that grazed on the then buried Forum. Poor and not so poor, but durable it still is, utterly indifferent to showing off —no Trasteverino "Festa di Noantri" with myriad light ornaments, an abattoir of *porchetta,* miles of pizza, stacks of rattan ornaments, and "souvenir art" to sell to hot, happy tourists inhaling and sweating Italianism. The Suburra prefers to hide its sunken streets and their bedraggled palazzi behind the large avenues that run between S. Maria Maggiore and the Colosseum, keeping its shops and trattorie and night-haunting girls and medieval houses supported by stubborn will power, to itself. It will neither frown at you nor embrace you, in the manner of Trastevere. Its total indifference to its own blandishments and yours is its greatest charm.

As good a place as any to start is outside the unused atrium of S. Prassede, on the Via S. Martino ai Monti, and to follow that short street to a sudden largesse of space that centers on a freestanding tall tower and another flanked by lesser houses, the *torre* of the Capocci, yet another family of medieval strivers and battlers. Across the square, a more authentic medieval monument (the towers have obviously been considerably patched up), the round Romanesque apse of the church of S. Martino ai Monti, all that is immediately visible of its early life except a stiff painting inside the church, done centuries later, of what it might have looked like when its altar held the traditional tabernacle and the ceiling was plain-spoken wooden beams. No need to linger in the church. Find one of the Carmelite brothers who may be sweeping or straightening up in the sacristy and ask that he open the gate to the rambling, disorganized crypt that holds shreds of history in its confused walls. First of all, be warned that the descent is steep and slippery. If you've made it successfully, you should be staring at a small marble figure that came from Trajan's baths or Nero's Golden House or the Gardens of Maecenas a few paces back of the church. In the dank, not unpleasant smell of sunless antiquity you will find remnants of early murals, arches successively opened and closed for the constant reshaping of the fourth-century church, Romanesque window-patterns in abstract designs, echoed in S. Sabina (and the work of the American architect Edward Durell Stone), remnants of primitive murals, several tombstones— one of them an impressive portrait of a long-bearded sixteenth-century savant—and a square vent in the floor which might have been a conductor of steam for a sauna used by Trajan and his guests. Tell the brother when you leave so that he can lock the gate, drop a couple of hundred lire in one of the numerous offering boxes, and go out to admire, once more, the adjustability of Rome which accommodates a movie house in the church-monastery building, and, coming up the Via Equizia, notice that one of S. Martino's "monti" is an outcropping of massive blocks that dates back to the Roman Republic.

The Via in Selci which introduces itself with a conspicuous white pissoir takes its name from the Roman pavement not too far under your feet that led from the lowly Suburra to the extravagances on the Esquiline Hill. It is, for a way, a "don't touch" street of tall, almost windowless monastery walls with traces of Romanesque openings rather like a back street in Siena. As it reverts to indigenous character with signs advertising beds and rooms to rent above auto repair shops, near its meeting with the Largo Visconti Venosa, there is a steep flight of stairs (look for the endless depth of a cellarful of wood as you climb, and give the gnomes who work in the gloom a cheerful "Buon giorno") that finishes on the Via Sette Sale, the route of the water that supplied Nero's house and Trajan's baths and the site of the vineyard from which the snake-ridden Laocoön arose. Suddenly you are in a green suburban street that gives glimpses of small houses and gardens high above the low network of Suburra alleys; to your left and at the right, the extensive green park built over Imperial high life.

S. Pudenziana

Sette Sale returns to S. Martino and the proximity of the Via Quattro Cantoni, which hasn't much to offer except an exceedingly pretty rococo palace which needs fresh powder and rouge for its neglected face. It is now a government office, and if you climb the hospitable stairs some gentleman or other will invite you in to see the ceilings that roister and giggle above the hard gray files. Daring the traffic on the Via Cavour and turning right on the Via Urbana, you should find a set of gates held by columns of green and white stone and a dignified set of angled stairs that walk down to the yard, well below street level, of the church of S. Pudenziana, the sister of S. Prassede.

The fruitful compound of legend and wisps of fact which functions as early Church history tells of the family of the Senator Pudens who sheltered St. Peter and the existence of a Christian place of worship as early as the mid-second century. S. Pudenziana, dedicated to one of the daughters of the family, might therefore be the earliest church in Rome. However, some authorities place Roman baths on the site, also of the second century, indicating that the oratory was short-lived or nonexistent at the time. In any case, it is a very old church with enough vestiges that outlived transformations to prove it. The attractive frieze above the door concerned with the sainted sisters and the Lamb of God framed in an animated floral design is comparatively young, of the eleventh century. The mosaics of the apse, originally of the fourth century, have been badly mistreated. Two of the Apostles were summarily dismissed in rebuilding and several of the heads of the sainted figures disconcertingly modernized, but shadows of the earlier work seep through. Overlooked in the late-sixteenth-century remodeling, or simply hidden from view because it was unmanageable, a dropped area behind the altar where sit the silent remains of timeless niches, apsidal Romanesque swells, scraps of early frescoes, and to support the thermal theory, a curved cut that suggests a nymphaeum.

The atrium returns one to another cluster of time with its beautiful portal, a faint smell of ageless sewage that seeps from neat apertures, and beyond a gate at the side, a glimpse of medieval wooden ceiling, indications of changes in height and shape of stone and brick used and reused, pieces of primitive Christian inscriptions, and as base for a vase of fernery, a Roman acanthus-leaf capital. The rest of the church is an imprisoned oratory on the Via Cesare Balbo, a unique street in itself and in its neighborhood. Turn-of-the-century rebuilding amassed more weighty ornaments per square foot than any other period and, having centuries of style to draw on, layered the walls with volutes as masks, sturdy male and female nudes, classical pillars for a synagogue, heavy balconies held by bold curved supports that spit flames, or feathers, or flowers, or stylized beards. The street has shed Suburra, Rome, and dressed itself as the 16th Arrondissement, Paris.

On the Via Urbana, near the Via Ruinaglia, there is the Hotel Etruria Pensione, one of several inexpensive hotels in the area, whose discouraged air does not altogether mask good columned windows or the shades of heraldic symbols, grotesques and half a nymph, pale survivors of a once galloping spread of painted façade. Urbana gives itself over to the homeliness of neighborhood-village mainstreet, contented with a few small trattorie, makers of keys, vendors of inexpensive yard goods, shoe repair dens, small garages, grocers, fruit and vegetable caves, butchers (one of these sports a kosher sign, a rarity in Rome), a modest hairdresser, and to complete the street's usefulness, a junk shop heaped to its low ceiling with pieces of cloth, scales, a pram, bits of copper and iron, and on a rack into the street, musty army jackets.

A few paces along the flavorful alleys of Caprareccia, Boschetto, Capocci, Cianceleoni, Cimarra (a not entirely reformed brothel quarter, as newspaper ads for "young, capable masseuse, no portiere," "very young manicurist, private entrance," many located on the Via del Boschetto, will prove), the twists of Clemente and Labre should slide you into an approach to the Piazza degli Zingari (gypsies), which has gathered to itself all the tonalities of Rome, the yellow gold, the red gold, the gold tinted with Neapolitan pink and the ocher of Siena in as many textures as time and weather can design. A wall that keeps its arm around the upper end of the piazza stops at a curve of wet-wash banners on slum buildings whose dented dainty balconies and dismayed plaster shells and swags speak of a happier century. The street gives out the noises of saws and the smell of varnish and glue, and again one feels that at least half of working-class Rome is an immense congregation of carpenters and finishers. A break to the right of the street of the gypsies opens to stairs and the Via del Sambuco, a slot of high walls brightened by laundry, the gleam of metal and glass toilet boxes and pots of geraniums on unsteady balconies. You may have to wade through small heaps of garbage, but not to mind; garbage is the landscape of secluded paths.

The rise from the other side of the Via Cavour (you may know it as the tunnel that has taken you to Michelangelo's *Moses* in St. Peter in Chains) has a holy name, S. Francesco di Paola, and an unholy history. In lost times, there lived on the Esquiline the king Servius Tullius, whose daughter Tullia found it difficult to wait for his death so that her husband, Tarquin, might become king. Between them they arranged to kill the unwanted father, and it was on this path that the loving daughter, to make certain her father was dead, dragged his body and rode over it in her cart. On one plateau of the hill, a large barrier of building, composed of a truncated tower, high arches, the relief of a white, feminine balcony, and an inimical blind silence.

This was the palace the Borgias bought of a failing medieval power, and it was here, they say, that Cesare Borgia and his brother, the Duke of Gandía, having supped with their mother, Vannozza (still important to their pope father as Concubine Number One), left on separate errands. The Duke proceeded to a street in the ghetto, where he was assassinated and his body thrown into the Tiber. After much searching a man was found who said he had seen a body dropped from a horse near the Cloaca Maxima, not far from the Isola Tiberina. He had been in no rush to report the event, it was so common. Of several possible assassins, history has chosen Cesare because it was he who profited from the death of his older brother. The imagination piercing the window of a room near the fateful dining hall, one can see the blond Lucrezia studying her Latin and Italian, in addition to the family's Spanish, so that she might some day be her father's capable assistant.

S. Lorenzo in Panisperna

A couple of streets to the north is the Via Panisperna, a main artery whose distinction lies in the mild roller-coaster effects of its rise to S. Maria Maggiore on the Esquiline, a dip and rise to the slopes of the Viminale, and down and up again toward the Quirinale, the only street that touches on three Roman hills. A second distinction is the picturesque if doubtful derivation of its name. Near the corner of Via Milano is the church of S. Lorenzo in Panisperna, where, in its original eighth-century version, the poor saint was grilled. At the side of the church there was a nunnery supported by alms given by the energetic Swedish saint Bridget. Whether it was her distribution of *panis* (bread) and *perna* (ham) or the act of a city official who gave food to the poor or the generosity of the church itself is murky and further dimmed by a scholarly source which insists that the name is a corruption of a word referring to a place covered with bits of wood. This doesn't sit well with Romans, and they will all quote, with pleased confidence, the bread and ham derivation.

Only the approach to this church, of the many dedicated to the saint who refused to turn over its holdings to officials of the third-century Empire and was roasted for his efforts, does him honor. The interior is a cliché of clichés surrounding a large, blistered apse mural of S. Lorenzo's martyrdom worked in perspectives imitative of Raphael and the musculature of Michelangelo. The position of the church at the top of dignified stairs, next to a vestige of tower whose small windows spray long, eager tentacles of geranium searching for air and sun, the minute medieval village at the side of the atrium, and the black, large, sharp curves and bundles of bound sheaves that compose a railing are all you need be concerned with.

Though it gives its rising and falling to TV repairs, wallpapers, auto mechanics, and a trattoria or two, Panisperna is one of the few streets in central Rome that lack bars. For a coffee, gelato, or *acqua minerale* break, go down the green Via Milano and look up at the great fans of trees that wave from its walled city of learned institutions, closed to you but not the boys who hustle coffee and apéritifs past the guards. Near the Via Nazionale, a coffee bar will teach you a moderately interesting lesson: the glass of *acqua minerale* that might cost as much as 150 lire on the Piazza di Spagna asks only 40 lire where tourists are too few for a special scale of prices to exist.

S. Agata dei Goti

St. Agatha, the patron saint of Catania in Sicily and a great beauty, caught the unrelenting Sicilian passion of a third-century Roman power whose name was Quintianus. When she wouldn't respond to his importunities he had her bound, beaten, and her breasts torn off (S. Stefano Rotondo depicts the event in lavish detail). That same night an angel and St. Peter carrying a vessel of healing balm came to her, and she was soon as complete and beautiful as before. Quintianus tossed her on a flaming heap of faggots. At that very moment an earthquake shook the site, and the Romans, linking cause and effect, took Agatha off the pyre and let her die in prison. Her church, S. Agata dei Goti (because it was a center of the Aryan cult of the conquering Goths in the sixth century) or S. Agata in Suburra, to place it with its neighbors, has closed the courtyard entrance on the Via Mazzarino, but the church can be approached through a yard on the Via Panisperna. Like innumerable early churches, S. Agata has been transformed, yet not offensively, except for the overlarge ceiling coffers. The basilica form is clearly marked by rows of ancient columns, the altar tabernacle has held tenaciously to its Cosmatesque bits, and the ancient porphyry urn still contains shreds of tormented saints. The court is an alluring, green, unobtainable thing, to be looked at through a closed door, unfortunately.

As you return to Panisperna and its meeting with the most complete street of the neighborhood, Serpente, a street that bounds, slopes, turns, opens to animated alleys from which the neighbors pour to buy their supplies and gossip in front of shops and the generous fountain, let your eyes connect two singularly Roman entities—a pride of the Empire, the Colosseum, which shuts off Serpente and, behind you, at the end of Panisperna, the pride of the Church as S. Maria Maggiore, sitting on its conspicuous mound.

Beyond affable, useful Serpente, the Via Madonna dei Monti breaks into a medieval island of house and attached wooden outhouse which looks as if it predated and withstood the Norman Robert Guiscard and as if it will hang, a thick, rough brown coffer, to outlive time itself. Share the

intimacy of the street—a drop of water from laundry
hanging overhead, a soccer ball rolled out of the reach of a
youngster, a greeting to the slack-bodied matrons who ooze
in and out of the market on Baccina, nod to the erased
ferocity of the Annibaldi family on their street, and, on the
other side of Via Cavour, a listless path in a secluded,
unambitious cluster that remembers the Frangipane of the
many fortresses. Somewhere in this ramble you should
collide with the Colosseum, or be ready to stride up the
Salita del Grillo or stare down into the forum of Augustus
and the long stretch of ruined temples and basilicas from
the Campidoglio to the arch of Titus and beyond.

NOTE: When you visit the *Moses* at S. Pietro in Vincoli make
an attempt to people the church with Jews, who, according
to an unreliable art historian, went "every Saturday in
troops to visit and adore it as divine, not a human thing."
There are people who see the profiles of Julius II, for whom
the unfinished tomb was meant, and that of the sculptor
in the beard of Moses. It requires a particular light, they
say—and a willing imagination.

Railroad Station and Environs

The crossings are broad rivers of peril, a clan of aggressive,
importuning gypsies mans the entrances to the station,
Gucci luggage on its way to the luxurious Sette Bello train
to Florence bangs against the rope-bound tattered paper
valises of country cousins and their bundles of country
sausage and flasks of country wine. Young American couples
bent in the shape of senility by the engorged carriers on
their backs search the information boards for trains to Siena.
On Sundays and Thursday afternoons the station is an
informal social center where lonely soldier and lonely maid-

servant with nowhere else to go in their time off eye each other, reject or accept companionship of one kind of another.

All this and much more can be enjoyed from the open caffè inside the station, and then, coffee cup long drained, explore the neighborhood beginning, to make an arbitrary choice, at a modern mosaic with a Byzantine overlay of St. Christopher, in the lobby of an insurance building at 26 Via Solferino. Returning toward the station, one sees great thrusts of Roman wall, rough blocks as old as the sixth century B.C. which became part of a later, smoother wall. Amble through the tree-shaded caffès, past the stalls of "souvenir" goods—inexpensive scarves, ties, miniatures of the late Pope John XXIII, and rosaries—and leaf through the bookstall prints (stamped in the millions) and the watercolors of the Spanish Steps and the Pantheon to find the not-impossible one or two to take home as unimportant gifts. If its cake cover of subway structure has been re- moved, observe the naiads in dalliance with watery male friends in the fountain of the Piazza della Repubblica, a work that scandalized Romans when the girls came into public view in 1901. Which goes to prove that most Romans were not aware of the goings on in paint and stone in their museums and galleries.

Museo delle Terme

The core of interest here is obviously the Baths of Diocle- tian, in which Michelangelo placed the church of S. Maria degli Angeli, leaving where he could the character of the Roman building, and where the government has gathered (and to a shocking degree cut off from the public eye) a rare collection of classical masterpieces. Were all the sec- tions and their hidden art available, the Museo delle Terme might rank with the world's great museums. Yet, in spite of inimical gates, and resolutely locked doors with exasperatingly seductive labels, the museum should not be neglected. There is considerable fascination in walking among sarcophagi, mosaics, sections of temples, chunks of statuary, tomb complexes, a few smallish colossi, friezes on remnants of pavement, among ruined compartments of baths under the grandiose cusps of distantly high ceiling. Try not to permit the strangeness of walking in a Piranesi print distract you altogether from the quality or rarity of some of the objects. A number of the sarcophagi are handsomely carved and, among them, a sarcophagus that describes in full detail a battle between Roman soldiers and Barbarians; on a marble cylinder that may have been part of a tomb, a light, airy Roman ballerina; and in a family sepulcher, second-century paintings of peacocks, birds, fruits, and people, each set in its own framed box.

Ultimately the vaults and defunct dressing rooms, gymnasia, and pools release you into a garden centered on a huge marble fountain vase very much like that in the courtyard of S. Cecilia and then return to a semicircular area paved in black and white mosaics which was the public toilet of the baths. The mind's eye or a visit to Ostia Antica must fill in the communal seats and the niches for companionable, homey gods.

The museum proper is entered from the garden, and you should be prepared not to see, or to glimpse with difficulty unless matters change radically and soon, the reputedly distinguished Ludovisi-Boncompagni collection, the frescoed room from the villa of Livia north of the city, and, possibly, the room of small, extraordinary mosaics. A whispered plea and several hundred lire may earn a quick look at Livia's room and the mosaics, but the Ludovisi collection has been locked up for years and promises to stay hidden. There are enough visible rewards, however, to keep one for an hour or so. In Room 2 of the Sale Nuove an Apollo dredged out of the Tiber whose marble is marred in red and yellow gouges and scars like recent injuries, as if he were pulled out yesterday, scraping along rocks and rusty nails in waterlogged planks. Near him an unearthly beauty, a vision dreamed in the fifth century B.C. and chiseled as a dancer in ripples of cloth as fresh as a light breeze.

The monumental works are gathered in Sala III, designed and lighted with special care to show superb Greek originals and Roman copies: the famous discus throwers, the heavily muscled bronze pugilist (found in the late nineteenth century near the Palazzo Colonna) sunk in exhaustion after a fight, still wearing a boxing glove, lifting his dazed face about to speak, if he could. And here the Hellenistic *Girl of Anzio,* called that because she was found (1878) when a violent wave demolished a corner of a submerged imperial palace on the beach of Anzio. She is a grave young girl whose face and bearing suit her serious purpose of carrying objects to a sacrificial altar. In the same dignified room the daughter of Niobe transfixed by an arrow from the bow of Artemis, intent on killing all her brothers and sisters to punish their mother, Niobe, for boasting of her numerous family. One could go on to describe a copy of a bronze Venus, of a Greek torso; there is no need but to urge a visitor to concentrate on the masterpieces in this hall and, if time is limited and a choice must be made, take this hall first.

Greek and Roman works of fine quality, though possibly of lesser impact and importance, stand in the set of rooms that follow and the Sale Minori delle Sculture. How much time you should spend among these displays returns us to an often iterated question: How much have you seen, how much do you want to see, of gods, emperors, mosaic pavements, and wall panels, choice as these are? The pace at which you go through these halls might depend on whether you have already seen some of the classical galleries of the Vatican and the museums on the Campidoglio. Whatever the decision—to saunter through or to concentrate—the exhibits on the upper floor, even if you have to stand behind ropes or under scaffolding for meager views, should be seen.

First of all, two sections of exquisitely fine mosaics in vivid color: a bright-eyed triumphant cat who has caught a quail, ducks, fruits, and flowers wreathed on pretty young heads, mythological figures and a pygmy hunt of hippopotami. A series of rooms on the same level *should* show paintings and plasterwork decorations that come from the house discovered at the edge of the Farnese Gardens. Romans have an understandable fondness for the unproven possibility that the house was that of Cleopatra, where she lived in the style that suited the queen of Egypt and the mistress of Julius Caesar. For proof they point to Egyptian elements in the beautifully executed luxuriance of decoration. It is weak proof, if any; Egyptian mannerisms in art were frequently used by Roman artists and decorators for their exoticism and novelty.

The high point of this section, a high point of the total collection, is the painted room from the villa of Livia, the wife of Augustus. The artist—Greek slave or Roman freeman—was done a disservice by history, which has forgotten to record his name, worth listing in the annals of art. Of a small closed room he made an enchanted garden whose dashing, confident drawing and youthful color carry over two millennia the scent of flowers, the fragrance of pomegranates ready for plucking, and the call of birds as they swing through the young blue sky.

A grander garden, pleasant though not half as enchanting, waits at the bottom of the stairs near the rooms of mosaics. There were the cloisters, purportedly designed by Michelangelo, whose arcades hold theater masks, statues whole and battered of Romans and Egyptian deities, mosaics —a potpourri of no major importance or interest except for the enormous white heads of bulls, a horse, an elephant, a rhino, a camel, that soar astonishingly out of the greens near the central fountain.

S. Bibiana

Southward on the Via Giolitti, beyond the airport buses, the snack bars, fruit stalls and vendors of packed lunches for railroad trips, the vivacious tone of the area slows, dulls, begins to smell of poverty and abandonment. Here, the young conscripts from the country, standing in protective huddles afraid of the big city, and the Toonerville trains that connect working-class suburbs and villages to jobs and relatives in Rome. To earn a few soldi from the rurals and the soldiers, Arab merchants establish their cheap wares —violently colored mats, crudely stamped purses, Woolworth jewelry, and always a few rosaries, on the narrow sidewalk, calling, cajoling in their strangely accented, limited, shrewd vocabulary. At a point where the street seems to have lost all life and meaning, except for the flinty highlights on railroad tracks, one comes on a small church said to contain 10,000 martyrs' bones, S. Bibiana, whose reconstruction was the earliest architectural work of Bernini. Should the church be open, you might see the statue of the saint, the first such commission for the young Bernini, and frescoes of her martyrdom (tied to a column and whipped to death during the persecutions of Julian the Apostate) by Pietro da Cortona.

The faceless street drags along decayed tenements and endless railroad tracks and springs the surprise of a round temple, as misplaced and lonely as its neighbor church. The denuded structure, which must have been imposing when it was dressed in marbles, was built in the fourth century. It then housed a statue of Minerva holding a serpent, a combination that had medical significance and therefore left the temple (an inspiration for many Roman painters, before it fell almost completely apart 150 years ago) the name of Minerva Medica.

Subterranean Basilica

One of those places where too much seems to be happening, as if the area had been picked up and whirled about by a typhoon to drop as a scramble of railroad siding, remains of Roman aqueducts and portals, and fierce converging flames of traffic scorching imperial highways, is the Piazza di Porta Maggiore. The face of this tangled Medusa head is the Porta Maggiore, an impressive gate of the Empire, a place where a number of aqueducts and supply roads met. From the time of Claudius through that of Hadrian (first to second centuries A.D.)—and one can observe advances in techniques and materials—the structure was shored up, improved, and enhanced and in the third century incorporated into the Aurelian wall. Passing through the gate from north to south, the feet feel uncertain, slipping over the smoothness of patient stone deeply rutted by the wagon wheels of supplies that came from the vineyards and orchards of Preneste (Palestrina). On the south side of the portal, a naïve and most endearing Roman monument—and few Roman monuments sit comfortably with that word. It is the tomb of a Virgilio Eurisace and his wife. He was a prosperous baker of the republic, apparently a wholesaler who supplied the state. Pillars and holes, quite like architectural ornaments on Mayan buildings, represent ovens and their vents and, to make matters explicit, a frieze that describes the baking and selling of bread.

An infinitely less overt monument, as seclusive and exquisite as the baker's tomb is open and homely, is the subterranean basilica achieved by negotiating the traffic and the meaningless buildings that trail off from the railroad yards, to number 17 on the Via Prenestina. Through the marble doorway, down several flights under the tracks, and into an enchantment of frail, artful plasterwork that tells the mysterious myths which sustained a mystical sect, probably Greek, that came to worship here secretly in the first and second centuries. From the remarkable condition of the basilica and its delicate friezes, it would seem that the house of worship was not used for too long a time but abandoned and untouched for nearly two thousand years until a landslide in the railroad yards brought it to view. Among superbly crafted scenes that may recall a simpler, bucolic life in a far country—a gay wedding, a group of mischievous schoolboys, artisans working, children playing with a dog, groups of dancers, and animals led to rural sacrifices—there are less comprehensible groups that suggest rites of ecstasy and blood compounded of Greek legends and the hidden religions of the East. These figures are touched with profound solemnity, the solemnity of preparation for departure, a departure into sacrifice or superhuman perfection or death. Ganymede is borne from earth by an eagle; Mercury leads a traveler (where?); a woman is raped by a god who is a deathlike figure, come to take her to another world. In the apse of the basilica a woman in a wild swell of veil stands with one foot on the shore and one touching the sea where Triton waits. High on a rock of the opposite shore a radiant Apollo beckons to her. To the right of the apse a woman stands hesitating before a guarded portal and two seated figures watch, judging, waiting for her to enter the momentous door. A glorious sea horse carries off another veiled woman accompanied by flights of bird-angels with broadly spread wings who direct and shield her passage.

Men astride swift leopards and griffons, motion, full veils, departures hesitant or forced, may mean the passing and changes of souls, transmigrations linked with a worship of Apollo, who appears frequently and always in a perfection of gesture and being. However, at the left of the apse there appears a rite that includes the worship of a sacred tree and women clapping and dancing around a central figure who holds a bloody mask in one hand and a knife in the other. Could these be frenzied Dionysian rites? And, might the structure of the basilica, which is like that of paleo-Christian churches, the presence of orants and the beckoning Apollo, perhaps a disguised Christ, point to an infiltration of Christianity?

According to some scholars, the figures refer to Greek myths in several versions and interpretations—a woman holding a figurine might be Helen protecting Troy (a far-fetched idea, since it was she who was an instrument for the city's destruction) or it might be Iphigenia trying to rescue her brother Orestes; a male figure might be Paris or Orpheus, both of whom carried off their women. The rescuing, the kidnapping, the carrying off, it is theorized, point to a neo-Pythagorean cult which believed in an immortality of supreme accord between the earthly and the magnificent unknown, the flights both transfer and linkage between one state and the other. With this early concept of heaven, based on a primitive cabalism and visions of the supernatural and eternal of Pythagoras, who lived in the sixth century B.C., there is an accompanying hell for the uninitiated, manifested in scenes of maddened cruelties.

No one knows surely; all that is sure is the incomparable beauty of the figures moving in sweet docility through pleasurable mortal life and those chosen to leave it movingly cajoled or guided or swept away into an unknown elsewhere.

NOTE: The basilica is not generally open to the public. However, the Foyer Unitas makes the trip quite frequently, as do other accredited guides. Not a certain thing, but the guardian has been known to admit unaccompanied visitors if they appeal to him. Tip, naturally.

Pantheon
Piazza Margana
S. Giorgio in Velabro
Largo Argentina
Via Funari
Piazza Campitelli
Circo Massimo
·Tribuna di Campitelli
Via dei Falegnami.
—Piazza Mattei
Teatro di Marcello
Piazza della Verità
Via Arenula
Ponte Fabricio
·Piazza Cenci
Clivo di Rocca Savella
Piazza di Prisca
Via di S. Sabina
S. Sabina
Piazza dei Cavalieri di Malta ·

Walk 6
S. Sabina to Pantheon

The abnormally sturdy, or those harried by the flight of
time, might combine this visit with the area around St.
Paul's Gate, but it does no justice to visitor or visited to
speed through the Aventine of barred villas guarded by
baying dogs, steep treed streets rarely disturbed by buses,
cloisters and nunnery gardens behind medieval walls; a
genteel place whose sparsely lighted silences make it a
popular haven for lovers in cars and on patches of shaded
grass, whom no one observes except a seminarist or monk
whose mind should be on other matters. Bus 94 currently
runs up the hill from the Pantheon, skirting an extensive
rose garden and streets named for uncommon saints—
Giosafat, Melania, Eufemia—to reach the peak of this unusually high area, the street of S. Sabina. It ends at a
sui generis piazza by Piranesi (1765), an early surrealist.
He was commissioned by the Knights of Malta (Cavalieri
di Malta is the name of the piazza) to build this anteroom

to their closed priory, gardens, and church which stretch to
the cliff above the river, a Piranesi etching translated into
obelisks, grotesques, plaques, stone balls, all in nervous
contrasts of heights and shapes and insistent chiaroscuro,
especially in its startling night illumination. The families
and tour groups stooping to the keyhole of the Priory gate
are looking at an artful miniature view of St. Peter's dome
perfectly framed in a bower of interlaced trees.

Returning on the Via S. Sabina, passing purposeful
churches, monks, and walls of villas should bring you very
soon to a formal park and a platform for following the bend
of the river, across into Trastevere and to rest on the triumphant gleam of St. Peter's. To experience one of the
many hidden passages that wrinkle the face of Rome, go to
the end of the park, away from the sturdy apse of S. Sabina,
find a break in the medieval wall and a slope—the Clivo di
Rocca Savella, named for the medieval fortress of the family
in control of the Aventine—which will slide you quickly
down to the river (note the masks on the chimney pots at
the end of the drop), a very short distance from the opening of the Etruscan-Roman sewer, the Cloaca Maxima.

But of that, elsewhere; several important matters have
been left at the top of the secretive passage from the park
also named for the Savelli. First, if there is a storm brew-
ing, the park next to S. Sabina makes a fine viewing point
for the drama of a flood of black sky which covers the
ocher of domes and picks up the white ribs, leaving airy
cages where there was, a moment before, solid roundness.
Second, third, and so on, this dominating hill was a place
of many and large temples. One street name and a piazza
indicate the probable site of a temple of Diana; some of the
marble columns in the church of S. Sabina are believed to
have supported a temple to Juno that, like the church, dominated the height above the river. Slaves came for sanctuary
to the temples on the Aventine, and Roman leaders fleeing
their enemies. There came, too, members of the Roman
middle class, not rich enough for the Palatine and too

prosperous for the tall, fetid insulae tenements that crowded lower portions of the city. In time the area became a minor Palatine, and when the sixth-century invaders plundered and burned the city they found rich rewards in the temples, palaces, and basilicas that lived together on the hill. Undis- couraged by the ensuing desolation, a wealthy priest from the Dalmatian coast named Peter built in the fifth century one of the most awesomely beautiful of early basilicas. According to Emile Mâle, it "calls up for us the times of St. Augustine, just as Vézelay recalls the century of the crusades and the Sainte-Chapelle the age of S. Louis." Peter built it over a Roman house of two or three centuries earlier (viewable), the home of a Christian lady, Sabina, who, as was the common practice, converted part of her house to the use of local coreligionists. Rebuilt in the ninth century and again in the thirteenth, plastered with gilt and curlicues in the sixteenth, S. Sabina was stripped of younger layers earlier in this century to return to its fifth- to ninth-century guise.

Stand away from it a while to enjoy the bounty and serenity of its brick height, the free curve of the apse, and, high up, the simple, geometric designs that shape its win- dows. Outside the portico, a reminder of pre-Church Rome in the form of a fountain of Egyptian granite faced with a large flat mask, something like the famous Bocca della Verità at the bottom of the hill and both very likely once sewer covers. The atrium and closed-in façade, supported by columns scored in spiral designs, make room for bits of fifth-century window, fragments of old plaques, and, most importantly, two wooden doors concerned with events of the Old and New Testaments that go back as early as the fifth century, thus the earliest examples of their type still in existence. Scholars have spoken of Eastern influences in the church, pointing out that it was originally built by an Illyrian priest, that the direct flow of arches between columns reflects the style used here for the first time in Christian Rome, and that the door panels treat of biblical incidents in keeping with Eastern legends. These are matters still in discussion, but one fact seems fairly sure: a panel near the top of the door of Christ nailed to the cross between two considerably smaller thieves is among the first crucifixions in Christian art.

The great, undisturbed length under the chaste wooden ceiling leads to a closed-off area that surrounds another unique entity, the tomb of a dourly displeased fourteenth-century church dignitary, a tomb portrait in mosaics, the only one of its kind in Rome. Its bits of stone, like the carved marble iconostasis and the unusual frieze of porphyry and serpentine in a repeated design of mirrors and cups, were rescued from the older versions of the church. Nothing much could be done about the decayed apse mosaic whose substitute, a sixteenth-century fresco, disturbs the perfection. Turn back instead to the fifth-century mosaics over the front portal, a solemn panel of strong, golden lettering on a deep blue ground and at each side a majestic female figure in the headdress of a nun or vestal who represent the church of the Jews (*ecclesia ex circumcisione*) and the church of the Gentiles (*ecclesia ex gentibus*), a concept later sweetened to intimacy as the sheep emerging from St. Peter's Jerusalem and St. Paul's Bethlehem. Having seen the distinguished particulars, stand under the mosaic and let the nobility of the basilica come to you.

If it is Sunday between 3:30 and 5:30 the cloister will be open. The monastery was founded by S. Domenico in the thirteenth century and, to judge from the number of bland white-cloaked friars who ply the streets and buses, is still a—or *the*—prime seat of the Dominican order, which continues to cherish the orange tree the saint brought from Spain, to honor his cell and the memory of a sojourn in the cloister of St. Thomas Aquinas.

The church of S. Prisca (a few streets below) is not impressive, although its history is. It was built on the house of a couple of Jewish converts, tentmakers who sheltered St. Peter when he was in Rome. Their chapel was unearthed very near the church in the eighteenth century and in 1940, practically adjacent to it, a Mithraeum which may have been part of a contemporary Roman household. The combination makes a telling example of the competition among religions which seized Rome when its pantheon of Gods proliferated meaninglessly and declined in power. (Petronius: "A land so infested with divinity that one might meet a god more easily than a man.")

A short distance from the Piazza of Prisca, the curved, dipping continuation of the street of S. Sabina becomes the Clivo di Publici, which has nothing to do with serving the public but repeats the names of the Roman brothers who built it. At a side of the curve there was, according to a doubtful source, a Jewish cemetery (where rose gardens now bloom) which Jews permitted to be used as a garbage dump by Romans for so much per sack. It is a curious piece of information difficult to credit or confirm; it may have been anti-Semitic gossip that arose from the presence of poor Jews and their cave-shops in the Circo Massimo below, near their old settlement at the Porta Capena.

This end of the Circus Maximus holds a shy speck of medievalism, the misleading remnant of a fortress owned by the Frangipane. Along the side under the Palatine's specters, a gallant, high curve of façade that screens a meaningless huddle of brick huts and, with the exception of a few boys bouncing soccer balls off their heads and clumps of azalea shielding sex, nothing but a broad, long, silent void, with not a fist of Roman stone left to remember its strident past. On this place where the Sabine women were chased and raped, a race course (circus) was already betting and roaring for its favorite charioteers in the second century B.C. It was Julius Caesar's choice (46 B.C.) for a staged battle that involved more than a thousand men and several dozen elephants. Augustus, who clothed his city in marble and works of art, embellished the circus and brought to it the obelisk that now stands in the Piazza del Popolo. The immortal Neronian fire destroyed it, to await reconstruction by Trajan and improvements ordered by Caracalla. During the third and fourth centuries, sporting another obelisk later moved to the Piazza of S. Giovanni in Laterano, the circus sat 300,000 people, a number that dwindled to reach a close with the last races arranged by Totila the Goth, in 549. Thereafter, for 1,400 years and probably years to come, a faceless waste.

Below the Circo Massimo, the city offers a handful of detritus and pearls. The gloomy, corpse-clogged, too old, too tired river, whose name is still thunderous and whose bizarre curves stretch, condense, and falsify distances; S. Maria in Cosmedin, a much manipulated church huddled under a fine tower, brought back recently to something of the early Eastern charms that sheltered Greek refugees from Iconoclasts and Arabs. (A Greek Orthodox service is still held on Sunday mornings.) Most travelers know of the Bocca della Verità, the broad moon-mask under the portico whose function is to bite the hand of a speaker of lies. There is more beyond, especially a Gothic altar tabernacle designed by one of the Cosmati, the early-twelfth-century Cosmatesque floor, Roman columns that supported establishments in the local grain market. Before the low, hooded church, an ebullient baroque fountain of tritons, fishy twisted tails, shells, rocks, and fancy. On a once lyrical slope from the river in the time of Augustus, the endearing toylike round temple of Vesta—which it is not, but no one surely knows how else to name it and a female name suits it best. Vesta's temple has a mate in the stolid, androgynously named Tempio della Fortuna Virile, quite Greek in style, built in Republican times (about a hundred years before its companion) and a favorite of Roman ladies because it was efficacious in blinding men to female faults. In the river, the hoary, broken mass of the Ponte Rotto, the remains of a bridge built in the second century B.C. and rebuilt frequently thereafter. It was for a long time the only stone bridge, a reliable place from which to throw the bodies of Christian martyrs and at least one emperor, the

strange Heliogabalus, and a useful site for belligerent encounters among the easily heated popoli. Having survived
centuries of activity, violent and peaceable, the bridge was
torn apart by river torrents late in the sixteenth century
and now points an accusing stump that begs to be etched,
painted, and photographed.

Up from the river and temples, the stocky white blocks
of the four-sided temple of Janus (late third century),
whose many niches were obviously meant for statues. Situated to straddle a number of important commercial streets,
it may have been a tax gate or simply a shelter and informal meeting place for merchants. Nor need it necessarily
have originally been so squat and earthbound. The Frangipani used it as a fortress in the Middle Ages, having lopped
off upper sections to suit more bellicose purposes. Nineteenth-century travelers complained about the hovels that
hid the temple of Fortuna Virilis and of the hideous bridge
and background gasworks that ruined the view of the
lovely ensemble below. We may complain of cars, buses,
the intrusive rigid shadows of Fascist buildings, but looking down from the gate still offers one of the most rewarding of Roman views, infinitely calmer in spite of cars than
when it was the Roman meat market, the Forum Boarium,
which, like present-day abattoirs and bullrings, was sig-
naled by a bronze bull. Legends speak of human sacrifice in
primitive days, the beginnings of gladiatorial games, and
forbidding rites in the local temples. Truth or fiction, it was
a robust place which changed its wares, as it moved up the
hill, to silver. Adjoining the felicitously placed and shaped
church of S. Giorgio in Velabro, there is an arch built by
the silversmiths in honor of Septimius Severus, his wife
Julia Domna, and their sons Caracalla and Geta. Heavily
ornamented, a bit like the plateresque work associated
with later silversmiths, its most interesting detail is the
fact that Caracalla's image and name remain while those
of the brother he killed were erased, as they were erased
on the larger arch of Septimius Severus in the main forum.

The holes that pierce the structure are the work of treasure hunters who were sure that the silversmiths stuffed their gift with treasure as had been the custom in the dedication of major Roman altars.

The picturesque S. Giorgio, made prettier by its green hill and the agreeable face of a gay villa across the piazza, supports the silversmiths' arch, the Arco degli Argentari. Other than the sturdy medieval tower that balances the horizontal of the marble-embroidered portico, there isn't much to see—unless you stumble on a fashionable wedding when the church is dressed in velvet, flowers, and hats (which Roman women never otherwise wear and wear oddly when they do)—except a few fragments of fresco attributed to Pietro Cavallini, and a pristine neatness to surround the marble columns and the Cosmatesque tabernacle.

The church figures importantly in early Roman history; it was here, in the marshes of the Velabrum, that Romulus and Remus were found, and on its portico Cola di Rienzo hung his inscription promising the people of Rome a new, just state. His memory lingers, quite erroneously, on another house just off the Piazza della Verità, the Casa dei Crescenzi, once called the house of Pilate and later that of Cola di Rienzo. It was probably a tower that surveyed the Tiber against the approach of the enemies of the autocratic Crescenzi and is now a wonderful hodgepodge of medieval and Roman bits, sections of cornices, arches, stubs of column, hints of balcony and parapet, and decorative scraps slapped together in the rough shape of a house.

There is a lucky dull moment with nothing much to look at except the stocky building of records (Anagrafe) until, once again, as again and again, the stunning blow—even if you have seen it a dozen times before—of the broken curve of the Teatro di Marcello and the superb tall podium and isolated tragic beauty of triple columns that were once, millennia ago, part of a temple of Apollo.

It has been described as a cheese riddled with mice, the

mice heaped, bedraggled shops pressed into the lower arches of the Teatro, recorded in innumerable yellowed photographs and paintings of the colorful Roman ghetto of *Roma Sparita*. Gone, the shops have left ruined caves, caged to protect shadowy stone hulks and another of Rome's many kingdoms of indestructible cats. It looks like a smaller, more desiccated version of the Colosseum, a poorer younger relation. In fact, it may have been a model of the Colosseum, since it was built earlier, begun by Julius Caesar, completed by Augustus and named in honor of the young man who he hoped would succeed him, his nephew and son-in-law. It is an infinitely sadder, more moving ruin than the Colosseum—darker, older, secretive, and its shape distorted, unlike that of the large arena which though stripped bare is clean and candid in its ample space. The Teatro di Marcello was not for long a successful showplace; the potential 10,000 or more customers had little taste for drama deteriorated to "star" declamation and balletic pantomime and preferred the greater excitements and crowds of the gladiatorial arenas and the racing stadiums. In the fourth century, already in disuse, it was partially stripped to shore up the bridge that led from the Isola Tiberina to Trastevere. The ruin was taken over in the twelfth century and held for two centuries by the Pierleoni, who built a fortress on the mounds of collapsed Imperial stone. Later came the Savelli, for whom Peruzzi built a palace viewing the Tiber, then the Orsini, Caetani, and now tenants of choice apartments that hide behind an irregularity of windows along the curve of the defunct third order of the theater.

All the earlier tenants were fascinating, conscienceless thieves and warriors, but the Pierleoni had a particular —and particularly appropriate to this mouth of the old ghetto—attribute. They were Jews, "the Rothschilds of the Middle Ages," converted in the eleventh century (although they were constantly referred to as members of the Jewish community), the lords of Trastevere which held the largest, oldest Jewish settlement. Bankers and minters, they con-

trolled both sides of the river from their castle in the
Theater of Marcellus, from the island where a tower of
their fortress still remains, looking down on the "Pons
Judaeorum" (the Ponte Fabricio, more commonly called
Quattro Capi), and from the Castel S. Angelo, where they
protected their popes.

Old stories interlaced with some fact tell us that the
Pierleoni were related by blood or marriage to three popes.
The first was believed to have been Gregory VI, whose
short reign was distinguished by gossip that the Pierleoni
had bought the former incumbent out of the papal seat to
make room for their candidate or relative. The next one is
the Hildebrand who became Pope Gregory VII, the strict
reformer of a corrupt church, who according to some
scholars inherited Pierleoni money from Gregory VI and
is actually mentioned in some annals as being a person of
Jewish origin. To deny the fact firmly, or enacting Jewish
anti-Semitism, or in a general cleanup of everything, he
issued an edict barring Jews from public office. The only
Pierleoni listed by name in the roster of popes is that of an
antipope, Anacletus II, who was according to his apologists a
liberal, a follower of Abelard, and consequently the butt of
the fulminations of the strait-laced, potent abbot of Cluny,
a vociferous stronghold of conservatism. Unfortunately,
Anacletus II became pope by devious means not at all unusual in papal history—which might have been overlooked
if he weren't worldly, rich, a cultivated gentleman, and a
Jew, open to all possible accusations from homosexuality
to desecrating the holy seat of St. Peter.

Returning from popes to emperors, one stumbles down
and up a few irregular paces to what is left of an arcade
built by Augustus in honor of, or to console, his sister
Octavia, the woman Antony left in Rome to keep the home
fires burning while he burned in Egypt. It was designed
as a public shelter and informal museum, furnished with
Greek and Roman art. For many years, into the late nineteenth century, it enclosed a smelly, noisy fish market

which fascinated travelers from cooler, less redolent and voluble countries. In this portico, according to Gregorovius, Titus and Vespasian celebrated their defeat of the Jews and the destruction of their temple, the festivities described by their friend the Jewish historian Josephus. Although there were Jewish spectators—the city may have had more than 10,000 Jews among its population of approximately 2,000,000 at the time—the public demonstration of joy and triumph in this place was not an extra fillip of cruelty. There was no movement of Jews to this "new" ghetto until the early Middle Ages, and a greater concentration after their expulsion from Spain at the end of the fifteenth century. The only present souvenir of the fish market is one marble slab left of many on which fish were measured; all fish heads that reached beyond a specific size had to be cut off down to the upper fins and presented to city officials. Embedded in the portico, another souvenir of medieval and Jewish history, the church of S. Angelo in Pescheria. It was at this church on a May night of 1347 that Cola di Rienzo met with his followers to march to the Campidoglio, to rid the people of Rome of the rule of the Colonna and Orsini and establish the "good estate."

For the Jews it was one of the local churches in which they were forced to listen to weekly sermons designed to convert them. John Evelyn wrote in the seventeenth century, "A sermon was preached to the Jews at Ponte Sisto, who are constrained to sit till the hour is done, but it is with so much malice in their countenances, spitting, humming, coughing and motion, that it is almost impossible they should hear a word from the preacher. A conversion is very rare." "The Jews in Rome all wear yellow hats, live only upon brokage and usury, very poor and despicable. . . ." Gregorovius, two hundred years later: "When we reflect that it is in Rome that this Jewry has maintained itself for eighteen centuries, its resistance excites astonishment."

Although there were Jews in the city before, the first recorded advent of a sizable number was their arrival as slaves captured by Pompey. They seemed to have been soon freed and established themselves well during the reigns of Julius Caesar (whose death they mourned in the week-long ancient rite of *shivah*) and Augustus in Trastevere and on the Aventine, conducting unremarkable and unmolested lives. Augustus went so far as to see that the grain distribution that fell on the Sabbath be arranged for another day among the Jews so that their religion not be offended. The Imperial court entertained Jewish nobles—Herod; his grandson Agrippa; Berenice, the daughter of Agrippa, who was purportedly the mistress of Titus; and Nero's wife Poppaea, who was a convert to Judaism. Caligula, who could let nothing peaceful rest, grew angry with the Jews because, unlike other peoples in the empire, they refused to permit him to put a gigantic god-image of himself in the inner sanctum of the Temple of Jerusalem. The whole population of the city went to Phoenicia, where they begged the governor, in charge of having the colossus erected, to kill them all rather than permit the desecration. It took time, patience, and diplomatic handling, but Agrippa, whom Caligula had named King of the Jews, finally persuaded the maniac that he could do without this one monument among the hundreds erected throughout his universe.

Later emperors, not sure who was Jew or Christian, mistreated them equally. Frequently exiled, both groups managed to return and grow, especially the Jews, whose numbers were increased by Titus' sack of Jerusalem, the slaves he brought back, and the refugees who made their way westward. Satisfied with their victories in the east, Titus and Vespasian contented themselves with using Jewish slaves to build their Colosseum and extracting a Jews' tax to be paid on the Capitoline, a tax continuously paid on the same hill until the ghetto walls were demolished toward the end of the nineteenth century. Through those centuries the seesaw went up and down; some emperors banished Jews; Hadrian brought in more in the course of his conquests. Hope and fear accompanied each new papal proces-

sion when the leaders of the community, surrounded by
jeering crowds, met the newly elected pope at Monte Giordano or the Castel S. Angelo, trying to judge from the
manner of accepting the Torah they offered (one pope threw
it to the ground), the tone of voice, the expression on the
face with which the acceptance formula was spoken,
whether they could look forward to misery or the hoped-
for indifference. Severe anti-Jewish laws were enacted by
one pope to be overlooked by the next. At times the condition of the Jews hung on the reputation and skill of the
Jewish physicians who tended the popes and on a few
essential moneylenders.

Not only revenue but amusement was derived from the
Jews; carnival was the time (from the late fifteenth century and for two hundred years thereafter) for elderly
Jews, in grotesque costumes or nude except for a loincloth,
to run with the horses and the donkeys as fast as they
could along the Corso during eight days of fun and games
which the Jewish community subsidized.

The abyss was not reached until 1555 with Paul IV. In
the words of Gregorovius, "This Neapolitan of the fanatic
and violent house of the Caraffa, a Theatine and an Inquisi-
tor, founder of the torture chambers and of the censorial
office in Rome, a pitiless reformer of iron determination,
had scarcely ascended to the papal throne when he issued
in 1555 the bull Cum nimis absurdum which regulated the
positions of Roman Jewry." No Jew could practice any
trade or handicraft, physicians could not treat Christians,
nor could any Jew associate with Christians. He required
that sums of tribute be increased and that Jews wear yellow hats and their women yellow veils should they leave
the ghetto in which he enclosed them, behind firm walls
and gates and with strict curfew hours. Among heaps of
forbidden books, Jews were burned on the Campo dei
Fiori. The light returned with Sixtus V, patron of the arts,
planner and enhancer of the city, and in the truest sense
of the word a humanist, the man whom Elizabeth I consid-

ered the only person worthy of her hand—were he not
pope. He tore away the imprisoning chains which, however,
were joined again, Caraffa style, a few years after his death.
It was about this time that the Saturday sermons began,
a Sabbath treat repeated for three hundred years.

Because of a rent law designed to keep Jews in local
houses owned by Christians who could not raise their rent
and therefore made no improvements in the crowded hovels,
the district still called the ghetto (roughly the river area
between the Portico di Ottavia and a short distance beyond
the large Via Arenula, revolving around the tall Orientalish
synagogue of this century) retains a good deal of medieval
and early Renaissance Rome. A few of its black, garbage-
ridden alleys (the vicolo in Publicis and those off the Via
dei Falegnami) are as desperate as they were centuries ago
when their inhabitants sat in the sunless, malarial paths
picking among heaps of rags, mending some of them for
possible resale—the only industry permitted in the ghetto
under the more sadistic popes. Ghetto place names, not
necessarily official, still remain; a restored antique building
on the Tribuna di Campitelli is called the Albergo della
Catena because of the chain that limited the area here; the
Via Catalana recalls Spanish Jews; the church of S. Maria
del Pianto faces a piazza popularly called Giudia. There was
a Piazza delle Azzimelle where matzo was made and a
piazza of the Cinque Scuole where five religious schools
under one roof taught children of Spanish origin, of Sicilian
Jews, and of Roman families as old as any in Rome. The
street from the Portico leads to the church of S. Maria del
Pianto, whose tears are generally attributed to a miraculous
image that wept on witnessing a murder. She wept also
because the Jews were so intransigent about conversion, or
perhaps because it was on her piazza that the Jews huddled
in a wailing, praying, frightened mob when they were
locked into the ghetto. You will have noticed on your way
from the Portico, showing itself grandly among the quiet
old houses, the late fifteenth-century small palazzo of

Lorenzo Manillio encrusted with Roman fragments of animals, heads, slabs, and in stentorian lettering, Latin and
Greek, proclaiming the owner.

It would be foolish to give precise instructions on exploring the ghetto except to say "meander," map in hand if you
become enmeshed, which you should. You may come on a
shoemaker who sits in half a metalwork tempietto which
may repeat the apse of a vanished church, or a street bulging with raw wool. Certainly you will come to the eternal
question of what does a Jew look like and decide he looks
like a Roman, or vice versa, and realize that for a Roman
child holidays mean balloons whether outside church or
synagogue, that there are no visible kosher butcher shops,
although one restaurant advertises itself as "Casher," and
that you hear no Yiddish, nor, except during a service,
Hebrew. The curious thing about this Jews' quarter is how
thoroughly—in speech, ebullience, crowded-togetherness on
summer streets—Roman it is.

There might be two goals in your free-form rambling, one
black and the other dazzling bright. Not far from the river,
off the eastern side of the Via Arenula, there is a shapeless,
sooty, sinister palazzo that spreads itself on a vicolo, a
piazza, under an arco and a rise (monte) all named for the
Cenci, who so fascinated writers and artists. The family
may have been no more decadent blood drinkers than their
ducal contemporaries, but somehow they, in company with
Borgias, lead among legendary Renaissance destroyers.
There were Cenci—the word, curiously enough, means
"rags"—malefactors as early as the thirteenth century, but
it wasn't until the sixteenth that they wove their immortality, textured of gloomy legends of madness, incest, and
murder, legends that persist in spite of questioning re-
search and contradictory facts. Francesco Cenci was the
illegitimate son of a father whose profitable church connections left the son very rich. Were he not so wealthy, the
owner of immense properties and of an illustrious name,
and were it today, he would early have been sequestered in

a detention home for young delinquents. Cruel, violent, and
with no necessity to control his princely impulses, he was
twice hauled into court on serious charges before he was
fifteen. His numerous sons, those who didn't die in infancy,
died violent early deaths, one of them on the scaffold. The
boys' activities in no way impeded their father, who was
sentenced to house arrest and later banishment, canceled
by the payment of enormous fines into the papal treasury.
This candidate for a hospital of the criminally insane kept
appearing in courts and paying for charges of brutalizing
servants and members of his family and, in 1594, for
"cruelty and unnatural crimes," which point to his daughter
Beatrice, whom he was forcing sexually—or so the story
goes. He paid an enormous sum, once again, for his freedom,
and continued beating, slashing, victimizing until, in 1598,
he was murdered outside the city by two hired assassins
who, according to one story, drove a nail into his eye and
threw him into a tree to make it seem as if he had fallen
and impaled himself on a branch. The confession of one
assassin implicated Beatrice (whose defense repeated the
charges of incest against her father), two brothers, and her
long-suffering stepmother, Lucrezia. Beatrice was tortured
into a confession of complicity in her father's death and
shortly after was taken to the piazza across from the Castel
S. Angelo to be quartered and then buried, by her own
wish, in the church of S. Pietro in Montorio, high above her
grim alleys.

Pearly, luminous joy invades the ghetto on the Piazza Mattei
as four graceful bronze youths, dancing in marble shells
where dolphins play, lift lithe, graceful arms to help turtles
drink from an upper basin. There are purists who say they
would prefer the fountain as it was designed in the late
sixteenth century by Giacomo Della Porta, without the turtles which were added somewhat later. With or without
turtles the merry faces and free gestures, the subtle con-

trasts of gently curved colored stone and greened bronze, the sheer innocent happiness, make it the loveliest fountain in Rome.

For a seriously overloaded, humorless courtyard of about the same time (the late Renaissance seemed capable of anything), go into the Palazzo Mattei di Giove at the corner with Via Michelangelo Caetani. The *cortile* is frantically stuffed with statues, reliefs, and sarcophagi for stiff Grant Wood Romans. Head for the Piazza Campitelli for calmer, less striving Renaissance palazzi which have adjusted their shapes and sizes to knots of medieval streets that run breathlessly, in the city's characteristic rhythm, to pause and breathe deeply, fully, on their piazza.

Several elements that might be discordant elsewhere but not in patchwork Rome live serenely and harmoniously together on the piazza. A small church, moved here during one of the restless rearrangements of streets, sits at an uncomfortable angle; a bright-umbrellas restaurant punctuates one corner; a merry, lavishly ornamented house of the early seventeenth century, built as his *staatspalais* by the architect Flaminio Ponzio, looks on a marble fountain designed by the master of the tortoise fountain and, along what might almost be considered a straight side, the soaring portals of two late-sixteenth-century palaces. These are accompanied by the church of S. Maria in Campitelli, built by the gifted Carlo Rainaldi in the seventeenth century as a papal offering to an image of the Virgin especially talented at allaying plagues. The detached columns, the placement of windows, and the flow of dark and light spaces create an unusually pleasing example of intellectual, restrained Baroque.

The adjoining Piazza Margana is used, from time to time, for sculpture shows and outdoor theater productions, to which its limited size and sense of enclosure adapt well, although it is best to see when nothing disturbs the view of its tower and the harmonious joining of houses of several periods.

Returning, possibly, by the street of the ropemakers (Funari) or the carpenters (Falegnami), or that of the dark little shops (Botteghe Oscure), one falls onto the terror and astonishments of the Largo Argentina, too frenzied for reflecting on how extraordinary a place it is. The traffic zooms around its perilous corners, buses thunder past its undistinguished shops and banks and bars from every direction, toward every direction, a few pausing to rest and fill up under crowded shelters. Harried two-legged beetles scurry past the newly refurbished eighteenth-century Teatro Argentina, where Rossini saw his *Barber of Seville* a failure, dismissed by a contemptuous noisy crowd on its first night, and a bounding success the second, while he sat in desperation in a room on the Via de' Leutari a short distance away. The prosaic, big-city, darting, preoccupied, frowning nervousness borders with sublime indifference a deep, open box of ruins, a medieval tower, cats, and spring grasses. The name of the big square, first; it has nothing to do with the South American republic but is the Latin name for the town of Strasbourg, the native city of Johannes Burckhardt, secretary and arranger of ceremonial meetings for Pope Alexander VI, the Borgia, and chronicler of his times in Rome. (On the other hand, the square may have been named for a Venetian Cardinal Argentino.) The original Largo was not especially large, and served mainly as a bottleneck for the increasing traffic carried by the broadened Corso Vittorio Emanuele. It was therefore decided by Mussolini's city planners to tear down the houses that fronted on the theater. The touch of a drill or a cut of a shovel is always likely in Rome, as in Mexico, to hit ancient city (a situation that seriously impedes the progress of subway construction), and so, in 1930, there arose from the deepening holes the sketchy remains of four temples of pre-Empire times. To whom they were dedicated, what their purpose was, has not been determined. Three are rectangular, one circular, and the deepest may go back to the fourth century B.C., which would make it one of the oldest unearthed relics of Rome. Some say it was here that Caesar was murdered; others place his perforated corpse in the lobby of the Teatro Argentina (the portico of the temple-theater of Pompey); others move it a short distance back toward the actual Roman theater. In any case the assassination took place near these ruins, a knowledge that makes for imaginative ruminating as one peers at the truncated columns on supports of ancient tufa and the medieval shadows of a church like many that sat in pagan remains.

It is possible to walk among the venerable stones, but, staring down from above, one hesitates. It is the cats, alert, fierce old pirates, ears chewed in fights, some filthy, some sleekly shining on their pedestals, the absolute lords of their manor of dark caverns and sun-splashed marble, terrifying in their numbers and confidence, sure of the old ladies who will bring plastic sacks full of entrails and last night's spaghetti for these kings of the jungle. Always mesmerizing and growing larger and more tigerish as one stares at them, they lose their menace only for a short time in the spring when the sterile old stones shoot forth flowers and the cats' tails swim through the blooms like swift, elusive fish. (Inhabitants of the neighborhood say they have observed an old woman creep into the ruins at night and out in the morning. They could be right. Between ruins Roman, medieval, Renaissance, and Hoovervilles, the city may have more than 50,000 squatters.)

Northward, off the Largo, a concentration of ecclesiastical dress and ornaments—if you've wondered about the underwear of priests and nuns this is the place to find out—and then the inexplicable dark spurs and blind arches that announce the Pantheon.

How to Live
in Rome

Turning a corner in Rome is a lovesome thing, God wot. It may open to a gentle, pale-blue canvas of sky embroidered with scallops of pale-gold dome, a flower stall splashed on the obdurate, gray stone of a Renaissance palace, a covey of medieval houses melting on each other in mutual support, zigzags of red tile and green terrace running together to greet a church steeple, a Roman column bound in an iron corset standing foolishly alone. The possibilities are endless and beguiling except one—the possibility of becoming oneself a decoration of blood red and entrail gray-yellow on one building or other. Before looking up at the enticements dangling in the sky, keep a sharp eye and a careful pace, particularly on sidewalkless, narrow streets, for the joy rider who has been imprisoned by enmeshed traffic, reunions of buses on main streets, unexpected arrows and barriers, to let loose in small side streets, gaily screaming around angles on two wheels.

Where there are sidewalks—and in most places they are too narrow—you may not be much better off: a boy delivering a large bundle may push you into the path of a car, or a postman's full bag, or a large pregnancy accompanied by two children. The major streets in Rome are nattily painted with zebras for pedestrian crossing. If you come from London you will have learned that they are your right to untroubled street crossing. Unlearn it in Rome, where they are yet another hurdle in the traffic game: can the car swing around you as you cross, can it tear through your territory before you can? You join in the game by not permitting yourself to be hurried in an undignified scramble for the sidewalk, or stroll across slowly holding up an august hand, which sometimes shocks drivers into slowing down. Carrying a cane and limping hideously sometimes helps. Or do the chic Roman thing and cross on the stripes, looking neither right nor left, like a lord sauntering through his own fields.

No matter what the attack or method, you may slow a car but never stop it. Nor will traffic lights help too much unless they are aided by policemen in hard white helmets and big white gloves. But police and traffic lights go off late in the evening, and with the feeble assistance of a yellow blinker here and there you are on your perilous own, contending to little avail with the great force of *gallismo,* the Italian version of the better-known Mexican *machismo,* which makes a Fiat Cinquecento the impenetrable armor of fearless, invincible condottieri not to be hindered by slow-footed serfs.

They will not necessarily love you, or hate you. Indifference is the prime Roman strength, and it makes the city a sterile place for the exhibitionist, for the traveler who expects his money to buy at least the aura of tender loving care, for those who insist that the citizens of sunny Italy always radiate good will and affection. They often do because it is a tangent of Italian politeness, because they like and are accustomed to that image of themselves, and because they are so thoroughly, securely uncurious and uncaring. You may easily come through a shower of smiling politeness and cordial words to the conviction that you have made a friend. Only for that encounter, however, which will end with "Ci vediamo" (We'll see each other) or "Ci sentiamo" (We'll hear from each other). The rest is silence. Besides the fact that he is of an ancient race that has been and seen everything, he really hasn't much time. His nonworking hours are full of large meals, eaten quickly but lingered on in long after-coffee conversations; he must do his frequent obeisances to his sanctified Mamma, in his mind and psyche a collage of the Virgin Mary, the many martyred female saints and heroic matrons of the Roman Republic. The tribe—parents, children, in-laws, grandchildren, spinster aunts, and a clump of distant cousins visiting from Pesaro —must spend Sundays and holidays together. Almost as rigid obligations are those imposed by the habit of meeting with old cronies at a bar to discuss football and of gathering after dinner and a light kiss on the brows of kiddies and wife, who are left at home, with those same cronies for long evenings of cards. It may or may not be your idea of a full life, but it suits a sizable portion of middle-class male Rome.

In the event that a friendship does develop, you will find it difficult to make a date for more than a day or two ahead. "When you ask me to do something a week from now I become anxious, sickish. I don't know what will happen between now and then, maybe something terrible or something fascinating." Anglos also play the "better offer" game, but are not as open about it. Here you are openly told, or as close to openly as is polite, that there is an expectation, a hope, of a brighter egg in the social basket than yours.

Assuming you can temper your need to plan ahead, have the time and flexibility to meet the impromptu invitation, the meetings will take place in a bar or restaurant, rarely at your friend's home. It may be that he is reluctant to make a *brutta figura* with his too many children tucked into too little space, or his wife too shy and naïve to cope with foreigners. But these are comparatively minor reasons; the home is sanctuary, reserved for a close inner circle, an ancient attitude reflected in Roman architecture and repeated in the atria and porticoes of early churches. The outer court was used for transacting business and treating with casual visitors, the inner court and rooms reserved for the family, and you are entertained in the outer court, the present-day bar or restaurant.

The Roman reluctance to plan also reflects a profound distrust of any moment that isn't now, immediately, being lived and a love of impromptu excitements as manifested in last-minute shopping. Shops open at about 9 and close at 1, reopen at 4 or 4:30 and close at 8; 12:50 and 7:50 are the preferred times for shopping, everyone scurrying, pushing, rushing; it puts a bit of pepper into daily life and makes one feel impulsive, energetic, and young, each time of the hundreds that the race is repeated.

Should you have to change a check at a bank—even if you have a local bank account and the check is your own made out to yourself—count on at least forty minutes for the transaction. This will allow for people to slip in ahead of you, the passion for the human warmth of crowding, the taste for Renaissance clusters and crowded baroque art resulting in an abhorrence of straight, long lines. Therefore, no queues in shops, box offices, train-ticket windows, bus stops, or staid banks. Someone who shouts at the teller for emergency succor, knowing which chords to strum—"I left the babies home alone," "I have to give some money to my mother in the hospital and it takes me hours to get there"—or a customer who flutters and smiles and swoops her low-cut neckline over the counter to make herself felt by a teller will get attention long before orderly you. Finally someone takes your check, examines it carefully, makes slow, studious searches of distant file boxes, returns to type out with one hesitant finger a large sheaf of forms which disappear into an invisible corner while you wait and wait for it to make its slow, mysterious progress through tubefuls of suspicious eyes to the desk of a cashier who will turn it into money. (If, by the way, you are cashing traveler's checks or collecting money transferred from a bank abroad carry your passport.)

From the leafy month of May to the cooling sun of October and often earlier and later, the money area on the upper floor of American Express on the Piazza di Spagna is a fair version of Gehenna. Low-ceilinged, not air-conditioned in the spring of 1971, the lines infinitely long, hot, and irritable, the sections not clearly categorized so that you often stand for a long time only to find out—brusquely—that you are at the wrong desk and must start all over again at another. Americans turn into Rome haters and say so loudly to anyone who will listen, and few will, because *they* are too busy tamping down their own impatience, shifting from one hot foot to another, searching for damp scraps of Kleenex to wipe the sweat off their faces. Behind the desk, tenseness, confusion, people appearing and disappearing to check American Express credit cards, to explain a complication to a new girl. The new girl (and there are always a number of them, since the turnover of employees is understandably high) shoots up in terror over some mistake she has made or may make, locks herself in the bathroom to weep, or runs to one of the older, harried employees for help. The heat comes down off the low ceiling hotter, denser, closer, nauseating, soon to become suffocating as the body odor of unwashed young nomads suffuses the steaming area. With all this, an unnatural-for-Italy degree of impoliteness, one percent to buy Express checks, a charge plus taxes to change them, one dollar off every hundred cashed on a credit card, erratic rules about maximum cashable amounts, and a lower rate of exchange than other banks offer.

Finding, maintaining, inhabiting an apartment in Rome is a large subject. To condense an encyclopedic range of possibilities and surprises: with enough time, patience, sturdy feet, and the wish to avoid agency fees, mark out the areas in which you would prefer to live (remembering that entire medieval streets around the Campo dei Fiori, the Piazza dell'Orologio, and the Piazza Navona are being rebuilt and prices soaring and that the Piazza di Spagna area, the Aventine and Parioli have for a long time been expensive) and search them. For this you will need to learn some Italian and develop an indifference to weather, but the compensation will be a growing intimacy with parts of Rome and encounters with diverse Romans.

As likely as not your landlady will have a title and a resounding historic name which needn't be too awesome since the famous condottiere dukes planted many peripheral lines which grew to forests of family trees through the centuries. Also, titles and imposing names were commodities that could be bought and sold. But you will be awed, too dazzled to see until a few sober days later that your smart, multilingual landlady has taken an empty apartment at a low rental, put in tremulously old furniture, and added to the feeble pieces improvisations that make bedside tables of boxes covered with old pieces of silk, a narrow hallway table of an unused loudspeaker box, decoration supplied by the amateur paintings of a friend. Be prepared for minimal heating, although you will pay an ample surcharge for it; be prepared for the electricity to go off if you burden it with the extra heater you will buy secondhand from an advertisement in the English-language daily.

Once the advance of rent and deposit are handed over,

Her Highness disappears and further inquiry, complaint, desperate pleas, advice are negotiated with her maid, a stimulating experience in traditional types. She may be a bland-faced country woman, whose face has a fresh openness that is as inexpressive as a field, who falls readily into the role of the favored house serf appointed to protect the lady of the castle from the rude world. She will improvise excuses and delays and small lies for her frail charge, not always so much out of devotion—though that exists—as in the knowledge, bred into her for generations, that this is her role and an essential part of her job. The other maid is the Susanna-Despina type, bright, chic, clever, who delays, deliberately forgets to transmit messages, and apologizes coquettishly. In her there is no fidelity; she plays the protection game for the love of darting between the two parties, of being messenger and maker of small intrigues and, if La Principessa becomes too exigent and you generous, she may become a strong ally, temporarily.

Never take an apartment without a working phone. Each room may be adorned with a telephone, but if it gives your expectant ear a breeze of dead silence, the likelihood is that that will be its condition for a long time, maybe the length of your stay in an area where new shops and reconstructed houses are making insupportable demands on the poorly equipped system. If you have a usable phone, expect to dial the same number several times, because a busy signal enjoys cutting in at the fourth or fifth digit. Each Roman has his own solution, which rarely works, but he enjoys believing in it, as he enjoys his many other superstitions. One dials very quickly, allowing no time for the impish signal to impede the run of numbers; others believe in banging the numbers out slowly and forcefully, thus battering down and smashing the interference. One refined system, and they swear it works, is to dial steadily in an even rhythm and hesitate before the fourth or fifth number. Whatever ritual works for you, the number once achieved, you will be confronted with conversation that has, besides its intrinsic self, a number of graphic possibilities. The words may come to you in thick, murky distortions, like slow bubbles out of a sulfurous swamp, or prickly crackles, or the voice may ebb to a distant whisper, rush back fast as a loud tide, and quickly ebb again. Nothing much to be done about it except to develop a capacity for extrasensory message transmission, which will also come in handy in London, Paris, New York, and all other places that have malingering telephones.

The interminable waiting for telephone installation can be sped up by ordering multiple extensions and by paying a larger deposit and extra monthly fee for a listing as a "private office" which puts one in the category of the "masseuses" and "manicurists" who top the AAAAAA (priority position) ads in an Italian newspaper.

A repairman never comes, never, when he says he will. Always there are monumentally important emergencies that tower above your flooded kitchen and icy radiators and windows that welcome knifelike winds. The great man arrives, finally, without tools. This is the time for diagnosis and discussion. *Va bene*, he knows what is required, but he can't possibly come back this week. "You know how it is with the pressure of work"—his tone implies the unspoken phrase, "with us famous neurosurgeons"—but "I'll give you a bit of advice. When you take a bath hang a big towel over the crack in the bathroom window so you don't catch cold. Don't, by the way, use any electrical appliances near the water in the bathroom." (Where, one is tempted to ask, but remains respectfully silent, is there space unrelated to water, in a bathroom?) "The charge of electricity is ten times as great when it is near water, and when people don't know that they run serious danger of electrocution. I wouldn't hurry to fix that lock in the kitchen window. You need a little air when you use gas so you won't be asphyxiated. No gas? All electricity? Well, fresh air never hurt anyone." And he puts on his cap and makes his regal departure. If the man in charge of repairs in your house is the portiere and his habit is to reassure you with "Ci penso io" (I'll take care of it), resign yourself to waiting and/or nagging, neither of which need necessarily have any effect at all.

Never assume you know where a bus stop is. In the constant, restless changes of traffic designed to so exasperate drivers as to keep them out of the center (diabolic means to a good, if fruitless, end), bus stops are uprooted, planted elsewhere, or dumped altogether.

To live successfully in Rome you must like to eat and never be, or appear to be, sated with the limited cuisine. Eating is the major social activity and an important topic of conversation. As everyone knows, there is an intellectual life in Rome; the city has museums in unused abundance, some theater, opera, concerts, movies, and art, many bookshops and periodical stands. Romans are capable of thinking well and quickly, and enjoy lengthy discussions. The discussions, however, usually concern themselves with choices of restaurants, their degrees of excellence and failure in certain categories, how fresh the supply of fish might be that day, and so on and on, animatedly, amusingly. The state of the world, of art, of literature, of politics—Che ne so io? Che me ne frega?—two Roman key phrases that sustain him well through an earthy, intellectually untroubled life.

As mentioned, many factors of Roman life are baroque. Consider the fact that tickets for a concert usually go on sale no sooner than three days before performance and must often be bought in an office completely detached from the auditorium. A theater series at reduced rates requires that you apply at one office for the privilege, not the tickets, and thereafter, precisely three days before each performance, buy the tickets separately at each of the theaters concerned. Or, for a concert series, you may have to be in line at 6:30 A.M. to receive a numbered slip of paper which, when the doors open officially an hour later, can be exchanged for another number for priority in line. A low number may mean nothing, in spite of the sacrificial offerings of gritty eyes and moaning feet; a good deal of horse trading impedes you. Latecomers will make deals with the few people ahead of you, and you're out unless you have a good loud command of Italian or, better still, a line companion who speaks both English and Italian and who will, in your defense, and to save the face of Italy, speak up for you.

An awed envy occasionally grips the Anglo when he observes the fluent ease with which Italians make and continue conversations, spinning and weaving to grandiose dimensions the thinnest of threads. Try to remember that, unlike you, he comes by it naturally; for many decades the most important branch of ancient Roman education was oratory.

The cleaning woman will inform you that her husband who is on a civil service job is studying for the examination in the next rank. He has been studying for years, is well prepared and optimistic, primarily because a professor he knows in Naples, a man with powerful connections, has promised to have one of *his* friends in a government office write a recommendation to the head of the office in which her husband works. But, you ask, if he is prepared and due for promotion, why all the complications? "Così è fatto"— that's the way it's done, Signora; you always have to have a *pezzo grosso*—big shot—to sponsor you. Otherwise, someone else with a *pezzo grosso* behind him will get the job whether he's qualified or not. A friend may phone to ask if you know someone who knows a *pezzo grosso* in the post office who might untangle the problem of no overseas mail received for weeks and weeks. The portiere says that he has an appointment with a local power to ask for a letter that urges his child be promoted in school. The child is doing fairly well, but it doesn't hurt to make sure with a strong word. In other words, the feudal habit of relying on the lord of the manor, the duke in power (translate it in terms of the Mafia, if you like), still pervades many phases of Italian life.

To feel truly indigenous, let the parish priest who rings your bell during Easter week bless your house. The fee is a contribution to his church.

The impromptu, improvised quality of Roman life becomes less joyful when you find that supplies you take for granted, like varieties of length and width in curtain rods, cannot be found at the shops and must be ordered of a specialist artisan. There is variety, though, where you do not expect to find it: two girths of neck for bulbs of the same size and wattage; two types of electric current, one cheaper than the other, and sockets in a diversity of design.

The appearance of the sweeper-upper of the stairs whom you never see, or the postman, ditto, at your door saying "Auguri" and smiling winsomely means that Easter is approaching, or Christmas or Ferragosto (mid-August), and a tip of about 1,000 lire is expected. The cleaning woman or steady maid is given more—3,000 or 5,000, depending on how simpatico you find each other.

Not only the children traipse through the streets in expensive *carnevale* costumes; their parents often dress up, too, for private parties. If the occasion should come your way and you can't or won't improvise, see what you can find at the costume shop in Bramante's arcades behind S. Maria della Pace.

Sixty-nine Via Caprettari (Pantheon) is the address of the package branch of the post office. They do—or did—the packing as well as the mailing. A shoplike section near the entrance to the main post office on the Piazza San Silvestro provides sealing wax for distinguished documents.

When you have been asked "Ce l'ha spiccioli?" or "Ce l'ha dieci [or venti or trenta] lire?" by the cashier in American Express, by the tobacconist, by the girl who sold you toothpaste, by a fruit vendor, by a newsstand keeper, and you've grown tired of digging into your pocket for the light, unfamiliar coins, say "No" and stand your ground. With a show of exasperated exhaustion, after a hopeful pause that waits for you to relent and produce the change, the vendor will scrabble under the counter for a cigar box more frequently than not full of coins. It must be a primitive compulsion, an atavistic faith in coins no matter how little their value, more intrinsically trustworthy than bits of paper which may represent money but have no metallic—even frail, tinny—ring. Or it may be the fact that small coins are used as a base for covered buttons, cheaper than cutting and shaping other bits of metal.

As a general rule, whiskey is served after dinner, although you may have it before if such is your primitive habit.

What makes conversation piquant is that there is never no answer and whether an answer makes sense or not matters very little. Scene: an accessories shop. Props: customer and saleslady and two shawls, one green, one black. The style and price are equal, but the weight of the wool is not —the green is more thickly woven and heavier. Customer mentions the fact and asks the saleswoman to lift both. She does, admits that there is a difference in weight, but adds that it is because of the color. But how can one dye weigh more than another? Surely it is the quality and quantity of the wool. No, Signora, it's the green color that's heavier. How can color make a difference in weight? Oh, yes, Signora, it's the color. Nothing moves her, nor will, and she has centuries of *pazienza* to draw on, so you buy, partly because your sales resistance or shrewdness has been engulfed in the swamp of her bizarre logic. Scene: the cleaners. Customer: But those big spots weren't on the dress when I brought it in. Answer: It's perspiration. How could I have perspired in the dress (the perspiration season is well over) while it was here in your shop? It's perspiration, and that's hard to get out. But I didn't bring it in this way. It's perspiration, etc., etc. And it's your turn to muster up *pazienza*.

There are at least three English-language libraries: the lending library (charge) of the Lion Bookshop, 181 Via del Babuino; at no charge, the library of the British Council, 20 Quattro Fontane, and that in the courtyard of the church of S. Susanna on the Via 20 Settembre.

It is easy to be sucked into the *bella figura* game. You do an Italian a small favor. He responds with a bottle of good French wine. You send a big, expensive box of chocolates to his children. He sends masses of rare flowers—and so it keeps spiraling. Watch early developments and resign immediately.

·   ·   ·

It is a comfortable thought that practically anything in Rome can be bought at a *sconto* (discount), including long-distance telephone calls, if you make enough of them. Ask a resident friend how it's done.

One of the penalties of living abroad is shuttling back and forth between home and the airport meeting visitors. An easy and cheap way to do it is to take the SARO bus that leaves from the terminal on Via Giolitti on the hour.

If you are the earnest parent of a number of children who have agreed to museum visits, best take them on Sundays when the fee is reduced to half-price or nothing.

Phoning for a taxi (stations are listed in the early pages of the yellow phone book) is the most efficient way of getting one unless it is raining. Then one must call several neighborhood numbers repeatedly in the hope that a taxi will come home to roost within some reasonable time, or scour the streets. Assuming the station phone is answered and the taxi arrives, be prepared to pay 50 lire extra for the telephone call charged to *your* bill. The reasoning is convoluted, following the baroque curves on churches, in traffic planning, arm gestures, the shapes of pears, and grapes.

In many Roman situations having a friend who has a friend has great value—to find a maid, a tailor, a dressmaker. It helps in shopping as well. To be introduced to a friend's fruit vendor or butcher puts you "in," and the service and quality are better than that given a total stranger. Have your friend's friend also introduce you to the well-stocked and inexpensive drugstore inside the Vatican gates.

. . .

All big cities can be lonely places for the person alone, but Rome is distinctly for togetherness of family and tribe. The summer pleasures of outdoor eating, the meetings in caffès, the walking arm in arm, and the inexhaustible conversations on benches, ledges of palazzi, corners of piazze, wineshops—everywhere, as a matter of fact—shape a large, noisy permanent festa in which the foreign loner may not join. He can stand outside the window looking in at the party, but no one will invite him in.

However, watching Romans is its own pleasure, and quite enough for a while. Every encounter is operatic, the voices carry, the gestures are oratorical, the face-to-face emotion intense—too intense for a screen, they belong on a stage, singing tragic stories of mad heroines and suicide heroes. Watch the progress of a conversation, the greeting always touched with pleased surprise, from a large smile to the Romanesco "ammazza," derived from a word for killing that expresses charmed amazement. Phase two is an *andante con brio*, heads nodding and eye caressing eye, and then a finger shoots up, and two, the whole hand lifts and turns, two hands now in a gesture of supplication ("per carità"— what the hell are you talking about?), the fingers bunched together and shaking like the beaks of nervous birds ("Listen, I'm telling you it's impossible"). The arms come into play, and the shoulders and the back, a vivacious dance on a tiny stage paced to the tune of rippling, cascading words.

As newspapers of other countries gleefully point out, some unit of Italian industry or service is on strike almost every day. Strikes came so thickly for a period that a phone number was assigned to strike information—dial and find out whether you walk to work, if there is work at all. Generally, strikes are well publicized so that the city can prepare; no schools open for a week, no mail for X number of days, no bus service between 10 A.M. and 4 P.M., general strike on Thursday. The Roman doesn't much mind; it's another holiday, and for a Roman there cannot ever be enough free days for walking, sitting in the park (closed caffès *are* something of a nuisance), taking a ride into the country if gas stations are functioning. A good number of strikes are political weapons; others break out for the usual causes —pay increases, shorter hours, expanded fringe benefits, and, peculiar to a people that have very little civic interest or pride and almost no sense of community, demands for improvements that serve the general good. A bus strike may have as one of its primary purposes the improvement of traffic routes in the center of the city. Bus drivers who know intimately the inextricable knots of traffic that mire their juggernauts suggest changes of traffic routes to the authorities, who pay no attention. Strike. Out come the night men who paint arrows and yellow lines and white bars, and the next morning there is complete chaos and paralysis except for those who studied the maps in the early morning papers. Pedestrians accustomed to watching one-way traffic on a particular street must train themselves to guard against assault from the other direction. Bus stops find themselves on unaccustomed corners.

It was usually said that everyone strikes but soccer players and priests. A union of soccer players issued a strike threat in the spring of 1971. Nothing came of it but pangs of misery in the hearts of male Italy. A few weeks earlier, on Easter Sunday, a sign protesting the low pay of parish priests was displayed immediately after the services outside St. Peter's. As irritating as they can be to visitors awaiting checks locked up in postal sacks behind shut doors, and to Italians as well, strikes usually produce the looked-for effects which an ineffective government and an inert citizenry should have seen to but didn't.

. . .

The noise of Rome—the shouting of "Senta" and orders, bellowings in and out of the kitchen in *casareccio* (home-style) restaurants, shrieking motorbikes, the blatting of hopped-up exhaust pipes on small cars, gears grinding their teeth, brakes shrilling, horns howling; big, round voices in the markets or shouting from window to street and across streets; televisions and radios turned up to near-explosion —is one of its major monuments, and venerable. The poet Martial, who wrote in the first century A.D., complained:

> *In Rome a poor man cannot find*
> *A place to think, or peace of mind.*
> *At dawn schoolmasters yak and clamor,*
> *Bakers bang pans, coppersmiths hammer,*
> *And all this din goes on all day*
> *If not all night. Across the way*
> *The moneychanger's killing time*
> *By rattling every phony dime*
> *In his tin coin box, and the sound*
> *Competes against the thud and pound*
> *As the gold-beaters grunt and groan*
> *Banging their mallets on the stone . . .*

and continues with his listing of

> *How many rapes my sleep endures*
> *In this metropolis of yours.*

Some years later, the satirist Juvenal: "Insomnia causes more deaths amongst Roman invalids than any other factor. The most common complaints, of course, are heartburn and ulcers, brought on by overeating." And he continues with his plaint of lack of sleep because of "the wagons thundering past through these narrow twisting streets, the oaths of draymen caught in a traffic jam," and much, bitterly, more. It was, it is, it will be, one of the noisiest cities in the world but—thin solace—without the noise it wouldn't be Rome.

. . .

The unnatives grow restless after two years, tired of big monuments and little lies. The Italian charm seems too practiced (Why is it that Italian children have so little appeal? Are charm and coquettishness learned as good, useful manners?) and grows tattered. The human and car noises no longer make a chorus of vivacity and are now merely nerve-plucking. The amusing evasions of the landlord have soured to greed. The summers are too damned hot and the winters not *that* much better than London's. And so on. It's time to leave, to go elsewhere, and wait for the inevitable yearning for Rome to attack.

Piazza del Teatro di Pompeo
Museo Barrocco
Via dei Baullari ☐ Pantheon
Vicolo Vittorio
Vicolo dei Bovari
Piazza del Biscione
Vicolo Cellini
Vicolo del Bollo
Piazza del Paradiso
Via dei Cappellari
Via dei Chiavari
Campo dei Fiori
Piazza dei Satiri
Via Monserrato
Via del Plebiscito
Palazzo Venezia
Palazzo Farnese
Largo Argentina
Via Capo di Ferro
Largo dei Librari
Palazzo Spada
Vicolo delle Grotte
Piazza B. Cairoli
Via dei Pettinari
Campidoglio
Via dell'Arco del Monte
V.Arenula
S. Salvatore in Campo
Via Giubbonari Vicolo de' Catinari

Walk 7

Campidoglio to Pantheon

Having fed on the rich mixture of Campidoglio, its museums, and the view of the battered Forum below, cross when and how you can to the Palazzo Venezia and enter the courtyard of its church, shaded by frayed umbrellas of palm. It will give you a bell tower brightened by ceramic disks (meant to ward off plagues) and the majestic procession of double arches usually attributed to Alberti, the fifteenth-century amateur who was most certainly a man of the Renaissance, rich, cultivated, painter, composer, writer, student of antiquities, and an accomplished architect who used Roman models but discarded the ponderous weights and encrustations to substitute light, ease, and Renaissance harmony. The creamy arches touched only by simple keystone ornaments, the contained extensions of ledges and loggia wall that hold the upward flight of stone for a pause, combine to make an oasis of calm reasonableness in a city of sharp marble stumps and dancing volutes.

The church of S. Marco, attached to the palazzo, has left some of its relics intact—Cosmatesque work, ninth-century mosaics, and a subterranean basilica of gone centuries. These are not, as you know, unique in Rome, and you might be satisfied with two objects under the portico, a medieval drum which was part of a well whose crude inscription invites passers-by to drink but not to sell (anathema to him who does) the water. Adjoining the ethical drum, a large plaque moved from S. Maria del Popolo that bears the name of Vannozza (Giovanna Cattanei), who was the "wife" of the Borgia Pope Alexander VI and the mother of his children. The incised letters are not smoothly worn but chipped by an instrument, fiercely gouged by an angry hand which resented her presence in a church.

The Palazzo Venezia and its eccentric collection drops you on the Via del Plebiscito, which rumbles past the church of the Gesù and into the Largo Argentina.

If you like the heated, acrid smell of cats, take the underpass (*sottopassaggio*) that leads toward Arenula. If you don't, dare your way through the maelstroms of traffic toward the street named for the jacketmakers, Giubbonari. The street takes its first deep breath at the Piazza B. Cairoli, which might ordinarily be dominated by the façade of S. Carlo ai Catinari (for the basinmakers in the neighborhood) were it not for the clothing racks and food stalls that clamor in voices, color, and vivacity from the piazza. The Via de' Giubbonari is a plump, glistening market street, garlanded with big beads of mozzarella and cables of sausage, stuffed with cakes and clothing, the modernity of frozen food cases and the traditional "confetti" (Jordan almonds) wrapped in little flowered tutus or dainty ceramic boxes to be given to guests at birth celebrations, first communions, and as invitations to weddings. To catch the 50- and 100-lire coins of the spenders of a thousand or two, there are the fringe vendors who have no shops or proper stalls and only pathos as lure. One set is an old couple who pile a small stock of inexpensive flowers on the street against the wall. The variety is more limited than that of any stall in the area, nor are they necessarily the freshest flowers or the cheapest unless you bargain hard. But who can bargain with an old man whose protection from the winter rain is a worn cap and a shapeless jacket and no gloves for the purple hands that bind a bouquet gathered by his wife, one of her eyes covered with a milky film, her hands knobbed with arthritis?

Before you are immobilized by saddened flowers, turn into the almost untouched, unimproved medievalism of the Vicolo de' Catinari, S. Salvatore in Campo (a group of garages lighten the local fatalism), the piazza of S. Salvatore, one of whose forgotten houses is wreathed in pretty plaster and ironwork, and S. Paolo alla Regola. There is a tradition that the Jewish-Roman citizen St. Paul lived where his minor church now stands, and there is contorted justice in the fact that this was one of the churches chosen for converting the Jews. Next to the church (16), a ladylike doorway and the approach to S. Maria in Monticello, a confusion of remade medieval at different levels, sketches of Gothic window, pieces of Roman column, and a spurt of modern smokestack, the ambiguous collection an eerie composition to confront in the course of a night walk under the pallid lamps. The street called Conservatorio has resigned altogether, most of its houses unused, which may, in time, be the fate of the Via dei Pettinari (combmakers), a strip that sustains life by selling basic shoes and clothing. Where it becomes the Via dell'Arco del Monte it turns to the buying and selling of jewelry and "antiques" as an adjunct to the Monte di Pietà, one of the most lordly pawnshops in the world and undoubtedly the only one that speaks its name—twice, in big bronze letters—in Latin: *Mons Pietatis et Depositorium.* Besides the refurbished yellow and white walls and gigantic clock and the Monte di

Pietà, the piazza sports a good palazzo and court (30) and then leaves you in a row of heavy beards of raw wool that fringe the mattress shops on the Via dei Pompieri.

The Vicolo delle Grotte and that of the Giglio return to shapeless antiquity, ameliorated at the Largo dei Librari, a wedge-shaped piazza that serves as community salon—therefore alert—still touched by traces of better-days volute and balcony.

The Palazzo Spada, fronting on the Via Capo di Ferro ("ironhead," the name of a cardinal), presents the usual problem. Its gallery is not large but crammed with Italian and some Dutch painting, mainly of the seventeenth century, and how much of that do you want to see? Should you choose to go you will find several Guido Renis, among them the *Judith* with sword in one hand and Holofernes' head in the other, bland face turned to heaven for approval; a landscape of Brueghel the Elder, and another by Poussin; a damaged *Portrait of a Musician* by Titian; a lively, curly-headed young man by Annibale Carracci; a strange *Saint Lucia*, paganized to a pearly back and shoulder touched by a seductive straggle of locks; the usual full supply of saints, Holy Families, cardinals, and a curious *Pietà* by Borgianni, a remarkable study in foreshortening that makes a pair of hard-working feet the focal point of the painting.

First things first, however. The palace façade is a sandwich of orders that enclose a yeasty mixture of ornaments —Roman emperors in niches topped with garlands, pediments that fly up to meet medallions, banners, festoons, and drapes in stucco, a fussiness that might have been better in ivory or, better still, cut velvet. Similar ornamentation by the sixteenth-century Mazzoni, who adorned the façade, seems to work more successfully in the entrance court, probably because of its limited size and the airy relief of three arches.

The palace, built for Cardinal Ironhead in the sixteenth

century, enlarged and restored by Borromini for the cultivated Jesuit Cardinal Spada of the collection, ultimately
became the seat of the Council of the State of the Italian
Government. For that reason, one cannot see all the rooms,
although the gallery is treated as a public museum and
open the ordinary museum hours. However, the hallways
offer enough examples of the decorative arts—ceilings of
several elaborate types, frescoes, skillful plasterwork, large
and frail chandeliers, gilded furniture, and, inevitably, white
noble Romans. If the Council isn't sitting you may be able
to go into the meeting room accompanied by a guide to visit
the superheroic oratorical figure dug out in the sixteenth
century from the Via de'Leutari, in the neighborhood. (One
sees that time as a long Judgment Day when the immense
stone ghosts rose in their mighty number from graves under
Renaissance palazzi.)

In the incessant uneasy effort to put the strayed bits of
ancient Rome together, to match if necessary round pegs
with square holes, the fast-spreading enamel of legend is
daubed on an awkward joint and soon one has a not quite
smooth but usable semifact. This practice assigned to the
Spada Colossus the role of Pompey's image at whose feet
Caesar fell. As always in these matters, why not?—until
someone unearths a more convincing statue and slicker
enamel. Whoever he is—warrior, god, or emperor in one
of his god phases—the figure had an eventful history. To
begin with, it may have been two statues, head and body of
different sources, or it may have been made in two parts, a
common practice. In a time of great demand craftsmen
prepared many colossal bodies (as itinerant New England
painters prepared figures and backgrounds beforehand in
considerable number) to be joined to a portrait-head. When
the nude colossus was found his head rested in Signore X's
soil and his body in that of a neighbor, Signore Y. Each
argued his right to the whole statue and brought the matter
to court, where it was decided, on the immortal example of
Solomon, that body and head be again severed and each

part revert to the appropriate owner. The Cardinal Capo-
diferro interfered in the neck of time (sorry) and spoke of
the matter to Pope Julius III, who bought the statue and
made a gift of it to the cardinal. The statue remained intact
in the palace until it was to be used as part of the scenery
for a performance of Voltaire's *Brutus* presented in the
Colosseum during the French occupation. In order to ease
the carting one of the arms was lopped off. So much for
reduced, putative Pompey whom Byron apostrophised as

> *Thou, dread statue! yet existent in*
> *The austerest form of naked Majesty,*
> *Thou who beheldest 'mid the assassins' din*
> *At thy bathed base the bloody Caesar lie,*
> *Folding his robe in dying dignity.*

In one of the galleries above the courtyard there are
eight marble reliefs and two casts of a mythological series
that represent a high development in Roman sculpture and,
in the garden bordered by architectural fancies of Borromini, a tiny court devised by the architect to perform the
most astonishing trompe l'oeil feat in Rome. One sees first
a long set of arches that enfold, at some distance, another
marble colossus. A minute back court reveals the statue
to be one yard tall, the arches and colonnades only seven
yards long, a wizard's faking of perspective which was
probably picked up by Bernini when he shaped his Scala
Regia at St. Peter's to appear a longer and wider set of
stairs than the space would normally allow.

The Burckhardt remembered for his book on the Renaissance built a strong little palace whose understated door,
rounded windows, ivied courtyard, traces of fresco and
graffiti, and carved, painted ceilings now serve to house
the city's theater library and small museum of theater arts.
Rarely will you find another visitor (from 9 to 3:45 except
on Sundays and holidays), and the attendant, bored with

the phone that rarely rings and the day's newspapers, will eagerly whisk you into all the rooms, behind the stacks, and into the corners of strayed objects waiting to be placed in a refurbished room.

The concentration is particular, but who isn't seduced by the theater, especially when its artifices are so engagingly scattered in an equally appealing house? Ring the bell at 44 Sudario, say no when the portiere-guide asks if you want to use the *biblioteca*, say *museo*, and proceed into a collection of theater programs in English and Italian printed on paper, cotton, and lace-edged silk. If you've seen a Palio in Siena or the tourney with the Moor in Arezzo or Renaissance football games in Florence, you will have learned that make-believe for Italians needs the stuff, the actual color and textures of reality, and you will observe this here again in magnificently embroidered velvet and satin gowns and the minutely, tightly stitched patches of a Punchinello costume. Before you mount the stairs, look into the courtyard and note the vestiges of towers hidden from the street and then return to a witty cartoon of Anna Magnani lost and wild in her storm of hair and Vittorio Gassman's profile thrusting forward its sharp definition. Opposing the worldly caricatures, a set of the naïve, as ugly, naturalistic southern puppets. *Pagliacci* is suggested in a painting of a Commedia del'Arte troupe alone in an endless plain, some clowning and dancing, others retired with a couple of bottles and a woman fiddler off to the side. No audience, no signs of surrounding life, no company but each other. Actors famous in Italian history—Ristori, Salvani—are shown in various roles in photos and miniatures, and we return to Commedia del'Arte figurines time and time again, with no boredom, since they were expressed in a great variety of materials and media and lent themselves so well to exaggerations of color and gesture. Their Chinese equivalent is a caseful of exquisitely gowned and masked puppets, a number of the more fiendish masks of carved ivory, the little white heroines' faces of fine porcelain.

Though the library is very orderly, there is no order, nor should there necessarily be, in the collection. Thus leather masks and remnants of classical mask and models of Roman theaters end their show with a large photo of Eleonora Duse and an enameled portrait as painted by an Italian Sargent. And we begin again with costumes, as perfect as before but this time in lustrous miniatures, turn to jewels worn by famous actresses, and enter a gallery of theater posters of a star in a Belle Epoque gown of peacock feather design, of engravings of climactic scenes in melodramas. As if it were planned, the show ends with a close view of the dome of S. Andrea della Valle, built into the minds of opera lovers as background for Tosca's glittering, susurrant entrance, calling, "Mario, Mario."

Working-class Rome—almost back into eternity to judge from the guild streets named for the makers of nails (Chiodaroli) and keys (Chiavari)—rears and roars up outside the enclave of romance and make-believe. The Via de' Chiavari snakes its way through basic shops, sliding past a hotel where no one should have to stay and probably no one does except for a half-hour of rapid dalliance, and a cave whose floor and walls are tattered books and pamphlets ready for pulping (and what sort of livelihood can such an enterprise earn?), and then slips into the Piazza dei Satiri and the Via di Grotta Pinta. The lean and curve of a set of houses on the street take their extraordinary form from the Theater of Pompey, into whose shape they settled, leaving uncovered early stone in the depths of a restaurant at the base of the eccentric, subtle slope. At the side of an abandoned church there is a passageway—closed at night because of a murder a few years back and, in any case, no longer of use to the scribes who once sat at the entrance—that introduces the dome of S. Andrea della Valle in its full might and, on the Piazza del Biscione (89), a painted house, varying the usual patterns with a tree that

gives birth to a goddess and a marble nameplate that features two realistic heads of horses.

At this point you might prefer to lose yourself in the
ebullience of the Campo dei Fiori market (closed afternoons except Saturday) or continue in its adjuncts of questionable *alberghi*, work pants, the hundreds of small lamps
several shops wear as bright necklaces, and on slats of
wood, in decayed prams, and on rags spread in the street,
lovely junk—old post cards, beakless vases, unattached
telephones, rusty keys in impressive numbers, lifeless
watches, and uncherished medals. (Piazza del Paradiso,
Vicolo dei Bovari, Piazza del Teatro di Pompeo.) Above the
yard goods, reduced from the secondhand silks and cut
velvets once displayed here, and shirts on the Piazza del
Teatro di Pompeo, a palazzo (18) whose round ornaments
echo the building glimpsed through the street, the great
Cancelleria, the papal offices for correspondence and
archives.

It does not matter in distance which path you follow;
these are not streets but elongated cells of a dense beehive.
The Via dei Pellegrini stops for a plaque which claims the
opening of the street for Alexander VI and might be a
veiled sentimental gesture for his Vannozza, who was the
hostess of an inn called The Cow on the Campo dei Fiori
when it was a jolly neighborhood, before it became public
execution ground. The street now blazes with high enamel
on secondhand furniture and mirrors where it doesn't glow
more subtly of conservative jewelry, some of it quite good.
Both 64 and 65 on Pellegrino show traces of painting, the
latter presenting chalky, abundant human bodies and volup-
tuous horses' behinds bearing warriors in combat. Above,
Picassoesque nudes just about contained by a reasonable,
earlier cornice. The street takes to scrap metal weighed in
huge scales as it is cut by the Vicolo del Bollo, which gives
all its attention to metal and junk and, as it becomes Montorio, gathers ladders, gutted refrigerators, sliding piles
of cartons, cut timber, and the odor of sawdust. All this

unambitious enterprise is crested by the symbols of the Chigi, who apparently had, in their time, as many palaces as the medieval Frangipani had fortresses.

Some measure of the amenities of the houses in the streets off the market can be judged by the hand-lettered posters on the walls. Among the announcements for Communist party demonstrations against the war in Vietnam and for freeing Angela Davis, complaints about the lack of nursery schools for the children of the many working mothers and the lack of hospitals, graphic protests against the unsanitary conditions of the houses, the constant struggles with rats and roaches, the inadequate kitchen and toilet facilities, and the fact that garbage is too rarely collected in the streets. (The old Russian Communist habit of self-criticism hasn't reached the party in Rome; they don't consider it necessary to examine the window-to-street sources of much of the garbage.)

The purest medieval street, the most picturesque, and one of the most diseased is the Via dei Cappellari (hatmakers), long, tight, winding, overarched like Siena and unlike Siena, crisscrossed in the Neapolitan pattern with permanent pennants of laundry. Archaeologists say that there is a Roman insula, apartments of low, crushed rooms, in these walls. It is still insula, tall, sunless warrens pitted with low arches around musty workshops or black mouths open to hunting grounds of rats and cats. Its jobs are hard unskilled labor, a bit of thievery, "reconstructions" of faked or stolen Etruscan pottery, and the inescapable poor-neighborhood prostitution. With luck you might be knocked down by a fat Medusa with black-ringed eyes clutching a dirty bathrobe over her jouncing breasts and belly as she tears after a co-worker and competitor, shrieking, "Pig-whore thief!"

· · ·

The long simple façade, cool and restrained, at the corner with the Corso is that of the Cancelleria, built in the late fifteenth century for the Riario whose name is engraved on the building. He was Raffaele Riario, a young nephew of Sixtus IV, who died in 1484 and was succeeded by Innocent VIII, who also had a nephew. Both young men, with limitless sums at their command and, like their peers in many places and centuries, steep gamblers, had one long session which resulted in an enormous coup for the Riario, a sum big enough to permit him to buy the property, on which some building had already begun, to complete and furnish as his private apartments. Whether he knew it or not, the gaming Riario was preserving the Roman spirit of the site which had been the training ground and headquarters of the Green team of gladiators, highly favored stars who were given sumptuous gifts and prizes, earned substantial sums in the betting, and, if they weren't killed too young, became —like survivors among bullfighters—very rich men. The wheel of Riario fortunes turned to the shade with the advent of the Borgias, back in the sun when Julius II, a relative, was crowned pope and again into thunderous cloud when the Medici (Leo X) accused the Riario of plotting against them and the palace was taken to be used to house important ecclesiasts. Since then it has served several purposes: as a court in the time of Napoleon and meeting hall for the brief Republican period of the mid-nineteenth century.

Like a number of early Renaissance buildings it is self-contained, its own integrated being which does not need, as Mannerist buildings do, the seduction of the spectator and his responses for effect. The lack of deep cornice, the flatness relieved by shallow pilasters and the subtle expansion and swell of papal shields at the corners, the understated window-surrounds, the felicitous spacing of the Riario rose, give the Cancelleria the look of a drawing, a blueprint of an ideal Renaissance building.

The courtyard, which may be the work of Bramante, is equally aristocratic. The many granite columns support sets of serenely balanced arcades that open to a grand stairway and a distinguished doorway. The provenance of the pillars, by the way, is still in dispute. They may have been brought from the Theater of Pompey to be used in the early church of S. Lorenzo in Damaso, part of the building, or may have been standing there as supports of the gladiators' buildings, or to surround temples and a Mithraeum still in a substratum of the building. There is less doubt about the other stones of the Cancelleria; they were pried off the Colosseum, that inexhaustible mine of marble and travertine.

A significant change in Renaissance architecture from "early" to "High" easing into Mannerism, occurs in a two-minute walk riverward to the stunning Palazzo Farnese, which drew on both the Colosseum and the Teatro di Marcello for its stone. The forceful building was designed by Sangallo the Younger in 1534 and completed on his death by Michelangelo, who was responsible for the deep cornice and the third story of the imposing court. It may mean returning on Sunday morning, strictly between 11 A.M. and noon (when the French Embassy, which inhabits the palace, admits visitors), if only to see the court, to observe the stone lilies both Farnese and French, the late Renaissance return to successive Roman orders. The street floor columns end at simple Doric capitals which curl as Ionic on the second and burst into Corinthian bloom on the third order. The columns serve to link and separate sets of lordly windows set above shapely arches. The interior need not concern one overly except for the length of the gallery and the splendid coffered ceiling in the double-storied salon. The art on view is in the "palazzo" convention—sarcophagi, Roman statuary in niches, tapestries which copy the Raphael *Stanze* paintings in the Vatican, and ceilings of Greco-Roman mythology as it bounds between wine and love.

The building qua building calls for and deserves major attention and should your time in the piazza be an early evening in the summer, the people in the piazza do too. Recently cut off from traffic, the wide piazza has become the local public park where grandpa, sitting on the palace ledge, reads his *Unità*, grandma crochets, and young mothers rock baby carriages while their sons, shouting for sheer explosive pleasure, churn their plump little legs on the pedals of never-fast-enough tricycles.

Continuing from the Palazzo Farnese, one is drawn into the suave curves and majestic doorways of the Via Monserrato, passing the English College, which grew from a hospice established by an English couple when the enclave of the Borgo S. Spirito had dissolved. Most of the courts are deep, broad, classical, and closed, but the small Palazzo Corsetti at 20 likes to show, in an attractive court, an engaging scatter of small friezes that depict a number of happy conditions and, to the searching eye, a touch of Roman obscenity. Numbers 111 and 112 combine as a pretty house of three flower-hung loggias in late medieval design, and at the end of Monserrato an incomprehensible imposing Roman slab marked large: CLAUDIUS.

The parallel street, the Via Giulia, planned by Julius II and related to impressive names—Bramante, Sangallo, Raphael—is considered a particularly handsome street by many; others are offended by the long strictness of glowering palaces threatening each other with their bulbous rustication. The courts, as always, are worth an occasional gloomy stare from a portiere, some of them regal, a few companionable (151, for example), some grotesque. The best grotesques are an eagle with a full bosom and, near the street arch, a wild-eyed, unintelligent fountain with lank hair, shocked at the ceaseless quantity of water pouring from her drooping mouth. Explore, if you can, the alleys that lead from the Via Giulia to the river. They have a forgotten air, a careless, tagged-on quality that is especially evocative after a few measures of the stern might of Pope Julius' row.

. . .

A twist, a turn, to a small building on the Corso Vittorio Emanuele at the end of the Via dei Baullari whose doorway introduces it as the Museo Barracco, a depository of "Scultura Antica." Shut, chained, mouth taped with the ominous sign "chiuso per restauro" (a word that often croaks "Nevermore") for a long time, it has again opened its doors to show a unique collection of original antique sculpture of several places and periods. The palace, attributed to Sangallo the Younger, uses rustication, alternations of triangular and arched pediments, unadorned portals, and simple ledges that add up to chaste Renaissance symmetry. The Italian-Victorian façade on the Corso is of the nineteenth century, arranged to accommodate the space needed by the broad avenue when it was pushed through the old city. Concentrate on the other sides of the palazzo, attempting to visualize the garden that flowed from the courtyard through the modern caffè and into the Via dei Baullari.

The building is referred to as the Piccola Farnesina or the Farnesina dei Baullari but actually has nothing to do with other palaces that bear the Farnese name. It was built by order of a French prelate who had the fleurs-de-lis etched as grace notes on his building. These were later identified with the Farnese lily as one sees it on the Palazzo Farnese, hence the name.

The collection is that of a Baron Giovanni Barracco of the nineteenth century, a member of an old family who, with the help of experts, amassed a group of sculptures which he gave to the city. After some peripatetic years that included a long imprisonment in the warehouses of the Capitoline Museum, the collection now rests in dignified rooms, intelligently placed and lighted to show authentic Greek pieces, a few archaic heads and statuettes, several Egyptian and Etruscan sculptures, Assyrian Babylonian—not too many in any one category and in general, an undemanding survey of choice pieces. As always—in the British Museum, in the Metropolitan Museum—one wonders how the gilded papier-mâché of an Egyptian mummy case stayed fresh and unspoiled, how a wooden lion's head maintained its form and ferocity intact for 4,000 years. True, they were deep in tombs, but how did they survive the later years of cartage, placing, replacing, and internment in cellars? One is confronted by the antique, persistent beauties that make vivid concepts of religion, social organization, ideals of physical perfection and techniques. A winged Assyrian genie with his careful alignment of minute curls in beard and hair and long, strongly marked eye speaks a strange language, but he speaks, as do the Assyrian ladies chatting in a palm grove. A bas-relief from an Egyptian tomb with sparsely placed, slender, slow figures and a fragment of Greek sarcophagus hum the plaintive music of sorrow of any age and place.

There are works that are their own lovely excuse for being, detached from funerary or documentary art—the girlish heads of young ephebi, a bearded, brooding head copied from a work by Myron, the smooth flow of cheekbone to tip of beard of a head from Cyprus, not yet ready for naturalism and in that unreadiness achieving a distant, godly tranquillity. Among the most attractive heads and figures are the archaic parents of classic Greek art. Certainly it is the archaic smile, especially joyous on a large-eyed, bright face pleased with the joke it just uttered, thoroughly amiable in its frame of jolly, curly red beard and hair, that creates the warm appeal. It is also, especially in the stelai, the equal emphasis on object and personage, the hand as schematic, no more and no less, than the lyre it holds, a rod between two men equally dominant with the men, a lack of emotive, dramatic stress that results in steady, quiet rhythms, which make the archaic Greek so peaceably pleasing. Contrast these, for example, with a later head believed to be that of Homer, a naturalistic portrait of a bearded old man with blind eyes, his mouth half open, ready to speak, expressive and capable of stirring emotion as archaic heads do not.

Since its size is humane, the Museo Barracco is a fine place to play the fascinating game of influences. Why is that Greek beard and mustache strange? It was probably copied from an Assyrian model. How is it that the small Greek figures on an altar seem so monumental? Archaic, and consequently more than touched by the hieratic attitudes of Egyptian statuary. An almost life-size Hermes, copied from a fifth-century B.C. bronze, carries a ram across his shoulders. Obviously, he is also the Good Shepherd who appears insistently in Christian art. He made his odyssey from Greek to Christian by way of a Roman coin of the second century A.D. which used as *its* model the older Greek figure. A Heracles of the sixth century B.C. stands like an Egyptian, but his fleshliness and close drapery recall Indian art, a stimulating, puzzling mixture. Among the "what does it remind me of" figures, two noble personages who might have been the honored donors of a Romanesque-Byzantine church but are actually of an earlier period, the third century A.D., and came from Palmyra.

In playing the game, don't overlook the long droop of a wounded dog, a thin, black basalt head which combines Egyptian and Roman mannerisms, purported to be a portrait of Julius Caesar. Nor should you miss a headless hermaphrodite who hangs abashedly high on one wall, nor the dead-white mummy head from Faiyum, eyes painted black, large, and staring in the style of that famous funerary art, the hair in the ringlets and curls of a Roman matron— as she may have been, the wife of a provincial Roman functionary or a dignitary exiled by the mistrust or greed of an emperor.

(There are indications that subterranean Roman rooms and paintings discovered when the street and building underwent changes at the turn of the century may be ready for the public soon. Inquire when you go: never on Monday; 9 to 1 on Sunday, 9 to 2 the rest of the week, plus 5 to

WALK 7: CAMPIDOGLIO TO PANTHEON

8 P.M. on Tuesday and Thursday. As mentioned elsewhere and repetitiously, try to go in the morning, however.)

The Vicolo Cellini, a few blocks westward, is a refined change from an earlier name, Calabraga (roughly, dropping pants), for a closed alley of brothels. The painted house a few doors from the Corso Vittorio Emanuele is called by the locals "The House of the Good Whore" because, one neighbor says, she was both kind and clean of disease.

The yeasty combination of art and sex should waft you across the Corso Vittorio Emanuele and, a short distance to the right, the Pantheon.

FOR THE
INDEFATIGABLE

Saturday: Culture in the Park

Sunday will not do because the museums in the park close at or before 1 P.M., and Saturday will because the museums last longer and, increasingly, the nonwork Sunday is expanding to include Saturday afternoon, which fills the zoo with children, the grass with picnickers, the paths with strollers to join after the museum pleasures and chores are done.

The infinite Villa Borghese was family country property in which Cardinal Scipione Borghese built a villa to hide from the teeming city and to give room to his collection of antiquities. In order that the collection be larger and better rounded, he coerced, bought, and commissioned additional art, which unfortunately began to disappear early in the nineteenth century when a scion, the Camillo Borghese who married Napoleon's sister Pauline, found it expedient to exchange for an extensive territory in northern Italy a considerable number of ancient works now in the Louvre.

What remains is primarily dedicated to Pauline, Bernini, and the proposition that no respectable palace may leave one inch of ceiling unpainted. After trial by colossal heads and a tropical forest of linked designs, one comes on Paolina lying on her marble chaise, raising her sharp little profile and Empire headdress à la Récamier from tasseled marble cushions. Except for nether drape she is quite nude, which does not matter as much as it might because the sculptor Canova legitimized her—or her effigy—as Venus. A close look will show that the couch, in spite of its wisps of marbling and gilded ornaments, is of wood, to substitute for the original marble kept, like Napoleon, in exile on Elba while the figure was returned to Rome.

The rooms that follow Pauline give Bernini center stage, occasionally obscuring an interesting painting or two. Guido Reni's *Moses with the Tablets of the Law*, forcefully colored and dramatic against a furious sky, suffers a bit in the concentrated attention given to Bernini's *David*, his face (said to be a self-portrait) and body contorted, strained in the effort of pulling his slingshot, in itself a remarkably skillful detail. The defeated, imprisoned Samson appears as an impressive painted nude by Annibale Carracci, and to emphasize the heroic, a set of sarcophagus panels carved at the time of the Antonines glorifies the labors of Hercules.

The virtuosity of the young Bernini is almost unbelievable in the *Apollo and Daphne* group. She, turning with a cry, feels her lithe body held in bark, her toes taking root, her hands and hair becoming leaves. The hair-leaves, the thin bark rising, and the tendril of root reaching down from one toe are marvels, though Apollo, modeled on the *Apollo Belvedere*, is a shade too unhurried, too calmly classic, to be completely effective.

Still with Bernini. In Room IV, a small bronze Neptune and his friend, an enthusiastic dolphin, and the renowned *Pluto and Persephone*. His body is that of an athlete in middle age, a faint shadow of fat at the waist, holding a struggling, weeping Persephone, her toes tensed with the effort to escape. But he holds her firmly, and the dents his firm fingers make in her thigh are a famous pinnacle of Bernini technique.

Bernini pauses for breath in Room V to take on the more casual job of retouching a copy of a Greek *Sleeping Hermaphrodite*, made of the original bought by Scipione Borghese from the friars of S. Maria della Vittoria and sold later to the Louvre. She is set at a side, part of her face and a slight swell of breast visible; the he is hidden, facing the wall and guarded from the inquisitive by two flanking busts. Among the Greek, Greek-inspired, and Roman statuary in this hall, notice an odd group of three women of different ages supporting a pine cone shaped like the magnificent bronze *pigna* found near the Pantheon and now sitting luminously in the gardens of the Vatican.

Aeneas carrying Anchises, who holds his household gods, and the terrified little Ascanius clinging to Aeneas, another work by the young Bernini and composed as a long column of figures, lacks the vividness of the other works but nevertheless shows a master's hand. In the same room, Bernini's *Truth*, a smiling, relaxed, well-fleshed nude who might be a Titian Venus were she not of stone. (We are in Room VI, whose walls also enclose, in a raised niche, three large Roman figures in a brisk free style.)

The next sala, which turns to Egyptian rigidities and Roman mosaics for décor, shows an archaic body in long, smooth regular folds of peplum joined to a later, unsuitable head and in the center of the room an effective, strange figure of a woman with a white head, white arms and feet, and the rest, vigorous cuts of dark marble drapery. Under a ceiling of vines and grapes and capering satyrs—the ceilings were painted to suit the art objects—there is a *Dancing Satyr* copied from a Greek bronze and improved early in the nineteenth century by the influential Dane, Thorvaldsen. Like the emperor-gods in the Vatican, this satyr has too old and wine-bloated a face to match comfortably his young body. More innocent merriment than that of satyrs appears in an appealing painting, *The Concert*, by Gerard van Honthorst. The cellist and the singers and the maid who beats time have pushed away their fruit plates and glasses of wine and are enjoying themselves decorously yet thoroughly.

One returns to Daphne and mounts a circular stairway that lets in a view of the fountain and formal gardens and continues mounting to the Gallery proper, for a Pinturicchio *Crucifixion* like a fine Flemish miniature and, on panels attached near the windows, a straightforward *Portrait of a*

Man by Raphael and a *Lady with a Unicorn* faced by an infrared photo of the painting which reveals that Raphael originally painted the unicorn as a lapdog and changed his mind, rather hastily to judge from the cracked, awkward symbol of virginity. In the same room (IX) a circular *Madonna and Child* by Botticelli surrounded by lovely, unusually large angels' heads.

An extraordinary palimpsest takes the place of honor next. She is a smiling girl of dark marble and contrasting alabaster in bronze sandals and a gilded bonnet, put together in the fifteenth century of a scrap here and a shred there found among unearthed caches of antiquity. With her, a disturbingly restored Andrea del Sarto *Madonna and Child*, a *Portrait of a Man* of the school, not the quality, of Dürer, and one of Cranach's endlessly repeated and endlessly diverting Venuses, nude and round-bellied and wearing her only hat, the broad red one with the plumes.

A terrace with deck chairs and a horizon of deep woods conducts one to an austere self-portrait of Lorenzo Lotto, whose hand rests on petals and a minute skull, and a moving *Portrait of a Young Man* by Savoldo, who also painted the *Tobias and the Angel*, a broad-winged, powerful angel clothed in a vivid robe. The paintings by Sodoma seem to have suffered from improving hands, and the Andrea del Sartos cannot refrain from prettiness, even when dealing with a Christ who though sad is mainly handsome. Under a dense, stolid family group (one young man holds a classic torso to show that the family were collectors), a window-panel holds a sure drawing of a woman's head that is not by Leonardo but might easily have been.

There is some irregularity of sala numbering at this point, XII reached by returning through IX and X, and into view of a clownlike *Laughing Youth* by Annibale Carracci and a *Sybil* by Domenichino in rich turban and robes, painted by order of Scipione Borghese. Tibaldi, of the early eighteenth century, obviously haunted by Michelangelo, borrows the tortured *Last Judgment* composition for his volatile, frenzied *Adoration* (XIII).

Caravaggio takes the next salon. *John the Baptist* was maimed by helping hands which spared his *St. Jerome.* Both his *Boy with Fruit* and the *Ailing Bacchus* seem ill, doughy-faced, the smile weak, an indication according to some authorities that these were self-portraits of a time when the young painter was sick. Caravaggio's *David* is indisputably sturdy, but the head of Goliath with its drooped eye suggests, again, long illness and, again, is said to be a self-portrait. The *Madonna*, a forceful composition of disturbing realism for its time, was rejected by the Vatican functionaries who had ordered it for St. Peter's: too earthy, too vehement, too emotional, the Holy Child too much a naked little boy; it wouldn't do.

Bernini shares some of the Caravaggio space, with the plump, listening, about-to-speak bust of Cardinal Scipione Borghese himself, in two versions. The original was cracked across the forehead and a copy hastily made which seems to lack the impact of the first. A smaller bust of Paul V is less intimate, more a court portrait and equally a masterpiece, unlike Bernini's unfortunate model of an equestrian statue of France's Louis XIV which displeased the King, who never gave it the place of honor in Versailles for which it was meant. Domenichino's *Diana Hunting*, wrested from another patron by the Cardinal, is broad, busy, noisy, entertaining, and in spite of its pallid color, zestily Trastevere moved to Olympus.

Bernini as painter hardly matched Bernini the sculptor, evidenced in three self-portraits (Room XV), of which the last lies under the heavy shadow of Velázquez. Rubens' *Mourning over the Body of Christ* is an early work, the tonalities already quite accomplished. For a mature work in every sense, turn to the portrait of Clemente Merlini by Sacchi, a confident portrait of a confident smiling man, painted with an intelligent economy of color and sharp insight. Jacopo Bassano's paintings almost fill the next section (XVI): a small and a large *Adoration of the Magi* and an enchanting *Adoration of the Shepherds.* The bustling *Last Supper* loses awe to naturalism in careful detail lavished on insignificant figures—a cat, a dog, the calf's head on the table. The painting is generally spoken of as Bassano's masterpiece, but you might prefer his intelligent, long-faced El Grecoish Madonna and the flamelike compositions of the *Adorations*.

The rest—Italian and Dutch and two unusual sculptured busts by Algardi—should not hold you too long, at least until you are confronted by the *Circe* of Dosso Dossi, a splendid luminous lady in a golden turban lighting a torch from the brazier whose embers illuminate her and, distantly, the turreted fairy-tale landscape which is her demesne. For once, a hefty *Judith* who looks capable of lopping off a head at one stroke and, to return to Circes, the seductive French-boudoir *Danaë* of Correggio, and a girl in near-black and white marbles who holds a dog and caresses a kneeling child, confected in the manner of the girl patched of archaeological finds you've seen before. Interrupted by a good portrait by Antonello da Messina and that of a saint by Titian, one is propelled again to the Loreleis, Titian's foamy ladies in *Venus Blindfolding Cupid*, his earlier *Sacred and Profane Love* (with a sadistic faint frieze at the base), and a Carpaccio *Courtesan* who, unlike her superbly vain sisters in Venice, has been, by retouching, reduced to the plain toughness of a Brecht tart.

To depart on a note of holiness, and the manifold pleasures of a majestic yet lyrical work, visit last Veronese's *St. Anthony Preaching to the Fish*. The saint stands on a promontory high above a group of Oriental listeners, his hand pointing to a low infinity of dark sea paling to blue at the horizon. The controlled colors have the depth of stained glass, and the placement of mass and figures high at one side, the rest of the canvas deep and flat, produces a bold, moving effect.

NOTE: The museum and galleries are closed Mondays, open weekdays 9 to 4 (make it 3), and 9 to 1 on Sundays.

A park is not for "go north," "turn southwest"; such instructions deny its purpose. But this is an extraordinarily large park cut into eccentric segments and requires a good map to tell you where you are and direct you to where you might possibly be going. If the sound of great names is for you follow the paths of Goethe, d'Annunzio, Victor Hugo, Corelli, Piranesi, George Washington, and Fiorello La Guardia. Or, you can have your picture taken with a lion cub in the zoo and watch the cats grab the fish near the seal pool and lie in wait for young ducklings. Or, call together a group to fill a family-sized rowboat and touch at a fake temple of Aesculapius. Find the yellow neoclassic toy building called the Casino del Lago clouded in white to shocking pink azaleas in the spring, surrounded by treed walks and manicured patches of flowers, and go diagonally right from the Casino, through formal cropped gardens to a family portrait of a Mama nymph, a Papa satyr, and a Baby faun with cloven hooves clutching a heavy bunch of grapes.

Take a voyeur's privilege of examining as thoroughly as you can the post-wine languors in the deep grass and under the trees. Join a group, called by music from a portable phonograph, watching the swift bare feet of transplanted Sicilians or Calabrians dancing their rural steps in a ferocity of nostalgia. Children own the area above the Piazza del Popolo, which feeds them ice cream and peanuts (parents settle for olives and broad beans in paper cones), merry-go-round rides in the latest models of station wagons, fire trucks, and airplanes and then turn to the most deeply traditional fun, the Punch-and-Judy show. Their names are not Punch and Judy, but it makes no difference in the immortal, unbeatable show, exactly the right mixture of menace, sadism, masochism, kissing, and making up for the joy of dancing and singing together and back to the quarreling and banging themselves and each other around. The enthralled audience, as uninhibited as the marionettes, shouts warnings, shrieks with horror, laughs from its pudgy toes, and applauds for a *bis*, the next round, due in a half-hour or so.

A logical return to the city below is a short zigging and zagging down to the piazza. If you intend to leave from the Borghese Gallery, walk toward the apartment houses to the left and through the Via Sgambati to the Via Po, whose buses go to the Piazza S. Silvestro and the central railroad station.

Museo Nazionale de Villa Giulia (Etruscan Museum)

This villa of spacious court bordered by rounded arcades painted with close latticework playgrounds for roses, babies, and birds, and the inevitable touch of the Pompeian, was the country retreat of Julius III, who was pope in the mid-sixteenth century.

Ingenious arrangements of glass cases, freestanding and in triangular and cross-shaped groups, the interruption of long space by one conspicuous object or an important few, erases the discouraging endless tunnel effect of other museums and galleries. The matter is Etruscan and somewhat repetitious. Although the precise provenance of vases in the Greek style, of punched bronze shields, of fibulae, nails, and funerary urns may differ, they partake essentially of the same culture. However, there are distinctions that derive from the luck and know-how of archaeologists and the contrasts of cosmopolitanism and wealth of a prosperous port town as opposed to a less worldly community inland.

The very first room (of a section dedicated to finds at Vulci) makes a dramatic statement with two figures of the

seventh century B.C., a crude, solid centaur and a boy riding
a sea-demon whose tail designs a strong, full curve. The
following two rooms, still Vulci, display bone containers
shaped like houses, bronze implements and ornaments,
pottery crude and delicate (twins and triplets of little pots
like modern salt and pepper holders), bronze pitchers with
light, long handles made of triple strips of metal, and one
round, flat vessel that might be the canteen of today's hiker.
The black bucchero ware was probably indigenous, but the
numerous Greek vases and plates may have been imported
or the work of Greek artisans in Etruria. Look for the
sophisticated drawing on a large three-handled jar decorated
with a group of women gathered at a well and a dashing
quadriga, obviously Greek in inspiration and skill. Room 4
shows charts of the positions of objects as they were dis-
closed in Vulci's tombs, skillfully formed leg armor, and an
extraordinary set of bucchero vases adorned with graceful
handles, primitive acanthus designs, and many small heads
pushing through the black clay. In the same area, a vase
etched in archaic animal figures like those in the early
tombs at Tarquinia, another shaped and painted like a
woman's head, ornately incised mirrors, and a curious rod
which ends in the long-fingered Etruscan hand held up in
a "stop" signal.

A breath of Egypt (the Etruscans were wide-ranging
traders, sometimes pirates, and always a collective sponge
that eagerly absorbed the habits and arts of other cultures)
comes with clay figures wrapped like mummies except that
the feet and heads are bare. The same room (5) changes to
alert realism in the figure of a fat laughing baby writhing
with pleasure, a little boy feeding a dove, a remarkable
bearded head, and a painted figure seated on a ceremonial
chair who resembles later representations of Christ. These
works may or may not be ex-votos, but there is no doubt
about the votive purpose of the plaques of clay intestines
that lie on one glass shelf. Egypt soon reappears (6) as
minuscule, stiff gods, then clears space for lesser Etruscan

humans, equally minute, who climb, work, and guide animals busily over the surface of a bronze urn mounted on wheels. A companion urn shows its industrious little men clambering around a bear chained at the crest of the lid. Among the bronzes and terra cottas, there is a pair of Etruscan sandals, the wood burned, but the bronze rim, articulated between heel and sole, still clearly defining the size and shape of a foot that died about 2,500 years ago.

Cases disappear in Room 7 to concentrate on segments of three masterpieces ("experimentally" restored, says a label) that were found at Veii, a short distance north of Rome. At one side, a goddess who once held a child—only its legs remain—and whose back is a graceful fall of long curls into swags of drapery that lightly cup the young buttocks. The other two facing personages are a Hercules and the commanding *Apollo of Veii*, a benign, virile young man with strongly marked eyebrows, a cleft chin, and the most amiable of archaic smiles. They both stood, to judge from the harplike ornaments at their feet, on suitably handsome bases, and were supervised by a long-tongued, snake-headed Medusa that stared malevolently from their temple roof.

From Cerveteri, also quite close to Rome, crude pottery, architectural ornaments and (Room 8) a charming little boy, a small figure of a bounteous nursing mother, and, the best piece in the room, a head of a thin-lipped man with a high-arched nose, as fine a sculpture portrait as the later Romans ever achieved. The long end room breaks at this point for the most famous of Etruscan sarcophagi, that of the *Spouses*. Innumerable Etruscan caskets bear semireclining effigies of couples, but these are young, sweetly smiling, his arm affectionately on her shoulder. Besides the stimulating mixture of cultures they represent—the advanced Etruscan women who sat at banqueting tables (which the bier represents) with their men, the archaic Greek smile, the Egyptian beard on the husband—one actively likes and regrets the loss of their bright good humor.

The end sala is mainly a repository for Greek vases and

plates designed around mythological drawings and, here and there, a cruder, down-to-earth Etruscan scene like that of women swimming under trees hung with their garments, a scene reminiscent of the boys diving and swimming in a famous fresco of Tarquinia. At the opening of this room, there is a stairway that leads to the Antiquarium, a miscellany of bronze figurines (notice the elongated forms created by Etruscan Giacomettis), arms, armor and jewelry, bronze funerary wreaths, pottery, funerary urns—in short, variations of themes stated before, with the addition of small, grotesque masks and, in Room 15, the shards of a vase with remarkable drawings of hunting scenes, griffons, and chimera masks.

A set of stairs leads to a curved gallery and its enormous, once private, collection of goblets, vases, platters with handles, and their renderings of mythology, many of them fine works but too many in their number. They stop at still another miscellany and to a double-leveled gallery (29) of distinguished pieces. On the walls, lacy temple ornaments of winged figures, bands of Greek keys, and stylized leaf patterns. In one case, four unusually advanced youthful heads; in another, a sturdy middle-aged head; and in a third, a superb warrior and the legs of another with whom he is fighting; on the wall above them, an equally well-modeled female figure wafting a veil. (All this highly developed art stems from as far back as the fifth century B.C.)

The gems from Palestrina (Praeneste) of the seventh century B.C. include a bronze chair, huge bronze bowls with chimera heads at their rim supported by conical bases worked in patterns of trees and animals, as well as exquisitely carved ivories, incised cylindrical containers whose lids are surmounted by three figures, frequently shaping a handle as two that support a horizontal third. In the cases that approach and face the entrance, look for a child's sandal, a dancing nude accompanied by her dog carved into an area about one and one-half inches wide and no more than two and one-half long, combs of wood and ivory, carefully graded necklaces, and a riot of figures—some in Indian plume headdresses—that tumble, lie about, roll into monster mouths as part of an ornament or handle. Several cases hold exquisite jewelry composed of rows on rows of almost microscopic lions, horses, and birds, a fine golden cup, two or three pins that are distinctly Art Nouveau, and two small, slightly flattened, beautifully stylized horses' heads. Before you leave, somewhere near the dancing miniature and the child's sandal look for the ultimate in Etruscan development—a set of four false teeth set in a gold band looped for attachment to other teeth.

NOTE: Open 9 to 3 weekdays; Sundays 9 to 1. Closed Mondays. The stairs to a reconstruction of a Cerveteri tomb below the first galleries are closed off by an easily lifted rope, and there aren't too many guards in attendance. Take a chance.

Galleria Nazionale di Arte Moderna

The usual neoclassic "temple of art" face—see the National Gallery in London, the Metropolitan Museum in New York, and at least a dozen similar replicas—ushers one into an unusual collection, unusual in the sense that the opportunities for seeing large samplings of twentieth-century Italian art are not normally visible elsewhere. From time to time, the gallery hangs large shows of foreign painters and keeps, a short distance beyond the entrance, models and photos of Le Corbusier's sculpturesque architecture. To counter the largesse, the nineteenth-century rooms are sometimes closed.

As "Arte Moderna," the collection includes samplings of landmarks in European and some American painting: a

Courbet, a Utrillo, a Van Gogh, a Monet water lily study, a Klimt, a Klee or two, two small Cézannes, two Pollocks, a Tobey, a Calder mobile. The shadows of Picasso, Renoir, Van Gogh, and Bonnard lie heavily on some of the Italian art, but where do they not in paintings of the twenties and thirties? The well-ensconced international Italian names are not numerously represented, so much of their work has gone abroad. De Chirico, for instance, shows a limited group of canvases; Marini appears in a case of busts and a compelling torso that implies a Crucifixion; Manzù's section is confined to several female portrait busts and a seated girl who lives in an aura of the untouchable primitive. The entertainment, however, for one who has not seen much modern Italian painting is to look for the Italian handling of cubism, the adaptations by Balla of pointillism, the habits of Mannerism clinging to the early twentieth century, and the always interesting changes in an artist's style. A painting of the thirties by Severini might be an eighteenth-century romantic vision of *Italy* complete with ruined arch, a cypress floating its black smoke into the clear air, a theater mask, a lute, and fruit. By the same artist, an abstraction of 1912; apparently he changed his mind or tastes. Lorenzo Viani, of the same period, worked in the expected progression of development and produced a group of skillful canvases to be savored and respected. As one expects, among the famous internationals there are groups by Campigli, Afro, and Music who should not overshadow for you the work of Scialoja, the inventive explorations of materials and textures of Lucio Fontana and Alberto Burri. And to know that Italy had not entirely lost her Cellinis, look for a case of artfully designed jewelry in gold and silver.

A spacious court furnishes seats, umbrellas, cool air, and a rest from painting; the entrance is well supplied with monographs, post cards, catalogs of former shows, and reproductions, all for sale at just prices. For fun or a nervous breakdown, "now" art—a square made of thousands of pins that seem to nod and dip irregularly, propelled by

their own slender, minute metal wills; a shockingly real
man and woman, separated figures waiting for a bus who
startle you from the mirrored end of a long corridor; a
"fun house" of hard maniacal lights flashing in a madness
of mirrors. There is a quieting mesmerism in watching sand
spill, creep, and separate in a moon landscape behind glass
or better still, the multiple paintings produced by German
kinetic art. A darkened room has been built around a
construction of turning geometric, metal shapes. These are
reflected on a screen and on the walls and ceiling by three
sets of rotating colored lights. The effects are an infinity
of colors and patterns, alone, in combination, meeting, separating, ceaselessly changing, a show of thousands of geometric paintings passing in the stately pace of Byzantine
royalty and LSD visions with the viewer as viewer, creator,
and core of the experience.

NOTE: The advertised hours are different, but go at about
10 or 11 to make sure. Positioned on the western (Flaminia)
edge of the Borghese gardens, the gallery is not far from the
Belle Arti bus stop of the 67, 2, and 26. Make sure to get off
near the Villa Giulia, the Etruscan Museum. Better still,
take a taxi from the Piazza di Spagna or the Piazza del
Popolo.

Vatican Museums

Then there are the Vatican museums and what to do about
them. There are several, spread over an athletic area, and
although they may combine as the "largest museum in the
world" it is not, in quality, "the greatest." The Mellon Collection in Washington, D.C. and the Metropolitan Museum,
to select two, have better collections of Italian art than the
Vatican's Pinacoteca, and certainly that is true of the

Uffizi, in Florence. The Etruscan Villa Giulia Museum will give you a broader range of Etruscology; the Egyptian collection of the British Museum far surpasses that of the Vatican and, for small objects, so does the Brooklyn Museum in New York. For a remarkably set and selected collection of Greco-Roman art, culled mainly from the great days of Magna Graecia, one might go to Taranto in the south. Roman portraiture and copies of Greek sculpture of unique interest and beauty appear in a few of the breathtaking rooms of the Museo Nazionale Romano (Baths of Diocletian). Furthermore, the Vatican seems to think that *all* reasonably valuable objects, whether for the antiquity or rarity, must be kept on public display. Thus, it houses numerous cold Valhallas of stony gods and semigods. Courage sinks and tourist conscientiousness flies when confronted by tons of white marble converted to portraits of Greek and Roman luminaries over and over and over again. It has been estimated that Imperial Rome had two million inhabitants (a figure not reached again until 1960), and each family must have been required, it would appear, to buy a blind bust for sitting with his household gods. Then one must consider public buildings, temples, inordinately large palaces with endless gardens, banqueting halls, and art galleries to sprinkle thickly with statuary, not necessarily the chill color they are now that their paint and gilt have been erased. And half of it all, the exhausted feet, eyes, and mind, say, found its way to the Vatican museums.

This does not mean that there are not alert, speaking heads among the dull and dour, nor that some marble drapery does not swing attractively with a well-turned limb, nor that all Apollos begin to look like spoiled, pretty boys, and all Minervas broad, implacable matrons, and all Venuses vapid young women. For the energetic and curious, there is always a masterwork, an astonishment, a curio to discover.

Pio-Clementino

Named for two late-eighteenth-century popes, Pius VI and
Clement XIV, who added space and objects scattered
throughout Rome to a fifteenth-century collection of antiquities. In the process of housing the collection they destroyed
invaluable frescoes by Mantegna and balanced that by
opening the collection to the public, an extraordinary gesture for its time, 1787. The aisles of frozen statuary and objects are not always as remarkable as their provenance but
they help make the impossibly sumptuous of Roman times,
difficult for an egalitarian present to imagine, take on reality. One knows, for instance, that the Domus Aurea of Nero
was one reflection of the Imperial mania for luxury. How
luxurious? A measure appears in the huge porphyry bowl
almost the size of a swimming pool that stands in the center of the Sala Rotonda, surrounded by stretches of Roman
mosaics designed by masters. One knows that a number
of emperors eagerly appointed themselves gods, some with
no doubts whatsoever. Here, one manner in which it was
expressed, not always successfully. Apollos and Joves with
the same youthful, tautly fleshed Greek body are matched
with grotesquely unsuitable heads—too old or too plain, or
both; a thin-lipped, wrinkled Galba, a flap-eared Claudius,
too blind to see the ugly humor of the combinations. One
knows that Hadrian deeply mourned the early death of his
young lover Antinous (540, 545), built and named a city in
his honor, and filled his world with statues of the boy, who
became a god-cult in time. Here he appears in several versions, as Hadrian and followers of the cult wished to
remember his brooding, doomed face under the wayward
hair held by a chaplet of flowers.

The Roman villas on the Appia reflect their luxury in a
remarkable mosaic of flowers in a basket that brightened
a wall or floor; the connoisseur's taste and impossible

dream of surrounding himself in total beauty that impelled Hadrian to build his boundless gardens and houses near Tivoli is evidenced by a number of objects labeled "Villa Adriana." The famous vanity and love of adornment among Imperial matrons is manifested in the astonishing varieties of hairdress—curls, deep waves, topknots, fringes, and tall embankments of tiny coils, the inventions of slaves whose lives in the golden boudoirs of the Palatine must have been trembling hells.

The museum is introduced by a pair of sphinxes at whose side stands a tall slender early Greek figure with a head that doesn't belong to it but is generally believed to be that of Cleopatra. The nose is, as usual, missing, but the mouth suggests a Negroid fullness and the expression is keen, aware, as she must have had to be. Two enormous porphyry boxes (you may already have seen a copy of one in the chapel of S. Costanza) deeply carved in paleo-Christian symbols of the vintage were meant for Costanza, the daughter of Constantine, and others, concerned with warriors and prisoners, for St. Helena, the mother of the Emperor, or for Constantine himself. A great bearded Jove (539) may remind you of Michelangelo's *Moses* were the Hebrew less anguished and without horns. A large Demeter (Ceres) looks quite like a fertility goddess should look, hardly a woman but a female abstraction of earth mother.

Did Hadrian (543) really have so intelligent and willful a face? The bronze Hercules with club in hand, lion skin in the other, and a wild, mad expression in his eyes, was this Caligula in one of his many god-guises? And was the pudgy-faced little man who looks like a well-steeped-in-drink Silenus (514) the great Socrates? Did Euripides, modeled after a fourth-century Greek original, actually have such a noble intellectual face, rarely the luck of writers? Homer with his closed blind eyes, was this from a portrait or an imagined vision of the legendary bard?

The Sala degli Animali is a stone and bronze zoo of animals of every sort, most of them engaged in eating each other or being killed by heroes. Don't run through, though; the walls bear a few distinguished mosaics that once decorated Hadrian's villa, a very large stupid camel's head whose loose, drooping lips were part of a Greek fountain, and a classic representation of Mithras in his Phrygian cap, accompanied by his dog and snake, in the act of killing the sacrificial bull. Spare a glance for a composition of waves, veils, curvaceous dolphin tail on a young Triton and his baby friends, ready to turn into a Bernini fountain.

Back among the statues and busts again, primarily Roman copies of Greek originals and in endless numbers. Having come this far, give some time to a simply modeled, sad young god who may actually be a mourner or himself a god of death (250) and to a curious pair (264 and 265), a smooth, soft Apollo with a girl's face and hair, copied from a bronze of Praxiteles, and at his side, an Amazon whose closely pleated drapery clings to a thoroughly feminine body attached to a head that is too large and masculine. A question of transposed heads? Hermaphrodites? Across the hall (395) an archaic Apollo holding a harp, and near him (405) an equally lovely work of a later time, a gentle, slender yet strong Hebe bending to place a bowl on a trunk of a tree. At the end of the hall a rare pair of candelabra which illuminated, at a distant time, a chamber in Hadrian's villa.

Make your way to the Cortile del Belvedere to dispel the marble chill in the sunshine, the silence of stone in the plash of water from the mossy craggy fountain, and the still statuary deadness in the sinuous movement of the fountain goldfish. This enclosed courtyard was replanned in the eighteenth century to create a portico and large and small niches for holding important works of antique art, each *gabinetto,* surmounted by a theater mask, open to the court. Here stands the Laocoön group found on the Esquiline in 1506 and immediately bought by Pope Julius II to add to his collection of antiquities, a core of the Vatican museums. The discovery of this work of the second century B.C. created by three sculptors of Rhodes, its intensity, the distortion of muscle in stress, the dynamic gestures, had a marked effect on Renaissance and Mannerist art and especially on Michelangelo. At a reasonable distance, the central figure might be judged his. (Laocoön was the priest who warned the Trojans against the famous wooden Greek horse. For this he was, according to one version, punished by Athena, who sent a snake to kill him and his sons. Another version has it that Apollo sent the snake so that Laocoön and his sons might become sacrifices to head off the total destruction of Troy and its people.) In the area next to the original group there stands a copy of a sixteenth-century reconstruction (Michelangelo made a tentative try at it) which distorted, it was later judged, the tight serpent-wrapped composition. The added sections were removed, an authentic fragment replaced, and the original is now fairly as Michelangelo and Julius II first saw it.

Another niche of the cortile encloses the equally renowned *Apollo Belvedere*, a Roman copy of a Greek statue found at the end of the fifteenth century not far from Rome. In another *gabinetto* the *Hermes*, said to be a copy from Praxiteles and a *Perseus* of Canova, standing between two glaring Canova athletes which served to replace antiquities carried off by Napoleon. Stendhal's informant thought the *Perseus* and the *Athletes* "the least good of Canova's works." "The *Perseus* is quite pleasing; women like it much better than the *Apollo*," he added. To one mind, a copy of Cellini's *Perseus* in Florence might have been a happier idea.

When the important subjects have been given their due, examine the lesser works. A frieze, probably the side of a sarcophagus, boisterous with musicians, actors, musical instruments, the playwright with his manuscript at the side, and every bit of remaining space filled with wide-mouthed masks; a simpler and more artfully made frieze shows two women involved in a rite with a bull. A figure in one of the smaller niches, as disturbing as the Apollos with soft chests and elaborate hairdress, has a long, bearded severe face, on his head a grape and flower headdress, in his arms fruits and flowers. His sex is covered with vine leaves that fall from the fruit, but the bulges on the chest definitely look like small breasts, fuller than is normal for a slender old man. It might be that he-she represents a fertility figure created by one of the "mystery" religions, or it might have originated in Rome, which at a late date in its Imperial life freely invented variations of the prime gods and new subgods to suit given occasions and circumstances.

Leaving the sunlit court, one goes to the Gabinetto delle Maschere, named for four mosaics that also came from Hadrian's country estate and, at this writing, lifted out of the floor in which they had been embedded. This is the room of the Venuses, inclined to be dull in spirit. The Venus who is tagged 474 is a replica of an Aphrodite of Praxiteles, important because this may be the first time she appeared altogether nude and because of her poised, wary movement as she steps into a pool. She has suffered through the centuries; the suspended motion is still sensed, but her face is meaningless and too much of her body is coarse plaster.

In the nearby Sala delle Iscrizioni a big athlete, copied from a bronze and lost for centuries under the cobbles and dirt of Trastevere, has the passive, wide-jawed face of any not-too-bright boy who has to make his way using a body that is more dependable than his mind. One should be able to use the handsome Bramante stairs from this room, but they are closed off. Take in the view from a nearby window, instead, and go back of the inscriptions into an area just about light enough to permit you to see three mosaic panels that describe Roman sporting life. A short distance away (ask the guard if your plan doesn't show it), the single most influential object in the collection: the Belvedere torso carved by a Greek working in Rome. Larger than life, headless, armless, back and shoulders twisted in agonized effort, the stubs of broken knee like massive tree trunks. You may have seen the strained, muscular turn of the back copied in

the body of a young man on the Sistine ceiling. Michelangelo was fascinated by this powerful stump, came back
time and again to study it, to stand in its mesmeric spell.
It doesn't require the eye and curiosity of a sculptor to
hold the image; once seen, it stays indelibly in the mind.

Museo Chiaramonti

The distinction is the fact that it was arranged by Canova,
and that it lives in clear light. The rest is dusty heads and
shoulders, fig leaves, godlike postures, sarcophagi, and the
irritated feeling that by neglecting the galleries one might
miss an indelibly notable object. Nothing indelible, but
among the Hercules, the heads of Tiberius and members of
his family, a family tomb (Section X) whose panels give
precise information about the grinding of wheat and the
utensils used in processing flour. A big head of Athena and
a Silenus with a panther, both copies of Greek originals,
point the way to several unique Roman portraits (XIX)
and, at XXI, a singular Eros and a statue of an athlete
inclined to be an ephebus, originally of the Age of Pericles.

The repetitions repeat beyond a gate, in an area called the
Braccio Nuovo, an addition of the early nineteenth century.
No dust here; the classics (in several senses) glow in pristine whiteness. Again, it is not necessarily the statuary but
the nearby places in which they were found that is of
interest. A portrait of Augustus, in early middle age,
about to address a group, was found north of Rome, in the
"villa of Livia," which yielded other treasures. A large
gentle mother of the Muses (23) was found in the Piazza
Mattei of the turtle fountain. A bitter, grotesque Medusa
once brightened a temple near the Baths of Maxentius,
adjoining the Forum. Of themselves compelling are the head
of a Barbarian (9), a toothless, sharp-faced old Roman of
the Augustan age (53), and (74) a portrait of Hadrian.

The gallery pauses to make space for a gigantic Nile
unearthed in the sixteenth century in the grounds dedicated

to Isis near S. Maria sopra Minerva and the Pantheon. The river, comfortably settled with a sphinx and a cornucopia, is the playground of myriad lively babes whose romping on his shoulders and hips don't ruffle the dignified old man at all. Below the god and his kindergarten, light-hearted reliefs of pygmies with fat behinds, fighting off, from the safety of their boats, a flotilla of threatening alligators and hippopotami.

Having committed yourself thus far, make the additional effort to look for the head of Dacius (115), strongly reminiscent of the large, rugged figure in the modern Lateran collection; the narrow, evil smile of the satyr in repose (117), a copy of a piece attributed to Praxiteles. A portrait bust of the Emperor Philip the Arab may fulfill your private portrait of Othello unless Olivier is already fixed in the frame.

The Biblioteca is quite close (unless you prefer—it seems unlikely—to pursue other multitudinous populations of eyeless, white people in additional galleries).

Biblioteca

Not as choice as the Morgan collection or as extensive as that of the British Museum, but if you are not acquainted with those collections, the selection of the Vatican's extraordinary archives opened to the public might be your opportunity to see a few of the treasures of European literacy. The first section of the gallery bears the name of Museo Profano della Biblioteca, a small collection of Etruscan and Roman bronzes, Roman ivories (try to find one that shows a griffon nursing from a lion, a Roman grotesque that may derive from voyagers' tales of the exotic animals or art in the stranger corners of the Empire), then the march past closed cabinets under painted vaults, accompanied by views of the Vatican gardens, to the cases of manuscripts and books, a very few highlights of a collection that was begun by the Church almost from the time it became the Church.

The display begins with very early fragments on parchment of Greek versions of the Bible, including a vivid seventh-century illustration of the Battle of Jericho. Of the fourth and fifth centuries, editions of Virgil, and a copy of Cicero of the fourth century, an indication that the Renaissance did not have to disinter, altogether, the classical world. That the so-called Dark Ages were not black pits of isolation and ignorance is suggested by an eleventh-century roll of parchment from the monastery of Monte Cassino which is illuminated by a large letter of intertwined bands like those designed in Irish monasteries—in the Book of Kells, for example. A book still in print, still authoritative in its field, the treatise on falconry by Frederick II, the Hohenstaufen known for his achievements and enlightenment as "the first Renaissance man" and, earlier, "Stupor Mundi," here appears in a thirteenth-century edition (very early, if not the earliest) illustrated with explicit demonstrations of the handling of falcons. Of the fourteenth century, Spanish astrological charts illuminated with figures that bring to mind William Blake, and of the same time, illustrations on golden backgrounds that reflect the influence of Duccio of Siena.

A large and superbly decorated edition of the *Divine Comedy* and as lovely, in their miniature fashion, the precise, elegant landscapes, courtly scenes, bands of flowers and fruits of French Books of Hours. Moving into more recent time: designs by one of the Sangallos, sketches and verses by Michelangelo, sketches by Raphael. A case of letters and autographs evokes the presence of Thomas Aquinas, of Savonarola, of Galileo, of Henry VIII and his Anne Boleyn, among others of the illustrious in history and art.

A Mantegna woodcut of the *Deposition of Christ* introduces a group of early printed Bibles, Gutenberg (1455) of course, a sixteenth-century Bible printed in Spain in several languages composed in various types and placed in an erratic arrangement of boxes and irregular columns. The first Bible printed in Rome (1471) was the work of two foreigners, Sweynheym and Pannartz, invited and housed by the Massimo family.

A display of fine dignified bindings leads to foreign books that include flowing Arabic calligraphy designed as perfect frames for choice illustrations. In this same exotic section a Chinese letter to a pope brushed on a gold sheet, a Mexican codex, Oriental writings on bark and palm leaves, as piles of flat sticks, as thick, folded screens, and from Japan a seventeenth-century letter on pale gold touched with faint cloudlets of gray and white.

Museo Sacro

The Biblioteca ends in the Museo Sacro, a collection of paleo-Christian art: reliquaries, shreds of ancient embroideries, enamels, ivories, terra-cotta lamps with curious inscriptions and symbols, the head of an apostle (about 800) from the Triclinium of the Lateran, the oldest representation of SS. Peter and Paul, of the fourth century, and among the most interesting objects, disks of third- to fifth-century gold-leaf figures embedded in glass, a number of them found in the catacombs. The last room, of later church art, ends in a tunnel that leads to and from the Sistine Chapel, a piece of information that may save you several weary kilometers. Before that, however, find the nearby room of the Nozze Aldobrandini, unearthed in the early seventeenth century on the Esquiline Hill and well enough preserved to represent Roman painting at its peak. As the title indicates, the paintings deal with preparations for a marriage: mythological figures bedecking the bride, others preparing household decorations, singing wedding hymns. In the solemnity of preparing the shy, fearful bride, the sobriety of ceremonials, one finds echoes of the rites described in the plasterwork of the subterranean basilica near the Porta Maggiore. From the same hill, a group of landscapes, found in the first half of the nineteenth century, that describe several stops made by Ulysses, and from the Porta S. Sebastiana, heroines of Greek tragedy caught at the shrieking, distorting climaxes of their terrible lives. Ostia left a line of babies playing a marching game. Hadrian's sumptuous villa yielded, as one would expect, an unusually fine mosaic of coiled bands that set off fruits and leaves and, from the Aventine, an equally effective collection of wild animals, including the lion and elephant of Africa.

Etruscan Museum

About as high as you can go up the stairs near the atrium of the Torso, you will find the isolated, never crowded, and not entirely Etruscan Museum. If your itinerary includes museums in Etruscan country—Volterra, Orvieto, Tarquinia, to select a few of many—your time might be better spent elsewhere. Should this be your only go at the Etruscans, climb the stairs which will open to you the possibility of seeing an Etruscan sarcophagus bearing a frieze of musicians and charioteers whose faces are still stained with immortal red paint and another sarcophagus surmounted by an alert Etruscan who refuses to lie down, a common resentful practice of the Etruscan dead. The cases on heavy cases of bronzes, urns, black pottery, and vases in the Greek manner sit in saddened rooms not yet released in the airy spacing afforded other parts of the collection. An important and strange object in this collection is the *Mars of Todi* of the fourth century B.C. In full armor, the top of his head gone, he is convincingly Greek. Was he an Etruscan work copied from the Greek, or was he brought from Greece, either as a purchase or among marauders' spoils? The rooms that have recently been rearranged leave the Etruscans and pick up vestiges of early Roman art and artifacts, displaying terra-cotta figurines inspired by

Tanagra, a good many appealing heads, pottery lamps of several degrees of refinement, some fine bits of glass and ivory, and cases full of hooks, knives, thimbles, needles, bolts, and quite modern-looking keys in bronze. One of the stars of the show is a dramatic bronze torso thrusting out of one of the walls and, beyond a group of early jewels, small heads and bronze figurines, an equally well-made huge bronze arm. The final rooms deal with Greek reliefs that include an especially well-preserved, attractive tombstone (fifth century B.C.) of a young Greek and his servitor in muted remoteness, the head of a mule, the head of a spirited horse not taken by Lord Elgin from the Parthenon, and an almost human head with eyes of contrasting marble pierced to make pupils, small, high ears, as bald as an unfinished mannequin. This embryonic entity, which may have been, in full attire, a Greek god or goddess, ushers you out.

Egyptian Museum

The Egyptian Museum (entered between the monumental Torso and the door marked "Toilettes") contains a surprisingly small though not dull amount of material when one considers the possibilities Rome had for removing countless masterpieces in its time as master of Egypt. Apparently the Romans were interested principally in the obelisks that told of the deeds of kings repeated in their arches and columns, and black lions and stone kings that answered their taste for monumentality. However, quantities of Egyptian objects may have been destroyed, stolen, burned, carried off by various conquerors, and certainly sold to private collectors and museums. At any rate, what is left is several mummy cases with an occasional blackened, petrified, shrunken face still *in situ*. To fill in the collection, several cases of Islamic majolica, small grotesques with Negroid features and Hellenistic in execution. Gold ornaments and small bronze gods, meshworks of faïence beads, chipped stones shaped as arrows and small hatchets, dried grain, and countless scarabs and seals lie in the blind sight of ghostly, bald basalt Egyptians. Household objects found in tombs—headrests, baskets—sit with crude, mysterious paintings and inscriptions on clay boxes and plaques. The next area of concentration is on the gods with animal heads —the many sacred cats in wood, bronze, clay, and mummified, and several representations of a hawk-headed deity.

A curved hall that holds another group of mummy cases makes respectful room for a group of gods standing and sitting, all as forbidding as they were meant to be, and hypnotizing. One tall, slender figure whose nipples are carved like flat, open-petaled flowers has the face of a movie vamp or, more truly, a vampire, the mouth reminiscent of the bloody jaguar gash of Mexican gods. A slickly wrapped body dexterously implies the nudity under the shining drape; a few economical lines and a broadening of nose make seated lions of a number of god figures. Continuing on to a room whose modern mural might be a set for *Aïda*, one is confronted with shriveled Egyptian hands, feet, and faces bared by their decayed wrappings, and fragments of Coptic cloth, and, for particular attention, a suave torso with the faintest of bulges above the edge of a garment. An Indian influence on the Egyptian, or vice versa? Inimical sphinxes greet one next, partnered by basalt figures which are odd hybrids of several styles. An Egyptian body carries a Roman or Greco-Roman head; an animal god is dressed in a Roman toga; a colossal Egyptian female head has the features of the Erechtheum caryatids in Athens; a black marble sculpture is a bull's head on one side and a Europeanized goddess on the other. Monkey gods and hawks in crowns neighbor obscene, repellent dwarf gods who resemble African pygmies elevated to portraits of the god Bes. (In spite of his looks he was a kind, lively fellow who protected the hunter and supervised home entertainment; the ancestor, perhaps, of the jester-dwarfs who entertained European courts in later centuries.) Just as the going becomes amusing, severe sphinxes intervene to conduct you to the stairs that lead down to the great red sarcophagi and Nero's lake-sized bowl in the Sala Rotonda.

NOTE: Buses 81 and 77 pass central areas to the Piazza Risorgimento, where the Vatican walls turn toward the Sistine Chapel, Raphael Stanze, and the museum's entrance.

A black-smocked, tall, starved crow of a man haunts the toilets near the turnstile. He stares hard as you emerge, jingles coins, stands in your way. Walk around him. There is no sign to say one must pay him anything. The 500-lire admission charge should cover this convenience. And remember that the ordinary bar *gettone* will not buy a telephone call from the Vatican. Only a Vatican *gettone* will do.

Palazzo Barberini

Leaving at your back Bernini's joyous Triton fountain on the Piazza Barberini, walk the slope of the Via delle Quattro Fontane, to arrive in a few paces at a bizarre, High Baroque set of gates held by huge columns that imprison terms with black embittered faces, the faces of Prometheus Bound. Actually these gates and bearded male furies were a work of the nineteenth century, trying to match the conceptions of the seventeenth-century baroque designers Maderna, Borromini, and Bernini, all of whom claim some part of the Palazzo Barberini.

There is an elevator that takes one up (prohibited, the going down), but it is more stimulating to walk up through the curious, dramatic perspectives of Borromini's double-columned stairway, then continue on an easy, noneccentric stretch of Bernini stairs to be greeted by an old lion, an intimate of Emperor Hadrian when they lived together in the villa near Tivoli.

The entrance proper to the galleries, hung with attractive posters of art shows in other parts of Italy and Europe, advertises the fact that there are, at least during tourist seasons, free guided tours conducted at 9:30 A.M. on Wednesdays and Fridays in Italian, French, English, or Dutch. If it shouldn't be the time of your tongue or day, it does not matter too much; most of the paintings—supplements to those at the Galleria Corsini—are usually well labeled. The collection represents paintings of the thirteenth into the eighteenth centuries. The early works, including a *Madonna and Child* attributed to Simone Martini, borrow from the seductive Sienese paintings, adding an angular touch of the Byzantine here, moving toward Giotto there. A triptych by Fra Angelico is dulled by a strict regularity of composition, and the young Filippo Lippi, experimenting in expressiveness, achieved his version of solemnity by making his Virgin and angels pout. To Piero di Cosimo, Mary Magdalene is a tastefully dressed lady reading a book, the Isabella d'Este of biblical times.

Our old friend St. Jerome makes his several appearances; in Room 3 his lion is wistful, in Room 4 the lion looks like the "Beast" in Cocteau's film. A third pet of the elderly saint is a stuffed toy lion. Before you look for him, though, linger a moment with a fresh-faced, beautifully dressed lady playing a lute. She may have been as respectable as bread, but costume and ripe fleshliness link her with portraits of other courtesans of the early sixteenth century. Her alluring music wreathes an even more superbly dressed lady in a jeweled crown, pearls marking the hem of her skirt and a moue of strong distaste on her face, as if she were in the aura of a stench which may emanate from the perforated St. Sebastian nearby. The only way you will know she was St. Catherine is that there are fragments of wooden wheel at her feet, and the label tells you so. There is no uncertainty of identity in the direct, unadorned planes of an accomplished Lotto portrait of a young man nearby. Next stop, several paintings by Sodoma, one of them replete with Sodoma idioms. Three seminude ladies begin as well-muscled boys with breasts tacked on to male pectoral swells; roly-poly cupids struggle with each other over a pile of coins behind a screen of the exotic birds the painter loved. For further exoticism, a very dark African, and all the exuberance threatened by a skull and scythe and a morbid fantasy of ruins in the background.

If you agree with Browning that Andrea del Sarto was the perfect painter, you will search out several of his canvases in Room 7. For other tastes, there is a portrait of Francesco Colonna dressed in armor, more *buona-forchetta* than warrior, his martial expression preparation for blasting out a slow waiter. An older Colonna, painted by Bronzino, also in armor, seems better to know what armor is for.

Room 8 contains the showpiece, alone on its own easel, the *Fornarina* of Raphael, the Trasteverino baker's daughter with whom the painter was in love, probably the woman, according to Vasari (he refers to her as *one* of the mistresses of the "very amorous" painter), who caused him to neglect his work for Agostino Chigi in the Farnesina. "Agostino, in despair, had the lady brought to his house to live in the part where Raphael was at work contriving this with difficulty by the help of others. That is why the work was completed." That she was not a shy virgin is immediately apparent in the large inviting eyes and the ready mouth and, particularly, the coy attempt to pull a transparent veil over one breast, the gesture less concealment than offer. That Raphael was proud to acknowledge her as painting and property is evident from the gold bracelet on which he etched his name.

The return to holy matters appears in a tranquil, controlled *Madonna del Silenzio* by M. Venusti, and continues in Room 9 with two soaring, churning El Greco paintings, a large St. Jerome by Tintoretto with masterly rendering of the cloaks and hats on a rack and birds on a withered tree. Tintoretto's, also, the *Woman in Adultery with Christ* set in a classical background, the woman a luscious, blond Venetian hetaera. Let her not distract you from the half-circle of apostles' heads, a singular group of small portraits. Titian's unmannered portrait of Philip II contrasts heavily with his *Venus and Adonis* and well-fed eager hunting dogs, the unconvincing passages to be blamed on the master's pupils. A Jacopo Bassano *Adoration of the Shepherds* combines chalky Venetian coloring, particularly in the white, white long-lidded Virgin, with Caravaggesque portraits of the shepherds, one of whom is so excited by the scene that he must relieve himself in a corner of the canvas.

Attractive, solid earth are the butchers and fish vendors (Room 11) painted by Passarotti. One of the butchers has a courtier's beard on an aristocratic face; his companion is an ex-prizefighter lacking a few teeth. The shining fish are supervised by a dignified old man with a gentle eye who apparently sells too cheaply, to judge from his contentious wife.

Dutch and Flemish painters absorb the next two galleries with their pale blue landscapes, painfully precise Gothic interiors, and long-nosed, pale saints. The Quentin Massys portrait of Erasmus, painted for Sir Thomas More, has the clarity, definition of telling detail, and sobriety that characterize the best Dutch portraiture; the books, the dark cloak, the contemplative face in its black cap present the indelible man and his meaning. Less attractive, equally revealing, are the portraits of the rough, pugnacious Bishop of Trent by Joos van Cleve and an anonymous portrait of an old Dutch lady. Next, the great Henry VIII, in yet another Holbein portrait. This one lacks his usual straddling, proud-paunched stance, but the fleshy face and the pursed mouth are here, and the jewels and brocades—this particular set worn for his wedding with Anne of Cleves.

In the progress from painting to painting, look up now and then at the painted and decorated ceilings, and glance at the small bronzes placed on side tables, several of them excellent examples of that métier. You should have arrived at a few lovely bonbons by Boucher, several "Roman" scenes by Hubert Robert—one painting chooses to place the Pantheon on the very edge of the Tiber—and, on an easel, an interestingly monumental, though actually small, Madonna and Child by Montagna. The French reappear with a charming Greuze girl, the romantic fragilities of Fragonard, and a trio of young singers by Le Nain. Two beguiling paintings by Guardi give way to a strange assortment of Renaissance religious works. (This latter group of mixed paintings, French and earlier Italian, are recent legacies and seem to be placed together temporarily.) Passing, slowly, a respectably painted nude female back by a Frenchman who worked and died in Rome, you are soon thundered at by the ceiling of Pietro da Cortona, in the big sala designed by Bernini. Mobbed, frenzied, and skillfully made, it wings symbols of Barberini might toward a smart, self-satisfied Divine Providence. The rest of the room is at the present in disorder, large paintings leaning upside down against scaffolding, but the Bernini works have not been disturbed. A portrait of Urban VIII by Bernini suggests again that painting was not his greatest strength. For proof, his marble busts of the same pope and of Antonio Barberini, which make a fitting close to a visit in a palace off a piazza that is, as much as any place in the city, Bernini country.

NOTE: Closed Mondays, and although official hours seem to be more permissive, go in the morning.

Museo di Roma

When the Palazzo Braschi is not busy with exhibitions—Dürer prints, scenes of Venice, the art of bookbinding, and the major effort: clever displays of Rome a hundred years ago or changes since—it keeps open on an erratic schedule the salons of its permanent collection. It is, as usual, unjust to promise that you will see everything at one go, but the possibilities include a group of near-life-sized, cheerful figures doing characteristic things of a century ago: making music, dancing, eating in an *osteria*, shopping at a pharmacy—and these accompanied and followed by an infinity of objects and pictures related specifically to Rome, a good number of them by the variously talented "Anonimo."

Whether the works are poor or rewarding as art is of minor importance, but it is interesting to see that there was jousting in the sixteenth century in the Belvedere court of the Vatican, and that Christian riders thrust lances at a mechanical Moor in the Piazza Navona. Il Signor "Anonimo" also recorded the games and contests on Testaccio in the seventeenth century. A festa in honor of Christina of Sweden in the Palazzo Barberini is a harsh-colored literal canvas which takes great care to show the vast court, the crowds on balconies and grandstands, the allegorical floats and bravura horsemanship.

The museum has picked up patches of a frescoed house, busts of cardinals, blocks used in printing on paper and cloth, tapestries, statuettes in china, antique pieces of furniture which lend variety to the main lode, portraits of Romans, Roman piazze, palaces, and churches as they appeared at different times, and among them a few rarities. Canova, you will find, was, like Bernini, not much of a painter, and if you would like to know the face of Piranesi, look for the only extant portrait (Room 12). Festas indoors and out, views of Rome straight and fancied, early nineteenth-century costumes, portraits dead, portraits alive (and these include important historians and archaeologists who worked in Rome). Further painted ceremonies bring one, or should, to the famous "Roma Sparita" watercolors of Franz Roesler, charming modest paintings of a bridge, a corner, a group of people gathered near a portico. If the three Roesler salons are closed, as they frequently are, visitors make do with the attractive post cards that reproduce the paintings, available at many post-card stands and that of the Museo as well.

The museum continues through several salons to celebrate Rome's great men, its ruins, streets, and spots of history, an omnivorous collection that may begin to pall except if you are with a group of Romans, your own or strangers, who take great delight—and lend you some of it —in the colors and figures of the enormous, richly textured tapestry that is its past.

Palazzo Venezia

One of the memorable portraits of Mussolini has him standing on a balcony of the Palazzo Venezia, the big jaw and forceful eyes like battering rams, exhorting thousands in the expansive piazza below. He chose well, not only for the space and numbers he could command, but also for the undisturbed Renaissance directness of the walls surmounted by crenelations that allude to a fortress. This earliest of Renaissance (mid-fifteenth century) palaces in Rome was designed by the great classicist Alberti for the Venetian Cardinal Pietro Barbo, later Pope Paul II, who left a colorful biography. He changed night into day, holding conferences and luncheon feasts at 3 A.M., and slept through the day, well protected from Roman noise by thick palace walls. A high and eccentric liver, his death was attributed to indigestion, translated by anticlerical Romans into a set of small devils piercing, pinching, chopping at his entrails.

The palace remained a Venetian stronghold for ecclesiasts and ambassadors of the Venetian Republic until the late eighteenth century; with turns of historical events since, it has become government property that now houses a museum and, in its many additional halls, changing exhibitions.

Closed Mondays, open 9 to 2 on weekdays, when admission costs 200 lire, and 9 to 1 on Sundays and holidays, admission 100 lire, and several rooms closed off "for lack of personnel," the museum offers an eclectic hodgepodge, rarely compelling and yet, for its variety, an informative long stroll interrupted only by a few eager words from the lonely guards. A well of pilastered stairs ends at Venetian fanfare as a faded red velvet banner which bears the golden lion, St. Mark, holding a sword and haloed in a ring of sainthood.

Against the walls—gray, dark brown, dark red Venetian velvet—lean unremarkable Venetian paintings, cases of Spanish majolica of the sixteenth and eighteenth centuries, and, everywhere, Renaissance chests, chairs, a credenza, a reading table. A "name" painting, like a *Christ* by Benozzo Gozzoli, who was better at Courts of Love full of the beautiful Renaissance people, shows now and then, though the galleries rarely display the highest achievements of a painter. These might be coupled with the work of lesser painters, sometimes anonymous, of essentially greater merit, or an entrancing oddity such as a miniature, no more than 7 or 8 inches high and an inch and a half wide, painted amply, sharply, with medallions, mythological figures, floral bands and arabesques, an astonishing rarity given to the state by the Orsini family. Suddenly a roomful of tapestries, followed by a large room devoted to Italian ceramics of the sixteenth century. At almost every turn, large Chinese vases, a lacquered Chinese box inlaid with mother-of-pearl and, again, Italian ceramics, from coarse rural to highly sophisticated in a great diversity of shapes, that date from the sixteenth, seventeenth, and eighteenth centuries. Among the paintings, there is a dark, entertaining Venetian work (sixteenth century) of a group watching the ascension of a soul, a few of the witnesses strayed from an El Greco canvas.

Under a ceiling of lozenges that frame satyrs and fauns and fun-loving nymphs, there are cases of small bronzes and, in the same room, a drawing by Mantegna of drooling

Silenuses and drunken young cupids dipping into, climbing around, and leaning on an enormous wine vat, one of the most Italian fervid hymns to wine. The subject changes rapidly: neatly arranged cases of china, a return to bronzes, which include a rather pedestrian bust of Michelangelo, and in the next room a gilded, beribboned, rosetted sedan chair painted with the pleasures of Elysian fields and a harpsichord to echo its charms. A door opening to the left takes one to the section referred to as the Palazzetto, and we are back in bronzes that run the gamut of conventional angels and saints, a small Laocoön, Europa on her bull, a sizable population of pagan roisterers. The pieces that will probably hold your attention longest are the carefully observed small animals and a lamp whose base is a sturdy chicken's foot clutching an athlete tightly folded on himself in order that he may balance on one knee.

The armory, the indispensable long hall bristling with armor, spikes, lances, and spears, stops at a display of carved wooden church figures of several backgrounds, techniques, and degrees of charm. Then, a return to ceramics and examples of old Italian weaving and embroidery and, moving back in time, the painted crucifixes and wooden Madonnas of the Middle Ages, some of them quite crude and rich in mystery. Of the same period, groups of finely carved ivories, several good pieces of medieval bronze, and a couple of carved wooden church ornaments as primitive as Easter Island heads; among Flemish and German paintings and wooden sculpture, a meticulously literal mob of six citizens, dressed in voluminous cloaks with sharply carved sleeves and broad headdresses, crowded together on a slim platform. A pregnant wooden angel who seems to be kneeling ungently on a child's head is from Lombardy, but one of her parents was almost certainly German.

The miscellany moves through the ever present Chinese vases, paintings in the style of Siena, boxes and chalices of gold and gilded bronze, and a remarkably decorated key plate wrested from a Renaissance palace. Farther on, a choice collection of medieval church crafts that includes enamels, an ancient crown, a lovely metal arch stamped with the busts of numerous saints, and a twelfth-century crucifix of enamels forced into silver. Gentile Bellini appears among these early chalices and reliquaries with a triptych of a *Virgin and Child with Saints,* not far from a much jauntier Venetian Virgin (fifteenth century) of painted wood who carries her baby on a flirtatious hip billowed in the provocative curve of an Indian goddess. In a case by itself is an extraordinary Venetian triptych of the fourteenth century, an amalgam of several media on a ground of gilded metal. A gem-studded Madonna and Child built up of clay are bordered by myriad tiny saints in enamel, carved wood, and paint, and in twenty small frames at the sides, against golden backgrounds, sharp miniatures of the life of Christ. An aloof lady is a painted wooden saint from Padova of a century later, contemptuous of her peasant ancestors, a Madonna and Child by Nicola di Nuto, both mother and babe silly, sweet, relaxed, and charming.

A change of concentration once more: tapestries, silver from northern Europe, Persian rugs, still more Chinese vases, a few conscientious Flemish portraits and Guercino's literal *St. Peter Weeping,* the virtuosity of tear-painting vitiating response to Peter's sorrow. The last room holds the fanciest of gondola hooks and a diverting *Rape of Europa,* a rural scene of startled fat ladies watching their placid friend amble off on the back of a Ferdinand.

A little of everything, little of major importance, a collection of this and that whose restless forays among disparate objects and periods saves it from monotony and provides a quiet, cool hour between the Forum and shopping, the Campidoglio and the Aventine, the Trevi Fountain and the Pantheon.

Buon Natale

A fervid schedule through masses, processions, benedictions, Te Deums rises to the capping ceremonies of Epiphany, the day of the Bambino of S. Maria d'Aracoeli which shares the Capitoline Hill with the Campidoglio. The Bambino was carved out of a piece of olive wood from Gethsemane in the fifteenth or sixteenth century, his face painted by angels. He is swaddled in gems—chains, brooches, loops of rings—a shapeless mass of glitter wearing a heavy, bulbous crown on a puffy little face which Dickens described as that of the famous American dwarf Tom Thumb. The Bambino was, in a more devout time, frequently called to cure the desperately sick. Any time of the day or night the dazzling bundle was taken by a priest in a waiting carriage to tear through the city to an agonized bedside. Stories are told of miraculous cures, of people literally frightened to death by the advent of this last, desperate measure, or turning to the peace of death to escape the commotion, the agitated crush of relatives and neighbors come to witness a miracle. He may not be so peripatetic now, but still receives—and one can see them in his chapel—hundreds of letters, undoubtedly prayers for cure and benediction, left unopened for three months and then burned. He apparently receives the messages and acts on them by spiritual osmosis, or, more simply, he betrays the fact in this fashion that he is a cynical Roman.

The Bambino opens the religious aspects of Christmas by appearing in a crèche near the entrance of the church, in the company of dark-skinned shepherds and a pale Mary who holds the armless, legless splendor of Her Son. Facing the crèche, across a respectful distance, is an improvised pulpit from which, especially on Epiphany, children address the Bambino and the Virgin in high, lilting, sentimental verse to a ground base of parental prompting.

The Rome of commerce and elaborations has already, for some time, been wearing its gems—dangles of metal streamers, free-form celestial plaques floating above the streets, boxes of light that greet passers-by with "Auguri." The Via della Croce lives in a soft twilight of bubbled light, the Via Margutta and its vicoli play decorative jokes in memory of its lost *vie bohème* by stretching across the streets lines of pots, pans, a papier-mâché leg, a bust, a washboard, a section of stovepipe, long underpants, bras, and socks, all stiff with gold radiator paint. The shops display their most explosive jewels, the glassware of gossamer, transparent china, and dresses of Medici velvets, and the butchers hang blood-dripping boars, like sentinels at baroque portals, at either side of their doors. An exotic import, Santa Claus (Babbo Natale) is reduced to a miniature plastic-bound figure impaled by the dozens on itinerant poles. Small Japanese toys clatter, mew, fly, flutter, dance to the voices of their vendors. Everywhere, inescapable, the bagpipes and fifes of the so-called Abruzzi peasants who appear in great numbers wearing sandals with pointed toes, cross-strapped to the knee, over heavy white stockings, broad knickers, sheepskin vests, and a jaunty repertoire of caps from knitted baby hoods to dashing, highwayman swoops of felt. They usually work in pairs, one to continue tootling a patiently repeated, thin air, the other to offer his hat and a spate of "Buon Natale" and "Auguri."

Buying goes on lustily into the twenty-fifth, so determined that for this time and this time only cars are bested, imprisoned, or forced out of a shopping street by the impenetrable mass of bodies. On Christmas Eve, women dash from the exhausted shops and markets to put the last touches on the pre-midnight-Mass dinner. The meal is always a large, festive one, the menu dependent on what a family can afford. It must, however, include one fish dish (symbolic of Christ's name), such as chunks of tuna among the antipasti or eel cooked on a spit with laurel leaves, or a dish of rice and seafood. Sparkling Spumante washes over the interminable feasting, which slows, but never quite finishes, with fruits, chocolates, nougat, and panettone, a light, puffy fruit cake attractively packaged and sold in the thousands at Christmas time. Time out for Mass and then the universal tombola, a traditional gambling game which may be a reminder of men gaming while the women attend a woman in labor. We are, after all, attending a birth vigil.

Tombola is bingo, but since it is also Italian, the caller shouts each number not as itself but as a description lost in time, and even if you have Italian, but no knowledge that 29 is, let us say, *il Mantovese,* or 11 is *gli amanti,* you're lost. The virtuoso who spins out every phrase roundly may be prevailed upon to call the number as well, but only after his cadenza has been permitted to hang awhile in the admiring air. The game (frequently relieved by horseplay which is more or less overt sex play—grabbing, pinching of genitals, lifting of skirts, and obscene words and gestures that have a distinctly incestuous cast) goes on into a somnolent, exhausted Christmas morning that rouses itself in time for the repetition of a gargantuan family meal and the distribution of presents, an innovation from abroad that clouds the newborn Christ child in whorls of Christmas wrappings.

Nothing stirs on the morning of the twenty-sixth except a few solitaries seeking the humanity of a coffee bar. Later in the day, rain or shine, the children are trotted out for a *presepio* (crib) crawl that requires energy, indifference to soggy skies, and a long muffler wrapped twice and thrice around young necks, once for the mouth and chin, around again for the snuffling nose, and again, to be tied as a fat knot in back, somewhere beween the shoulders and the top of the too-deep, too-large new hat, leaving free only a pair of wide eyes to peer out of the billows of wool. The itinerary varies, often beginning with the Bambinello of Aracoeli, and we might as well follow, stopping with the family to buy a balloon or a bag of chestnuts, then climbing at the side of the short round legs in new red stockings under the stiff new coat to the modest Romanesque façade sitting in the sky.

The right to house a miracle-making Roman folk figure justly belongs to S. Maria d'Aracoeli. Its centuries witnessed and projected important events in the religious and secular life of Rome, and had it not suffered tactless changes, it might be the compendium of church architecture it almost is. Depending on whom you read, again, it was a fortress of the Romans, the site of a majestic temple to the mighty Juno, the site of a palace of Augustus. As the most prominent height of the Capitoline Hill it was undoubtedly covered by major Roman structures, one of them a meeting place for the Roman Senate. During the Middle Ages, a time that gathered folk tales, ancient gossip, a taste for blood and mysticism to make a web of history, a legend was invented—with a little help from a friend, Virgil (the famous Eclogue IV)—that lent Augustus a Christian aura and Christianity a continuity with heathen antiquity. The Roman Senate, inspired by the burgeoning power and

wealth of the Empire, the transformation of the city by
Augustus from stone and brick to lustrous marbles on
superb monuments, possibly spurred on by a hand from
the Emperor or sly, menacing suggestions from his wife
Livia, proposed to deify their leader. Acting like the modest
man he could not altogether have been, Augustus recoiled,
hesitated, and then sought the advice of the trustworthy
Sibyl of Tivoli. After a three-day fast and a subsequent
trance she prophesied the advent of a King for the Ages
who would descend from the sky. Augustus was slow to
understand, so the sky parted, sending down a blinding
ray on which the Virgin and Child descended to a pagan
altar, while a great voice called, "This is the altar of the
Son of God." The trembling Augustus ordered a new altar
built, *"ecce ara primogenito Dei,"* thus "Aracoeli," the altar
of the heavens dedicated to the first-born Son of God.

Recorded history describes the church as "old" in the
sixth century, when it was supervised by Greek monks
who represented the Byzantine hierarchy. In the twelfth
century, the Jewish antipope Anacletus II turned church,
monastery, and the whole of the Capitoline Hill over to the
Benedictines, who lost the property a century later to the
Franciscans. They initiated an ambitious building program
and for the expenses secured a papal bull which granted
indulgences to those who helped finance the project. The
new building remained, as in Roman times, a center for
public governmental activity; priestly and lay powers designed their divers laws here. It was from these marble
steps, which he was the first to climb in 1348, that Cola
di Rienzo addressed his hordes of followers, and when they
abandoned him, it was at the bottom of these stairs that he
met his death. (An insignificant hooded figure on the side
of the rise to the Campidoglio shamefacedly acknowledges
his once potent existence.)

Most of the showpieces of the church are kept, as usual,
in barred darkness, waiting for release by a beadle or 100
lire in a light-controlling box. Do the best you can to see

the fluid figures and ripe color of Pinturicchio's murals that deal with S. Bernardino of Siena, and S. Antony of Padua as celebrated by Gozzoli against a star-studded sky and two worldly blond angels blessing S. Antony in the act of blessing. Near the entrance, a mistreated tomb portrait by Donatello and close to the altar, a wondrous amalgam of superstition and art through the ages. The Byzantine Virgin of the main altar shares with the Virgin of S. Maria Maggiore the responsibility of watching over the people of Rome. She may have been painted as early as the sixth century or as late as the eleventh, but the true believer knows that she was a much earlier creation of the gifted St. Luke. (The irreligious Napoleon ordered that her golden crown be taken to France, and there it stayed, to be restored about 150 years later.) Not far from the sacristy a classical tempietto surrounds the remains of St. Helena, the mother of Constantine. It is a crowded shrine, composed of elderly reliquaries, a modern St. Helena who shows the influence of Manzù, and below the saint and difficult to see, the altar supposedly built by Augustus, centered on a conventional Lamb of God. In one corner, a Babe and Virgin, in the other a kneeling king, all stiffly and crudely carved in Romanesque style. This might be Barbarossa humbling himself as he did once in a profitable while or Charlemagne at his devotions, but Augustus, no, not by a millennium of time and art style, infinitely more polished and elegant in the Emperor's day. No one argues with legends, however.

As neighbor the humbled Emperor has a pope who admired Imperial habits and had himself portrayed as a blind Colossus to symbolize for the Church the power and divinity that once pertained to the weird and the worthy who ruled the Empire. The giant pushes into obscurity a tomb designed by a Cosma in the early fourteenth century and a beguiling panel of Virgin, Child, and saints by Cavallini. Among the infinitely more to see of paintings, mosaics, and memorials—some designed by Bernini and Michelangelo—stop for the enchanting tomb designed by Arnolfo di

Cambio supported by a rampantly joyous Roman sarcophagus and over the side door (the easiest approach to the
Campidoglio from the church) a thirteenth-century Virgin
so battered by exposure that only golden aureoles and
edgings of robes show clearly. No one seems to care about
her progressive mortal disease, understandable in a place
whose taste for the arts has been ebbing for some centuries and, in any case, is overpopulated with aged and
ailing Virgins.

The *presepio* viewers are ready for other churches, the
length of the tour dependent on how long a child can stay
awake and how tired Mamma and Babbo become lifting
their young above the entranced heads of adults. The next
stop might be the Gesù whose animated Holy Family and
astonished shepherds live among hovering doves and falls
of ivy. The children are caught and held by a smoking,
flickering fire, a large, luminous angel, and a comet that
slowly crosses the sky and, most of all, by a button that
makes snow fall on the scene.

Given the number of churches in Rome, Italian crafts-
manship, and its love of minute detail, one expects and gets
a considerable set of variations on the Nativity theme.
S. Alessio on the Aventine, for instance, makes a serious
effort at biblical history and authenticity of detail without
losing aesthetics and subdued appeal. A section of the crypt
is set aside for panoramic windows, each accompanied by a
piped-in, appropriate biblical text that begins with Adam
and Eve in Paradise, a place of primordial hills, palm trees,
and lush jungles where elephants rove, and finishes with
Chinese pagodas, Mexican pyramids, Egyptian obelisks, and
African hills to portray the Universal Church.

Gifted monks often invite the public to see their crèches
(listings appear in newspapers, and a good concierge should
be helpful) of beautifully detailed and cleverly devised
scenes. The long night of searching for an inn is marked,
at its darkest time, only by the movement of a lantern, the
desert is hot and dry, and the Egyptian obelisks scored with

tiny hieroglyphs. S. Carlino is young and "now," a background of modern buildings, a working class crowd holding placards calling for "Pace" and "Libertà" that almost succeed in hiding the Mother and Child relegated to an inconspicuous corner. S. Marcello on the Corso clings to the luminous and mystical in the principal figures and lets go with a group of hearty peasants listening to a vivacious group of shepherd pipers and bagpipe players as they eat on a porch of the inn.

The airy railroad station matches its restrained modernity with a modern, metal crib, the wax museum mechanizes its figures, and a group of ceramicists (entrance to the Torre delle Milizie) present stunning large personages and animals in a diversity of masterly techniques and subtle glazes. The same delight in rendering, using other images and techniques, appears in S. Maria in Via (near S. Silvestro), which has two presentations, one that treats of Trastevere in the late nineteenth century and the other of an eighteenth-century Neapolitan hamlet, its inn a many-roomed house busy with animated aspects of living—robust women cooking and arguing among heaps and dangles of sausages and salamis, people eating, shouting, tootling on pipes, boys chasing dogs, drovers, and water carriers about on their business, and one amazed old man among the energetic lusty stopping to gaze in awe at the Holy Family and the superb angels with long Mannerist fingers and gentle, patrician faces.

The Commune of Rome erects one of its cribs on the Spanish Steps and engagingly resurrects Rome of a century ago guarded by policemen in Napoleonic hats who glance, as calmly as they do now, at a drunk wobbling out of a wineshop, a chestnut vendor, the singers and dancers in an *osteria*, and a nobleman who rides his horse briskly out of the gates of his villa. Somewhere there is a Nativity, but it hardly seems to matter.

The apogee of the development from humble Nativity scene to a streetful of citizens, to a hillside of peasants, to a world of plasterwork figurines, is the famous *presepio* to be seen all year round behind the church of S. Cosma e Damiano in the Foro Romano. This, too, is Neapolitan and contains one thousand figures gesticulating, eating, working, calling, and feeling. In the distance, neighboring hill towns, clumps of cypress, and desolate castles; below, houses, inns, flocks of sheep, green-mouthed caves, a curve of ruined aqueduct, crenelated towers, shops hung with goods purchased by a bustling populace; in a ruined temple, the Holy Family guarded by flights of spirited angels and, waiting to present themselves and their gifts, the richly robed Magi and their attendants, all exquisitely made, each body sinewy and in suave, natural movement.

What has this ebullient show to do with Christ, the mysteries of his birth and death, his miracles, and the validity of his teachings? For the non-Catholic, and non-Italian especially, very little but a response to boundless appeal and respect for admirable, meticulous workmanship. For the religious it has significances which developed in the Middle Ages when St. Francis and his followers made all of life a manifestation of Christ's love. The saint's canticles to the sun, the moon, animals, and flowers linked man with God in an intimacy that had been lost for centuries. The figure on the criminal's cross had become proud and remote as Teacher of the Church and stern Pantocrator. He was brought back by St. Francis and other mystics to a closeness which could admit a Christ baby like any other but prettier and haloed. The conception suits the earth-based Italian who likes his religion palpable, visible, not abstract, and thus, by extension, why shouldn't Bethlehem have been a village like his, with street lamps and ruins and old men smoking pipes and women stirring pots, and everyone excited and readying for the great day?

The toys continue peeping and croaking, the pipers' sounds become desultory, as if under water, the Befana market begins to raise its slats and canvas. The Befana (a corruption of Epifania-Epiphany) has evolved from the Magi to a spectacled benevolent witch who brings gifts to children, and around her grows a yearly market and fairgrounds with shooting galleries, machines for testing a boy's strength, big blocks of candy, buckets of beans and olives. But Epiphany is not just yet. The second climax of the season comes at New Year's Eve and is celebrated with fireworks and showers of bottles and crockery, sometimes garbage, into the street, ostensibly to rid the house of the evils of the old year but also to release some energy and the anarchist latent in every Roman. The sky is torn with banging rockets and streaks of colored light. From balconies and terraces cascades of sparkling lights and the brief jumping streaks of sparklers. Noise of bottles and rockets finished, one sits down to a meal of pork sausage and lentils, the lentils prophecies of gold coins which will become a pile of riches in the coming year.

Those with the energy to rouse themselves go near noon of New Year's Day to the bridge of S. Angelo to watch a *belga pazzo* leave his top hat near the foot of an angel and leap into the icy river to bring from its depths a happy and prosperous year. Climbing up from the riverbank, he reaches for his top hat, passes it among the crowd and, in reward, delivers himself of a speech or two of good wishes, and everyone goes back to lunch and an afternoon of sleep. The following days are devoted to complaints of colds, exhaustion, and liver irritations, the result of overeating, they all say as they continue the family rounds of prodigious meals. The kids are complaining of nothing except delays in taking them to the Befana market on the Piazza Navona.

Each year the displays become increasingly like those around S. Giovanni on his festa day and of Trastevere during the week of Noantri, leading one to suspect that all the ties, scarves, wooden ladles, North African pocketbooks, and ceramics with serious birth defects come from the same warehouse. The children see none of the shoddy; their eyes are glued to one goldfish in one plastic bag, to pink, yellow, and purple balloons with rabbit ears, to cotton candy that manages to look both fluffy and limp; unaware of the deafening noise—without which any Roman place is empty and might be said hardly to exist at all—that comes from blaring phonographs, the pop of rifles, squeaking miniature bagpipes, loudspeakers beckoning to bargains.

After the children have carried their gifts out of the piazza, holding their boxes before them like solemn offerings, it will soon be time to visit the Bambino in Aracoeli again.

The dark crib shepherds are now robed as Oriental nobles, and two Negroes in savage finery have come to join the scene. At about 3:35 organ music sounds across the deep aisles to introduce a sermon that booms out of the loudspeakers. The doors constantly open and close to admit twittering young nuns and dashing foreign monks in three-tiered black cloaks and black skullcaps set on keen, cool heads. Tourists, Italian and foreign, with guidebooks in hand, try to push their way to a glimpse of art. A balloon pops in the back of the church and a firecracker barks. As the door opens, the wail of an Abruzzi fife sneaks into the church. The young nuns begin to fly ecstatically about, exclaiming over everything. Young soldiers stroll in for shelter and inexpensive entertainment. The sermon goes on.

Below the children's pulpit a group of relatives and child-lovers assembles to listen to the young declaim while the cameras click. Some of the orators are very young—four or five years old—and hang desperately to the string of a balloon as if it were a parent's hand. They smile feebly at the crowd below, forget why they've mounted the terrible tall place, and look frantically for a familiar, helping face. The boys of seven and eight are already poised talkers and, confidently dressed in their new Wild West outfits, complete with badge and two heavy guns, make their speeches in clear voices, without hesitation. Their sisters, the passive, shy women some of them will become, begin a verse of adoration and burst into frightened tears after the first trembling words. There is always, though, a frilly Lolita, petted, praised, and beruffled all her seven years, who twinkles and flirts with her charmed audience as she makes love to the Virgin and Child.

In the meantime, the elderly members of the congregation, the sermon ended, join in the singing of "Adeste, Fideles" and "Silent Night." The nuns have settled in places near the aisle where the Bambino will pass in procession. The clever foreign abbots in their romantic cloaks look at a fresco or two and smile indulgently at the naïve Italian fervor. The procession begins more or less at 4 o'clock, led on by a long red banner, priests, and acolytes in several qualities of white, lacy, gold-embroidered splendor, brown-clad monks, and a trail of the faithful. The Bambino is taken from the crèche and is placed in the arms of a very old dignitary. Out one side door and in another the procession goes and out again. This time the holy figure is raised and lowered in a gesture of benediction over the city and brought back on the main aisle slowly so that those close by can genuflect and touch the sacred jeweled wood and carry the touching hand to their mouths in a kiss. The many chandeliers of the church are lit, and several large candles throw an aura of light around the Bambino, who is placed on the high altar where he looks small and defenseless under the black-eyed stern Madonna, the spreading chandeliers, and the noble spaces of the apse vault.

Suddenly, barriers appear at the altar and the openings of the side aisles, and a crush of people behind them. As suddenly as the barriers, several young men in uniform have appeared, three or four to hold back the crowd and three to guard the extravagantly dressed Bambino who has been robbed of his jewels before and may be again. By now balloons have floated from drowsy hands; the babies are asleep or whimpering while they are carried through the mob to mount the altar stairs and must be nudged awake and urged to kiss the image. The stage-struck older children climb up to their pulpit two and three and four times to say their say to the unabating admiration and congratulations of parents and grandparents.

The season ebbs slowly, reluctantly; the Saturnalia of shopping and force-feeding grinds to a drowsy halt. The street ornaments disappear, piece by piece, the last survivors the underwear near the Via Margutta, tired and limp, all the gilded impudence gone. The last of the glass is swept off the streets, sales signs fill shop windows, traffic again steps on the gas. The skiers are back in their insulting tans, the coffee bars are alive again, people compare diets of several fanciful kinds. Everyone diets for two days, gives it up as a bloody bore, and Rome is back to its unique version of normal.

Index

A Note on the Type

The text of this book was set on the Linotype in
Aster, a typeface designed by Francesco
Simoncini (born 1912 in Bologna, Italy) for
Ludwig and Mayer, the German type foundry.
Starting out with the basic old-face letterforms
that can be traced back to Francesco Griffo
in 1495, Simoncini emphasized the diagonal stress
by the simple device of extending diagonals to
the full height of the letterforms and squaring off.
By modifying the weights of the individual
letters to combat this stress, he has produced a
type of rare balance and vigor. Introduced
in 1958, Aster has steadily grown in popularity
wherever type is used.

*Composed by Cherry Hill Composition
Pennsauken, N.J.*
*Printed and bound by The Colonial Press, Inc.
Clinton, Mass.*

*Typography and binding design by
Virginia Tan*